The New Science of Marketing

State-of-the-Art Tools for Anticipating and Tracking the Market Forces That Will Shape Your Company's Future

Vithala R. Rao
Joel H. Steckel

IRWIN
Professional Publishing®

Chicago • London • Singapore

TO OUR PARENTS,
four of the greatest people the world ever knew.

V. Kameswaramma (Mother) and V. Sitaramamurty (Father)

Hazel and Phillip Steckel

Table of Contents

Preface   *ix*

1 *The Role of Analysis in Strategy Formulation*   *1*

Introduction   1
Boundaries of Strategic Marketing   3
Classification of Strategic Situations   6
Analysis and the Process of Strategic Thinking   12
Framework of the Book   17
Bibliography   19

2 *Segmenting Markets: Who Are the Potential Buyers?*   *21*

Introduction   21
Bases of Segmentation   24
Benefit Segmentation   37
Segmenting with Other Behavioral Bases   49
Selecting Target Segments   51
Bibliography   52

3 *Identifying Unmet Needs: What Do the Customers Want?* *55*

Introduction   55
Methods for Identifying Unmet Needs   60
Problems with Existing Offerings   62
Changes in the Environment   82
Methods for Identifying Solutions   82
Other Methods   88

The Role of Creativity   91
Conclusions   93
Bibliography   94

4   *Identifying Competitors: Who Will We Compete Against?*   **97**

Introduction   97
Identifying Competitors inside the Industry or Product
    Category   100
Identifying Competitors outside the Industry or Product
    Category   110
Predicting Competitors' Actions   115
Conclusion   117
Bibliography   117

5   *Understanding and Forecasting External Environment—I*   **121**

Introduction   121
Situations Where Environmental Understanding Is Critical   122
Overview of Methods for Understanding
    and Predicting Environmental Factors   124
Methods for Analyzing Demographic Factors   127
Methods for Analyzing Social/Cultural Factors   137
Methods for Analyzing Economic Factors   151
Methods for Analyzing Political Factors   153
Summary   156
Appendix: A Guide to Information Sources for Marketing
    Strategy Analysis   157
Bibliography   161

6   *Understanding and Forecasting Market Environment—II*   **163**

Forecasting and Design of Strategies   163
Uncertainty and the Role of Judgment   164
Forecasting Technology   164
Selected Formal Forecasting Methods   169
Scenario Analysis Methods   189

Methods for Forecasting Sales of Durable Products   199
Summary   204
Appendix: Descriptions, Advantages, and Disadvantages of
    Selected Methods of Forecasting   205
Bibliography   206

7   *Analyzing Strengths and Weaknesses: How Will We Compete?*   **209**

Introduction   209
Skills and Resources on What Dimensions?   211
Assessing Strengths and Weaknesses in Competitive Position   221
Assessing Strengths and Weaknesses in Performance Outcomes   232
Assessing Strengths and Weaknesses with Managerial Judgment   233
Summary   238
Bibliography   239

8   *Resource Allocation*   **243**

Introduction   243
Principles of Resource Allocation   247
Methods for Allocating Resources among SBUs   249
Allocation of Resources across Multiple Brands of One Product
    (SBU)   281
Methods for Allocating Marketing Expenditures for a Brand   283
Methods for Allocation of Resources across Geographic Markets   292
Summary   292
Bibliography   293

9   *Analyses in Action: Case Examples*   **295**

Introduction   295
Sports Apparel Industry Study   297
The Victoria Moore Activewear Line   307
Citibank Photocard Focus Group Project   310
Holdzer Catering   313
Summary   318
Appendix   320

Index   **335**

Preface

Marketing touches every person in one way or another. Marketing and innovation are perhaps the only two significant engines for growth of any economy. Successful growth of an industry (and an economy) will depend heavily upon insightful, systematic, and scientific application of marketing principles and methods.

But, the word "marketing," to a lay person, is likely to elicit thoughts of commercials with special effects, catchy slogans, and celebrity endorsers touting new and improved products and services. This visible output of the marketing process is a creative and artistic activity and implies a sole purpose of persuading the customer to buy things. Fortunately, those of us who are marketing academics or practicing professionals know better. Behind those enticing commercials are often hours of quantitative analysis attempting to uncover what customers will want, how alike people or organizations who want the same things are, how to design a new product or improve an existing one, and how successful a new or improved product is likely to be. These analyses are necessary not only to be successful. What the lay person sees as art is often the result of hours of scientific work.

The distinction between art and science in marketing is reflected in the evolution of marketing practice. In the first half of the twentieth century, the task of marketing began with the product as given. The main job was to think of "artistic," creative, and often clever ways to persuade customers to buy a product or service. With technological and industrial progress, new industries have evolved leading to ever-changing ways to satisfy customer needs and wants. The structure of competition among firms has also changed due to the emergence of new competitors and the eventual exit of some old ones. Existing boundaries between industries and product markets has blurred. Firms have to seek new ways for satisfying the needs and wants of customers better than their dynamic competitors do. Accordingly, focus has shifted to the importance of gaining deeper understanding of customer behavior (by discovering new product opportunities to satisfy unmet customer needs) and understanding of the anticipated behavior of competition. Both the academic community and consulting firms, often in cooperation, have developed newer sets of analytical and scientific methods directed towards assisting firms to tackle the newer challenges.

Marketing executives make decisions for their products and services both at tactical and strategic levels. The tactical decisions are often the day-to-day tasks for managing an existing business with more attention paid to current problems. These include designing price promotions, formulating advertising slogans, and identifying and targeting market segments. These managerial tasks fall under the rubric of brand or product management and planning. Strategic decisions consider issues such as how the market and industry will change in the future, what competitive advantages are sustainable, which newer product markets to enter and how the firm may compete in those markets. Strategic marketing is more concerned with the long-term viability of a business and even the corporation as a whole.

Needless to say, effective planning is required to implement decisions at both the tactical and strategic levels. In order to survive, the modern corporation must search continually for new product opportunities. Once a firm enters a new market with either a new or a modified existing product, the markets must be managed effectively. Both levels of planning also require relevant and intelligently performed analyses to be successful. To be useful, analyses must provide information that impact corporate decisions. This book was written in response to a perceived void in the literature related to effective analyses for the strategic marketing function.

Two sets of books are related to the specific niche we are interested in, those on strategic marketing and those on marketing research. Books on strategic marketing tend to describe frameworks and paradigms that emphasize the questions that management ought to consider while formulating a strategic decision. However, they generally do not provide sufficient detail about specific research approaches that are needed to answer these questions. In contrast, most marketing research books are oriented toward techniques of data collection and analysis. They concentrate on formulating research designs and technology of conducting research projects.

No book exists which takes the questions relevant for strategic market planning and describes precisely how to conduct the research and analyses needed to answer them. That is . . . until now. This book starts with issues faced by and decisions to be made by a strategic marketer and describes various methods of analyses that can be done to assist the management in this endeavor. After reading this book, the manager will:

1. gain a deeper understanding of the issues that encompass marketing strategy (e.g., investigating product/market opportunities, discovering unmet consumer needs, analyzing competitors, determining competitive advantage, predicting environmental changes so as to be proactive in the marketplace, forecasting results of strategies and allocating resources);

2. have at his or her disposal a set of well-tested methods that address each of the issues; and

3. be able to implement or guide the implementation of research with these methods.

It is an exciting time to be writing this book. Several developments have either occurred or are on the horizon that will facilitate the kinds of analyses described in this book. Generally speaking, the seeds for a marketing information revolution are sown in a fertile environment amply supplied by technology, communication, and brain power. Using supermarket scanners to collect data on customer behavior is now commonplace; new, interactive computer-aided interview methodologies have emerged; and who knows what new opportunities the information superhighway will bring for collection of data which can help one address strategic questions related to customers and competitors? Further, decision support systems are being designed to implement the results of various analyses in a more or less routine manner.

One of the attractive aspects of the material in this book is that it is quite robust to all of these changes. The tools and techniques described herein will be as applicable in the future as they are today. The thing to look forward to is that the future will bring richer data collected by better methods for applying the methods in this book for strategic marketing.

Our thinking on this subject has of course been shaped by each other as well as generations of students, consulting clients, teachers, and colleagues. We particularly want to acknowledge the inspiration of Professor Paul E. Green of the Wharton School of the University of Pennsylvania. Paul served on both of our doctoral dissertation committees respectively as Chair and a member. His example in thought and deed has been felt by every marketing academic, practicing researcher, consultant, and manager in the United States and indeed the whole world. He has provided us with a model to emulate. People who have read his extensive contributions to the marketing literature will undoubtedly see his influence in various parts of this book. We also thank Saroj V. Rao for her help and patience throughout this project.

Vithala R. Rao
Ithaca, New York

Joel H. Steckel
New York City

CHAPTER 1

The Role of Analysis in Strategy Formulation

INTRODUCTION

Formulating marketing strategy is a difficult task. Managers will rarely have all the information they would like to have in order to make the necessary decisions. Furthermore, the information they do have may be difficult to interpret, especially if it relates to future business environments. Consider the following scenarios as illustrations.

The **VICTORIA MOORE** Company* designs and manufactures women's dress and casual clothing, shoes, jeans, accessories, men's wear, and children's wear. The vast majority of its business is in women's clothing, the area in which the company began. As the company wants to continue growing, it needs to investigate whether new products or new markets will best fuel that growth. If new products are the answer, the company needs to determine what new products will best serve the company's purposes. Victoria herself wondered whether activewear was a future growth opportunity. In order to determine the appropriate course of action, she needed to answer the following questions:

1. How should we identify our target activewear customers? What is the potential they represent?

2. Who will our competitors most likely be, other fashion designers of casual wear or sports apparel manufacturers?

3. What benefits do potential customers look for in leisure sports apparel: fit, fashion, comfort?

4. Is the Victoria Moore brand name an advantage in this category? If so, how much would the brand name contribute to the company's performance?

In the early 1990s, **CITIBANK** was attempting to differentiate their classic Visa and MasterCard by placing a photograph of the customer on

---

* Victoria Moore is a fictitious name for a real company. The company has provided data that is used later in the book and has asked that its name be withheld.

1

them.** The credit card market has become extremely competitive, and competitors such as Citibank had to find reasons for potential customers to choose their card. The intent behind the photo was to appeal to security-conscious consumers who might be afraid of fraudulent charges made with a lost card. The bank felt that the new card would reinforce the positioning statement of its Bankcard Division: "No other credit card gives you the security and confidence of Citibank MasterCard and Visa because no one is as responsive to your needs." Before the photocard was introduced on a wide scale, Citibank was interested in customers' reactions to various aspects of obtaining and using their cards. In particular, the bank wanted some insight into the relative importance of the photo in acquiring and using the card.

In the early 1990s, the athletic footwear industry entered its mature stage. Growth in sales flattened as the number of people participating in exercise peaked and the domestic economy began to falter. After a decade of double-digit retail growth, 1993 saw essentially no growth at all. Sales to women actually declined. Recognizing clouds on the horizon, **REEBOK**, the number two company in this industry (behind Nike) recognized the need to identify the growing market segments in the industry. This involved two subtasks: segmenting the market and forecasting each segment's growth.

During the 1970s, **XEROX** customers had become disappointed with Xerox quality and service. The company's early competitive advantage was gone. Consequently, the company lost its leadership in the copier industry it had created with the introduction of its 914 in 1959. In 1983, Xerox began to regain lost share by initiating a "Leadership through Quality" program, which emphasized product quality, customer satisfaction, and new products. In order to monitor the success of the program, Xerox felt they had to develop a set of tools to continuously measure customer satisfaction. In their view, customer satisfaction was a leading indicator of financial performance.[1]

In the first half of the 1990s, many electronics companies were investigating high definition television (HDTV), a new technology that produced higher picture resolution in addition to superior digital stereo sound. **ZENITH**, as the only American owned television manufacturer, was particularly interested in this development. In order to best make a decision about whether and how to proceed, they had to forecast demand for the new technology and study consumer preferences for the new format.[2]

---

1   This example is fully discussed in "Xerox Corporation: The Customer Satisfaction Program," Harvard Business School Case #9-591-055, Boston, 1991.

2   This case is discussed in "Zenith: Marketing Research for High Definition Television (HDTV)," Harvard

** Photocards were available in the early 1980s from some regional banks (e.g., Baybank in Boston). These cards were abandoned because of excessvie production costs. In the early 1990s technology

Coffee is the largest product category in the portfolio of **GENERAL FOODS**. Unfortunately for them, however, health concerns have led to a national decline in coffee consumption. These trends have not affected all aspects of the coffee business equally. In particular, decaffeinated brands are less affected than caffeinated ones. Gourmet brands, such as the General Foods International Coffees, are less affected than mass-market ones. General Foods, and the Maxwell House division in particular, must decide how to allocate its resources among its brands so as to maximize its performance.[3]

These situations differ in a wide variety of ways. They involve distinct strategic decisions. Some involve market entry (e.g., Zenith), others involve product differentiation (e.g., Citibank), and others involve resource allocation (e.g., General Foods). The role the company plays in its industry differs. Some of the situations involve companies that are market leaders (e.g., Citibank), while others involve companies that are market challengers (e.g., Reebok). The situations represent industries in different stages of growth. Some involve mature industries (e.g., General Foods), while others involve embryonic industries (e.g., Zenith). The situations also differ with respect to issues as fundamental as whether or not the company is a participant in the industry in question. Some involve companies contemplating entering an industry (e.g., Victoria Moore), while others involve companies already there (e.g., Xerox). Still, despite these many differences, they all have one thing in common, and that one thing provides the basis for this book. They all require the collection and/or analysis of information (data) in order to make the appropriate decision. That is what this book is about, the analysis of information necessary to make strategic marketing decisions.

In this chapter, we begin by outlining what a strategic marketing decision is. We continue by classifying strategic situations and demonstrating that specific needs for analysis vary systematically across these situations. Then we show what role analysis plays in the process of strategic decision making. The chapter concludes with a bridge between these issues and the remainder of the book.

BOUNDARIES OF STRATEGIC MARKETING

If you ask most managers what a strategy is, you will invariably elicit a response such as: "It's the way you go about accomplishing your objectives." This is rather vague, and for good reason. The word *strategy* is ubiquitous in common language. It is used not only in conjunction with business in general and marketing in particular; it is also associated with politics, military action, and sports. For example, consider the longtime rivalry between tennis players

---

Business School Case #9-591-025, Boston, 1990.

3 This example is based on "U.S. Retail Coffee Market (A)," Harvard Business School Case #9-582-087, Boston, 1982; "U.S. Retail Coffee Market (B)," Harvard Business School Case #9-582-088, Boston, 1982; and "Brim (A)," Harvard Business School Case #9-582-089, Boston, 1982.

Martina Navratilova and Chris Evert. Each match they played followed the same pattern. Martina would try to attack the net and either hit a winning shot or make an error; she tried to shorten the points as much as possible. In contrast, Chris would try to hit the ball deep and keep Martina away from the net until she made a mistake; she tried to lengthen the points as much as possible. Each player tried to establish the pattern of points in which she had the best chance of winning. Martina wanted short points because she was a dynamic, attacking player who could hit winning shots with great skill; if the points were determined by who could hit the first winning shot, her skill at attacking would be the determining factor, and she would most likely win. Chris wanted long points because she was steady; if the points were determined by who made the first mistake, her steadiness made it unlikely it would be her, and she would most likely win. In this context, strategy reduces to the pattern of points (short, long) and the method of winning points (attacking, steadiness).

In marketing, the pattern of points reduces to the selection of markets that companies will compete in, the products they design, and the companies they acquire. The method of winning points becomes the way companies get sales from customers, what skills they employ to get customers to buy. These ideas are reflected in the strategic game board designed by Roberto Buaron, the well-known McKinsey consultant. As shown in Figure 1.1, strategic choice can be boiled down to two issues, where to compete and how to compete.

The question of where to compete can manifest itself in a variety of forms. It can be a question of whether or not to enter a new industry, as is the case with Victoria Moore. It can focus on the pursuit of certain segments within a given industry, as is Reebok's task. Finally, given that a firm may compete in several industries and/or segments, it must decide on the relative emphasis to place on each. Such is the situation confronting the Maxwell House division of General Foods.

Although the question of how to compete seems to encompass almost an infinite number of alternatives, Michael Porter argues that there are really only two general classes of options.[4] One is to be the low-cost producer. If a firm is the low-cost producer, it will perform at or above the industry average if it can sustain prices at or near the industry average. The second way for a firm to compete is by differentiating its product or service from its competition. Some companies, such as Xerox, attempt to do this by making their product objectively better. Others simply make their product different and then see whether consumers value their differences. This is the case with the Citibank photocard. The choice between these two ways to compete should be dictated by the skills and resources a firm possesses that allow it to play the appropriate game well.

Formally then, we define the boundaries of strategic marketing as those issues that either directly or tangentially impact decisions on either or both of:

---

4   Michael E. Porter, *Competitive Strategy* (New York: Free Press, 1980).

FIGURE 1.1
THE STRATEGIC GAME BOARD

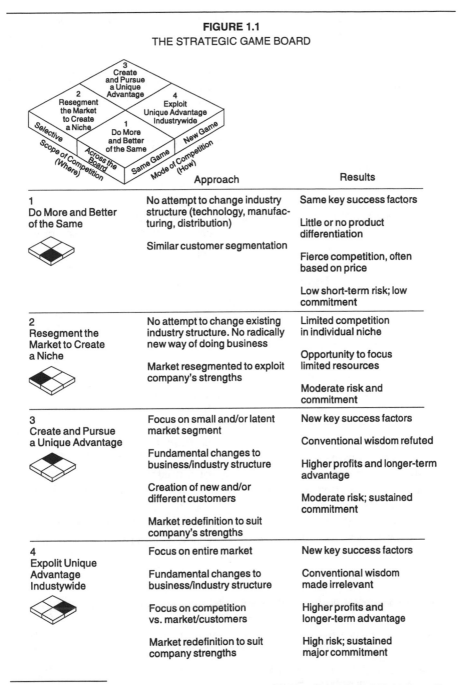

	Approach	Results
1 **Do More and Better** **of the Same**	No attempt to change industry structure (technology, manufacturing, distribution) Similar customer segmentation	Same key success factors Little or no product differentiation Fierce competition, often based on price Low short-term risk; low commitment
2 **Resegment the** **Market to Create** **a Niche**	No attempt to change existing industry structure. No radically new way of doing business Market resegmented to exploit company's strengths	Limited competition in individual niche Opportunity to focus limited resources Moderate risk and commitment
3 **Create and Pursue** **a Unique Advantage**	Focus on small and/or latent market segment Fundamental changes to business/industry structure Creation of new and/or different customers Market redefinition to suit company's strengths	New key success factors Conventional wisdom refuted Higher profits and longer-term advantage Moderate risk; sustained commitment
4 **Expolit Unique** **Advantage** **Industywide**	Focus on entire market Fundamental changes to business/industry structure Focus on competition vs. market/customers Market redefinition to suit company strengths	New key success factors Conventional wisdom made irrelevant Higher profits and longer-term advantage High risk; sustained major commitment

Source: Roberto Buaron, "How to Win the Market-Share Game: Try Changing the Rules," *Management Review* 70 (1981): 8–19. Reprinted with permission, AMACOM, American Management Association.

1. Market Scope. Those markets that a firm wishes to target. Market can be defined with respect to customers, products produced, needs satisfied, or technologies employed.

2. Competitive Advantage. The assets, skills, and resources a firm possesses and the positional (differentiation, low cost) advantages they lead to that enable a firm to achieve superior performance.

CLASSIFICATION OF STRATEGIC SITUATIONS

The specific strategic issues a firm faces in its choice of market scope and competitive advantage will differ as its circumstances differ. Charles Hofer surveyed the business strategy literature and uncovered a set of 54 variables that marketing, policy, and economic theorists have determined to be of major importance to a firm's choice of strategy. These include broad-based environmental variables (e.g., economic, demographic, sociocultural, political, and legal), supplier variables (e.g., degree of supplier integration), industry structure variables (e.g., degree of product differentiation, price/cost structure), competitor variables (e.g., number of competitors, aggressiveness of competition), consumer variables (e.g., buyer needs, market size), and firm characteristics (e.g., market share, quality of product).[5] Some of these variables are faced by *all* firms in an industry (e.g., environmental and industry structure variables), while others are *unique to each firm* in an industry (e.g., firm characteristics). Fortunately, as Hofer points out, these factors are not completely independent. Many of the factors faced by all firms in an industry are systematically related to the stage of an industry's development. Furthermore, industry progressions are not completely random. Much commonality exists across them. For example, early in its development, *any* industry will tend to have few competitors and low degrees of product differentiation. This commonality and the relationship of stage-of-industry development to other important strategy determining factors make it a useful variable on which to characterize strategic environments.

There are many ways to categorize industry development.[6] These schemes differ according to the number of discrete stages, what their names are, and what determines the transition from one to another. We use the approach suggested by Philip Kotler. His framework suggests that an industry evolves through four stages: emergence, growth, maturity, and decline.[7]

Before a market emerges, it exists in a latent condition: A group of people have an unmet need or want that no existing product currently satisfies. The people who have this need may not even recognize it themselves. Some

---

5   See Charles W. Hofer, "Toward a Contingency Theory of Business Strategy," *Academy of Management Journal* 18 (December 1975): 784–810.

6   *Ibid.* mentions several alternatives.

7   See Philip Kotler, *Marketing Management: Analysis, Planning, and Control* (Englewood Cliffs, NJ: Prentice-Hall, 1994): 374–377.

entrepreneur, however, does recognize it and derives a way to fill it. The need exists in a general form, and general satisfaction of it will usually suffice. The Bowmar Brain (the first hand-held calculator) was developed in response to a latent need for people to perform calculations more rapidly than could be done with a paper and pencil, abacus, or slide rule. The precise form of a product in the **Emergence Stage** is not usually a major issue. Buyers' preferences will in some sense be formed to fit the alternatives the market provides.[8] If that is indeed the case, the forecasts Zenith needs to make for its HDTVs should not depend on the precise formulation of the product as much as the generic need it satisfies. A firm's ability to gain competitive advantage in the emergence stage is largely keyed to its ability to satisfy a generic need. Satisfying it better than others is not that great a problem at this point, since there are no others. One of the major risks the entrepreneur faces here is a lack of knowledge of how extensive the generic need is. The extent of the need determines the potential size of the market.

If sales in an emergent market are good, other firms will enter the market and help it grow. Often, this will occur because the market recognizes there is something that the product(s) in the market could do better. For example, hand-held calculators could be made smaller than the original Bowmar Brain. Many firms entered the market making smaller and smaller calculators. As a market gains experience with a product, it learns how to use it and begins to understand its requirements. A key to the market's development is to recognize that not all consumers will have the same requirements. Different segments will have different needs unmet by existing offerings. These unmet needs represent opportunities for potential entrants. A potential entrant's ability to gain competitive advantage in this **Growth Stage** is therefore keyed to its ability to recognize and satisfy diverse consumer preferences. The Bowmar Brain was not only too large, it did not perform enough functions. Calculators with more scientific functions than addition, subtraction, multiplication, and division began to emerge. Normally, the number of competitors increases rapidly during the Growth Stage. Industry sales generally increase in this stage as well since the latent need capitalized on in the emergence stage is becoming more obvious to the population as a whole. For example, the Victoria Moore company is trying to enter a market where more and more customers are recognizing the need to integrate fashion with athletic activity. Since the market is still evolving in a turbulent manner, its ultimate potential and the depth of the underlying need is still uncertain.

When most of the population has recognized the need the product satisfies and consequently has entered the market, sales increases will necessarily slow or perhaps even disappear. Industry sales levels become predictably stable, and

---

8   For example, Gregory S. Carpenter and Kent Nakamoto, "Consumer Preference Formation and Pioneering Advantage," *Journal of Marketing Research* 26 (August 1989): 285–298, suggest that consumers' preferences in an emerging market are labile and influenceable by the specific design of the pioneering product. Uneducated consumers are not really capable of understanding the variety of potential benefits a product can offer and therefore need the manufacturers to tell them what is really important.

the industry enters the **Maturity Stage.** The only way firms can increase their revenues here is to take them from existing competitors. Customer requirements will become more and more precise largely because customers will understand the product and how it performs better. They will know more about what they want in the product. Firms will be willing to tailor their offerings to more refined segments because it is the only way they can continue to succeed. Unfortunately for them, the degree of potential success decreases. As a segment's requirements get increasingly refined, the segment will usually fragment. Furthermore, satisfying these requirements will usually entail research costs to modify existing products and develop new ones. In the wake of these dynamics, profits may not be as large as they were previously. But because the industry is still profitable, firms will continue to enter the industry.

Consider the credit card industry. Profits have traditionally come from retailer discounts, annual fees, and interest on balances. A casual visit to one's own mailbox should demonstrate that more and more companies are offering cards every day. These offerings waive annual fees, charge lower interest rates, and decrease retailer discounts. This forces traditional competitors to either match these terms and/or provide customers some other incentive to use their card. In the face of sharply declining profits, Citibank is trying to satisfy the precise needs of a security-conscious segment with the photocard. They first must discern if the card would actually satisfy this need.

Eventually, markets enter a **Decline Stage**. Often, new technologies emerge that make previous products obsolete. New competitors no longer enter the market; in fact, existing competitors may leave it. A firm can remain in the market only if it either looks for an enduring pocket of demand in the declining market, such as General Foods has done with their decaffeinated brands of coffee, or if it becomes the dominant competitor in the declining industry. The choice of which of these, if either, a firm should do is contingent on its forecast of how fast the decline will be and how strong it is relative to its competitors.[9]

In sum, a firm's decisions related to market scope and competitive advantage vary as the stage of development of its industry evolves. Firms in an emergent industry face different circumstances than those in a mature industry. Consequently, a firm's specific needs for information and analyses related to customers and competitors and its ability to forecast the market will also vary as the industry evolves. Table 1.1 summarizes the major variations in these situations that in turn affect a firm's need for analysis.

The type of research and analysis a firm needs depends not only on its stage of development, but on the role it plays in its industry as well. A firm participating in an industry can be a leader, challenger, follower, or nicher.[10] In addition, there are potential entrants to any industry.

---

9   See Kathryn R. Harrigan and Michael E. Porter, "End Game Strategies for Declining Industries," *Harvard Business Review* 61 (July–August 1983): 111–120.

10 This classification is proposed in Philip Kotler, *Marketing Management: Analysis, Planning and Control,* 8th edition (Englewood Cliffs, NJ: Prentice-Hall, 1994): 382.

TABLE 1.1

STRATEGIC ENVIRONMENTS AT DIFFERENT STAGES OF DEVELOPMENT

Stage of Industry Development	MARKET SCOPE RELATED			COMPETITIVE ADVANTAGE RELATED	FORECASTING RELATED
	Segments	Buyers' Needs and Wants	Product Variety	Ability to Gain Competitive Advantage	Difficulty
Emergent	None	Undefined, but to be developed	None	Easy once need is identified	Extremely high
Growing	Beginning to form	Defined but need to be differentiated	Limited but growing	Keyed to differences in customer preferences	Uncertain— errors still likely
Mature	Many and diverse	Differentiated	High (may be in terms of cosmetic features such as size, flavor, or technical features)	Difficult	Straightforward
Declining	Many (perhaps fewer) and diverse	Changing in dramatic style	High at first, but eventually small as brands begin to evaporate	Very difficult	Straightforward

The **Market Leader** is the firm with the largest market share. It is an orientation point for competitors to consciously challenge, imitate, or avoid. In general, the strategies available to a leader include increasing market share, defending market share, and expanding the market by attracting new users, developing new uses, or increasing current users' use of a product or service. Citibank is the market leader in the credit card industry. The photocard is Citibank's attempt to increase market share by differentiating its product in a meaningful way.

A **Market Challenger** holds the second, third, or sometimes lower rank in market share. Its strategic objectives are usually framed in terms of increasing market share, with the underlying assumption being that increased market share will lead to increased profits.[11] The tasks that a market challenger must face include identifying which competitor or class of competitors the challenger will try to take share from and whether the challenger's attack would be pitting its strengths against the competitor's strengths, pitting its strengths

11 For a discussion of the market share–profitability relationship, see Robert D. Buzzell, Bradley T. Gale, and Ralph G.M. Sultan, "Market Share—A Key to Profitability," *Harvard Business Review* 53 (January–February 1975): 97–106.

against the competitor's weaknesses, or applying its strengths to areas the competitor has not yet taken advantage of. Reebok has consistently been a challenger to Nike's position in athletic footwear. In attempting to identify growth segments, Reebok is attempting the last of the above options.

Market Followers tend to follow rather than challenge the market leader. Their philosophy is that a market leader will react strongly to any threats. If a firm does not have the ability to seriously threaten a market leader with a product innovation or distribution breakthrough, it may be better off recognizing that any attempt at challenging the market leader's position can at best be a Pyrrhic victory. Market followers usually clone, imitate, or adapt the leader's products.

An alternative for the smaller firm to being a market follower is to be a **Market Nicher.** Firms can avoid major competitors in two ways. They can deliberately not be a threat in the overall market, or they can target small segments (niches) of the market that have little or no interest to the leader. They become specialists in some end use, customer group, quality level, or channel. In producing the General Foods International Coffee line, the Maxwell House division of GF is acting like a market nicher by going after the gourmet segments and other consumers who entertain often.

Finally, any industry is subject to potential entrants. As suggested by Michael Porter's Five Forces of Competition (see Figure 1.2), potential entrants are one of the basic forces that determine an industry's long-term profitability. The seriousness of the threat of new entrants depends on the barriers to entry present and the degree to which potential entrants can expect harsh retaliation from firms already in the industry. High barriers to entry exist when there are large economies of scale, customers have high degrees of brand identification, there are large capital requirements or set-up costs, entrenched companies have cost advantages, access to distribution channels are scarce, and government has placed regulations on the industry.[12] Harsh reactions from incumbents can be expected when the incumbents possess substantial resources or have excess capacity, or when industry growth is slow.[13]

Potential entrants can come from almost anywhere. However, the firms that are most likely to enter a given market are those that operate adjacent to the market. Two of these classes of firms can also be found among Porter's five forces: the suppliers and customers of those firms that operate in the industry. These firms would enter if the benefits of buying a buyer or seller (e.g., operating economies, access to supply or demand, control over the product system) justify the increased costs (e.g., operating costs, inexperience in a new business, reduced flexibility). Other potential entrants operating adjacent to a given industry include firms that sell different products to the same market and firms that make similar products and sell them to different markets.

---

12 These conditions are outlined in more detail in Michael E. Porter, "How Competitive Forces Shape Strategy," *Harvard Business Review* 57 (March–April 1979): 139–140.

13 These conditions are outlined in more detail in Porter, *Ibid.*, 140.

FIGURE 1-2
PORTER'S FIVE FORCES OF COMPETITION

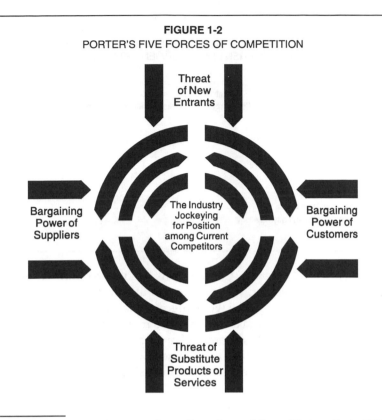

Source: Michael E. Porter, "How Competitive Forces Shape Strategy," *Harvard Business Review* 57 (March–April 1979): 141. Reprinted with permission.

Victoria Moore makes products similar to activewear in manufacturing process (apparel) and sells them to the same market (the upscale consumer). Thus, Victoria Moore is a potential entrant.

Industries at different stages of development will have different concentrations of firms with given roles. Emergent industries usually have one or maybe two firms competing. Even after technology and design have been established, an emergent industry may have no competitors for a while until a product is commercialized. Such is the case with the HDTV market, as described in the Zenith vignette. As an industry grows, other firms enter to challenge and imitate the leader. Once an industry matures, niche players emerge. Finally, as an industry declines, there is rarely room for more than one or two competitors. These stages are summarized in Table 1.2.

The important point to remember here is that the analysis needs of a firm depend not only on the stage of development of its industry, but on the role the firm plays in that industry. For example, Citibank and Reebok both compete in mature industries. Citibank is a market leader; Reebok is a market

TABLE 1.2
STRATEGIC RELEVANCE OF COMPETITIVE ROLES
AT DIFFERENT DEVELOPMENT STAGES

Stage of Industry Development	Market Leader	Market Challenger	Market Follower	Market Nicher	Potential Entrant
Emergent	?	?	—	—	X
Growing	X	X	X	—	X
Mature	X	X	X	X	X
Declining	X	?	?	?	—

X = Strategically most relevant
— = Strategically least relevant
? = May or may not be strategically relevant

challenger. As a market leader, Citibank was looking to reinforce its positioning statement. In particular, they wanted to affirm its "security and confidence" aspects. That is why they were interested in establishing the role of the photo in card usage. In contrast, Reebok, as a market challenger, had to try to do something substantively different. Thus, they began to look for growth segments. More specifically, they needed new ways of segmenting the market and selecting some of these segments for intensive pursuit.

ANALYSIS AND THE PROCESS OF STRATEGIC THINKING

As implied by the situations described at the outset of this chapter, good judgment is not enough to make good strategic decisions without the benefit of thorough analysis. When a strategist views a situation primed for a strategic decision with respect to market scope and/or competitive advantage, he or she generally encounters areas of uncertainty that directly affect the decision. This uncertainty can usually be captured in the form of strategic questions such as in Table 1.3. Formal analyses are often necessary to answer these strategic questions. The manager then uses the answers to these questions in making decisions. For strategic questions to be meaningful, they must relate to a firm's ability to attain a competitive advantage within a given market scope. The general entities that primarily influence this ability are customers, competitors, the firm itself, and the external environment. (See Figure 1.3.)

Strategic questions relating to customers tend to focus on defining market segments and understanding their motivations. Market segments can be defined in terms of customers, products, technologies, or needs. Segments are important because they provide a framework for defining market scope (i.e., What segments will be served?). Customer motivations are important to understand because the skills and assets needed to address these motivations

---

TABLE 1.3
EXAMPLES OF STRATEGIC QUESTIONS

Customer Related

> Who are the potential customers?
> Are there any customers not being served adequately?

Competitor Related

> Who are the potential competitors?
> What is the basis of the firm's advantage over its competitors?

Environment Related

> What factors in the external environment influence how the firm will perform?
> How will these factors change?

Company Decision Related

> How should a firm decide how much emphasis to place on each market it participates in?
> What are the expected results of any given strategy?

(which may currently be unmet by existing competitors) present the key to a firm striving for competitive advantage in a given segment.

Those strategic questions relevant to competitors generally come in two forms, Who are they? and What are their strengths and weaknesses? The notion of competitive advantage usually involves exploiting a competitor's weakness or neutralizing a competitor's strength. The importance of the Who are they? question comes from the observation that firms often define their competition too narrowly. For example, the myopia of the railroad industry in the middle of the 20th century in not recognizing the competitive threat of the airline industry is well documented.[14] Activewear manufacturers would be remiss if they ignored companies such as Victoria Moore.

---

14 See Theodore Levitt, "Marketing Myopia," *Harvard Business Review* 38 (July–August 1960): 45–56.

FIGURE 1.3
FRAMEWORK FOR ANALYZING MARKET SCOPE AND COMPETITIVE ADVANTAGE

External Environment

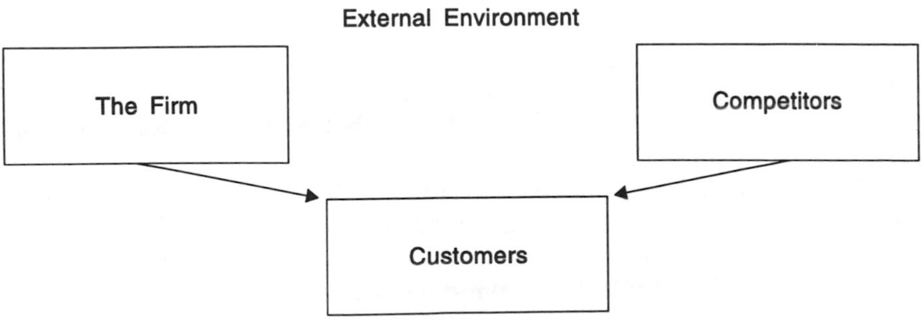

Strategic questions about the firm itself are essentially the same as the strengths and weaknesses questions about competitors. These again provide the basis for assessing competitive advantage. The major difference between answering questions about your own strengths and weaknesses and those of your competitors lies in the level of information available.

Finally, each firm faces important forces outside it that shape its strategic options and choices. These forces include political, economic, social, and technological factors. Strategic questions about these forces focus on how they will change and what impacts they will have on particular markets. Do they present any new opportunities or threats? For example, the last 20 years have seen an increase in the fitness consciousness of many Americans. This as much as anything has produced the opportunity for Victoria Moore to come into the market.

We should keep in mind however that firms usually participate in multiple markets. Therefore, the framework presented in Figure 1.3 has to be replicated as many times as the number of markets the firm is considering. From an analytic perspective, each replication has its own set of strategic questions. From a decision-making perspective, this leads, of course, to the question of how much effort the firm should allocate to each market.

Thorough Analysis Does Not
Always Lead to Good Outcomes

Unfortunately, after all is said and done in obtaining the best answers to the strategic questions posed, a manager may still make a decision that has a bad outcome. This can occur because the analyses cannot eliminate uncertainty, the analyses lack relevance, or the managers are incapable of interpreting the results accurately.

The first reason that thorough analyses do not guarantee success is that they do not eliminate uncertainty. Consider Zenith and the HDTV. It would be surprising indeed if any forecast were perfectly accurate. There are so many unknowns, so many strategic questions. How will the technology develop? What competitive technologies (if any) will emerge? How will consumers react to the technology? How will it be priced? Each of these areas will affect the number of HDTVs sold. Not knowing the answers to these questions necessarily imparts some uncertainty to the forecast. Whether a manager likes it or not, decision making usually takes place in the face of uncertainty. In fact, if there were no uncertainty in a situation, a manager probably would not be needed. All decisions could be made by a robot or a computer that could unambiguously interpret the appropriate information.

What then, if not to eliminate uncertainty, is the role of analysis? Analysis provides information in a form that **REDUCES** the uncertainty implicit in the strategic questions. The manager's job then is to take the information and exercise his or her judgment in making decisions. The good decision maker acknowledges that uncertainty is unavoidable and that each decision is a risk.

Therefore, we distinguish between bad decisions and bad outcomes. Good decisions can have bad outcomes if the uncertainty gets resolved in a manner that was both unlikely before the decision was made and unfriendly to the chosen strategy. Suppose that before the decision, we could have said that it was likely that the uncertainty would be resolved in a manner friendly to the chosen strategy. In this case, the decision would still be correct; it would just have turned out wrong. More likely than not, this decision would have produced a good outcome.

Suppose, for example, that Zenith used consumer surveys to forecast HDTV demand and that these revealed a lucrative market. Suppose further that Zenith interviewed television network representatives and determined they had a 90 percent likelihood of being able to develop transmission procedures that would take advantage of the high-resolution properties of HDTV. This hypothetical example twists on a final supposition—that the networks could not develop appropriate transmission procedures. In this case, HDTV would provide no benefit to the consumer, and sales would fall far short of the forecast. The decision was the right one because it was likely the uncertainty in transmission would be resolved in a manner friendly to HDTV. The decision would have been bad if the unfriendly manner in which the transmission uncertainty was resolved could have been viewed as likely before the fact.

A second reason that thorough analyses frequently do not lead to success is that they are often conducted without a direct link to the decision involved. For example, suppose Citibank was reluctant to pull the trigger on the photo-card line. Feeling nervous, bank management requested a study of how other banks solicit new cardholders. The connection between this and the go/no-go decision for the photocard is tangential at best. This story demonstrates an all too common function of research and analysis. It serves to postpone the decision for managers who have cold feet. Furthermore, the lack of a direct relationship to the decision renders the analysis relatively useless. An analysis should have a direct impact on the decision. For example, Citibank's attempt to determine whether the photocard generates feelings of security and confidence is more directly related to the card's introduction. If it does, the appropriate decision is to introduce; if it doesn't, the appropriate decision is to pull back. This last statement indicates one way to ensure that analyses are relevant to a decision at hand. If a manager can make a statement of the form, "If the results of the analysis say X, then I should do A; if the results of the analysis say Y, then I should do B," she knows that the forthcoming information is relevant to her decision.

A third reason that thorough analyses do not always produce successes is that the information contained in the results may be difficult for managers to interpret, and the problem lies in the managers! Unfortunately, managers (and humans in general) are not nearly as smart as they think they are. This is ironic in light of the fact that we all accept the deficiencies and limitations in our memory. We all use aids (e.g., address books, daily calendars, etc.) to help us avoid the penalties of faulty memory. We seem to be unwilling, though, to acknowledge that our judgment might be faulty or biased.

For example, managers tend to complain that they do not have enough information on which to base their decisions. Russell Ackoff suggests that just the opposite is true. His contention is that managers often have *too much* information at their disposal. Their difficulty is in determining which precise pieces of information are most relevant to their current decisions. Consequently, they may base their decisions on the wrong information.[15]

The view of the Nobel Prize winning scientist Herbert Simon is consistent with this view.[16] He argues that managers face a very complex world. Even when they have complete information about this world, they cannot make the appropriate decisions because their abilities to mentally process this information are limited. In order to deal with this limitation, they simplify the world to make it more manageable. They then make the correct decisions given the way they have simplified their world. However, there is no guarantee that these decisions are correct for the actual, complex world. Simon calls this *bounded rationality*; the manager is rational within the bounds of the way he or she views the world.

Simplification of information about the world for judgment and decision often results in the use of simple rules or *heuristics*. These simple rules introduce bias into a decision maker's activity. For example, suppose that a Reebok executive was on a flight to Miami Beach. On that flight, he notices a number of senior citizens all wearing athletic shoes. He makes the simplification that the proportion of senior citizens on that flight is typical of the proportion in the population as a whole. He therefore assumes that senior citizens are a growth market for athletic shoes. What he has done is use a rule that states that specific instances that are easily observed or recalled can serve as a basis for future-oriented decisions. This is an example of the well-known *availability* heuristic and *availability* bias.[17] The Reebok executive is focusing on the mental availability of the number of senior citizens on the flight wearing athletic shoes and ignores the possibility that a flight to Miami Beach might have a higher proportion of senior citizens than does the population as a whole. Similar results would occur if the executive conducted a consumer survey with a sample that did not reflect the population at large.

The Remedy: Planning Processes

As indicated earlier, uncertainty is something we can never eliminate. There are ways, however, to ensure relevance and minimize a decision maker's

---

15 See Russell L. Ackoff, "Management Misinformation Systems," *Management Science* 14 (1967): B147–B156 (C) for a complete discussion.

16 See Herbert A. Simon, *Administrative Behavior*, 3rd ed. (New York: Free Press, 1976) for a complete presentation of Simon's viewpoint.

17 See Amos Tversky and Daniel Kahneman, "Availability: A Heuristic for Judging Frequency and Probability," *Cognitive Psychology* 5 (1973): 207–232 for a more complete discussion.

susceptibility to the limitations in information-processing abilities. These can be accomplished with the aid of a formalized, structured, comprehensive planning process. Structure ensures that many of the "right" strategic questions get asked. This in turn ensures that any analysis done is relevant. The Citibank study of competitors' solicitation procedures proposed in the previous section would never be allowed. Comprehensiveness ensures that enough pieces of information are seen so that the decision maker can best approximate the complex world she or he operates in and avoid biases such as availability. It is important that enough gets seen and no more! If too much gets seen, the decision maker may see the world as more complex than she or he needs to and be vulnerable to bounded rationality.

Planning processes are usually conducted according to strict guidelines and follow a strict schedule. Companies have formal how-to type planning manuals that dictate how the process is to be conducted.[18] The product of the process is usually a formal, written document that reflects and justifies the firm's strategic intentions.

Unfortunately, too often in corporate America, the product (the plan) is emphasized at the expense of the process (planning). After all, planners are hired to prepare plans. When the plan itself takes on paramount importance, the planning process usually turns into one of essentially completing a checklist of separate tasks prescribed by the manual without paying attention to whether the thinking behind it is coherent. As General Eisenhower said during World War II, "Planning is everything, plans are nothing." Although this is somewhat of an exaggeration, it emphasizes the point that the decision-making activity is more important than the written document. In fact, one could argue that if the planning process were conducted properly, the decisions that emerged from it would be logically based as well as understood and accepted by everyone involved. The written document would almost be superfluous except as a historical record. The purpose of planning is not to create a plan. The purpose of planning is to ask the right strategic questions, answer them to the extent possible, and use those answers in making decisions.

FRAMEWORK OF THE BOOK

This book is structured around formal analytic methods that can be used to answer the strategic questions described in Table 1.3. As noted, these questions all relate to customers, competitors, the company itself, and the external environment.

Who are the potential customers? Analyzing the marketplace begins with a thorough understanding of the behavior of a firm's customers and their needs. Part of determining market scope is deciding which customers will comprise the firm's future. In order to do this effectively, the marketing strategist must

---

18 David S. Hopkins, *The Marketing Plan* (New York: The Conference Board, 1981) presents some excerpts from some of these manuals.

first determine what segments currently exist in the marketplace. This is the task facing Reebok at the beginning of the chapter. Only then can intelligent choices be made with respect to whose needs the firm will meet. The identification of these segments is the subject of Chapter 2, Segmenting Markets: Who Are the Potential Buyers?

Are there any customers not being served adequately? In order to grow, a firm must expand its portfolio of offerings by modifying existing products and services as well as adding new ones. A change in its market scope must constantly be under consideration. Whether products and services are modified or changed, the firm must understand the current and future needs of various customer segments, such as the security-conscious segment Citibank is interested in. The firm's objectives must then include both the satisfaction of needs currently met by other firms, perhaps inadequately, and the satisfaction of needs not currently being met in the marketplace. Chapter 3, Identifying Unmet Needs: What Do the Customers Want? is devoted to methods of identifying both classes of need.

Who are the potential competitors? In order to attain growth objectives, firms must strive to enter new markets as well as strengthen their positions in existing ones. Marketing strategists searching for new markets must identify the existing and potential competitors in them. For example, Victoria Moore wanted to know who her competitors would be. Similarly, firms defending their positions in existing markets must be able to anticipate potential entrants. Thus, maintaining viable market positions requires careful analysis of present and potential competition. The identification of both types of competitors forms the subject matter of Chapter 4, Identifying Competitors: Who Will We Compete Against?

What factors in the external environment influence how the firm will perform? Any given industry's fortunes naturally depend on the behavior of its customers, competitors, and suppliers. At a macro level, these behaviors are influenced by a variety of environmental factors, including demographic, economic, social, political, and technological factors. Such factors can be instrumental in providing opportunities for and imposing threats on the firm. General Foods was faced with a health-conscious population decreasing its consumption of coffee. Determining the critical environmental factors represents a major component of so-called S.W.O.T. (strengths, weaknesses, opportunities, and threats) analysis. Chapter 5, Understanding and Forecasting External Environment, describes analytic methods for identifying which factors are most important to the firm. It also touches on ways of determining the likely future trends of these factors.

How will these factors change? Effective marketing strategy requires more than just an understanding of the current environment. Only a vision of the future can enable management to assess any market's attractiveness appropriately. Methods useful for this generally fall under the heading of forecasting. When forecasting for established products and markets, standard techniques such as regression, which rely on historical data, can be used. When dealing with new products and new markets such as is Zenith's task for the HDTV, forecasting can be particularly difficult because less historical data will generally be available. Here creative thinking is required. Issues related to these tasks form the basis for Chapter 6, Understanding and Forecasting Market Environment.

What are the bases of a firm's advantage over its competitors? Analyzing the environment will generally reveal the opportunities and threats facing a firm. Its ability to capitalize on those opportunities and avoid those threats hinges on the skills and resources it has relative to its competitors. Chapter 7, Analyzing Strengths and Weaknesses: How Will We Compete? is devoted to the measurement of these skills and resources and completes the S.W.O.T. analyses that form the basis of strategic market planning. Such an analysis enabled Xerox to become aware of its problems.

How should a firm decide how much emphasis to place on each market it participates in? Strategic decisions based on previous analyses require an allocation of resources among competing activities. These allocations are performed at various levels within the organization. In general, resources at the corporate level are allocated among divisions and among the different strategic business units (SBUs) within each division. Allocation decisions are also made among existing products and new opportunities. Furthermore, new opportunities may reside within existing SBUs or lead to the creation of new SBUs. Methods of allocating resources have to account for possible interdependencies and synergies among the SBUs, for existing brands, and for new opportunities. Of course, the resources allocated to a brand or opportunity has to depend in part on the return expected from it. The expected return is in turn a function of the specific marketing activities on which the resources are spent. This is essentially the question, *What are the expected results of any given strategy?* For established brands, this question translates to modeling marketing mix response. (Forecasting this return is part of the subject matter of Chapter 6.) For development projects and new brands, this translation is not as precise. Therefore, we may need different approaches to allocate resources in different circumstances. These approaches provide the subject matter for Chapter 8, Resource Allocation.

The concluding chapter of the book, Chapter 9, Analyses in Action: Case Examples, presents a series of studies the authors are aware of that use methodologies discussed in Chapters 2 through 8 to address strategic questions posed in Table 1.3. The assumption here is that the reader will better learn from real-world examples.

BIBLIOGRAPHY

Ackoff, Russell L. "Management Misinformation Systems." *Management Science* 14 (1967): B147–B156 (C).

"Brim (A)." Harvard Business School Case #9-582-089. Boston, 1982.

Buaron, Roberto. "How to Win the Market-Share Game? Try Changing the Rules." *Management Review* 70 (January 1981): 8–19.

Buzzell, Robert D., Bradley T. Gale, and Ralph G.M. Sultan. "Market Share—A Key to Profitability." *Harvard Business Review* 53 (January–February 1975): 97–106.

Carpenter, Gregory S., and Kent Nakamoto. "Consumer Preference Formation and Pioneering Advantage." *Journal of Marketing Research* 26 (August 1989): 285–298.

Harrigan, Kathryn R., and Michael E. Porter. "End Game Strategies for Declining Industries." *Harvard Business Review* 61 (July–August 1983): 111–120.

Hofer, Charles W. "Toward a Contingency Theory of Business Strategy." *Academy of Management Journal* 18 (December 1975): 784–810.

Hopkins, David S. *The Marketing Plan.* New York: The Conference Board, 1981.

Kotler, Philip. *Marketing Management: Analysis, Planning, and Control.* Englewood Cliffs, NJ: Prentice-Hall, 1994.

Levitt, Theodore. "Marketing Myopia." *Harvard Business Review* 38 (July–August 1960): 45–56.

Porter, Michael E. "How Competitive Forces Shape Strategy." *Harvard Business Review* 57 (March–April 1979): 137–145.

———*Competitive Strategy.* New York: Free Press, 1980.

Simon, Herbert A. *Administrative Behavior.* 3d ed. New York: Free Press, 1976.

Tversky, Amos, and Daniel Kahneman. "Availability: A Heuristic for Judging Frequency and Probability." *Cognitive Psychology* 5 (1973): 207–232.

"U.S. Retail Coffee Market (A)." Harvard Business School Case #9-582-087. Boston, 1982.

"U.S. Retail Coffee Market (B)." Harvard Business School Case #9-582-088. Boston, 1982.

"Zenith: Marketing Research for High Definition Television (HDTV)." Harvard Business School Case #9-591-025. Boston, 1990.

CHAPTER 2

Segmenting Markets: Who Are the Potential Buyers?

INTRODUCTION

Market segmentation involves identifying subgroups of consumers who respond differently to a given marketing strategy. The response, which can range from sensitivity to price to desired benefits within a product category, is conceptualized as homogeneous within a segment and heterogeneous across segments. Recall from the first chapter that much of strategic decision making is devoted to determining market scope, i.e., deciding which markets to invest in. Segmentation then structures these decisions by defining the alternative product markets. Consequently, it is one of the most fundamental concepts in marketing strategy. Without it, marketers would have to treat the market as uniform.

For example, people buy automobiles for a variety of reasons: style, reliability, price, or perceived status. Identifying segments of consumers who desire certain benefits can be essential to marketing strategy. In particular, a company can only effectively design and market a stylish automobile if it knows there is demand for it. Furthermore, knowing who in general demands it, where they live, and what they read are critical for deciding what geographic areas it should be shown and sold in and where it should be advertised.

Furthermore, segmentation can be the key to developing a competitive advantage in and of itself. Kenichi Ohmae, the well-known Japanese consultant, tells a story about a forklift firm that focused on the retailing and construction industries.[1] It let its competitors handle the more demanding segments in the heavy-duty harbor and logging markets. The focused product line was able to achieve a 20 percent cost advantage and develop a dominant position.

Market segmentation has become even more important in recent years for four reasons:[2]

---

1 Kenichi Ohmae, *The Mind of the Strategist* (New York: Penguin Books, 1982) for more details.

2 Orville C. Walker, Harper W. Boyd, and Jean-Claude Larreche, *Marketing Strategy: Planning and Implementation* (Homewood, IL: Irwin, 1992): 176.

1. Populations are not growing as fast as they have been and many standard product-markets are maturing. The Census Bureau projects the American population will grow just 7.2 percent during the 1990s. Consequently, competition is becoming more and more intense. To survive, firms must pay attention to the precise needs and wants of their customers. If needs differ from those of the population at large, they must be addressed.

2. Expanding disposable incomes and higher education levels have produced consumers with sophisticated (and varied) tastes and lifestyles.

3. New technologies such as computer aided design and modular assemblies have enabled manufacturers to customize a wide variety of products.

4. New advertising media appealing to special-interest groups (e.g., magazines, cable TV, radio, direct marketing, etc.) has emerged, facilitating the implementation of narrowly targeted marketing programs.

While making segmentation more important, some of these reasons also make it more difficult. The increased variation in tastes and lifestyles makes it more difficult to determine the correct way to segment a particular market. In addition, the purchase criteria that consumers use in making brand choices are constantly changing. For example, one survey shows that in 1992 "a reasonable price" had become a more important determinant of brand choice in general than "manufacturer's reputation for quality." In 1985, the opposite was true.[3] However, we might not expect the dominance of price to hold across all demographic and socioeconomic groups. Thus, a marketer must have a comprehensive set of segmentation bases.

Market segmentation derives its value from three assumptions:

1. Consumers are different in many ways.

2. Many of these differences are related to demand in some manner.

3. Consumers that are different in ways related to demand can be isolated within the marketplace.

Some of the differences referred to in the first assumption are visible to the naked eye (e.g., sex, race, age); others are not (e.g., personal values). These differences produce the variables we use to segment markets, in other words, provide the bases for segmentation. The second assumption simply implies that segments should have different demand characteristics. For example, people who live in Minnesota will have greater demand for heavy winter coats than those who live in Arizona. People who are weight conscious will leave the store with grocery bags filled with very different items than people who are not weight conscious. The third assumption is a practical one. A firm needs a way to reach specific segments of customers—either by placing products in

---

3   This study is described in Holly Heline, "Brand Loyalty Isn't Dead," *Brandweek* (June 3, 1993): 14–15.

a given type of store or by advertising in certain media. Suppose an insurance company wanted to sell term life insurance to financially secure consumers who are emotionally insecure in that they worry about dying. If these insecure consumers are no different from secure ones with respect to media and shopping habits, it would be very difficult to communicate to them. The company would have to resort to a mass marketing approach.

A well-planned study designed to uncover market segments consists of the steps outlined in Table 2.1.

Since our focus is on marketing strategy, the managerial questions we will concentrate on are those related to strategy: Structuring the market with an eye towards identifying target segments. Among the wide variety of available segmentation variables or bases, we emphasize benefits sought by the consumer. A company should target only those segments for which it has the assets or skills to build sustainable competitive advantage. The most direct road to satisfying these consumers is to simply provide the benefits they seek. Thus, benefits sought is **THE** critical segmentation base for strategy development.

In discussing the formation of segments, we present a variety of analytic methods that can be used to accomplish the task. Of course, the appropriate analytic technique depends on both the managerial question that needs to be addressed and the segmentation bases chosen. The relevant data collection procedures depend in turn on the analytic method chosen. In this chapter, we mostly discuss steps two (segmentation variable or base selection) and four (analysis) from Table 2.1. We take step one (the managerial question) as given

TABLE 2.1
MAJOR STEPS IN A SEGMENTATION STUDY

Step		Examples
1)	Pose managerial questions to be answered by study.	What are potential target segments?
		Who is buying our product?
		Are there subgroups of the market who are price sensitive?
		What are the media habits of our customers?
2)	Select potential segmentation variables or bases.	Consumer markets: Age, sex, usage rate, benefits sought.
		Industrial markets: SIC code, organization size, benefits sought.
3)	Collect data.	Surveys, syndicated data sources, scanner panel data.
4)	Analyze data.	Perceptual mapping, conjoint analysis, laddering, cluster analysis, regression analysis.
5)	Interpret data.	Provide meaningful answers to managerial questions posed in step 1.

by those questions implicit in strategy development, discuss step three (data collection) only as it relates to steps two and four, and briefly address step five (interpretation).

BASES OF SEGMENTATION

There are literally thousands of dimensions on which consumers differ (e.g., age, sex, religion, etc.). Each can serve as a basis for segmenting markets. Not all dimensions will be equally useful in all situations. Nevertheless, Table 2.2 presents some of the more popular ones.[4]

The table divides the variables in several ways. First, it separates those more useful for consumer markets from those more useful for industrial markets. Some variables (e.g., geographic location and benefits sought) are useful for both. Others (e.g., race and SIC codes) are more specific for one. Second, the table separates out those variables that describe the consumer in general from those that specifically relate to various aspects of the consumer's choice and behavior. This distinction will become very important shortly.

Consumer Markets

Demographics are among the most popular variables used in segmenting consumer markets. Several reasons account for this. First, demographics are easy to measure, and segments defined this way are often very large and accessible by various communications media and distribution channels. Furthermore, demographic data can be very inexpensive. Relevant publications, such as the *U.S. Statistical Abstract, Rand McNally's Commercial Atlas and Marketing Guide, Sales and Marketing Management's Survey of Buying Power,* and the *U.S. Census of Population and Housing,* are available at almost every library in the United States. Finally, demographics are often projectable. Consider, for example, that today's male teenager will be a young adult male in 10 years.

Nevertheless, the question arises as to whether demographics-based segments have differences that are significant to the marketer. One might suspect that the young are different from the old but whether this is relevant in marketing a specific product may not be obvious. Do adults between 20 and 40 differ in their purchasing of headache remedies from those between 40 and 60? At best, the answer is unclear.

Many demographic variables can be conceptualized as composites of others. For example, *stage in life cycle* can be defined in terms of age, marital status, and number and age of children. This is also true with socioeconomic variables where social class can be defined in terms of income, education, home ownership, family size, and occupation. Donnelly's ClusterPlus project has used these socioeconomic variables to define 47 distinct social classes.[5]

---

4   This table presents an updating and expansion of the typologies developed in Ronald E. Frank, William F. Massy, and Yoram Wind, *Market Segmentation* (Englewood Cliffs, NJ: Prentice-Hall, 1972).

5   These classes are fully described in Art Weinstein, *Market Segmentation: Using Niche Marketing to Exploit*

TABLE 2.2
BASES OF SEGMENTATION

A. CONSUMER MARKETS

GENERAL DESCRIPTIVE CUSTOMER CHARACTERISTICS

Demographics
  Sex
  Age
  Marital status
  Number and age of children
  Stage in life cycle
  Subcultures
    Race
    Ethnic group
  Geographic location

Socioeconomic characteristics
  Income
  Education
  Occupation
  Social class

Psychographics (personality and lifestyle characteristics)
  Personality
  Attitudes
  Interests
  Opinions
  Lifestyle

Occasion

CHARACTERISTICS RELATED TO CONSUMER BEHAVIOR

Benefits sought

Desired application

Purchase and loyalty patterns
  Usage characteristics
    Heavy vs. Light
    User vs. Nonuser
  Store loyalty

Participation in the adoption and diffusion process
  Information and influence patterns
  Innovativeness

Brand behavior
  Loyalty
  Attitudes
  Intentions
  Perceptions
  Preferences

Sensitivity to marketing mix elements
  Price
  Advertising
  Promotion

B. INDUSTRIAL MARKETS

GENERAL DESCRIPTIVE CUSTOMER CHARACTERISTICS

General organizational characteristics
  SIC Code
  Size
  Geographic location
  Structure
    Power relationships
    Reward system
  Technology

Psychographics
  Direction
  Achievement motivation
  General degree of conflict
  Organizational climate

CHARACTERISTICS RELATED TO CONSUMER BEHAVIOR

Benefits sought

Product usage

Source loyalty

Buying process

Attitudes

Perceptions

Preferences

Sometime during the late 1960s and early 1970s marketers accepted the fact that demographic prediction of consumer behavior, though essential, could be improved upon. It seemed that individuals who had similar interests, enjoyed similar activities, and had similar outlooks on life might respond similarly to marketing stimuli. Researchers and practitioners began to use a collection of variables based on consumers' personalities; values; and activities, interests, and opinions (often referred to as AIO). Lifestyle is another composite variable that captures elements of all of these.

Companies routinely take advantage of life-style elements in marketing. Quaker Oats has gone to great pains to make its sports drink Gatorade available at what the company calls "points of sweat": sports clubs, gyms, any place people exercise and get thirsty.[6] Coca-Cola does the same with its PowerAde brand. Coke had the advantage of having vending machines already in place.

The term *psychographics* emerged to describe these sets of variables. There is no universally accepted definition of psychographics.[7] Despite this, the area has thrived over the last two decades. It suffices to say that psychographics are simply psychological elements such as personality, values, and lifestyle that can be used to describe consumers. They are intended to supplement (not replace) demographics. The two sets of variables should be used together, not independently.

Psychographic variables are not nearly as easy to identify as demographic ones. The usual approach is to ask a sample of consumers a large battery of AIO questions, some homemade and others taken from standard attitude or personality tests used in psychology, and use factor analysis to uncover whatever underlying psychographic dimensions dictated the responses to the questions asked. This is done by grouping together those items to which consumers respond similarly.

Table 2.3 presents the results of a factor analysis designed to consolidate psychographic dimensions to be used in segmenting the market for department stores in a large Southwestern community.[8] The table summarizes a psychographic analysis of 29 statements given to 754 residents of that community. Such an analysis could impact strategy in several ways. For example, a new department store might choose to carry quality old-fashioned merchandise if there is a large enough segment in its region that scores high on the statements comprising the traditionalist dimension.

New Markets (Chicago: Probus, 1987): 75–81.

6   "The Third of Champions," *The Economist* (June 6, 1992): 83.

7   William D. Wells, "Psychographics: A Critical Review," *Journal of Marketing Research* 12 (May 1975): 196–213 for a discussion of this issue and some interesting case studies.

8   This example is taken from William O. Bearden, Jesse E. Teel, Jr., and Richard M. Durand, "Media Usage, Psychographic, and Demographic Dimensions of Retail Shoppers," *Journal of Retailing* 54 (Spring 1978): 65–74.

TABLE 2.3
PSYCHOGRAPHIC ANALYSIS FOR SOUTHWESTERN DEPARTMENT STORES

Dimension	Sample Statement*	Number Items
Traditionalist	I have some old-fashioned tastes and habits.	11
Outgoing/ Individualist	I would rather fix something myself than take it to an expert.	5
Quality/Service	I will go out of my way to find a bank with good service.	5
Socially Conscious	If my clothes are not in fashion, it really bothers me.	5
Other-Directed	I usually ask for help from other people in making decisions.	3

* All AIO statements were operationalized as five-point scales ranging from strongly disagree to strongly agree.

Syndicated Services

As is apparent from the above description, psychographic studies can be very complex and costly. Syndicated or standardized research services can often provide lower (but still high) cost substitutes. Instead of hiring someone to take a survey, you subscribe to a survey already taken. Suppliers such as Yankelovich, Clancy, and Shulman, and Donnelly Marketing Services have derived general lifestyle segments that can be used as possible segmentation bases.

Probably the best known of these is Stanford Research Institute's VALS (Values and Lifestyles) program.[9] The latest version, VALS2, proposes the eight lifestyle segments illustrated in Figure 2.1. These segments, each ranging from 8 to 16 percent of the population, were derived from people's responses to a set of AIO items.

Suppliers such as Claritas, Donnelly, Mediamark, and Simmons characterize each respondent to their survey by VALS2 type. This allows the cross-classification of VALS2 type with all the product usage and personal information these companies collect. Researchers can see which VALS2 type bought which products, viewed which media, and so on.

For example, standard share data tell us that Advil is the market leader in ibuprofen (19.2 percent share); Nuprin is a distant second (6.4 percent share).[10] Furthermore, Simmons and Mediamark tell us that actualizers have the highest percentage of heavy ibuprofen users. They also tell us that Nuprin's

---

9   Rebecca Piirto, *Beyond Mind Games: The Marketing Power of Psychographics* (Ithaca, NY: American Demographics Books, 1991) provides a superb discussion of the history of the VALS program along with its criticisms and modifications. She also outlines several examples.

10 This example is discussed in more detail by Piirto, *Ibid.*, 88–90.

FIGURE 2.1
THE VALS2 TYPOLOGY

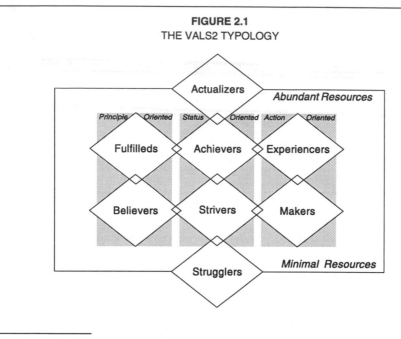

Source: SRI International. Reprinted with permission.

penetration of this segment is 15 percent below that of the U.S. national average across segments. Nuprin should be curious about why. In contrast, Advil's penetration of this segment is 5 percent above the national average. A possible first step in Nuprin's development would be to analyze its presentation relative to Advil's to find its flaws with respect to the actualizer group.

Services such as VALS2 are still growing in popularity. However, in the end, their effectiveness may be still be somewhat limited since the lifestyle research is general in nature and not really directed to purchasing behavior in any particular product or market category.

Another syndicated service that attempts to describe consumers at a much more micro level is Claritas Corporation's PRIZM (Potential Rating Index for Zip Markets) clusters. In 1974, Jonathan Robbin, a computer scientist, devised a system that matches zip codes with census data and consumer surveys (which measure VALS2 typologies among many other things). He sorted the 36,000 zip codes into 40 lifestyle clusters. Each zip code belongs to one of the clusters. The idea is, as Robbin says, "Tell me someone's zip code, and I can predict what they eat, drink, drive—even think."[11] Claritas updates the PRIZM clusters with every census. The 40 PRIZM clusters are fully described in a popular press book by Michael J. Weiss.[12] Clients of Claritas, though, can

11 Quoted in Michael J. Weiss, *The Clustering of America* (New York: Harper & Row, 1988): 1.

FIGURE 2.1
THE VALS2 TYPOLOGY (Contiued)*

Actualizers: 8% of population. Median age is 43. Highest income, median is $58,000. Successful, take-charge individuals interested in personal growth and exploration. Image is more of an expression of cultivated tastes than a status symbol. Wide interests. Enjoy finer things in life.

Fulfilleds: 11% of population. Median age near 50. Mature, comfortable, reflective people. Median income $38,000. Interested in broadening knowledge. Have strongly held principles and appear self-assured. Demand value and durability in products.

Believers: 15% of population. Many are retired. Median income $21,000. Conservative, conventional people with concrete beliefs. Few have any college. Follow established routines surrounding family, religion, and social groups. Favor known brands.

Achievers: 13% of population. Mostly in 30s. Median income is $50,000. Self-definition comes through career success. Like to feel in control. Image is important as a status symbol.

Strivers: 13% of population. Mostly in 30s. Few have college experience. Median income $25,000. Money is measure of success. Most feel cheated by their limited resources. Concerned about opinions of others. Like style and emulate those with higher means.

Experiencers: 12% of population. Mostly in 20s. Median income is $19,000, but disposable income is high since they share living quarters. Vital, enthusiastic, rebellious. Savor what is new, offbeat, and risky. Sports and outdoors provide outlets for abundant energy.

Makers: 13% of population. Median age is 30. Median income is $23,000. Craftspeople and do-it-yourselfers. Practical, self-sufficient people. Like to build. Conservative and suspicious of new ideas. Few have college background.

Strugglers: 12% of population. Have hard time making ends meet. Chronically poor, low skilled, poorly educated. Two-thirds are women. Median age over 60. Median income below poverty level. Focused on meeting urgent needs of moment. Concerns are for security and safety. Cautious consumers who are limited but brand loyal.

* Source: Descriptions are based on those from Rebecca Piirto, Beyond Mind Games: The Marketing Power of Psychographics (Ithaca, NY: American Demographics Books, 1991): 80–83.

access their database in much more detail. They can find out what people in a single zip code buy, what zip codes tend to buy their products, what people in a zip code read, and so on.

There is one final variable among those that describe consumers that deserves special mention: occasion of product use. Up to this point, we have been describing the consumer. However, it is a fact of life that in many product categories (e.g., soft drinks) consumers switch brands from one occasion to another. Coca-Cola no longer really competes for customers (or users); they compete for drinks (or occasions)![13] For example, a consumer might be price sensitive for soft drinks for his or her own consumption but not price sensitive when he or she serves guests. Coke and Pepsi compete with store brands for usage occasions on which the consumer is alone. Furthermore, they may need to be on promotion to even be in the running. On the other hand, Coke and

12 *Ibid.* The clusters described are *not* the most current ones.

13 Joel S. Dubow, "Occasion-Based vs. User-Based Benefit Segmentation: A Case Study," *Journal of Advertising Research* 32 (March–April 1992): 11–17.

Pepsi compete with each other for the usage occasion on which guests are served. The occasion-based usage notion is just emerging in the field. With the increasing importance of market segments, occasion-based analyses can only prosper. It remains to be seen, though, exactly what the proper unit of analysis is for a given category. Is it user? Is it occasion? Or is it some combination of occasion and user?

The second major group of segmenting variables consists of those directly related to consumer behavior. These are important in that they are related to the focus of the marketer's activity: buying the firm's products and services. Unfortunately, these variables are often not easy to relate to communications media and distribution channels that allow one to approach the consumer of interest.

Two exceptions are the usage characteristics: user vs. nonuser and heavy vs. light user. Many research suppliers, including the Market Research Company of America (MRCA), NPD, National Family Opinion (NFO), and Simmons have standard products that allow for relating usage characteristics to communications media, and distribution channels. All except Simmons employ a consumer panel, a group of individuals who report their purchases of a certain product category (or categories) over time. This is done either by phone interview, mail questionnaire, or a diary that a consumer completes as he or she shops. Simmons uses a one-time large-scale personal interview. All these services either relate usage characteristics directly to media or channels or they provide demographic characteristics that can then be related to media or channels if typical profiles of particular media or channels can be found (and they usually can be).

Perhaps the most commonly used usage characterization is the "heavy half." The term *heavy half* refers to the fact that if a company ranked its customers according to how much of its product they bought, the top half of the list, the heavy half, would necessarily account for more than half of the product's sales. In fact, the heavy half is so skewed that marketers often speak of the "80/20 law," that the top 20 percent of a product's customers account for 80 percent of the product's sales.

Industrial Markets

The state of knowledge regarding industrial market segmentation is not nearly as well developed as that of consumer market segmentation. That is one reason why the industrial bases are not structured as well. There are some clear parallels between the two, however, in particular as they relate to general customer descriptive characteristics. Industrial markets have their corresponding demographics. One study on hospitals used size, number of beds, budget, percent occupancy, teaching vs. nonteaching, and community size as demographic variables (and explicitly called them so).[14]

---

14 Thomas S. Robertson and Yoram Wind, "Organizational Psychographics and Innovativeness," *Journal of Consumer Research* 7 (June 1980): 24–31.

Perhaps the most often used industrial demographic is the SIC (Standard Industrial Classification) code. The SIC code is a hierarchical numerical classification system controlled by the Statistical Policy Division of the Office of Management and Budget. It divides all economic activity into major categories (e.g., agriculture, manufacturing, construction, mining, wholesale trade, retail trade, etc.). It further subdivides each activity into major groups, each identified with a two-digit code. For example, the two-digit number 35 represents General Industrial Machinery and Equipment under the manufacturing major category. The major groups are divided into subgroups, and a third digit is added. Subgroup 357 represents the Office, Computing, and Accounting Machines subgroup of group 35. A more and more detailed industry classification emerges when more digits are added to the code. Category 3572 denotes typewriter manufacturers; 3573 denotes manufacturers of electronic computing equipment, and so on. The level of detail can extend to the seventh digit. In any event, industrial marketers have been using SIC codes as tools for segmenting their markets for many years.

Beyond demographics, organizations, like consumers, can be described on nondemographic, psychological descriptor dimensions (e.g., openness of communication, clarity of organizational objectives, achievement motivation, resistance to change, and maybe even strategy). Thus, we can also have an organizational analogy to psychographics.[15]

The parallels between industrial and consumer segmentation bases begin to lessen, though, when we turn our attention to characteristics related to buying behavior. As complex as consumer buying processes may appear, they pale in comparison to industrial buying processes. There are usually many more people involved in industrial buying; a wider variety of technological and economic factors must be considered; large sums of money are frequently involved; and the duration of some buying processes can exceed a year.

Often, the most difficult task is for a marketer to discover who in an organization influences the buying decision and who is responsible for eventually making it. Imagine the difficulty of a salesperson trying to interest a prospect in a product as he or she gets to the front door of the company's building, looks at the directory, and cannot figure out who to go see. One of the keys to the early success of Federal Express in the 1970s was their understanding that the decisions to use some of their products (e.g., Standard Air Services and Priority One mail) were made by traffic managers, and the decisions to use others (e.g., Courier Pak) were made by executives and secretaries.[16]

Fortunately, it is often possible to segment potential customers by the identities of the decision makers. For example, one study on industrial air conditioners, described in Table 2.4, found four segments. The raw data for the analysis that produced this table were collected via a survey in which

---

15 See *Ibid.*

16 See *Federal Express*, Harvard Business School Case Series (1977): Case 9-577-042.

TABLE 2.4
MAJOR SEGMENTS OF ORGANIZATIONS IN THE
INDUSTRIAL AIR-CONDITIONING STUDY

	Segment 1	Segment 2	Segment 3	Segment 4
Segment Size (% of Potential Market)	12%	31%	32%	25%
Major Decision Participant Categories in Equipment Selection Decision (Frequencies of Involvement)	Plant managers (1.00)	Production engineers (.94)	Production engineers (.97)	Top management (.85)
	HVAC consultants (.38)	Plant managers (.70)	HVAC consultants (.60)	HVAC consultants (.67)

Source: Jean-Marie Choffray and Gary L. Lilien, "A New Approach to Industrial Market Segmentation," *Sloan Management Review* 19 (Spring 1978): 17–30. Reprinted with permission.

respondents from the potential market were asked who (in terms of job title) would influence the purchase decision. A cluster analysis was then performed to group the respondents into segments.

Selecting a variable or set of variables to use as bases of segmentation for a specific product category can be problematic. Where to start? Which are more likely to be useful, descriptor variables or behavioral variables? The answer to this is that

BOTH ARE NECESSARY!

This is implicit in the *American Demographics* characterization of consumer information in Figure 2.2.[17] Their philosophy is that all four types of information described in the figure are necessary in order to know your customer, and knowing your customer is a prerequisite for success.

It is common, though, for a company to start with just a set of descriptor variables (usually demographics) as a basis for forming segments. This might be all well and good if we knew that segments formed this way behave differently. For example, we know that African Americans make fewer impulse purchases and time their purchases to plan for sales less often than other Americans.[18] We also know that New York Hispanics consume a disproportionate amount of Mazola Salad Oil, Libby's Canned Fruits, and Hawaiian Punch.[19] The Simmons Market Research Bureau publishes data collected from a large-scale survey that allows us to make inferences of this type where appropriate. For example, data from their 1989 survey imply that single, male

17 See American Demographics, *The Insider's Guide to Demographic Know-How* (Ithaca, NY: American Demographics Press: 1990), and Peter Francese and Rebecca Piirto, *Capturing Customers: How to Target the Hottest Markets of the '90s* (Ithaca, NY: American Demographics Books, 1990).

18 "Where Blacks, Whites Diverge," *Brandweek* (May 3, 1993): 22.

19 Elisa Soriano and Dale Dauten, "Hispanic 'Dollar Votes' Can Impact Market Shares," *Marketing News* (September 13, 1985): 45.

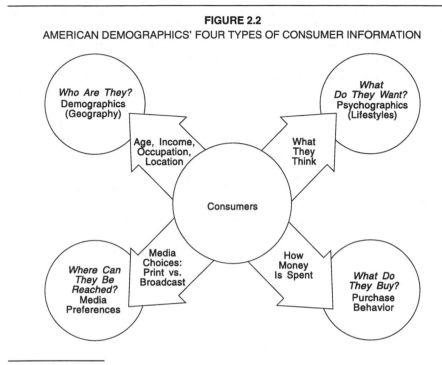

FIGURE 2.2
AMERICAN DEMOGRAPHICS' FOUR TYPES OF CONSUMER INFORMATION

Source: American Demographics. Reprinted with permission.

college graduates consume a disproportionate amount of Becks beer: 91.1 percent of Beck's customers are white, 75 percent are male, 50 percent are married, and 38.3 percent graduated college. Beer drinkers as a whole are 86 percent white, 62.9 percent male, and 30.4 percent college graduates.

Unfortunately, many attempts to use descriptor variables to segment buyer behavior fail. In an industrial marketing study of the nonintelligent data-terminal market published a decade ago, 300 recent buyers of this product category were surveyed about the major benefits they sought in their terminals.[20] While the customer company's size was somewhat related to benefits sought, its industry, as reflected by SIC code, was not very helpful. Retail establishments, financial institutions, and manufacturers all reported similar relative importances for several characteristics (e.g., speed, service, reliability, delivery, etc.).

The company that sponsored the study segmented the market by SIC code. The results of the study implied that the company was designing product and promotional programs for very specific segments of the market that do not behave differently than the market as a whole! Or perhaps the company is

---

20 This study is fully described in Rowland T. Moriarty, *Industrial Buying Behavior: Concepts, Issues, and Applications* (Lexington, MA: Lexington Books, 1983).

designing multiple programs for multiple segments that all behave in the same way. Nature's Bounty, the vitamin company, sells its product through seven brands, each in a different distribution channel.[21] The vitamins are identical, but they have created seven different brands with seven different marketing campaigns. They obviously believe their strategy is paying off. Indeed, the company is doing well.

Segmentation is an expensive proposition. It not only requires the financial costs of creating multiple programs, it also requires time and effort, which result in opportunity costs. The costs of segmentation need to be balanced by benefits. The company has to be able to create an offering more tailored to the way a consumer behaves. That behavior might be reflected in benefits sought or the way a consumer responds to other marketing variables (e.g., price sensitivity), any behavioral variable. That is why behavioral variables are important. They reflect the behavior the company has tailored its offering. Now the company has to find those consumers that respond to the new tailored offering in the way the company has predicted. That is why descriptor variables are important. They allow the company to pinpoint those consumers that will have the desired response.

Consider chewing gum. One brand, Cry Baby, made by the Philadelphia Chewing Gum Corp., has an extremely sour taste.[22] It makes your eyes water and your body sweat. Why would anybody buy it? The company (behaviorally) segments on two benefits sought: the desire to prove that you can "take it" and the opportunity to play practical jokes. Who seeks these benefits? Twelve- to thirteen-year-old junior high school students, of course. They want to prove they're adults. That is why the gum does not sell much to younger children (who have no illusions of adulthood) or older children (who do not need to resort to these symbols).

This interesting (if unconventional) example illustrates a further point. Not only are both descriptor and behavioral variables important, but the link between them is essential. What good would it do the company if they just knew the benefits without knowing who sought them? They would not know how to promote or distribute the product. Figure 2.3 summarizes these ideas.

Given the importance of both sets of variables, we are essentially left with two choices. We can form prototype segments with descriptor variables and search for commonalities in behavior among consumers with common descriptors, or we can start with behavioral variables and search for descriptors that correspond to the relevant behavior.

The first approach has the advantage of easily formed prototype segments. It is usually developed with the use of a classification table where one or more (usually more) descriptor variables are laid out as the rows and/or columns. The entries in the table are some behavioral variable. Table 2.5 presents an example. Household beer purchase is cross-classified by income and educa-

---

21 Richard S. Teitlebaum, "Companies to Watch: Nature's Bounty," *Fortune* (May 18, 1992).

22 "Tastes Yucky, Sells Like Hotcakes!" *Business Week* (May 18, 1992): 56.

FIGURE 2.3
RELATIONSHIPS FOR SEGMENT TARGETING

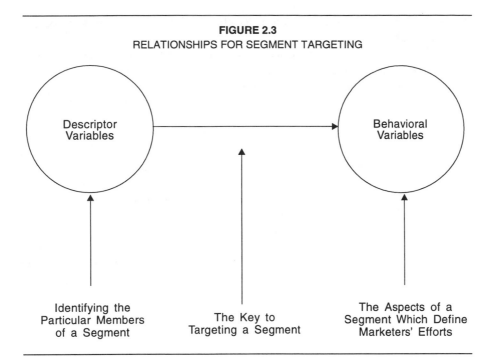

Descriptor Variables → Behavioral Variables

Identifying the Particular Members of a Segment

The Key to Targeting a Segment

The Aspects of a Segment Which Define Marketers' Efforts

TABLE 2.5
HOUSEHOLD BEER CONSUMPTION BY INCOME AND EDUCATION

Annual Family Income	Years of Education (Head of Household)				
	6	10	12	14	16
Less than $9,000	$ 30.03	$19.59	$18.54	$ 36.81	$46.53
9,000–14,999	$ 83.22	$60.81	$35.10	$ 52.20	$ 5.37
15,000–23,999	$ 75.69	$78.09	$67.89	$ 72.81	$50.40
24,000–29,999	$ 83.16	$72.63	$96.42	$ 63.84	$69.69
30,000–44,999	$102.72	$72.15	$64.62	$ 61.89	$72.54
45,000+	$109.74	$37.50	$70.47	$117.51	$53.58

Source: Adapted from Frank M. Bass, Douglas J. Tigert, and Robert T. Lonsdale, "Market Segmentation: Group versus Individual Behavior," *Journal of Marketing Research* 5 (August 1968): 264–270. Reprinted with permission, American Marketing Association.

tion of the head of the household. The table shows the mean purchases for each cell. As implied by the table, consumption varies widely according to socioeconomic characteristics. Cross-classification and the descriptor to behavior approach is useful in this example, but it has the drawback in general of being potentially inefficient. As with SIC codes in the nonintelligent data terminal market, there is no guarantee that different segments will exhibit different behaviors.

With the second approach however, we *are* guaranteed divergent behaviors among segments. Consider the industrial air conditioner example discussed earlier in this chapter. Table 2.6 provides descriptor variables that distinguish between the segments defined in Table 2.4. For example, companies in segment 4 tend to be smaller, more satisfied with their current air-conditioning system, and more concerned with the economic consequences of their decisions. Accordingly, the managerial function is more involved in the purchase, with expertise being provided by external consultants. On the other hand, in larger companies (e.g., segments 2 and 3) the decision is essentially made by engineering people who are less concerned with economy. Therefore, knowledge of the size of a company tells the marketer a great deal about how to market air conditioners to that company.

In this chapter, we advocate the second approach, that of beginning with behavioral variables and searching for commonalities in descriptors. We now discuss what we believe is the most useful behavior for marketing strategy: benefits sought.

TABLE 2.6
CHARACTERISTICS OF EACH INDUSTRIAL AIR-CONDITIONER SEGMENT

	Segment 1	Segment 2	Segment 3	Segment 4
Satisfaction with Current A/C System	Medium–High	Low	Low–Medium	High
Consequence if A/C System Is Less Economical Than Projected	Medium–High	Low	Low–Medium	High
Consequence if A/C System Is Less Reliable Than Projected	Medium–High	Low	High	Low–Medium
Company Size	Medium	Large	Large	Small
Percentage of Plant Area Requiring A/C	Medium–Large	Small	Large	Medium
Number of Separate Plants	Medium–Large	Small	Large	Small–Medium

Source: Jean-Marie Choffray and Gary L. Lilien, "A New Approach to Industrial Market Segmentation," *Sloan Management Review* 19 (Spring 1978): 24. Reprinted with permission.

BENEFIT SEGMENTATION

Of the myriad bases of segmentation, benefits sought is generally the most relevant for marketing strategy. The benefits a company decides to provide can determine its entire marketing strategy. For example, toothpaste users can be divided into those who want whitening power, those who want decay prevention, those who want good taste, appearance, and so on. When the company decides to provide one of these benefits, other decisions such as target segment (in terms of descriptors) and product positioning follow immediately.

Tables 2.7, 2.8, and 2.9 contain the results of benefit segmentation studies of toothpaste, financial aid management services for educational institutions, and electrical components.

The segments in the first two examples are very useful in that the benefits are tied to specific descriptor variables, which are useful in uncovering potential market opportunities or identifying target segments. In the toothpaste example, there is probably an opportunity for a brand to better provide the benefits of the sensory segment than Colgate, its favorite brand, does. A financial aid package stressing aid dispersement (concept 5) would best be targeted to small schools with a high percentage of their students applying for financial aid.

The electrical components study proved to be a major boom to its sponsor, a company with a 24 percent market share and a 10 percent price premium that covered special features and services the company provided for makers of high-quality specialty products (e.g., Segment D). The company found it

TABLE 2.7
TOOTHPASTE MARKET BENEFIT SEGMENTS

	Sensory Segment	Sociable Segment	Worrier Segment	Independent Segment 4
Principal Benefit Sought	Flavor and product appearance	Brightness of teeth	Decay prevention	Price
Demographic Strengths	Children	Teens, young people	Large families	Men
Special Behavioral Characteristics	Users of spearmint flavored toothpaste	Smokers	Heavy users	Heavy users
Brands Disproportionately Favored	Colgate	MacLeans, Ultra Brite	Crest	Cheapest brand
Lifestyle Characteristics	Hedonistic	Active	Conservative	Value oriented

Source: Russell I. Haley, "Benefit Segmentation: A Decision Oriented Research Tool," Journal of Marketing 32 (July 1968): 30–35. Reprinted with permission, American Marketing Association.

TABLE 2.8
FINANCIAL AID MANAGEMENT BENEFIT SEGMENTS

Characteristics	Segment 1	Segment 2	Segment 3	Segment 4
Potential Benefits Sought	Accuracy	Accuracy	Accuracy	Accuracy
	More time to counsel students	Consistency in award making	Consistency in award making	Consistency in award making
	Stored data	More time to counsel students	Better control of funds	More time to counsel students
	Speed & time savings			
		Speed & time savings	Cost savings	Better control of funds
Institution Type (Predominantly)	Public (54%) Private (46%)	Public (64%) Private (36%)	Public (56%) Private (44%)	Public (68%) Private (32%)
	Four-year and two-year colleges	Four-year and two-year colleges	Vocational/ technical schools	University and two-year colleges
Undergraduate Enrollment	Under 1,500	Under 1,500	Under 1,500	Over 1,500
Number of Financial Aid Applications Processed/Year	Under 500	Over 500	Under 500	Over 500
Purchase Intentions*	Concepts 6 and 7	Concepts 3,5,6,7	Concepts 3 and 6	Concept 6

* Intentions were measured for eight service concepts: 1) Data storage and retrieval; 2) Applicant ranking; 3) Needs matching; 4) Financial aid correspondence; 5) Aid dispersement; 6) Aid profile; 7) Special request report; 8) Custom survey.

Source: Mark Moriarty and M. Venkatesan, "Concept Evaluation & Market Segmentation," Journal of Marketing 42 (July 1978): 82–86. Reprinted with permission, American Marketing Association.

had only an 11 percent share in the price-sensitive Segment A. Furthermore, its average order from Segment A was only $2,260, while its competitors were getting $20,000 per order. Recognizing that the company could not compete in Segment A because of its antiquated facilities, top management decided to price itself out of Segment A by raising prices 25 percent. As expected, none of the major competitors followed. The company retained essentially all of its specialty business at a significantly higher margin.

In general, to perform a benefit segmentation study, we must take an appropriately chosen sample of consumers, measure their benefits, group them according to similarity in benefits sought, and search for other (descriptor) variables to profile each group. Of course, these descriptors should be useful for marketing action.

We first focus on three ways to measure benefits sought: direct questioning, perceptual mapping, and conjoint analysis. We then briefly discuss the group-

TABLE 2.9

SEGMENTATION BY KEY BUYING FACTORS—ELECTRICAL COMPONENTS

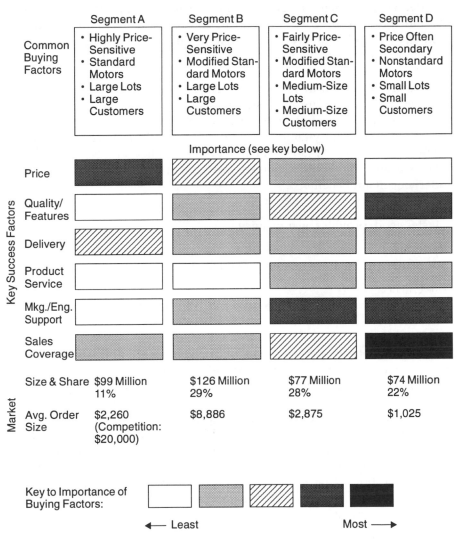

	Segment A	Segment B	Segment C	Segment D
Common Buying Factors	• Highly Price-Sensitive • Standard Motors • Large Lots • Large Customers	• Very Price-Sensitive • Modified Standard Motors • Large Lots • Large Customers	• Fairly Price-Sensitive • Modified Standard Motors • Medium-Size Lots • Medium-Size Customers	• Price Often Secondary • Nonstandard Motors • Small Lots • Small Customers

Importance (see key below)

Key Success Factors: Price, Quality/Features, Delivery, Product Service, Mkg./Eng. Support, Sales Coverage

Market	Segment A	Segment B	Segment C	Segment D
Size & Share	$99 Million 11%	$126 Million 29%	$77 Million 28%	$74 Million 22%
Avg. Order Size	$2,260 (Competition: $20,000)	$8,886	$2,875	$1,025

Key to Importance of Buying Factors:

← Least   Most →

Source: Robert A. Garda, "Strategic Segmentation: How to Carve Niches for Growth in Industrial Markets," *Management Review* (August 1981): 21. Reprinted with permission, AMACOM.

ing of consumers with respect to benefits sought and the describing segments steps.

Direct Questioning

The easiest way to get some insight into the benefits people seek is to ask them directly. A survey might include a section where a list of potential benefits in a specific product category is provided, and respondents are asked to rate them on a five-point (or any other number for that matter) scale according to how important they are in making a choice between products.

These responses can then either be used directly or be further reduced by factor analysis to see if there is any underlying structure to the benefits. For example, suppose we are interested in segmenting the snack market. We might come up with the following list of potential benefits: tastes good, filling, nonfattening, contains vitamins, easy to serve, provides energy, clean, inexpensive, good for teeth, can be eaten out of hand, juicy, and easily available. After analyzing the survey responses, we might find that there are really three underlying major benefits:

Taste:
   tastes good, provides energy, juicy.

Nutrition:
   nonfattening, contains vitamins, good for teeth.

Convenience:
   filling, easy to serve, clean, inexpensive, can be eaten out of hand, easily available.

Each respondent can be given a score reflecting his or her average importance rating on the specific components that make up each major benefit.

Direct questioning suffers from two major limitations. First, people are sometimes unwilling to say what is really important to them. Their answers may have what is called a *social desirability bias*. Indeed, researchers have shown that fewer mothers serve their children nutritious snacks than would be indicated by their direct importance ratings.[23] Second, they may not really know what is important to them. People sometimes make product choices without reflecting on the benefits of the products. When asked why they made a specific choice, they may not have a good answer, or they may tell you why they think they made a choice without it being the real reason.[24]

Perceptual Mapping

A perceptual map is a visual representation of consumers' perceptions and preferences of a given set of products or brands. Products are plotted as points on a set of axes. The distance between two products can be interpreted as the

---

23 James H. Myers and Edward W. Forgy, "Getting More Information from Customer Surveys," *California Management Review* 18 (Winter): 66–72.

24 R.E. Nisbett and T.D. Wilson, "Telling More Than We Can Know: Verbal Reports on Mental Processes," *Psychological Review* 84 (1977): 231–259, provide evidence of this point.

psychological similarity between them. Consumers are plotted as ideal points on the same axes. A consumer's ideal point represents the location on the map that his or her ideal product would occupy. Products located closer to the ideal point are preferred to those further away.

As an example, consider the hypothetical perceptual map of seven American cars and three respondents in Figure 2.4. The ideal point for respondents I, J, and K indicate that their favorite cars are the Ford Thunderbird, the Chrysler Imperial, and the Chevrolet Camaro, respectively, although it appears that there is room for a car that would better satisfy K. This example incorporates the frequently made assumption that consumers are homogeneous in perceptions (i.e., they all have the products on the same place on the same map) but heterogeneous in preferences (i.e., they each have their own ideal point).

Many mathematical techniques have emerged for constructing perceptual maps. These include multidimensional scaling, factor analysis, and multiple discriminant analysis.[25] These are complex, computer-intensive techniques that we unfortunately can only convey limited insight into here. Fortunately though, specialized computer packages, including MARKPACK and PC-MDS, have emerged that can produce perceptual maps from either simple, overall similarities and preferences or from ratings from several people on a large number of attributes that account for all the potential ways in which the set of products might differ from each other.

In Figure 2.4, the labels *luxurious* and *sporty* are the key in determining the benefits that respondents I, J, and K seek. What combinations of dimensions will satisfy the consumer? Unfortunately, these labels are not direct results of any perceptual mapping procedure but rather of further analysis (often subjective) of a map after it is produced. Managers who have studied the products mapped will hopefully look at the map, recognize intuitively what the axes stand for, and apply some meaningful labels.

Conjoint Analysis

Conjoint analysis is a technique useful for sorting out the relative importances of a product's attributes (benefits). It starts with a consumer's overall preference judgments about a set of complex products with common attributes. It then decomposes these evaluations into separate and comparable utility scales, which can be used to either reconstruct the original preference judgments or predict preferences for a new set of alternatives with the same attributes.

Suppose a company wants to decide what benefits to include in a new credit card.[26] Management believes that consumer preference is dictated by five

---

25 For a complete exposition of these techniques, see the classic book by Paul E. Green and Vithala R. Rao, *Applied Multidimensional Scaling: A Comparison of Approaches and Algorithms* (New York: Holt, Rinehart, and Winston, 1972).

26 This example is adapted from Paul E. Green and Yoram Wind, "New Way to Measure Consumer

FIGURE 2.4

HYPOTHETICAL PERCEPTUAL MAP OF AUTOMOBILES

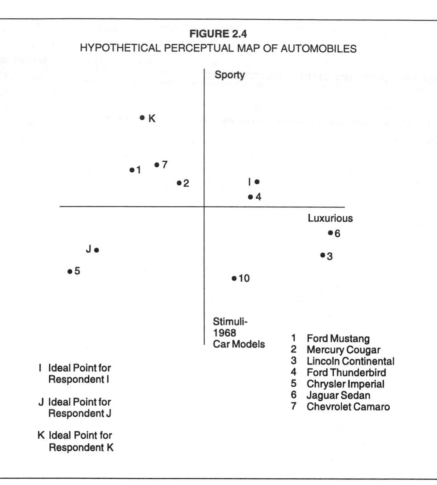

Stimuli-
1968
Car Models

I Ideal Point for
   Respondent I

J Ideal Point for
   Respondent J

K Ideal Point for
   Respondent K

1 Ford Mustang
2 Mercury Cougar
3 Lincoln Continental
4 Ford Thunderbird
5 Chrysler Imperial
6 Jaguar Sedan
7 Chevrolet Camaro

factors: annual fee, the size of cash rebate (if any) given at year's end, establishments accepting the card, whether or not the card carries retail purchase insurance, and whether or not the card carries rental car insurance. For simplicity, suppose there are three potential annual fees ($0, $20, $50), three potential cash rebates (None, 0.5 percent, 1 percent), three categories of card acceptance (AHC—air, hotel, rental cars; AHCR—AHC plus most restaurants; AHCRG—AHCR plus most general retailers). In addition, the only option for retail purchase or rental car insurance involves a 90-day expiration date, and the only option for rental car insurance has a $30,000 maximum.

Management is concerned with how consumers value the various benefits. Relevant questions might include:

Judgments," *Harvard Business Review* 53 (July–August 1975): 107–117 and Paul E. Green and Abba M. Krieger, "Product Design Strategies for Target-Market Positioning," *Journal for Product and Innovation Management* 8 (1991): 189–202.

- Is retail purchase insurance worth more than rental car insurance?
- Would a consumer pay 50 dollars annual fee to get cash rebates?
- What is more important, annual fee or card acceptances?
  Conjoint analysis can answer all of these questions.
  The basic conjoint model is called the part-worth model:

$$U_i = \sum U_{ij}$$

where U_i is the utility for the ith brand (credit card) and u_{ij} is the utility of the jth attribute possessed by card i. The u_{ij} are usually called part-worths. They reflect the part of the total worth of the brand contributed by the jth attribute.

In a typical conjoint study, a respondent would be presented with some well-constructed fraction of the $3\times3\times3\times2\times2=108$ total possible credit cards.[27] See Table 2.10. The respondent then either ranks or rates them according to his or her preference. These play the role of the left-hand side of the part-worth equation. Conjoint analysis then derives the part-worths. Many mathematical procedures are available, but multiple regression is the easiest and works as well as any.

The data in Table 2.10 were analyzed to reproduce the part-worths shown below:

Annual Fee	Cash Rebate	Acceptance	Retail Insurance	Rental Car Insurance
$50=0.0	None=0.0	AHCRG=0.9	No=0.0	No=0.0
$20=0.5	0.5%=0.1	AHCR=0.6	Yes=0.1	Yes=0.5
$0=0.9	1.0%=0.3	AHC=0.0		

These in conjunction with the part-worth equation can be used to answer the above questions. Indeed, rental car insurance is worth more than retail purchase insurance (it adds more to overall utility); annual fee is more important than cash rebate (the range of part-worths for annual fee is 0.9 and cash rebate is 0.3; thus fee has a larger effect on utility than rebate); and a consumer would be indifferent between a $50 fee with AHCRG acceptance and AHC acceptance with no annual fee (they have the same part-worth sums).[28]

---

27 To see how to construct these fractions, see Paul E. Green, "On the Design of Choice Experiments Involving Multifactor Alternatives," *Journal of Consumer Research* 1 (June 1974): 61–68.

28 For more information about conjoint analysis, see Paul E. Green and V. Srinivasan, "Conjoint Analysis in Consumer Research: Issues and Outlook," *Journal of Consumer Research* 5 (September 1978): 103–123; Paul E. Green and V. Srinivasan, "Conjoint Analysis in Marketing Research: New Developments and Directions," *Journal of Marketing* 54 (October 1990): 3–20; Phillipe Cattin and Dick R. Wittink, "Commercial Use of Conjoint Analysis: A Survey," *Journal of Marketing* 46 (Summer 1982): 44–53; and Dick R. Wittink and Phillipe Cattin, "Commercial Use of Conjoint Analysis: An Update," *Journal of Marketing* 53 (July 1989): 91–96 study the state of industry practice.

TABLE 2.10
CONJOINT ANALYSIS OF CREDIT CARDS

	Annual Fee	Cash Rebate	Card Acceptance	Retail Purchase Insurance	Car Rental Insurance	Respondent Evaluation (rank number)
1	$50	0.5%	AHCRG	No	No	13
2	$50	None	AHCR	No	Yes	11
3	$50	1.0%	AHC	Yes	No	17
4	$20	0.5%	AHCR	Yes	Yes	2
5	$20	None	AHC	No	No	14
6	$20	1.0%	AHCRG	No	No	3
7	$0	0.5%	AHC	Yes	Yes	12
8	$0	None	AHCRG	No	No	7
9	$0	1.0%	AHCR	No	No	9
10	$50	0.5%	AHC	No	No	18
11	$50	None	AHCRG	Yes	Yes	8
12	$50	1.0%	AHCR	No	No	15
13	$20	0.5%	AHCRG	No	No	4
14	$20	None	AHCR	No	No	6
15	$20	1.0%	AHC	Yes	Yes	5
16	$0	0.5%	AHCR	No	No	10
17	$0	None	AHC	No	No	16
18	$0	1.0%	AHCRG	Yes	Yes	1*

* Highest rank.

Grouping Consumers

Cluster analysis is the standard method used for grouping consumers into segments. Any (or all) of our measures of benefits sought (importances elicited through direct questioning, perceptual map ideal points, or conjoint analysis part-worths) for each consumer can be input into a standard computer program that will group them according to similarity and derive discrete clusters (or segments) of consumers. Three examples in the case of perceptual maps are shown in Figures 2.5, 2.6, and 2.7. In the perceptual map of the Chicago beer market, ideal points tended to group themselves into clusters (circles). Certainly, many ideal points are found outside the circles, but the picture provides an excellent approximation.

The picture implies there may be an opportunity for a new beer on the heavy side of the space, approximately neutral in price/quality, to appeal to the relatively large segment 3.

A similar picture is presented for the candidates in the 1968 presidential election. In the main election (Richard Nixon vs. Hubert Humphrey), voters whose ideal points were on the left side of the space tended to vote for Humphrey; those with ideal points on the right tended to vote for Nixon.

FIGURE 2.5
DISTRIBUTION OF IDEAL POINTS IN CHICAGO BEER MARKET

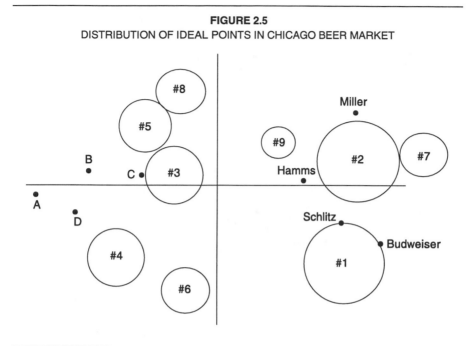

Source: Richard M. Johnson, "Market Segmentation: A Strategic Management Tool," *Journal of Marketing Research* 8 (February 1971): 13–18. Reprinted with permission, American Marketing Association.

Finally, the machining center picture demonstrates there is a perceived economy/performance relationship. Those suppliers highest on the economy dimension tended to be lower on the performance dimension and vice versa. Segment 2, prospects desiring high-performance and high-economy machining centers, are left unsatisfied. Warlock, Adaptive, and Terrific 300, all competing for segment 3, are perceived to have approximately the same levels of (high) performance. Terrific, though, is thought to have the poorest economic product. They have a job to do in altering the market's perceptions of their product. The wisdom of these three suppliers, though, can be severely questioned when one recognizes that segment 3 represents only 15 percent of the market.

These are very nice pictures in the sense that the clusters come out very neatly. This need not be the case. For example, one study presents the distribution of importances of nutrition and convenience stated by mothers choosing snack foods for their children.[29] This study shows much more of an amorphous mass of benefits sought than others.

29 See James H. Myers and Edward W. Forgy, "Getting More Information from Customer Surveys," *California Management Review* 18 (Winter): 69.

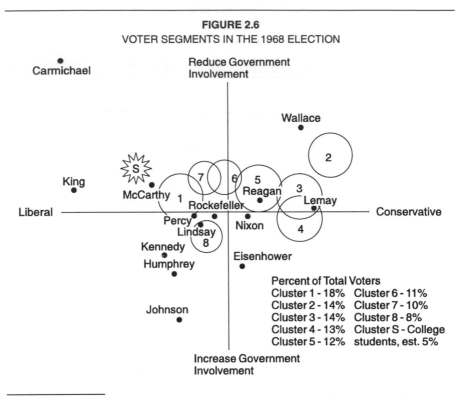

FIGURE 2.6
VOTER SEGMENTS IN THE 1968 ELECTION

Source: Richard M. Johnson, "Market Segmentation: A Strategic Management Tool," *Journal of Marketing Research* 8 (February 1971): 13–18. Reprinted with permission, American Marketing Association.

Describing Segments

Once the segments are formed, the analyst or manager has the task of describing them. They must decide which of the descriptor variables discussed earlier in this chapter differ among (at least some of) the segments. This can be done by visually inspecting the descriptors for the consumers in each segment. Table 2.11 presents a set of descriptions of two statistically distinct benefit (convenience or service) segments for banks. Convenience-oriented bank customers are more likely to have fewer children, lower incomes, and unemployed spouses than service-oriented bank customers.

The two major PC software conjoint analysis packages, those produced by Sawtooth Software in Idaho and Bretton-Clark in New Jersey, both have the facility to cluster respondent part-worths and relate them to descriptor variables.

Multiple regression affords the opportunity to describe segments sometimes without even the clustering step. Consider a regression model of the form:

FIGURE 2.7
MACHINING CENTER MARKET STRUCTURE

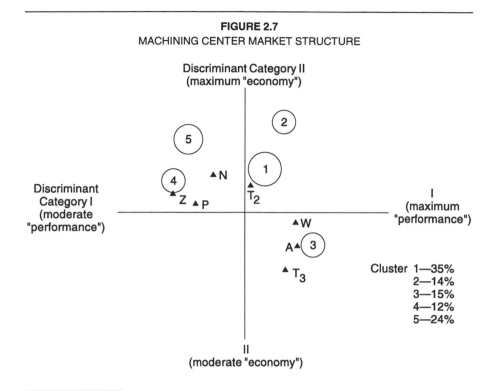

Benefit Sought$=a_0+a_1X_1+\ldots\ldots\ldots+a_kX_k$,

where the X's are descriptor variables and the a's are regression coefficients. The statistical significance of the a's should provide insight into which descriptor variables are related to the particular benefit sought (be it a stated importance, ideal point coordinate, conjoint part-worth, or ladder). This would be sufficient to create a table that would provide insights similar to those of Table 2.9. Unlike in the analyses leading to Table 2.9, we would not know which consumers belonged to which segments but we might not have to. This approach may also prove useful when distinct segments (clusters) cannot be found.[30]

---

30 Some relatively recent developments in marketing science have modeled benefits sought directly as a function of descriptor variables rather than trying to relate derived benefit measures to descriptor variables after the fact. In these cases, the parameters of interest are those that relate the descriptors to (say) conjoint part-worths, as in Paul E. Green and Wayne S. DeSarbo, "Componential Segmentation in the Analysis of Consumer Trade-Offs," *Journal of Marketing* 43 (Fall 1979): 83–91 and Paul E. Green, "Hybrid Models in Conjoint Analysis: An Expository Review," *Journal of Marketing Research* 21 (May 1984): 155–169

TABLE 2.11
PROFILES OF DISTINCT BANK BENEFIT SEGMENTS

Variable	Segment 1: Convenience-Oriented Bank Consumers	Segment 2: Service-Oriented Bank Consumers
Deal with one of the five principal downtown banks	51% yes 49% no	21% yes 79% no
Frequency of downtown shopping	56% twice/week or more often 18% 2–3 times/month 13% once a month 8% 2–6 times/year 5% almost never	5% twice/week or more often 15% 2–3 times/month 14% once a month 16% 2–6 times/year 50% almost never
Marital status	76% married 14% single 10% other	86% married 9% single 5% other
Stage in the family life cycle	13% single 30% childless 23% preteenage children 17% teenage children 7% postteenage children 10% other	9% single 28% childless 32% preteenage children 18% teenage children 9% postteenage children 4% other
Family member selecting principal bank	67% husband 9% wife 22% both 2% other	69% husband 14% wife 15% both 2% other
Annual family income	20% above $20,000 53% above $10,000 and lower than $20,000 27% below $10,000	31% above $20,000 46% above $10,000 and lower than $20,000 23% below $10,000
Employment status of the spouse	27% full time 20% part time 53% not employed	42% full time 14% part time 44% not employed
Source of information concerning bank selection	10% television 1% radio 8% newspapers 78% conversations 3% billboards	5% television 0% radio 3% newspapers 90% conversations 2% billboards

Source: Thomas W. Anderson, Jr., Eli P. Cox III, and David G. Fulcher, "Bank Selection Decisions and Market Segmentation," *Journal of Marketing* 40 (January 1976): 40–45. Reprinted with permission, American Marketing Association.

In a study performed by one of the authors, segments based on conjoint analysis derived part-worth importances for the inclusion of certain features (e.g., built-in exposure meter, automatic focus adjustment, shutter speed adjustment, and built-in automatic flash) were related to camera ownership, film usage, photography as a hobby or profession, and magazine readership.[31] One of the more interesting findings of this study is that the only segment responsive to the inclusion of an automatic flash were heavy readers of *Popular Photography* and the *New Yorker* magazines. This has direct implications for where cameras with built-in flashes should be advertised as well as for where cameras without them should not be advertised.

Before we end this section, we would be remiss if we did not point out that attempts to relate measures of benefits sought to descriptor variables have met with mixed success. In one perceptual mapping study of computer buyers, for example, it was found that all classes of consumers essentially sought hardware reliability as the most important benefit.[32] Different types of consumers had different second most important benefits; buyers who were employed as data processors were more concerned with technical backup features while buyers who were employed in other capacities were more concerned with a performance/cost ratio. Regression studies demonstrate that the amount of variation that descriptor variables explain is small—statistically significant yes, but small nevertheless.[33] Similar comments can be made about cluster analyses of conjoint part-worths.[34] The major conclusion seems to be that descriptor variables can be useful in discriminating among benefit segments but often not nearly as useful as we would like.

SEGMENTING WITH OTHER BEHAVIORAL BASES

Of course, the particular variables included in a segmentation study depend on the purposes of the study. If, for example, a company were interested in measuring consumer satisfaction as a precursor to product improvement or perhaps attempting to uncover an unmet need, brand attitudes and perceptions would be appropriate. If a company were interested in growing essentially with its current products, it would be most interested in identifying its current markets, and usage characteristics would be most relevant. From a

---

or ideal points as in Wayne S. DeSarbo and Vithala R. Rao, "A Constrained Unfolding Methodology for Product Positioning," *Marketing Science* 5 (Winter 1986): 1–19.

31 Vithala R. Rao and Frederick W. Winter, "An Application of the Multivariate Probit Model to Market Segmentation and Product Design," *Journal of Marketing Research* 15 (August 1978): 361–368 for full details on this study.

32 This study is fully described in Paul E. Green, Donald S. Tull, and Gerald R. Albaum, *Research for Marketing Decisions*, 5th ed. (Englewood Cliffs, NJ: Prentice-Hall, 1988): 682–684.

33 For examples, see William F. Massy, Ronald E. Frank, and Thomas M. Lodahl, *Purchasing Behavior and Personal Attributes* (Philadelphia: University of Pennsylvania Press, 1968).

34 See William L. Moore, "Levels of Aggregation in Conjoint Analysis: An Empirical Comparison," *Journal of Marketing Research* 17 (November 1980): 516–523.

more tactical perspective, a company interested in evaluating a pricing schedule, promotion, or media plan would be interested in responsiveness to
specific marketing mix elements.

In terms of growing with current products or services, companies can
proceed in two ways. They can either pursue people who do not use the
product or light users (a potentially useful behavioral variable). Pursuing
people who do not use the product does not imply that companies should
target the nonuser segment and create a communications program to reach
them, but quite the opposite. Better logic dictates that future customers are
likely to be similar to current customers. Reaffirming a marketing program
directed to current customers appears to be the way to go. Indeed, Yamaha
uses this approach for choosing sites for new dealerships.[35] They identify the
demographic characteristics (descriptors) of previous buyers (behavior). They
then use Census Bureau data to search for geographic areas with similar
demographic profiles.

Finally, marketers can better fine-tune their tactics if they know the characteristics of those consumers who are more sensitive to specific marketing mix
elements. Consumers can be segmented by responsiveness to any one of a
large number of marketing stimuli: price, coupon, advertising, even package
size and variety.

Consider a study conducted by AT&T after a rate increase.[36] The company
contacted a sample of those customers who maintained (or *even* increased)
their usage (behavior) after the rate increase and a sample of those who
decreased their usage. They found that members of the price insensitive
segment had a higher income and were either single, newly married, or had
teenagers living in the house (descriptors). One of the implications of this
study was to inform lower-income customers about lower rates for off-peak
and weekend calls.

Response segmentation of this type is likely to increase greatly in the
coming years with the growing availability of scanner data. These are essentially sales data obtained from optical scanners at the cashier or the consumer's
home. Two research companies, A.C. Nielsen Inc. and Information Resources
Inc. (IRI), have set up some markets in which consumers present a magneti-
cally coded identification card when they buy their groceries.[37] The research
company can then determine exactly what a consumer buys, at what price,
and under what competitive conditions in the store that day, all of which are
known to the research company. These consumers can then be characterized
by descriptor variables also known to the research company. Subscribing

---

35 See "Computer Mapping of Demographic Lifestyle Data Locates 'Pockets' of Potential Customer at
Microgeographic Levels," *Marketing News* (November 27, 1981): 16.

36 For a detailed description of this study, see Henry Assael and A. Marvin Roscoe, Jr., "Approaches to Market
Segmentation Analysis," *Journal of Marketing* 40 (October 1976): 67–76.

37 Nielsen's SCANTRACK markets include Sioux Falls, SD and Springfield, MO. IRI's INFOSCAN markets
include Cedar Rapids, IA; Eau Claire, WI; Grand Junction, CO; Marion, IN; Midland, TX; and Pittsfield,
MA.

companies can then identify segments that switch brands in response to a promotion, price change, end of aisle display, and so on.[38] The representativeness of such analyses is increasing as Nielsen, and IRI are continuing to add more and more markets to their operations.

This section has merely scratched the surface of behaviorally based segmentation. No matter what the variables of interest are, though, the overall philosophy remains the same as in benefit segmentation:

1. Identify the behavior of interest.

2. Measure it for a sample of consumers.

3. Cluster the sample into segments.

4. Find descriptors that are appropriate for each segment.

SELECTING TARGET SEGMENTS

After segments have been defined, the next step in the strategic process is the selection of those segments in which the company wishes to compete. That selection should be based on the answers to three questions for each segment:

1. Is the segment attractive?

2. Does the firm have a competitive advantage in the segment?

3. Is that competitive advantage sustainable?

If the answer to any one of these questions is no, the segment in question is probably not one in which the company should compete.

Although as the noted author George Day says, "Attractiveness will ultimately be in the eye of the beholder,"[39] all firms look for segments that exhibit growth prospects and they believe have above-average profitability. Such segments may be large, such as the price-sensitive retail segment pursued by Wal-Mart. It may also be a small segment in which the firm can command a large price premium. Witness Ford's entry into the luxury car segment via the purchase of Jaguar. A firm might also find a segment attractive if it does not have any dominant competitors. Such was the case with the authors' decision to write this book. There was no dominant book in the strategy market that treated the subject from an analytic viewpoint.

In order for a company to be successful in a given segment in the long run, it must have some competitive advantage in that segment. This can only be determined after a thorough analysis of the company's (and its competitor's) strengths and weaknesses. The central question is What assets or skills does the company possess that allow it to provide the benefits desired by the consumers in that segment? Analyzing strengths and weaknesses is the topic studied in Chapter 7 of this book.

---

38 David J. Curry, *The New Marketing Research Systems* (New York: Wiley, 1993), discusses these research suppliers and their capabilities in great detail.

39 George Day, *Market Driven Strategy: Processes for Creating Value* (New York: Free Press, 1990): 201.

The final question in the assessment of a segment is whether the advantage a firm has in it is sustainable. Wal-Mart's early strategy made its advantage sustainable by not leaving any room for competitors. They deliberately located their early stores in small towns with populations that were not large enough to support a second large-scale mass-merchandiser. Thus, they avoided competition by selecting segments they knew would not be attractive to potential competitors.[40]

BIBLIOGRAPHY

American Demographics. *The Insider's Guide to Demographic Know-How*. Ithaca, NY: American Demographics Press, 1990.

Anderson, W. Thomas, Jr., Eli P. Cox III, and David G. Fulcher. "Bank Selection Decisions and Market Segmentation." *Journal of Marketing* 40 (January 1976): 40–45.

Assael, Henry, and A. Marvin Roscoe, Jr. "Approaches to Market Segmentation Analysis." *Journal of Marketing* 40 (October 1976): 67–76.

Bass, Frank M., Douglas J. Tigert, and Robert T. Lonsdale. "Market Segmentation: Group versus Individual Behavior." *Journal of Marketing Research* 5 (August 1968): 264–270.

Bearden, William O., Richard G. Netemeyer, and Mary F. Mobley. *Handbook of Marketing Scales: Multi-Item Measures for Marketing and Consumer Behavior Research*. Newbury Park, CA: Sage Publications, 1993.

"Where Blacks, Whites Diverge." *Brandweek* (May 3, 1993): 22.

"Tastes Yucky, Sells Like Hotcakes!" *Business Week* (May 18, 1992): 56.

Cattin, Phillipe, and Dick R. Wittink. "Commercial Use of Conjoint Analysis: A Survey." *Journal of Marketing* 46 (Summer 1982): 44–53.

Choffray, Jean-Marie, and Gary L. Lilien. "A New Approach to Industrial Market Segmentation." *Sloan Management Review* 19 (Spring 1978): 17–30.

Curry, David J. *The New Marketing Research Systems*. New York: Wiley, 1993.

Day, George. *Market Driven Strategy: Processes for Creating Value*. New York: Free Press, 1990.

DeSarbo, Wayne S., and Vithala R. Rao. "A Constrained Unfolding Methodology for Product Positioning." *Marketing Science* 5 (Winter 1986): 1–19.

Dubow, Joel S. "Occasion-Based vs. User-Based Benefit Segmentation: A Case Study." *Journal of Advertising Research* 32 (March/April 1992): 11–17.

"The Thirst of Champions." *The Economist* (June 6, 1992): 83.

---

40 Wal-Mart Discount Store Operations, Harvard Business School (1987): Case number 9-387-018 for a full discussion.

Federal Express, Harvard Business School Case Series, Case 9-577-042, 1977.

Francese, Peter, and Rebecca Piirto. *Capturing Customers: How to Target the Hottest Markets of the '90s.* Ithaca, NY: American Demographics Books, 1990.

Frank, Ronald E., William F. Massy, and Yoram Wind. *Market Segmentation.* Englewood Cliffs, NJ: Prentice-Hall, 1972.

Garda, Robert A. "Strategic Segmentation: How to Carve Niches for Growth in Industrial Markets." *Management Review* (August 1981): 15–22.

Green, Paul E. "On the Design of Choice Experiments Involving Multifactor Alternatives." *Journal of Consumer Research* 1 (September 1974): 61–68.

Green, Paul E., "Hybrid Models in Conjoint Analysis: An Expository Review." *Journal of Marketing Research* 21 (May 1984): 155–169.

Green, Paul E., and Wayne S. DeSarbo. "Componential Segmentation in the Analysis of Consumer Trade-offs." *Journal of Marketing* 43 (Fall 1979): 83–91.

Green, Paul E., and Abba M. Krieger. "Product Design Strategies for Target-Market Positioning." *Journal for Product and Innovation Management* 8 (1991): 189–202.

Green, Paul E., and Vithala R. Rao. *Applied Multidimensional Scaling: A Comparison of Approaches and Algorithms.* New York: Holt, Rinehart, and Winston, 1972.

Green, Paul E. Donald S. Tull, and Gerald R. Albaum. *Research for Marketing Decisions.* 5th ed., Englewood Cliffs, NJ: Prentice-Hall, 1988.

Green, Paul E., and V. Srinivasan. "Conjoint Analysis in Consumer Research: Issues and Outlook." *Journal of Consumer Research* 5 (September 1978): 103–123.

Green, Paul E., and V. Srinivasan). "Conjoint Analysis in Marketing Research: New Developments and Directions." *Journal of Marketing* 54 (October 1990): 3–20.

Green, Paul E., and Yoram Wind. "New Way to Measure Consumer Judgments." *Harvard Business Review* 53 (July–August 1975): 107–117.

Jones, J. Curtis. "Market Segmentation Strategy Decisions." *Combined Proceedings of the American Marketing Association,* Thomas V. Greer (ed.), 35. Chicago: American Marketing Association, 1973: 114–117.

Haley, Russell I. "Benefit Segmentation: A Decision Oriented Research Tool." *Journal of Marketing* 32 (July 1968): 30–35.

Heline, Holly. "Brand Loyalty Isn't Dead." *Brandweek* (June 3, 1993): 14–15.

Johnson, Richard M. "Market Segmentation: A Strategic Management Tool." *Journal of Marketing Research* 8 (February 1971): 13–18.

"Computer Mapping of Demographic Lifestyle Data Locates 'Pockets' of Potential Customer at Microgeographic Levels." *Marketing News* (November 27, 1981): 16.

Massy, William F., Ronald E. Frank, and Thomas M. Lodahl. *Purchasing Behavior and Personal Attributes*. Philadelphia: University of Pennsylvania Press, 1968.

Moore, William L. "Levels of Aggregation in Conjoint Analysis: An Empirical Comparison." *Journal of Marketing Research* 17 (November 1980): 516–523.

Moriarty, Mark, and M. Venkatesan. "Concept Evaluation & Market Segmentation." *Journal of Marketing* 42 (July 1978): 82–86.

Moriarty, Rowland T. *Industrial Buying Behavior: Concepts, Issues, and Applications*. Lexington, MA: Lexington Books, 1983.

Myers, James H., and Edward W. Forgy. "Getting More Information from Customer Surveys." *California Management Review* 18 (Winter): 66–72.

Nisbett, Richard E., and T.D. Wilson. "Telling More Than We Can Know: Verbal Reports on Mental Processes." *Psychological Review* 84 (1977): 231–259.

Ohmae, Kenichi. *The Mind of the Strategist*. New York: Penguin Books, 1982.

Piirto, Rebecca. *Beyond Mind Games: The Marketing Power of Psychographics*. Ithaca, NY: American Demographics Books, 1991.

Rao, Vithala R., and Frederick W. Winter. "An Application of the Multivariate Probit Model to Market Segmentation and Product Design." *Journal of Marketing Research* 15 (August 1978): 361–368.

Robertson, Thomas S., and Yoram Wind. "Organizational Psychographics and Innovativeness." *Journal of Consumer Research* 7 (June 1980): 24–31.

Soriano, Elisa, and Dale Dauten. "Hispanic 'Dollar Votes' Can Impact Market Shares." *Marketing News* (September 13, 1985): 45.

Teitlebaum, Richard S. "Companies to Watch: Nature's Bounty." *Fortune* (May 18, 1992).

Walker, Orville C., Harper W. Boyd, and Jean-Claude Larreche. *Marketing Strategy: Planning and Implementation*. Homewood, IL: Irwin, 1992: 176.

Wal-Mart Discount Store Operations, Harvard Business School Case number 9-387-018, 1987.

Weinstein, Art. *Market Segmentation: Using Niche Marketing to Exploit New Markets*. Chicago: Probus, 1987.

Weiss, Michael J. *The Clustering of America*. New York: Harper & Row, 1988.

Wells, William D. "Psychographics: A Critical Review." *Journal of Marketing Research* 12 (May 1975): 196–213.

Wittink, Dick R., and Phillipe Cattin. "Commercial Use of Conjoint Analysis: An Update." *Journal of Marketing* 53 (July 1989): 91–96.

CHAPTER 3

Identifying Unmet Needs:
What Do the Customers Want?

INTRODUCTION

In order to grow, a firm must design a strategy for expanding its portfolio of offerings. Ansoff[1] product-market matrix provides a useful way for a firm to identify growth options for a business. Ansoff classifies a firm's current products as "existing" and calls all the future products (including those yet to be developed) as "new." He uses a similar terminology for the markets currently served by the firm and for those yet to be developed. The resulting 2×2 combinations form the product-market matrix. The strategies corresponding to the four cells are: market penetration for expanding existing products in existing markets; product development for developing new products for existing markets; market development for marketing existing products in new markets; and diversification for marketing new products in new markets. The "product development" growth direction involves modifying existing products and/or developing new products and services for current markets. However, in the process of developing new products, the firm may seek entirely new markets (not served by the firm so far) or investigate segments in markets it currently serves. Internal development of products is a viable option if the firm has the technological capabilities. If not, it may need strategies of strategic alliances, licensing, or acquisition. When a firm engages in acquisition, it may also be diversifying its product portfolio.

To achieve success with the product development strategy (product modification or creation of new products), the firm must understand the current and future needs of various customer segments. Its objectives must include both the satisfaction of needs currently met by other firms, perhaps inadequately, and the satisfaction of needs not currently being met in the marketplace. Many companies in a wide variety of industries have used the satisfaction of unmet needs as a major vehicle to growth. The following are some examples.

---

1   See Igor Ansoff, *Corporate Strategy* (New York: McGraw-Hill, 1965).

Light Beer Industry. Although the light beer market is sizable and growing in the United States, the most significant unmet need is for a low calorie beer (lower than the present 90 or so calories for 12 oz.) with the robust flavor of a full-calorie beer. At the same time, no light beer is sold in countries such as Trinidad, and the need for a light beer may not even be perceived in these countries.

Ice Cream Industry. The U.S. ice cream industry is somewhat stable, but there are segments that may offer growth potential because they are not served with appropriate products. These include vegetarian and vegan populations.

Personal Computer Industry. In the PC market, the unmet needs include total software compatibility between the MacIntosh and DOS systems, standardized open architectures, standardized networking solutions between DOS and Mac, and standardized ISDN and multimedia solutions with adequate communication bandwidths.

Notebook Computers. In this industry, there is an unmet need for low-priced machines as well as longer-lasting batteries.

Cellular Phones. Two unmet needs with regard to the use of cellular phones are automatic number identification (ADN) and security.

Ready-to-Drink Tea. In the growing ready-to-drink tea industry, a significant unmet need is a 100 percent natural product as well as good-tasting diet alternatives.

Pay Phones in Remote Places. Hikers, boaters, and other travelers sometimes need to call friends and families. Currently, phone lines do not exist in remote places. Perhaps cellular phones will fill this need (*WSJ*, July 1, 1993).

Self-Moving Industry. Ryder Truck Rental, Inc., recognized an unmet need of customers for an easy and convenient moving experience and repositioned its truck-renting operation accordingly (*Brandweek*, January 25, 1993).

Health Care Industry. Doctors and nurses always want to be sure about a diagnosis. The use of developments in artificial intelligence (e.g., computer-assisted diagnosis) can prevent not only misdiagnosis, but misadministration of drugs. The Discern program of the Kansas City-based Cerner Corporation is an example of this; it uses Boolean algebra to take advantage of what computers can do best and leaves to human doctors what they can do best (*Forbes*, March 14, 1994).

Van Design. The General Motors remote-controlled side passenger door in its new minivans meets van drivers' previously unmet need of being able to open and close the side door with ease (*New York Times*, March 24, 1993).

Energy for Electric Vehicles. Energy Partners, Inc., and other companies are pursuing the development of a fuel cell as a lighter-weight, higher-power, long-lasting alternative to batteries in an electric vehicle; the progress in the use of electric vehicles has been slow, owing to the significant unmet need for a suitable energy source (*New York Times*, March 3, 1993).

Battery Discharge in an Automobile. Many motorists have experienced the unmet need of their car battery remaining charged even though they have left the car headlights on by mistake. A new product, Battery Buddy, developed by Masco Industries, offers a neat solution to this need. It switches off the flow of electricity before it is drained too far. It consists of a microprocessor that monitors the electrical flow and outside temperature. It is strapped to the battery and connected to the terminal (*New York Times*, February 14, 1993).

Computerized Auto Service Systems. The development of a computer chip as a nerve center for an automobile will save a lot of time and energy in diagnosing problems. Rather than replacing a faulty computer chip to correct how a car runs, the new technology will allow mechanics to diagnose the problem and reprogram the chip by downloading a new program onto it. The process takes only a few minutes (*New York Times*, November 7, 1993).

Genetic Engineering of Foods. The food industry (e.g., tomatoes, corn, milk, raspberries, food oils, and potatoes) is likely to be revolutionized by the developments in gene-splicing technology. The gene-spliced tomato, called Flavr Savr—the product of eight years and $20 million in research by Calgene, Inc., in Davis, California—is one example; Flavr Savr has been genetically engineered to retard rotting (*Business Week*, December 14, 1992).

Classifying Unmet Needs

One way to organize the sources of customers' unmet needs is from the perspective of a firm marketing a product for a specific consumption situation. Figure 3.1 shows a convenient way to categorize customer needs. In general, customers recognize a majority of the (potential) needs existing in a situation.[2] Further, because existing products in the marketplace meet most of the needs recognized by customers, the opportunity for developing new products based on meeting such needs is rather minimal. However, firms can either modify/reposition their existing products or develop new products to meet those needs recognized by firms but not served by current products. In a similar vein, some of the needs yet to be recognized by customers are, in fact, recognized and understood by firms; this is due to the research and development efforts of the firms that produce new technologies. Finally, there is a group of unmet needs that are not known to either customers or firms.

For example, consider the development of the cordless telephone and various features during the last 10 years or so. Assume that the current product with the ability to store numbers in memory is produced by several firms and meets customers' need for flexibility in using the telephone. Nevertheless, the product can be modified to include an answering machine (a need that is unmet and recognized by customers). Similarly, the cordless telephone can be redesigned to have the capability of sending/receiving a facsimile; but it may require designing an entirely new product. Among the possible developments

---

2   We use the term *needs* very broadly; it is not restricted to essentials for survival.

FIGURE 3.1
A CLASSIFICATION OF CUSTOMER NEEDS

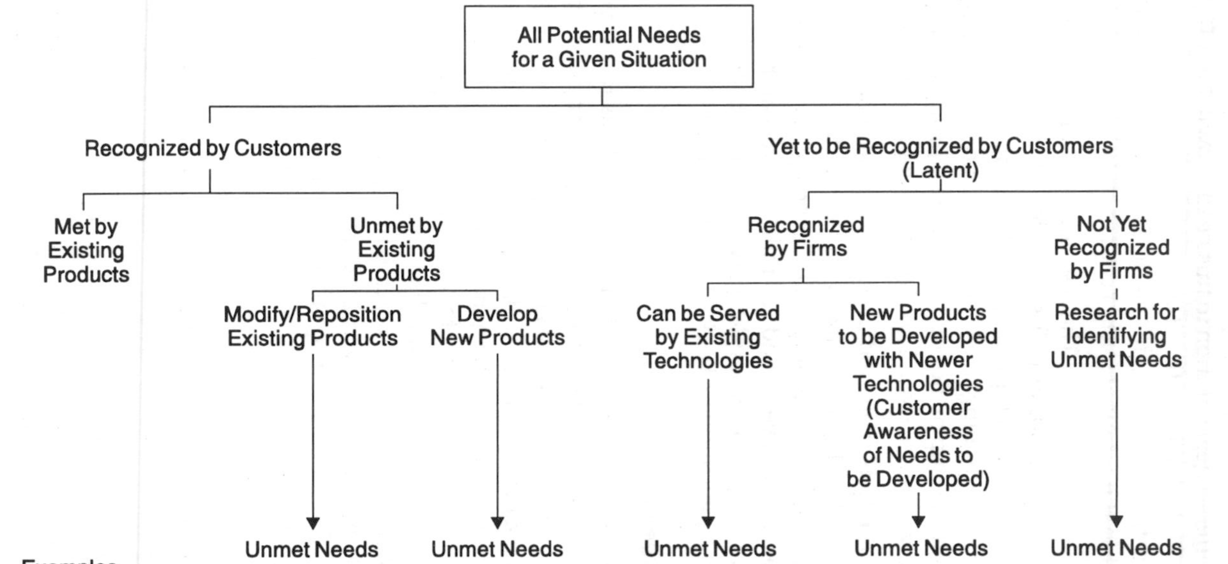

	All Potential Needs for a Given Situation					
	Recognized by Customers				**Yet to be Recognized by Customers (Latent)**	
	Met by Existing Products	**Unmet by Existing Products**		**Recognized by Firms**		**Not Yet Recognized by Firms**
		Modify/Reposition Existing Products	**Develop New Products**	**Can be Served by Existing Technologies**	**New Products to be Developed with Newer Technologies (Customer Awareness of Needs to be Developed)**	**Research for Identifying Unmet Needs**
		Unmet Needs	Unmet Needs	Unmet Needs	Unmet Needs	Unmet Needs
Examples	A cordless telephone meeting the needs of being able to receive/ send calls within a certain range and being able to store up to 10 numbers in memory.	A cordless telephone with the additional feature of answering machine included.	A cordless telephone with the additional feature of sending/ receiving facsimile messages.	A cordless telephone with the additional use as a tool for "banking from home."	A cordless telephone with the additional use as a palm-top computer.	A cordless telephone with the additional feature of simple printing capability.

that would meet needs not yet recognized by customers are a cordless telephone with the previous enhancements *and* the capability for use in home banking and a phone unit that performs as a palm-top computer with printing capabilities. The first modification utilizes existing technology, while the second might require technological development.

Developments in the computer industry offer another illustration of our categorization of unmet needs (see Table 3.1). Examples range from product repositioning (e.g., modification of Novell software) to the potential develop-

---

TABLE 3.1

CLASSIFYING UNMET NEEDS FOR THE COMPUTER INDUSTRY

Case	Category of Potential Needs	Case Example
1	Recognized by customers but unmet by existing products; served by modifying/repositioning existing products	While popular with scientific users, Novell Inc.'s Unix operating system software has not been used greatly in business because of incompatibilities in different versions. Thus, there exists a need to standardize. Novell is planning to modify the software to a standard, ready-to-ship product. ("Novell to Try to Make Unix More Acceptable," by Lawrence M. Fisher, *New York Times*, September 22, 1993.)
2	Recognized by customers but unmet by existing products; served by developing new products	Recognizing the need of travelers to send faxes to the hotel front desk to get printouts, Canon introduced a powerful 7.7 pound laptop with a built-in inkjet printer. ("Canon's New Laptop Packs a Nice Printer Inside," by Peter H. Lewis, *New York Times*, April 18, 1993.)
3	Yet to be recognized by customers but recognized by firms; served by existing technologies	Understanding the potential demands placed on computer terminals not in use yet turned on, Berkeley Systems developed screen savers such as their tropical fish-decorated After Dark product. ("Microsoft into Saving Screens," by Terry Lefton, *Brandweek*, July 26, 1993.)
4	Yet to be recognized by customers but recognized by firms; new products to be developed along with increasing customer awareness	In response to its perception of the ways people naturally share and swap information on a network, Lotus developed Notes, a product that enables large groups of users to collaborate on projects. Documents can be created, revised, and organized with a minimum of meetings and management interventions. Lotus's intent was to minimize the need for bureaucracies. ("Products That Make Markets," by Belinda Luscombe, *Fortune*, June 14, 1993.)
5	Yet to be recognized by customers and yet to be recognized by firms	Recognizing the coming need for increased user-friendliness of the point and click features of the Windows operating system, Microsoft developed the Word for Windows word-processing package. This pulled the rug out from under WordPerfect's DOS market leadership position. ("The Glitch at WordPerfect," *Business Week*, May 17, 1993.)

ment of a product that would cater to needs yet to be recognized by customers or firms (e.g., Word for Windows).

Characteristics of Situations for Study of Unmet Needs

A question may arise whether one could identify a set of general characteristics of market situations for studying unmet needs. Leading off from our previous discussion, a firm may first wish to explore strategies for market expansion (i.e., in current markets with current products) before considering product development. Beyond that, the following may represent opportune situations for studying unmet needs:

- Current markets are reaching a high level of saturation.
- Customers are highly dissatisfied with current products (of the firm as well as its competition).
- New technologies are emerging that may significantly alter the production processes of current products.
- New societal trends are emerging that alter the lifestyle of current customers.
- New geographic markets are opened up for foreign products, but cultural differences exist between these markets and the markets currently served by the firm.

We proceed from the premise that studying customers and other groups in a creative manner will enable the strategic market planner to uncover these opportunities. The remainder of this chapter will be devoted to methods for identifying unmet customer needs.

METHODS FOR IDENTIFYING UNMET NEEDS

There are two broad sources of unmet needs: (1) manifest or latent problems with the currently available offerings designed to solve a set of customer needs and (2) general changes in the environment that lead to changes in consumption habits. Several research methods exist for identifying the unmet needs that may arise from these two sources. Table 3.2 categorizes selected research methods for identifying unmet needs.

The first group of research methods shown in Table 3.2 involves insightful analyses of various aspects of the consumption process of the available product offered in the marketplace and the degree to which these products satisfy customer needs. We identify four specific aspects of consumption process: how customers evaluate products offered in the marketplace; the problems customers experience during the actual transaction of buying; the difficulties customers experience while using or disposing off the products; and how well customers are satisfied with the products. A range of research methods exists for studying these aspects of consumption with an eye to identifying problems (and, implicitly, unmet needs). Focus groups,[3] perceptual mapping methods,

TABLE 3.2
SELECTED METHODS FOR IDENTIFYING UNMET NEEDS

Source of Unmet Needs	Associated Aspects of Buying/Consumption Process	Research Methods	Examples of Unmet Needs Uncovered
A. Problems with existing offerings (own and competitor's)	Evaluation of existing alternatives	• Focus groups	Identification of the need for a warranty program for items bought on a credit card.
		• Perceptual mapping methods	Identification of locations in the perceptual map not well served by existing products.
		• Benefit structure analysis	Identification of gaps in the benefits wanted versus offered by existing products.
	Transactional aspects of buying (mechanics of buying)	• Mystery shopper surveys	Unmet need for a totally courteous service while shopping for goods.
	Aspects of use and disposal of a product	• Problem research (detection analysis and inventory analysis)	Unmet need for an environmentally safe product (e.g., paper towels or baby diapers).
	Satisfaction with use of a product	• Customer satisfaction surveys • Customer complaints analysis	Unmet need for a defect-free automobile at a "reasonable" price.
B. Changes in the environment	Some fundamental changes in various aspects of consumption process	• Environmental scanning • Analysis of trends in population changes, society, and technology*	Unmet needs for nutritious and convenience food products (arising due to both adults working outside home).

* These methods are covered in Chapters 5 and 6.

and benefit structure analysis are generally suitable for studying how customers evaluate existing offerings. Mystery shopper surveys are an interesting way to understand any problems during the actual transaction process. The techniques of the so-called "problem" research, involving detection and inventorying problems, are perhaps ideal for studying customers' difficulties with using or disposing of products. The methods of customer satisfaction research (i.e., surveys and complaint analysis) are relevant for studying the degree of satisfaction with products. Table 3.2 gives examples of the unmet needs that could be uncovered with these methods. These methods are described more fully in the following sections.

3   The focus group is only one of the methods available to the strategic analyst for exploring unmet customer needs. In practice, it is a variation of the brainstorming method.

The second set of methods involves tracking and analyzing changes in the environment and evaluating them for identifying any of the customers' unmet needs. This research requires studying environmental factors relevant to the business under review. In addition to studying demographic trends of the market, the strategic analyst should identify and evaluate the effects of various environmental trends; these include economic, social, technological, and legal factors. Environmental scanning can help forecast potential changes in consumption habits, which may lead to identifying unmet needs. While our discussion in this chapter is confined only to this technique, we cover the variety of methods for studying and forecasting the environmental factors in Chapters 5 and 6.

PROBLEMS WITH EXISTING OFFERINGS

Following from our categorization of methods in Table 3.2, we will describe in this section various methods available for identifying problems with existing offerings in the marketplace. These methods are focus groups, perceptual mapping methods, benefit structure analysis, mystery shopper surveys, problem research methods, customer satisfaction surveys, and customer complaint analysis.

Focus Groups

Developed as a basic qualitative research technique in marketing research, focus groups are an effective way for a firm to gain insights and to generate hypotheses on customer behavior toward its products. This technique, when skillfully administered, can help identify unmet consumer needs. Focus groups are quite widely employed in marketing; because they are based on small samples, we must caution that they are not to be used as a substitute for large-scale quantitative studies.

American Express used insights gathered from focus groups as an important input when developing the program that extended warranties.[4] In this endeavor, the marketing department at American Express first developed a set of 10 ideas potentially valuable to its customers. Using focus groups, it reduced this list to a handful to ensure that the firm was pursuing ideas of some interest to customers. The reduced list of ideas were subsequently tested using quantitative research techniques. The result of this research process, of which focus groups played a significant part, was the design of a buyer's assistance program that extended warranties on products bought with an American Express card. The program was successful; it increased both card usage and card sales.

Focus group methodology was also instrumental in understanding the users' problems in using shampoo by Johnson Wax.[5] Having identified that

---

4   Jeffrey A. Trachtenberg, "Listening, the Old-Fashioned Way," *Forbes* 140 (October 6, 1987): 202.

5   See "Key Role of Research in Agree's Success Is Told," *Marketing News* (January 12, 1979): 14.

the oiliness problems were major for teenage users of shampoo, the company developed a successful formulation for its Agree Creme Rinse, a brand that took a significant lead over its competitors in the market.

Recently, one of the authors conducted a focus group among executives of biotechnology companies to ascertain how Cornell's Center for Advanced Technology (CAT) can serve their unmet needs in research and technological support. This exercise identified a significant unmet need for networking among companies and CAT to exchange information more effectively.

The emphasis in this technique is on group interaction, *focused* on a series of topics introduced by an experienced moderator. The discussion is open-ended and takes place among the members of the group with minimal input from the moderator. The group size is about 8 to 12 people, and each group is relatively homogeneous in terms of background characteristics (users or nonusers of a product, age, social status, and so on). Homogeneity of a group enables easy exchange of views among the members. To ensure that focus groups generate a wide spectrum of insights, it is necessary to conduct several focus group sessions. At least four group discussions are held for a given project, and groups vary in their composition; for example, only users of the firm's products, only users of competitive products, and mixed.

Screening interviews are conducted, usually by telephone, to determine which individuals will participate in a particular focus group. It is important to avoid individuals who have participated in prior focus groups because some of them may second-guess the purposes of the focus group study and may express opinions simply to be consistent with such purposes. A focus group of members who behave like "experts" will not provide useful information.

The moderator directing the focus group attempts to follow a rough outline of issues while simultaneously directing that each member's comments be considered by the group. Each participant in the focus group is thereby exposed to the ideas of others in the group and offers his or her own ideas to the group for consideration. A typical focus group lasts from one and one-half to two hours. The participants are typically compensated for their time, the amount depending on the subject matter of the focus group and therefore, the type of participant (e.g., secretary versus physician).

The moderator of a focus group should be cognizant of the meanings behind nonverbal communications from the group members and direct the group so as to enable open exchange of ideas.[6] Two significant aspects of nonverbal communications are the signs/signals used and posture of the members of the group. Various nonverbal communications that arise in a group discussion context can be illustrated in a 2×2 chart such as Figure 3.2. If a group member uses closed signs (e.g., legs crossed, arms folded across body, and so on) with a tense posture (e.g., symmetrical body position, vertical

___
6   See Wendy Gordon and Roy Langmaid, *Qualitative Market Research: A Practitioner's and Buyer's Guide* (Aldershot, UK or Brookfield, VT: Gower Publishing Company, 1988): Chapter 7.

FIGURE 3.2
MEANING OF NONVERBAL COMMUNICATIONS
SIGNS/SIGNALS

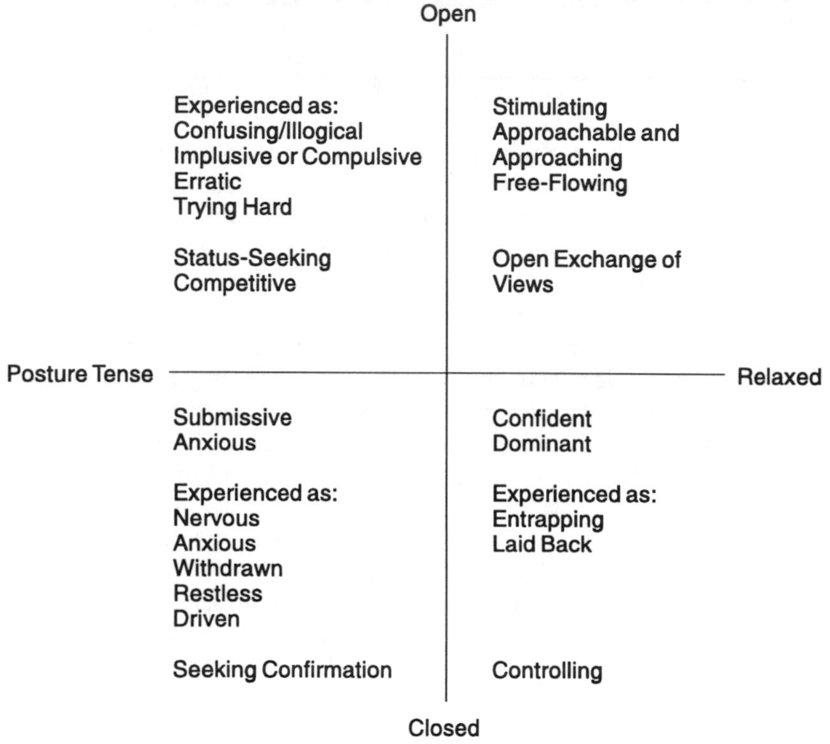

Open

Experienced as: Confusing/Illogical Implusive or Compulsive Erratic Trying Hard	Stimulating Approachable and Approaching Free-Flowing
Status-Seeking Competitive	Open Exchange of Views

Posture Tense ───────────────────────┼───────────── Relaxed

Submissive Anxious	Confident Dominant
Experienced as: Nervous Anxious Withdrawn Restless Driven	Experienced as: Entrapping Laid Back
Seeking Confirmation	Controlling

Closed

Source: Wendy Gordon and Roy Langmaid, Qualitative Market Research (Brookfield, VT: Gower Publishing Company, 1988): 88. Reproduced with permission of the publisher.

posture, tense hands, etc.) he or she may be seeking confirmation of his or her views. On the other hand, he or she may be controlling the group by using closed signs with a relaxed posture (indicated by asymmetric body posture, leaning or head tilted backwards). Open signals (e.g., maintaining eye contact, arms at side, etc.) and relaxed posture will enable an open exchange of views among the group. The goal of the group moderator is to create an atmosphere of open signals and relaxed posture; the moderator should recognize the signals conveyed by the participants at any given moment in the group discussion and take appropriate steps to move the interview along. He or she should use own body language to help discussion going using movements either to mirror others' postures or to contradict them. Further, pacing may be a useful technique to help group members verbalize their thoughts.

An Illustration of the Use of Focus Groups[7]

The following is an illustration of how focus groups were used to determine the unmet needs of commercial vehicle operators: truckers, product delivery salespeople, and parcel delivery salespeople employed by firms such as UPS and Federal Express. Assume that an electronics firm has several technological capabilities and can develop various tracking and monitoring systems that could be installed in both existing and future commercial vehicles. The company is interested in knowing more about the unmet needs of these commercial vehicle operators. How will it go about this task? A suitable technique is focus groups among commercial operators. In fact, the firm conducted several such focus groups using the procedures described earlier.

In this case, these focus groups revealed a number of unmet needs of the commercial vehicle operators, including the following:

- **Communication with the Base.** An operator needs to let the base personnel know how much of the work has been completed and to receive any new or revised directions (for example, to change the route to perform an urgent task).

- **Routing.** The firm managing the commercial vehicles needs to identify the optimal route for each operator in the local area; using the information on the particular deliveries that need to be made in the area, one may develop a route that minimizes either the total driving time, considering the traffic patterns, or the number of deliveries made later than the expected or promised time.

- **Safety and Security.** The operator needs to contact the base quickly and perhaps unobtrusively when there is a danger on the road. This need may be critical for a vehicle that carries valuable goods or cash.

- **Locating.** The home base needs to locate each vehicle in a local area.

With this information, the electronics firm can design suitable tracking and monitoring systems that could be installed in commercial vehicles.

Perceptual Mapping

Perceptual mapping methods are used to develop maps that show various competitive products as points in order to describe their relationships; for example, the degree of similarity between them. The axes of these maps are the salient attributes of the products. Consumers are positioned as points in the perceptual maps to describe their most desired combination of the attributes. A mapping study on a product category will reveal gaps in the current attribute combinations offered in the marketplace and therefore can suggest potential new products.

---

7 This illustration is patterned after a real application conducted for a large corporation. Owing to confidentiality, only cursory information is provided.

We will illustrate the perceptual mapping method with applications for food products and cars. The first illustration of a product perceptual map given in Figure 3.3 shows the derived perceptual positions of six brands of a food product labeled A through F (shown as dots in the figure) and a test product, located by an asterisk.[8] The analysis was based on data on attribute ratings by a sample of consumers, and data on their preferences toward the existing brands (A–F). The perceptual map was derived using multidimen-

8   This illustration is drawn from Henry Assael, "Evaluating New Product Concepts and Developing Early Predictions of Trial," *Marketing Review* (May 1975): 13–18. See also, Martin R. Lautman, "The ABCs of Positioning," *Marketing Research* 5: 1 (Winter 1993): 12–18 for a method for screening potential positionings of a brand in the perceptual space.

FIGURE 3.3
PERCEPTUAL MAPPING TO POSITION A NEW PRODUCT
RELATIVE TO EXISTING BRANDS

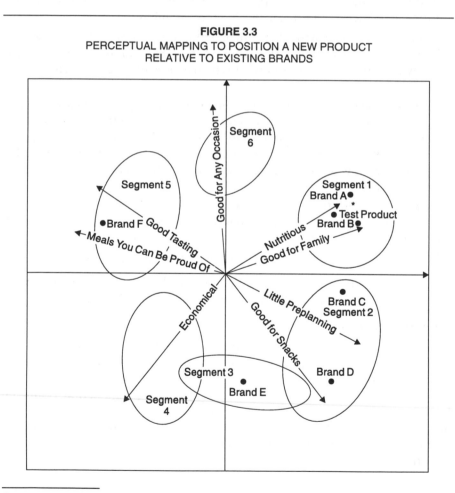

Source: Adapted from Henry Assael, "Evaluating New Product Concepts and Developing Early Predictions of Trial," *Marketing Review* (May 1975): 13. Reproduced with permission of the publisher.

sional scaling methods. The arrows show the attributes in the space; for example, brand F, positioned in the direction of "good tasting," is rated highest on that attribute. Brand E does not have a distinct position in the market.

Each consumer is represented in this map as an ideal point, which represents a product most preferred by the consumer. The preference for actual brands decreases in relation to the distance of the actual brand from the ideal point. The ideal points of the consumers are clustered into six segments of consumers, and these segments are also positioned in the perceptual map. The segments labeled 1 through 6 are shown as circles or ellipses in the figure, the size of which represent the relative size of the corresponding segment. For example, the largest segment, Segment 1, which encompasses brands A and B, prefers these two brands as well as the test concept. The second largest segment, Segment 2, prefers brands C and D, and so on. Further, this map suggests that the test product may need to compete head-on with brands A and B in order to achieve any realistic market share. On the other hand, positioning the test product as "good for any occasion" may establish itself as a viable choice alternative for Segment 6, which is not essentially well served by the current brands (i.e., there is an unmet need for Segment 6). Similarly, there is an unmet need for Segment 4, which is seeking a more economical product.

Figure 3.4 maps preferences of existing cars (i.e., Brazilia, Beetle, Datsun, and Renault) in relation to three new car concepts (S-car, T-car, and V-car) under consideration by an automobile manufacturer in a foreign market.[9] The perceptual map, developed from responses of 1,000 automobile owners, shows four distinct segments of car owners. It clearly points out that the T-car concept is not meeting the needs of any group of consumers, while there is a clear unmet need for Segment 4 (about 22 percent of the sample) which may be served by the S-car concept.

Benefit Structure Analysis

Benefit structure analysis[10] is a survey-based approach developed especially to find new product opportunities (presumably based on unmet needs) in broadly defined product/service categories, such as household cleaning products, banking services, or tools for home repair or redecoration. The method involves two phases. In the first phase, some 50 in-depth interviews (or six or so focus groups) elicit information on all possible occasions for the product category, products used, benefits sought, and product attributes. (This phase may be omitted entirely if a company already has extensive information about the product/service area from previous research.) A comprehensive questionnaire on various benefits wanted versus received for a number of alternative products for several consumption occasions is developed with the information

---

9 See Henry Assael, *Consumer Behavior and Marketing Action*, first edition (Belmont, CA: Wadsworth, Inc., 1981): 464.

10 See James H. Myers, "Benefit Structure Analysis: A New Tool for Product Planning," *Journal of Marketing* (October 1976): 23–32.

FIGURE 3.4
POSITION OF SEVEN POPULAR CAR CONCEPTS
BASED ON CUSTOMER PREFERENCES

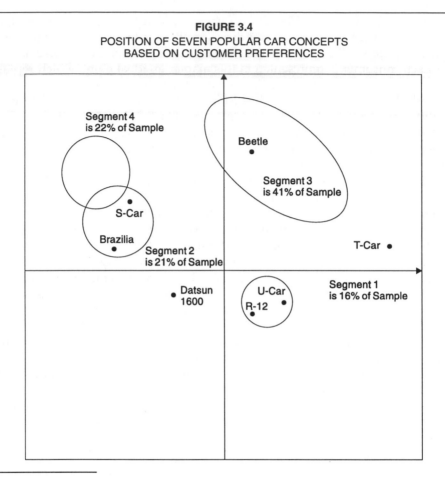

Source: Adapted from Henry Assael, *Consumer Behavior and Marketing Action* (Belmont, CA: Wadsworth, Inc., 1981): 464. Reproduced with permission of the publisher.

from the first phase. Using this questionnaire, a large-scale survey among 500 or so prime users of the product category is conducted in the second phase. Data collected in this phase form the major source of the benefit structure analysis. The data collected can be analyzed in terms of the following dimensions:

- Benefits wanted.
- Benefits received.
- Ratings on product characteristics.
- Product(s) used by use occasion.
- Brands chosen by use occasion.

- Various background data on respondents.

Each dimension in these data may have 5 to as many as 100 categories, depending upon the context. Data combined on all of these dimensions, called the complete benefit matrix, are analyzed using various univariate and multivariate methods. The objectives of these analyses are to explore various gaps in the product available in the market, to identify deficiencies in existing brands with regard to benefits delivered by them versus those wanted, and to identify any use occasions that can be exploited for future product development. In addition to simple cross-tabulation, factor and cluster analyses are used to identify gaps.

One analysis of interest is cross-tabulating the degree to which a benefit is wanted versus received in the products in use and summarizing the table into a deficiency index for each benefit. Simply stated, a benefit deficiency index is the average of the score "benefit wanted minus benefit received" for a benefit. The benefit wanted and benefit received are usually rated on a four-point scale: (1) not at all; (2) somewhat, (3) pretty much, and (4) a whole lot. The difference score will have seven values ranging from –3 to +3. The numbers of respondents with each difference score are computed from the cross-tabulation. This cross-table is called a *benefit deficiency matrix.*

Next, various plots show the average benefit-wanted score versus average deficiency scores for each benefit, the average positive deficiency score versus the proportion of sample with some deficiency, and the average benefit-wanted score versus the proportion wanting the benefit "pretty much" or "a whole lot" that felt some deficiency. Similar plots can also be made for product characteristics. These plots enable a market planner to identify "opportunity points": benefits that are wanted but not received or product characteristics that are received but not wanted and that are wanted but not received. The analyses for product characteristics may help direct the research and development labs to modify existing products by either adding or removing certain product characteristics.

Third, various benefits can be clustered into benefit groups using the information on benefit wanted, and the resulting benefit groups can be analyzed to show which group is more important in size with respect to wanted versus deficient for the sample as a whole. Finally, a combined linkage analysis of use occasions and benefits wanted can reveal at a glance which general types of use occasions require which general types of benefits.

As an illustration, consider the category of household cleaning products. The qualitative phase would identify various use occasions such as cleaning windows, cleaning appliances and broiler pans, cleaning floors, and cleaning bathrooms. Further, it would identify various benefits and product characteristics for this product category. In a study reported by Myers, over 25 benefits and product characteristics are reported; a subset of these are shown in Part A of Table 3.3.

TABLE 3.3
ILLUSTRATION OF BENEFIT STRUCTURE ANALYSIS:
HOUSEHOLD CLEANING PRODUCTS

A.   **Benefits and Product Characteristics**

Benefits	Product Characteristics
Bleaches	Strong smell
Removes stains	Abrasive/scratchy
Removes grease	Can wipe on
Cleans tub ring	Self-polishing
Doesn't leave residue	Biodegradable
Doesn't streak	Can spray on
Doesn't hurt hands	Economical
Seals porous floors	Stains
Strips wax	Contains deodorant
etc.	etc.

B.   **Benefit/Deficiency Matrix**
Benefit #49: "Removes grease"

	Received				Marginal Sums	
Wanted	"Not at all" (1)	"Somewhat" (2)	"Pretty Much" (3)	"A Whole Lot" (4)	Wanted	Got
Not at all (1)	108	13	10	12	143	187
Somewhat (2)	22	15	13	6	56	84
Pretty Much (3)	23	30	25	20	98	75
A whole lot (4)	34	26	27	109	196	147
Total	187	84	75	147		

Wanted minus Received = (Deficiency)		−3	−2	−1	0	1	2	3
Number of Respondents[*]		12	16	46	257	79	49	34
Averages: Wanted: 2.70					Received: 2.36			

[*] These numbers are obtained from different combinations of the table above; for example, 49 is obtained as the sum of 26 (wanted "a whole lot" and received "somewhat") and 23 (wanted "pretty much" and received "not at all").

C.   **Comparative Size of Major Benefit Wanted Segments and Benefit Deficiencies**

	Benefit Grouping	% Sample Wanting Benefit Pretty Much or More	% Sample Having Deficiency
A.	Removes dust/dirt/film	76%	32%
B.	Removes porcelain stains	63	28
C.	Leaves no film/residue/scratches	61	26
D.	Removes grease/wax/stains	59	41
E.	Convenient to use/store	58	34
F.	No unpleasant odor during/after use	54	62
G.	Gentle on hands/skin	35	56

Source: James H. Myers,"Benefit Structure Analysis: A New Tool for Product Planning," *Journal of Marketing* 40 (October 1976): 23–32. Extracted with permission of the publisher.

Part B of Table 3.3 shows the benefit deficiency matrix for the benefit of "removes grease," using data from 493 respondents. About 59 percent (= (98+196) ÷ 493) respondents wanted this benefit "pretty much" or "a whole lot," while 45 percent of the respondents got this benefit "pretty much" or "a whole lot." While a large majority of these people are satisfied with the amount of benefit received versus wanted, there is a subgroup who find deficiencies in the benefit.

For the benefit, "removes grease," the average benefit-wanted score is 2.70 versus the average benefit-received score of 2.36, yielding a deficiency of –0.34. From this table, the average positive deficiency computed by ignoring negative deficiencies (setting them equal to zero) accurately reflects the extent to which respondents wanted a particular benefit and did not get it; its value for the "removes grease" benefit is 0.57. For this benefit, 15 percent of the sample have a negative deficiency score. Also, the number of respondents with some deficiency in this benefit is 162 (= 34 + 26 + 27 + 23 + 30 + 22), about 33 percent of the sample.

In this cleaning study, the primary benefits that people want in cleaning products are grouped into seven categories, A through G, shown in Part C of Table 3.3. Here, not only are the percentages of the sample wanting a benefit pretty much or more shown, but the importance of making an improvement in the benefit is gauged by the percentages of the sample having a deficiency (i.e., wanted more than received). While 75 percent of the sample wants the benefit group, "removes dust/dirt/film" pretty much or more, only 32 percent of the sample finds deficiency in this benefit in the existing products. On the other hand, although only 35 percent of the sample want more of the benefit "gentle on hands/skin," 56 percent of the sample finds deficiency in this benefit received from various products. Thus, a marketer may need to evaluate which of these two product improvements offers greater economic potential.

Mystery Shopper Surveys

This method is useful in determining whether there are any deficiencies in the services delivered in a retail environment. It involves sending a few individuals who are trained to describe various special needs to pose as shoppers and gather information on the way the firm's products are described relative to those of competition. The data gathered here can reveal areas where existing products can be improved. If these studies are done by a retail organization, they will indicate areas where service improvements are perhaps necessary.

For example, this approach can profitably be employed by a firm such as IBM in exploring how its ThinkPad laptop computers are being described by salespeople in such retail stores as CompUSA. The firm can recruit interviewers who are dispatched to shop for a laptop computer at the stores identified. These "mystery shoppers" will keep track of their interaction with the salespeople, particularly with respect to the way the IBM laptops are described and are compared with the other laptops in the store. The resulting information can be valuable for IBM in its communication with the stores and also in providing appropriate information to the stores for their use in training sales personnel. It is also worth pointing out that company executives can gain some first-hand knowledge of the happenings in the market with regard to their products by visiting stores as mystery shoppers.

Another natural application of the technique of mystery shopper surveys is in the context of evaluating how franchises are implementing the policies of the franchisor such as the McDonalds' Corporation. In this case, a sample of franchise locations can be visited by a number of interviewers who "shop" and gather information on the relevant policies being evaluated (e.g., prices, displays, and premium offers).

Problem Research

There are two basic ways of researching consumer problems to identify unmet needs. The first method is to ask consumers what problems they encountered with each of the existing products they use and to have them rate the severity of each problem identified. Each solution may lead to a new product idea or opportunity. We call this the product problem detection system. The other method is to present to consumers a long inventory of problems and ask them to identify what product comes to their mind as having each problem; this approach is called problem inventory analysis.

Problem Detection System

Developed in the late 1970s by BBDO Advertising Agency, the problem detection system involves two major steps: (1) problem generation and (2) problem evaluation. (The method was formerly called problem detection analysis.) The first step is to develop a long and thorough list of possible problems for a particular product or service (or with a broadly defined end-use area such as cooking or housecleaning). This is done by such methods as focus group interviews among prime prospects for the product or service, analysis of secondary sources such as past consumer surveys, expert judgment, and researcher insight.

The second step of problem evaluation involves reducing the list developed in the first step to yield a list of "big" or "major" problems. For this purpose, personal interviews among 150–200 prime prospects are conducted. Each problem generated is put on a separate card, and three questions are asked for each problem. These questions elicit informaion on the perceived importance of the problem, frequency of occurrence, and preemptibility (whether the solution to the problem was preempted by some other product or service). Using these data, two scores—the problem score (PS) and the opportunity score (OS)—are computed for each problem. The problem score is a weighted score of frequency of occurrence by importance, while the opportunity score is a weighted score of all three items of data including preemptibility.

The formulae for computing these scores for a sample of n respondents as a whole are as follows

$$PS_j = \frac{1}{n} \sum_{i=1}^{n} (\text{IMP})_{ij} * (\text{FREQ})_{ij} \text{ and}$$

$$OS_j = \frac{1}{n} \sum_{i=1}^{n} (\text{IMP})_{ij} * (\text{FREQ})_{ij} * \text{PREEMPT}_{ij}$$

where

IMP_{ij} = importance rating given by the ith respondent for the jth problem (on a 0–10 point scale, 10 being high).

FREQ_{ij} = frequency of occurrence of the jth problem as experienced by the ith respondent (measured in terms of number of times per month).

PREEMPT_{ij} = 1 if no product or service has preempted solving the jth problem and 0 otherwise according to the ith respondent.

The larger the PS score for a problem, the more severe the problem is from the consumers' perspective. Various problems can first be ranked on the problem scores. Those with high opportunity scores can be chosen for possible product enhancements or for the development of a new product. Usually, the top two or three problems are identified for this purpose.

These computations are illustrated in Table 3.4 for five respondents, using hypothetical data for a banking service. These five respondents are assumed to have equal sales potential. The problem, "Lines are too long" receives the highest score on both problem score and opportunity score as compared to the other two problems, "Service is too slow" and "Banking is too complicated." The bank under consideration may benefit by taking steps to correct the problem of too-long lines.

It is worth noting that problem detection can also be conducted for industrial products. For such products, the sample of respondents will typically be small, and the relative weights of the respondents in terms of their sales potential will need to be incorporated in the computation of the scores.

BBDO has used this technique for several of its clients. It claims that the problem detection approach is superior to the approach of asking customers the benefits desired in a product or service because customers simply play back benefits previously heard in advertising. These distinctions are quite apparent for the two cases—dog food and banking—shown in Table 3.5. While the benefit approach uncovered "good" aspects of a product or service, the problem detection system identified those areas where a firm can improve a product or develop a new product to solve the problems.

TABLE 3.4

ILLUSTRATIVE COMPUTATIONS OF SCORES IN PROBLEM DETECTION ANALYSIS
FOR A BANKING SERVICE

			Problem	
Respondent	Measure	Service Is Too Slow	Banking Is Too Complicated	Lines Are Too Long
1	Importance	8	6	10
	Frequency	3	2	4
	Preempt	1	1	0
2	Importance	7	8	9
	Frequency	2	1	4
	Preempt	1	0	0
3	Importance	7	8	7
	Frequency	3	3	5
	Preempt	0	1	1
4	Importance	4	4	6
	Frequency	1	2	2
	Preempt	0	0	0
5	Importance	8	7	5
	Frequency	3	3	6
	Preempt	0	1	1
	Problem Score	17.4*	14.6	30.6
	Opportunity Score	7.6+	11.4	13.0

* 17.4 is computed as $\frac{1}{5}$ $(8 \times 3 + 7 \times 2 + 7 \times 3 + 4 \times 1 + 8 \times 3)$.

+ 7.6 is computed as $\frac{1}{5}$ $(8 \times 3 \times 1 + 7 \times 2 \times 1 + 7 \times 3 \times 0 + 4 \times 1 \times 0 + 8 \times 3 \times 0)$.

Although we have developed aggregate measures for various problems, the analysis can be done at an individual respondent level in order to identify those customers with the most severe problems. Such an analysis can lead to identifying segments of customers who may be good prospects for improved products.

We conducted a small scale study with the problem-detection approach for the product category of laundry detergents. The results (both the consumer problems identified and potential product enhancements needed to solve these problems) are shown in Table 3.6. Also shown in this table are descriptions of selected brands that seem to address some or all of the consumer problems.

Undoubtedly, the success of the problem-detection approach depends on the customers' ability to tell their needs and problems in the first stage of the method. Once a list has been identified, the data collected and analyses in the second step seem quite straightforward.

TABLE 3.5

ILLUSTRATIONS OF PRODUCT DETECTION SYSTEM APPLICATION

Product/Service Category		Problem Detection System: "Biggest" Problems	Benefit Identification Approach: Most "Desired" Benefits
Dog Food	1.	Is expensive.	1. Balanced diet.
	2.	Does not smell good.	2. Nutrition.
	3.	Does not come in different sizes for different dogs.	3. Contains vitamins.
	4.	Does not keep teeth clean.	4. Tastes good to the dog.
	5.	Does not chew like a bone.	5. Easy to prepare.
Banking	1.	Service is too slow.	1. Modern.
	2.	Banking is too complicated.	2. Innovative.
	3.	Lines are too long.	3. Friendly.
	4.	Can't get a loan.	4. Low interest rates.

Source: Extracted from "BBDO's Problem Detection System," a presentation by BBDO, June 1993 (with permission).

TABLE 3.6

ILLUSTRATION OF PROBLEM RESEARCH FOR LAUNDRY DETERGENTS

A. Problems and Product Enhancements

Selected Consumer Problems	Potential Product Enhancements
Brighter clothes Whiter whites	Include bleach in detergent, add optical brighteners
Cleaner clothes	Add phosphates
Use any water temperature	Add cleaning agents geared for any water temperature
Allergic reactions	Eliminate dyes and perfumes, eliminate enzymes
Softer clothes	Add fabric softener
Convenience: all in one	Add softener, bleach, and phosphates
Smaller package	Superconcentrated formulas

B. Description of Selected Brands

Selected Brands	Powder (P)/ Liquid (L)	Bleach	All Temp	Non-Allergy	Softener	Super Concentrate
Tide Ultra	P	Y/N	X			X
Cheer Free	P/L		X	X		
Solo	L		X		X	
Yes	L	X	X		X	
Dash	P		X			X
Bold Ultra	P		X		X	X
All	L		X	X		

Problem Inventory Analysis

This approach is aimed at rectifying any difficulties in developing a list of consumer problems when the problem-detection method is employed. Rather than asking consumers to indicate problems with a specific product or service, this method presents a list of problems and asks a consumer to indicate what products come to mind as having that problem. The method is implemented in a self-administered survey using the sentence completion technique of data collection.

The method was implemented by Tauber for food products in a survey among 200 women using the mall-intercept method.[11] Tabulated results for 10 statements are reproduced in Table 3.7. These results indicate possibilities for product enhancement. But caution must be exercised in making changes to existing products from these results without further analysis. Certain "stock" or "expected" results may not represent true opportunities because they may not be important problems to consumers. For example, as Tauber reports, General Foods introduced a "compact" cereal box, which was a failure.

Customer Satisfaction Studies

Perhaps a more fruitful way for a firm to uncover the unmet needs of customers is to study the degree to which current customers are satisfied with its products as well as the sources of dissatisfaction. The topic of consumer satisfaction/dissatisfaction (under the acronym S/D) has received more prominence in the last 10 years or so. Simply stated, if a product performs higher than a level expected by a consumer (or buyer), the consumer is satisfied; otherwise, the consumer is dissatisfied. Of course, the expectation of performance and the observation of performance do not necessarily occur in the same time frame. While an analysis of sources of dissatisfaction can identify problems with the firm's products and areas of improvement, it can also identify customers' unmet needs.

Sources of Data

Firms can use one or more of the following sources of data to identify problems with existing products and to identify sources of consumer dissatisfaction. Analyses of these data using simple statistical methods can identify consumers' potential unmet needs.

- Consumer panels and consumer surveys to track market shares.
- Consumer surveys of customer satisfaction.
- Consumer complaint letters.
- Warranty claims.

---

11 Edward M. Tauber, "Discovering New Product Opportunities with Problem Inventory Analysis," *Journal of Marketing* 39 (July 1975): 67–70.

TABLE 3.7
ILLUSTRATION OF RESULTS OF A PROBLEM INVENTORY STUDY ABOUT FOOD

Questions Asked and % of Respondents Answering

1.	The package of _____ doesn't fit well on the shelf.		6.	_____ makes a mess in the oven.
	cereal	49%		broiling steaks	19%
	flour	6%		pie	17%
				roast/pork/rib	8%
2.	My husband/children refuse to eat _____.		7.	Packaged _____ tastes artificial.
	liver	18%		instant potatoes	12%
	vegetables	5%		macaroni and cheese	4%
	spinach	4%			
3.	_____ doesn't quench my thirst.		8.	It's difficult to get _____ to pour easily.
	soft drinks	58%		catsup	16%
	milk	9%		syrup	13%
	coffee	6%		gallon of milk	11%
4.	Packaged _____ doesn't dissolve fast enough.		9.	Packaged _____ looks unappetizing.
	jello/gelatin	32%		hamburger helper	6%
	bouillon cubes	8%		lunch meat	3%
	pudding	5%		liver	3%
5.	Everyone always wants different _____.		10.	I wish my husband/children could take _____ in a carried lunch.
	vegetables	23%		hot meal	11%
	cereal	11%		soup	9%
	meat	10%		ice cream	4%
	desserts	9%			

Source: Edward M. Tauber. "Discovering New Product Opportunities with Problem Inventory Analysis," *Journal of Marketing* 39 (1975). Reproduced with permission of the publisher.

The firm is better off developing an information system to maintain these databases and enhancing their accuracy over time. Care must be taken to assure comparability over time by using the same questions in repeated surveys.

Measures of Customer Satisfaction

As shown in Table 3.8, measures of customer satisfaction can be either objective or subjective. Various measures are self-explanatory. The statistical techniques called for in building these measures are generally quite straightfor-

TABLE 3.8
SOME MEASURES AND ANALYSIS METHODS OF CUSTOMER SATISFACTION

Measure of CS/D	Satisfaction (S) or Dissatisfaction (D)	Type of Measure	Source of Data	Analysis Method
Market share	S	Objective	Share data obtained through surveys or panels	Computation of market share using a relevant competitive set of items
Repeat purchase	S	Objective	Data on consecutive purchases of items obtained through surveys or panels	Analysis of a brand switching matrix and transition probabilities
Switching out rate	D	Objective	Data on consecutive purchases of items obtained through surveys or panels	Analysis of movements relative to a random switching model
Frequency of unsolved "objective" problems or complaints	D	Objective	Consumer letters, consumer surveys	Content analysis of letters received and open-ended data in surveys
Stated satisfaction or dissatisfaction	S/D	Subjective	Consumer surveys	Means and distribution of overall satisfaction ratings
Frequency of consumer problems	D	Subjective	Consumer surveys, consumer letters	Frequency analysis over time
Frequency of warranty claims	D	Objective	Data on warranty claims settled	Frequency analysis over time

Source: Adapted from Alan R. Andreasen, "A Taxonomy of Consumer Satisfaction/Dissatisfaction Measures," *Journal of Consumer Affairs* 11, (Winter 1977), with permission of the publisher.

ward; they include developing profiles of the firm's products against competing products, developing frequency counts of various problems experienced by consumers, analyzing the content of letters received from customers, and so on. Also, some comparisons of actual consumer switches from the firm's brand to a competing brand can be made relative to a model of random switching. For example, one may compute a measure such as

$$F_{ij} = \frac{N_{ij}N_{..}}{N_{i.}N_{.j}}$$

where N_{ij} is the number of consumers switching from brand i (the firm's) to another brand j (a competitor's) over two purchase occasions; $N_{i.}$ and $N_{.j}$ are the number of consumers who purchased brand i in the first occasion and brand j in the next occasion; and $N_{..}$ is the total number of consumers. If this measure exceeds 1.0, the firm marketing brand i should examine its product more carefully to understand the reasons for this high switching out of i to j. This measure may indicate potential problems with brand i and perhaps some unmet needs among buyers of brand i.

It is important to develop the F-measure using brand-switching data of a longer duration (e.g., panel data for a year) to reflect "stable" market conditions. Measures based on shorter intervals are subject to the effects of sales promotions and other tactical marketing variables and will not be useful for identifying potential problems with a brand.

Consumer Satisfaction Study

Studies of customer satisfaction are becoming very popular in almost every area of marketing. The methodology of conducting such studies is quite similar to that of any marketing research survey (for details, see Hayes, 1992).

We will illustrate this research with a study by the Bank Marketing Association.[12] The Bank Marketing Association's 1992 National Consumer Study on Service Quality in Banking surveyed by mail over 20,000 consumers across the United States. Questionnaires were mailed to a nationally representative sample of consumers throughout the nine census regions of the United States. Survey respondents included customers of commercial banks, thrifts, and credit unions.

Consumers' views were elicited on eight service areas: accessibility, appearance, clarity, competence, courtesy, features, reliability, and responsiveness. Each service area was measured by multiple questions ranging in number from 6 to 11: Accessibility (10 questions), Clarity (6 questions), Competence (7 questions), Courtesy (8 questions), Features (10 questions), Reliability (9 questions), and Responsiveness (11 questions). Questions included the importance of various attributes and satisfaction ratings of the consumer's financial institution. The survey data were weighted to reflect the true distribution of the U.S. population. A number of statistical analyses were performed to search for differences by region, type of financial institution, and/or customer demography.

The analyses relevant to customer satisfaction included computation of five measures of consumer satisfaction for each of the eight service areas:

1. Service Magnitude (importance weighted by the degree of satisfaction).
2. Service Gap (the distance between maximum satisfaction—a "10"—and expressed satisfaction weighted by importance).
3. Maximum Attainable Satisfaction (customer satisfaction standards).
4. Improvement Potential (room for improvement).
5. Satisfaction Impact (effect on overall satisfaction).

---

12 "BMA National Service Quality Study . . . ," *Bank Marketing* (March 1992): 37–38.

These five measures can be computed for each financial institution and its particular competitors (or more generally national and regional institutions as a whole). Table 3.9 presents illustrative results on the first three measures for customers of Bank A and customers of its competitor B. It is clear from these data that customers of Bank B are more highly satisfied relative to Bank A. These data reveal areas where Bank A can improve so as to satisfy its customers' unmet needs. Bank A is considered by its customers to be highly deficient in clarity (e.g., providing clear statements and the like), courtesy (e.g., friendly tellers), and responsiveness (e.g., being able to react to suggestions). Bank A can meet its customers' unmet needs by designing appropriate programs such as training its personnel, redesigning its statements, and inviting suggestions on a routine basis.

Consumer Complaint Analysis

There has been extensive research on consumer complaint behavior. Andreasen and Best's 1977 study[13] (sponsored by the Call for Action and the Center for Study of Responsive Law), based on a telephone survey of 2,419 households in the continental United States, contains interesting information on the incidence of nonprice problems and the actions consumers undertake to solve them. Nonprice problems are problems mentioned by consumers regarding the quality of product or service but not price; an example of a nonprice problem is "The product did not last long." In this study, consumers were asked to indicate their degree of satisfaction, any problems they experi-

---

13 See Alan R. Andreasen and Arthur Best, "Consumers Complain—Does Business Respond?" *Harvard Business Review* (July–August 1977): 93–101.

TABLE 3.9

ILLUSTRATIVE RESULTS OF CUSTOMER SATISFACTION STUDY FOR TWO BANKS

Service Area	Customers of Bank A			Customers of Bank B		
	Service Magnitude	Service Gap	Maximum Attainable Satisfaction	Service Magnitude	Service Gap	Maximum Attainable Satisfaction
Accessibility	5.7	4.3	9.0	6.7	3.3	8.0
Appearance	8.2	1.8	9.0	7.5	2.5	9.5
Clarity	3.7	6.3	8.0	6.3	3.7	7.6
Competence	5.0	5.0	9.0	6.0	4.0	7.5
Courtesy	4.0	6.0	10.0	4.5	5.5	9.2
Features	7.2	2.8	7.0	6.0	4.0	8.5
Reliability	7.5	2.5	8.0	8.5	1.5	8.5
Responsiveness	4.5	5.5	7.0	5.5	4.5	9.0

Data shown are average ratings.

enced (by simple questioning and by probing), and whether they took any action to solve the problem. Among over 20,000 purchases analyzed in the Andreasan and Best study, about 12 percent were considered "unsatisfactory" by the respondents and 20 percent of purchases resulted in nonprice problems. While dissatisfaction with purchases ranged from about 3.0 percent (lamps) to 23 percent (car repair service), consumers experienced problems of a non-price nature at a much higher level. For example, only 8.5 percent of lamp purchases resulted in nonprice problems, while consumers experienced non-price problems in over a third of the car repair purchases. Furthermore, consumers tend to voice only about half of their complaints. This study reveals two important facts for a manufacturer to keep in mind: (1) Even when consumers are satisfied with their purchase, they can still experience problems with the products, and (2) Frequency of complaints is not a full measure of the problems with a manufacturer's products. With respect to immediate han-dling of consumer complaints, a firm is well-advised to set up a system to achieve maximum synchronization between the type of complaint and the type of response.[14]

Thus, while studies on consumer complaints can be a valuable source for uncovering consumer problems with a firm's products, they may not fully represent all of the dissatisfaction among customers. Nevertheless, such infor-mation can lead to identification of consumers' potentially unmet needs.

Warranty Claims

In 1993, based on five cases of warranty-claims reports, the Chevrolet division of General Motors took preventive action by advising its dealers of a potential problem involving automatic transmissions offered on the full-size Caprice sedan, and on its C, K, S, and T series of trucks. The company said that it was not recalling the vehicles, but only advising dealers what to look for in making transmission repairs to prevent future problems. This example is illustrative of the use of even limited data on warranty claims in the prevention of consumer problems.

Studies focusing on purchase encounters, rather than global assessments on consumer satisfaction, can be a valuable method of uncovering problems with products and services. Further, there could be trade-offs between achiev-ing consumer satisfaction and market share goals.[15]

---

14 See Alan J. Resnik and Robert R. Harmon, "Consumer Complaints and Managerial Response: A Holistic Approach," *Journal of Marketing* 47 (Winter 1993): 86–97 for an exploratory study that examined the perceptions of managers and consumers regarding complaint letters. Also, see William L. Wilkie, *Consumer Behavior* (New York: John Wiley and Sons, 1986): 558–583 for a comprehensive discussion of consumer satisfaction/dissatisfaction research.

15 See Eugene W. Anderson, Claes Fornell, and Donald R. Lehmann, "Economic Consequences of Providing Quality and Customer Satisfaction," Working Paper (Cambridge, MA: Marketing Science Institute, Report Number 93–112, August 1993).

CHANGES IN THE ENVIRONMENT

Consumer needs change as changes occur in the environment. These changes provide opportunities for new products. In Chapters 5 and 6, we will discuss methods for understanding and forecasting various environmental forces. Here, however, we will describe a simple method known as environmental scanning.

Environmental Scanning

Environmental scanning involves the strategic marketer keeping abreast of various environmental trends and identifying any consequent unmet consumer needs related the firm's product line. For this purpose, the firm should have a system for compiling data on various demographic, social, political, technological, and other trends in the United States and around the world and should analyze their implications for its several businesses. Sources of information include newspapers such as *The Wall Street Journal* and *New York Times*, weeklies such as *Business Week* and *Newsweek*, television reports from different networks, analyses of congressional proceedings, and the like. It is worth pointing out that organizations exist that make it their business to analyze and report on major trends in the society at large; one of these is Megatrends, Inc. which published the book, *Megatrends 2000: Ten New Directions for the 1990s*. There are also newsletters such as *John Naisbitt's Trend Letter* and *Kipplinger's Letter*, which report on trends on a regular basis.

METHODS FOR IDENTIFYING SOLUTIONS

A firm needs to find solutions to identified unmet needs (which will ultimately lead to the design of new products or processes). In order to be successful, a firm needs to adopt a systematic process for translating identified needs into solutions. The various steps of the new product development process are well suited for this translation (see Urban and Hauser 1993 for a comprehensive discussion on new product development). Usually, the steps involve internal research and development. In some cases, however, a firm may be able to license products or processes or join alliances with other firms for developing new products and processes. (A successful example of alliance is the development of the Power-PC by a consortium of microcomputer firms including Apple and IBM).

Customers play a significant role in finding a solution to their unmet needs. In fact, studying customers is one of the phases of new product development process. Table 3.10 illustrates three methods in which customers play a significant role in finding solutions to unmet needs. The methods are studies among lead users, brainstorming techniques, and synectics. While the last two are, in general, extensions of focus group techniques, lead-user research methodology is a composite of several research techniques. It not only includes focus groups, but involves conducting surveys among current users of

TABLE 3.10

SELECTED METHODS FOR IDENTIFYING SOLUTIONS TO UNMET NEEDS

Methods	Examples
Lead-User Analysis	Seeking a solution to problems experienced by users of scientific instruments by studying lead users.
Brainstorming Techniques	Seeking solutions to the general problem of making a household's life easier and better (by redesigning existing appliances or by adding new appliances).
Synectics	Seeking a solution to the problem of car leaks with a group discussion method.

the firm's and competitors' products to identify a group of users who are much more sophisticated than others. The solutions developed by this group of users (called the lead users) to solve problems encountered with the current products are then used to develop and test new products.

Lead-User Analysis

Lead users, a term coined by Eric von Hippel, are current users of a firm's products whose present strong needs will become general in the marketplace months or years in the future.[16] Since lead users are more knowledgeable about future conditions of product use than most others, they can serve as a laboratory for testing future (and currently unmet) needs.

Lead-user analysis consists of three essential steps: (1) identifying an important trend that affects the firm's current markets; (2) identifying lead users; and (3) conducting extensive surveys and focus groups to determine how the lead users are solving problems (or needs) not yet clear-cut in the marketplace. The lead-user data on usage collected through surveys in step 3 are also employed for projecting future market demand for the solutions developed by lead users, should they be commercialized by the firm. Further, lead users can become a sounding board for evaluating the viability of new product concepts under development. Open-ended data collected in lead-user surveys on need statements also contain information about possible solutions to the need under consideration.

Lead-user research methodology employs focus groups among other marketing research techniques. Studies on lead users are more advantageous than focus group studies on customers in general because members of focus groups are generally constrained in their discussions by the current uses and current products. It requires a creative moderator to bring out the future use situations

---

16 See Eric von Hippel, "Lead Users: A Source of Novel Product Concepts," *Management Science* 32 (July 1986): 791–805. See also Eric von Hippel, *The Sources of Innovation* (New York and Oxford: Oxford University Press, 1988).

in focus groups similar to those experienced by present lead users. Further, lead users' experience is needed for conducting marketing research in fast-moving product categories such as semiconductors.

Two examples illustrate successful applications of lead-user research. The first was the development and marketing of an automated optical pattern generator by GCA/David Mann and Company in 1967 for the manufacture of semiconductor masks, which involved projecting on a photographic plate mounted on a X–Y table; such a design can be adjusted to obtain any desired mask pattern. Initial development of this product occurred at IBM (a lead user) in the mid-1960s and perhaps elsewhere. The second was Monsanto's introduction of butyl benzyl phthalate (BBP) in 1946 as a plasticizer for several rubber and PVC products, which enabled processing of PVC at lower temperatures (110° to 130° C rather than 150° to 160° C) on standard rubber-processing machines. The BBP was developed initially by Bayer in the 1930s as a plasticizer for cellulose nitrate.

The lead-user analysis method is well illustrated by the study reported by Urban and von Hippel (1988) for the development of computer-aided design (CAD) systems used to design printed circuit boards (PC-CAD).[17] The methodology involved conducting a survey among current users of a product in order to identify a group of lead users and designing and testing new product concepts based on the solutions of lead users. The survey was conducted among 136 respondents who are users of a PC-CAD system. The sample was grouped into two clusters of 98 and 38 users on the basis of characteristics measured in the survey such as building own PC-CAD, innovativeness, satisfaction with commercial products, and year of first use of a CAD. The smaller cluster was labeled lead users because it tended to be set apart from the first cluster on a number of characteristics; this cluster is also highly consistent with prior assumptions/conjectures of lead users. For example, 87 percent of the lead-user group builds their own PC-CAD systems compared with 1 percent for the first cluster. The lead user group is more innovative and is less satisfied with commercially available systems. Also, they used PC-CADs many years earlier than the other group. Using various group discussion techniques among a sample of the identified lead users, Urban and von Hippel developed a concept for a new PC-CAD system. The "lead user" concept was tested against other product concepts in a questionnaire survey in order to test the validity of this method for identifying new product possibilities (or stated differently, users' unmet needs). The lead user concept received 78.6 percent first choices as against 9.8 percent for respondents' current PC-CAD; only 4.9 percent preferred the best system commercially available, and 6.5 percent preferred a specialized user system. This illustration shows a firm (particularly one marketing technological products) can not only identify unmet customer

---

17 See G. L. Urban and E. von Hippel, "Lead User Analysis for the Development of New Industrial Products," *Management Science* (May 1988).

needs, but can design products to satisfy such needs using the methodology of lead users.

Brainstorming

Brainstorming is a group discussion method specifically developed to generate creative solutions to problems. The brainstorming technique developed by Osborn[18] has become quite popular in various segments of society including business. Under the general direction of an experienced moderator, groups in a brainstorming session solely devote their energies to creative thinking, each building upon the ideas expressed by the other members. We will describe how it may be used to identify unmet needs among consumers.

First, a few important rules for a successful brainstorming session: criticism is ruled out; freewheeling is welcomed; quantity of solutions is explicitly sought; and combination and improvement of previously expressed ideas is sought. A brainstorming session may be held among 10 people or so at a time and may last about 90 minutes. The moderator of a brainstorming session should explain these rules at the beginning of the session and should try to maintain an informal atmosphere during the session. Participants should be encouraged to express any and all ideas that occur to them because one can never really tell how one idea (good or bad) may lead to another that may be worthwhile. The subsequent idea may not occur to another without the stimulus of a prior idea. Osborn presents considerable evidence that application of these rules generates a large number of ideas for solving problems.

Assume that a brainstorming session is planned for identifying unmet needs in a household to make its daily life a little better. First, the moderator may write a background memo prior to the session to each recruited participant, laying out the purpose of the session and asking him or her to think about any ways in which his or her daily life can be improved by either new products or services. The moderator may also suggest some examples to facilitate individualistic new products for various rooms in the house (e.g., electronic faucets that are turned on and off automatically; an electronic fence for the yard, etc.). The moderator should also come up with a set of ideas; some of these may be suggested during the session when the flow of new ideas has slowed down. Once the session is over, the whole set of ideas may be grouped under various categories that may become the starting point of "unmet needs" in a household. This list may be refined with the information gathered in subsequent discussion groups.

Synectics

Synectics, a word of Greek origin, means joining together of different and apparently irrelevant elements. The group discussion theory of synectics applies to the integration of opinions and judgments of diverse individuals

---

18 Alex. F. Osborn, *Applied Imagination: Principles, Procedures of Creative Thinking*, revised ed. (New York: Charles Scribner's Sons, 1957).

into a problem-stating or problem-solving context. The application to the problem-stating context is relevant to finding unmet needs for a firm. The method is systematic and consists of establishing a synectics group in three distinct phases:[19] (1) selecting people from the firm's personnel such as salespeople, managers, and so on, or a sample drawn from customers at large; (2) training the group of selected people in the theory and methods of synectics; and (3) reintegrating the group into the firm's environment.

The technique of synectics was developed using two basic and interrelated approaches to encourage creativity: (1) procedures, such as the use of analogy and other indirect means, that lead to imaginative speculation and (2) disciplined ways of behaving in the group so that speculation is not cut down, but is valued and encouraged. In this endeavor, an experienced group leader is critical.

Three stages are critical in a synectics session: (1) choice of a goal as understood by the group members, (2) generation of ways to view the unfamiliar (strange) problem in familiar ways and to view familiar solutions in a strange manner so as to come up with several "solutions," and (3) examining closely one solution and force fit it to develop a worthwhile viewpoint by group. The group leader asks several types of questions to make the strange familiar and the familiar strange. These questions fall into three categories: asking for specific examples, asking for personal analogies, and asking for a book title (a two-word phrase) to capture the idea. As an illustration, when the group is trying to find a solution for a thermos-bottle closure, a specific example for a closure could be a door or a mental block. While door may be a familiar concept, the stranger example of a mental block may lead the group into a new line of speculation that may result in a novel solution. Personal analogies can aid in developing material to help look at the problem in a strange, new context. In response to a personal analogy question, group members may simply describe facts, may describe emotions in the first person, or may identify empathetically with the subject matter. For example, for the leader's question "You are a tuning fork. How do you feel?" these three types of responses could result:

- *Description of facts:* I am made of metal and have very precise dimensions. When struck, I vibrate with a fixed frequency.

- *First-person description of emotions:* I feel sensitive, but only to very special things. You can hit me with a hammer and I do not care at all, but if you whistle just the right note, I feel I am going all to pieces.

- *Empathetic identification with the subject matter:* My nerves are shot. Here I am, a high-grade piece of steel, and when the right tone sounds, I have a breakdown! But, I am intensely responsible and narrow-minded. Dead to anything until my frequency comes around and then WOW![20]

---

19 J.R. Gordon William, *Synectics: The Development of Creative Capacity* (New York: Harper & Brothers, 1961).

20 See G. Prince, *The Practice of Creativity* (New York: Harper & Row, Publishers, 1970): 82. See also pages

The third option of empathetic identification generally produces more useful material.

Various principles and cautions should be followed while conducting a synectics session. These include such obvious things as avoiding impatience, acknowledging the contribution of others to the session, and listening attentively as well as more subtle things such as temporarily suspending all feelings of disbelief, avoiding negative evaluation of one's own thoughts and of others' suggestions, and not insisting on precision.[21]

A company with the same name as the technique, Synectics®, was founded in 1960 by George M. Prince and three of his colleagues (all former members of Arthur D. Little). This company sought to explore innovative thinking and how it could be applied reliably to organizations. The firm focuses on the research and new product development areas.[22]

Synectics® involves consumers and experts in three major ways: (1) consumer exploratory sessions; (2) use of customers and experts as creative resources; and (3) consumer development labs. As stated in their brochures, details for these three methods are as follows:

Consumer Exploratory Sessions

Before undertaking any concept generation process, Synectics® works with groups of targeted consumers to uncover needs, tap insights, and catalyze their creative thinking in direct and indirect ways. The Synectics® team applies many of the techniques the company is best known for, such as utilizing metaphors and analogies, to uncover frustrations and wishes that direct questions do not surface effectively. They then discuss, learn from, and translate this information to maximize the usefulness of consumer and client team insights in subsequent idea generation and development work.

Customers and Experts as Creative Resources

Since the early seventies, Synectics® has incorporated outside experts, customers, and other resources to think with clients in the invention and development phases of new product development projects. These "outsiders" provide depth and unexpected creativity to the client team. Synectics® continues to utilize this very successful approach in Innovation and Development Sessions using their ability to draw on over 200 diverse "expert thinkers," based on project need or client request.

In addition, the firm frequently works with clients and relevant outside experts to creatively explore new directions, strategies, trends or hypothe-

---

146–169 in that book for complete transcripts of some synectics sessions.

21 For more discussion, see G. Prince, *The Practice of Creativity* (Harper & Row, Publishers, 1970) and R.A. Procter, "The Use of Metaphors to Aid the Process of Creative Problem Solving," *Personnel Review* 18:4 (1989): 33–42.

22 The following information is from several brochures from Synectics® Inc., Cambridge, MA 02138. We thank Ms. Pamela W. Moore of Synectics® Inc. for sharing these materials. Used with permission.

ses their clients believe represent fertile opportunities. These short sessions usually precede new product idea generation, allowing them to prepare a synthesis of the discussion and learnings as stimulus for generating ideas.

Consumer Development Labs

For the last 10 years, Synectics® has expanded its new product development services to involve consumers in the development and refinement of concepts created by our clients. Typical groups include internal and external customers or consumers, the trade, distributors, and other important constituents of the concepts generated. Using its proprietary approach, Synectics® works with these groups to creatively transform beginning ideas into workable concepts by incorporating the consumer's needs and wishes. Typical projects have included refining new product or service concepts for quantitative or qualitative testing and creating innovative promotions, positionings, and names.

This firm has successfully implemented the synectics approach for the design of such products as Silkience by Gillette, which became one of the 10 top selling brands of shampoo.[23] Synectics® Inc. has worked in most major industries and has served such organizations as NYNEX, AT&T, Black & Decker, Gillette, Kodak, and DuPont.

OTHER METHODS

In this section, we will describe two miscellaneous research methods that are useful in the identification of potential products that could meet certain unmet needs. The methods are morphological connections and Kansei analysis. The former is a technique of systematically enumerating all possible products that could be developed from various product attributes and locating potential new products. The second method utilizes some behavioral concepts to identify product features that could enhance a new product's appeal to potential customers.

Morphological Forced Connections

The method of morphological forced connections will enable a strategic marketer to identify new product possibilities.[24] This method involves identifying a list of salient attributes in the current alternatives used to solve a consumer need (or problem). For each attribute, a number of alternative possibilities are also identified. Given the premise that all new inventions are

---

23 Magalay Olivero, "Get Crazy! How to Get a Breakthrough Idea," *Working Woman* 15 (September 1990): 144–147, 222.

24 See James L. Adams, *Conceptual Blockbusting: A Guide to Better Ideas* (Reading, MA: Addison-Wesley, 1986): 109–110.

merely new ways of combining old bits and pieces, the method looks for new combinations not yet available as possible solutions.

The example, drawn from Koberg and Bagnell, shows how a new ballpoint pen can be developed[25] (see Figure 3.5). For this purpose, one first lists all of the attributes of a ballpoint pen. Below each attribute, one then lists all the possible alternatives one can think of. Once these lists are completed, many random runs are made through the alternatives, one from each column, in order to assemble the combinations into entirely new forms of the original ballpoint pen. The attributes and levels along with a potential invention are shown in Figure 3.5.

The first row in Figure 3.5, marked with rectangles, shows the combination of an existing ballpoint pen; whereas, the combination resulting from those alternates marked with ellipses is a potential ballpoint pen. This combination

---

25 Don Koberg and Jim Bagnell, *The Universal Traveler* (Los Altos, CA: William Kaufmann, 1980).

FIGURE 3.5
ILLUSTRATION OF MORPHOLOGICAL CONNECTION METHOD

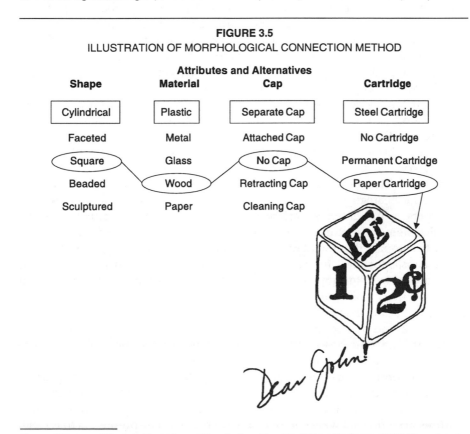

Source: Koberg and Bagnell, *The Universal Traveler* (Los Altos, CA: William Kaufmann, 1980). Reproduced with permission of the publisher.

led to the invention of a square ball-point pen, made of wood, with a paper cartridge, and no cap. When this product was designed, it led to a cube pen, one corner of which writes, leaving six faces for ads, calendars, photos, and so on, as shown in the figure.

The recent introduction of AT&T international fax service is an example of a service design intended to solve business users' unmet need to send facsimile documents when either the receiver's international fax number or the telephone line is busy or not operational. In this situation, the sender of the fax can transmit his or her facsimile document to the number 1-800-THRUFAX, which transmits the fax at a later time to the receiver when the lines are free. The morphological connections method can be used in the identification of the features of such service innovations.

Kansei Analysis

Given the concern that verbal reports are not always accurate predictors of purchase behavior, methods have been developed that probe into people's feelings. One such method is Kansei analysis—a technique developed in Japan. *Kansei* ("sensitivity" in Japanese) is a successor to the popular phrase *human engineering*. Mazda Chairman Keinchi Yamamoto gave speeches in 1986 on the need to understand the rapport between the driver and the car and the need to appeal to his senses or his Kansei. Two main branches of this method are in vogue: methods for evaluating abstract feelings about a product and methods for analyzing facial muscle movements when people look at products or discuss various products.

In the first branch of Kansei analysis, the researcher first develops a list of abstract constructs of feelings (e.g., elegance, sportiness, comfort, feel, noise, shape, color, etc.) and identifies one or two abstract constructs of relevance to the product category under study. For ascertaining feelings, a sample of customers is presented a variety of alternatives in the product category (physical items or pictures or models, e.g., coffee cups or sports cars) and are asked to compare them with respect to an abstract construct (e.g., elegance for coffee cups, sportiness for cars). The responses (recorded on 10-point scales) are analyzed to determine the features of the product that most contribute to the construct. (In this sense, the method is quite similar to a regression analysis of judgment data in conjoint analysis.)

In the second branch, sensors are put on customers' faces to record movements of facial muscles as they test prototypes of products. The data are collected through a telemeter system. Customers speak into a microphone to give their spontaneous reactions while using the product. In this approach, the manufacturer can determine which aspects of the product are causing difficulty for the customer. Mazda used this approach to identify which features of shift gears were cumbersome for drivers. The premise is that facial muscle data give more accurate readings on subtle nuances than verbal reports do.

Mazda recently adopted these approaches to determine physical and emotional responses to noise, shape, and color in its automobiles, according to Shuji Mata, senior research engineer, at its Yokohama Research Center.[26] The procedures consisted of testing its image creative system and vehicle sound synthesizer. In the image creative system, a group of 20 people were shown slides of places, objects, colors, and shapes and were asked to provide written responses to each image. Cameras were also used to follow eye movements stimulated by each image. The vehicle sound synthesizer, on the other hand, was used to determine the "ideal blend" of engine noise and miscellaneous sounds for different car models; a sample of mixes of engine noises and other sounds were tested.

In a similar vein, Nissan Motor Company employs the "kansei factor" in developing new technologies. It uses kansei methods to determine the look and feel of the exterior or interior of a car. Its approach uses more personal judgment than Mazda's.

Kansei approaches are also useful in developing strategies for customer satisfaction, according to professor Jack Matson.[27] In this context, kansei means being "in congruence with nature and natural harmony." Given that hassles at the time of a sales transaction can be a serious turnoff for a customer, firms can satisfy their customers by understanding their feelings using the nonverbal methods. For example, the policy of Radio Shack to collect personal data such as name and address of a customer when even a small item such as a phone jack is purchased can be a turnoff for obtaining repeat business. Understanding such reactions can be valuable in developing appropriate customer-satisfaction strategies.

THE ROLE OF CREATIVITY

While certain streamlined research methods exist for uncovering consumers' unmet needs, the foregoing discussion makes it clear that the process for identifying unmet needs is undoubtedly a creative one. It is, therefore, essential for a firm to foster an environment among its employees that encourages creativity. Several volumes have been written on different aspects of creativity of the human mind. We will offer a brief account of a few of them.

Using their experience in a graduate course at Stanford, Ray and Myers suggest the following ideas to encourage creativity in business: (1) Have faith in your own creativity by letting things follow their own course and surrendering to your creativity even after initial failure; (2) Make an all-out attack on barriers to your creativity by destroying judgment of things or people; (3) Pay attention by using all five sensory skills: sight, sound, smell, hearing, and

---

26 See Mary Ann Maskery, "Mazda Looks for Numbers to Explain Kansei Concept," *Automotive News* (January 1994).

27 See Thomas L. Brown, "A Job for Management: Eliminate the Hassles," *Industry Week* (September 20, 1993): 23.

touch; and (4) Ask questions even if they seem dumb. They further identify several ways, some of which appear somewhat philosophical, for developing inspiration and implementing creative ideas. These include methods for reducing stress, methods for being in the world at large but not belonging to it, and methods for developing a sense of balance and purpose in life.[28]

In a similar vein, Ackoff presents a number of illustrations and a potentially rational approach to problem solving in management. His approach is derived from a paradigm: objectives/controlled variables/uncontrolled variables, relationships/outcomes. But he suggests some useful ways of developing insights from any given situation. The following are some of the "principles" or morals he offers: (1) Irrationality is usually in the mind of the beholder, not in the mind of the beheld; (2) That which is lost may not be found where the loss is found; (3) It is often harder to solve a problem created by others than it is for them to solve the problem created by the solution; and (4) The way variables act may not be nearly as important as how they interact.[29] These ideas are generally useful in guiding one's own thinking about things in general and in spotting needs unmet by existing products. They are useful while employing group discussion techniques described earlier in the chapter.

The business press contains several articles describing ways in which firms devote resources of time and money to come up with breakthrough ideas.[30] These methods are the brainstorming techniques described earlier or some variations of them. A recent technique is the use of metaphors, called the ZMET.[31] This technique offers a systematic way to elicit nonverbal communication from customers and to understand their opinions. It uses personal interviews among a sample of product customers to elicit the metaphors, constructs, and mental models that drive customers' thinking and actions. Customers are asked to bring pictures on a topic of the study, which then form the basis of the interview. The customer is asked to sort the pictures in order to develop connections between them that tell a story. To facilitate this process, the customer is asked to compare three pictures at a time and is asked to indicate which two are similar to each other but different from the third and why. The metaphors used by customers are elicited during a series of interviews, and a mental map is produced from them. Digital imaging techniques are also used in the process of summarizing images of consumers' thinking.

---

28 See Michael Ray and Rochelle Myers, *Creativity in Business* (New York: Doubleday & Company, 1986).

29 See Russell L. Ackoff, *The Art of Problem Solving* (New York: John Wiley & Sons, 1978).

30 See, for example, Magaly Olivero, "Get Crazy! How to Have a Breakthrough Idea," *Working Woman* (September 1990): 144–147, 222; Nellozuech, "Identifying and Ranking Opportunities for Machine Vision in a Facility," *Industrial Engineering* (October 1992); Mark McLaughlin, "It Is OK to Say Oops: Consultants Encourage Creativity by Easing Fear of Making Mistakes," *New England Business* (February 2, 1987): 50, 53.

31 Gerald Zaltman and Robin A. Higie, "Seeing the Voice of the Customer: The Zaltman Metaphor Elicitation Technique," Working Paper, Report Number 93–114 (Cambridge, MA: Marketing Science Institute, September 1993).

For example, in a study of assessing financial success, a participant whose assignment was to take/collect pictures of "financial success" brought 23 pictures; she further sorted them into eight groups such as social things or situations (two pictures), living spaces (six pictures), personal grooming and health (six pictures), family (one picture) and so on before developing connections among them. The constructed mental map for financial success for this participant included such constructs as achievement, confidence, being responsible, excitement, indulging, and so on. Further, the composite picture developed using digital techniques was that of a decadent dinner with friends in a fancy dining room, music, and lots of attention by a waiter. A consensus map developed from mental maps of a sample of participants will reveal ingredients of financial success as expressed by the participants. Proprietary data indicated that ZMET generates more ideas than focus groups and that the consensus map includes constructs generated by focus groups. Thus, ZMET enables a firm to gain more insights. The technique, although in its early phases of development, has been used by a few companies in helping a variety of marketing decisions. It can potentially be employed for identifying unmet customer needs.

CONCLUSIONS

Because growth of a firm's revenues will naturally involve new products, identifying unmet consumer needs is an essential step in the market research process. In this chapter, we have classified the sources of unmet needs into two groups of problems with existing offerings in the marketplace and changes in environment. We have described a wide range of methods for identifying problems with existing products; these included focus groups and mystery shopper surveys as well as more formal methods such as perceptual mapping, benefit structure analysis, and problem research. Further, analysis of data on customer satisfaction, both objective and subjective, can offer clues on the sources of customer dissatisfaction, which can also lead to an identification of unmet needs. Problems arising out of changes in environment can be ascertained by the general method of environmental scanning. The methods for understanding various environmental factors and forecasting trends in environment are extensively covered in Chapters 5 and 6.

We have also identified a set of methods for identifying solutions to unmet needs. These included lead user research, brainstorming techniques, and synectics. The group discussion techniques of brainstorming and synectics (which may be thought of as extensive modifications of focus groups) are also productive ways to generate ideas; they can therefore be used to identify potential lists of unmet needs. We have also described two miscellaneous methods, morphological connections and Kansei analysis, which are useful in identifying new product possibilities.

We concluded this chapter with a brief discussion of methods for increasing creativity among consumers or managers. We now turn to a discussion of methods for identifying competition to a business.

BIBLIOGRAPHY

Ackoff, Russell L. *The Art of Problem Solving Accompanied by Ackoff's Fables.* New York: John Wiley & Sons, Inc., 1978.

Adams, James L. *Conceptual Blockbusting: A Guide to Better Ideas.* 3d ed. Reading, MA: Addison-Wesley Publishing Company, 1986.

Andreasen, Alan R. "A Taxonomy of Consumer Satisfaction/Dissatisfaction Measures." *Journal of Consumer Affairs* 11 (1977): 11–24.

Andreasen, Alan R., and Arthur Best. "Consumers Complain—Does Business Respond?" *Harvard Business Review* (July–August 1977): 93–101.

Andriole, Stephen J. *Handbook of Problem Solving: An Analytical Methodology.* New York: Petrocelli Books, 1983.

Bearden, William O., and Jesse E. Teel. "Selected Determinants of Consumer Satisfaction and Complaint Reports." *Journal of Marketing Research* 20 (1983): 21–28.

Elizur, D. *Adapting to Innovation: A Facet Analysis of the Case of the Computer.* Jerusalem: Jerusalem Academic Press, 1970.

Folkes, Valerie S. "Consumer Reactions to Product Failure: An Attributional Analysis." *Journal of Consumer Research* 10 (1984): 398–409.

Gordon, William J. *Synectics: The Development of Creative Capacity.* New York: Harper & Row, 1961.

Hayes, Bob E. *Measuring Customer Satisfaction.* Milwaukee: ASQC Quality Press, 1992.

Levenstein, Aaron. *Use Your Head: The New Science of Personal Problem-Solving.* New York: Macmillan, 1965.

Makridakis, Spyros G. *Forecasting, Planning, and Strategy for the 21st Century.* New York: Free Press, 1990.

Martino, Joseph P. *Technological Forecasting for Decision Making.* 3d ed. New York: McGraw-Hill, 1993.

Mason, Joseph G. *How to Be a More Creative Executive.* New York: McGraw-Hill, 1960.

Morgan, Gareth. *Imagination: The Art of Creative Management.* Newberry Park, CA: Sage Publications, 1993.

Morgan, Gareth. *Riding the Waves of Change: Developing Managerial Competencies for a Turbulent World.* San Francisco: Josey-Bass Publishers, 1988.

Myers, James H. "Benefit Structure Analysis: A New Tool for Product Planning." *Journal of Marketing* 40 (October 1976): 23–32.

Norris, E.E. "Seeking Out the Consumers' Problems." *Advertising Age* (March 17, 1975): 43–44.

Oliver, Richard L. "A Cognitive Model of the Antecedents and Consequences of Satisfaction Decisions." *Journal of Marketing Research* 17 (November 1980): 460–469.

Osborne, Alex F. *Applied Imagination: Principles and Procedures of Creative Thinking.* New York: Scribners, 1957.

———*Applied Imagination.* Third edition. New York: Scribners, 1963.

———*Your Creative Power: How to Use Imagination.* New York: Scribners, 1952.

Parasuraman, A., Valerie A. Zeithaml, and Leonard L. Berry. "SERVQUAL: A Multiple Item Scale for Measuring Customer Perceptions of Service Quality." *Journal of Retailing* 64 (1986): 12–40.

Prince, George M. *The Practice of Creativity: A Manual for Dynamic Group Problem Solving.* New York: Harper & Row, 1970.

Ray, Michael, and Rochelle Myers. *Creativity in Business.* Garden City, NY: Doubleday, 1986.

Resnick, Allan J., and Robert R. Harmon. "Consumer Complaints and Managerial Response: A Holistic Approach." *Journal of Marketing* 47 (1983): 86–97.

Russ, Sandra W. *Affect and Creativity: The Role of Affect and Play in the Creative Process.* Hillsdale, NJ: Lawrence Erlbaum Associates, 1993.

Stein, Morris I. *Stimulating Creativity, Volume 1: Individual Procedures.* New York: Academic Press, 1974.

———*Stimulating Creativity, Volume 2: Group Procedures.* New York: Academic Press, 1975.

Tauber, Edward M. "Discovering New Product Opportunities with Problem Inventory." *Journal of Marketing* 39 (1975): 67–70.

———"HIT: Heuristic Ideation Technique—A Systematic Procedure for New Product Search." *Journal of Marketing* 36 (1972): 58–73.

Taylor, Irving A., and J.W. Getzels, eds. *Perspectives in Creativity.* Chicago: Aldine Publishing Company, 1975.

Urban, Glen L., and Eric von Hippel. "Lead User Analyses for the Development of New Industrial Products." *Management Science* 34 (1988): 569–582.

von Hippel, Eric. "Get New Products from Customers." *Harvard Business Review* 60 (March–April 1982): 117–122.

———"Lead Users: A Source of Novel Product Concepts." *Management Science* 32 (1986): 791–805.

———"Successful Industrial Products from Customer Ideas." *Journal of Marketing* 42 (1978): 39–49.

———*The Sources of Innovation.* New York: Oxford University Press, 1988.

————."Users as Innovators." *Technology Review* (January 1978): 31–39.

Wheelwright, Steven C., and W. Earl Sasser, Jr. "The New Product Development Map." *Harvard Business Review* (May–June 1989): 112–125.

Zangwill, Willard I. *Lightning Strategies for Innovation: How the World's Best Firms Create New Products.* New York: Lexington Books, 1993.

CHAPTER 4

Identifying Competitors: Who Will We Compete Against?

INTRODUCTION

Competitive analysis has become more than just a job activity these days. It's a job description as well. Many firms have employees whose formal responsibility is to analyze competitors. These include Citicorp, Mitsubishi, Adolph Coors Co., Motorola, McDonnell Douglas, and Marriott. Employees in these firms have job titles like Manager for Competitive Intelligence.

Suppose now that you are a consultant at Great Spring Waters of America, Inc. You have been charged with the apparently simple exercise of profiling the competition for its Poland Spring brand. Your first decision relates to which brands and firms should you collect information on. You likely begin with Great Spring Waters' other brands: Deer Park and Great Bear. Not only are these marketed by the same company as Poland Spring, they come from springs in the same state: Maine. You might also want to profile Vermont Pure Spring Water. It comes from a nearby state. Other American brands like Spa are probably relevant too. Should you consider non-American brands like Naya from Canada and Evian from France? Probably yes. After all, these brands are bottled water. People who prefer one are probably not likely to turn another down if offered it at a party. Now what about Perrier? Is this a competitor of Poland Spring? It is essentially water; it is clear; but it contains carbonation. Furthermore, it comes flavored, fruit flavored no less! How can a carbonated fruit flavored beverage compete with bottled waters? Nevertheless, a bottled water drinker who is really thirsty is not likely to refuse a lemon flavored Perrier when offered. They might even buy it at a restaurant if that is the closest thing to bottled water that is available. So include it. Now what about Seven-Up or Sprite? They are also clear, carbonated, and fruit flavored. If Perrier is a competitor of Poland Spring, why not Seven-Up or Sprite? Maybe you should not include them since they have calories. If calories are so important, there's Diet Seven-Up and Diet Sprite. If these are included, then why not Diet Coke and Diet Pepsi or Coke and Pepsi? Most people, if thirsty enough, would be likely to drink any one of them. Not to mention beer. Where do you stop? The seemingly simple exercise has become a nightmare.

Two principles emerge from the previous discussion. First, *competition is a matter of degree*. It is not realistic to say that products are either competitors or not. A more accurate picture emerges if you allow Evian to be a more serious competitor to Poland Spring than Perrier than if you are forced to make a yes or no decision on each. With this in mind, we still characterize a *competitive set* as those brands or products that are the most serious competitors of a given brand or product. We must never lose sight though that this concept, while often useful to managers because of its simplicity, is an approximation to what is really a continuum.

Second, *competition is governed by consumer behavior*. If a consumer views Poland Spring Water, Perrier, and Caffeine Free Diet Pepsi all as capable of quenching her thirst without providing calories or caffeine, and that is all she cares about, these brands all compete with each other *for that customer!* One implication of the dependence of competition on consumer behavior is that competitors can often be found outside the primary product category. Consider the story of the demise of the railroad industry as chronicled by Ted Levitt.[1] Thirty-five years ago the major railroads fell upon hard times because they "assumed themselves to be in the railroad business rather than in the transportation business."[2] They never considered the airlines as potential competitors and consequently never saw the coming threat. People did not need to take the train to get from New York to Washington or Paris to London. They could fly.

Success in any given industry depends largely on an understanding of the relevant competitors. Whether these competitors are inside or outside the industry, the strategist must recognize that if her or his product were not available, the consumer would not be without choices. The effective manager's task is to ensure that the manager's product has the best chance of being chosen over alternatives both in her or his product category and in other product categories.

The primary objective of this chapter is to describe those methodologies and frameworks useful for identifying current and future competition from both inside and outside the product category. These methods are listed in Table 4.1.

They use data from a wide variety of sources: managerial judgment, consumer judgment, secondary data, financial data, and scanner panel data. There are important trade-offs among these data sources. Consumer judgments may provide the most explicit information into how products compete for choices. They can also provide insight into the potential acceptability of products that

---

1 Theodore Levitt, "Marketing Myopia," *Harvard Business Review* 38 (July–August 1960): 45–56.
2 *Ibid.*, 45.

TABLE 4.1
METHODS FOR IDENTIFYING COMPETITORS

Methods Applicable within an Industry or Product Category

Method	Data Source(s)
Strategic groups	Secondary data, product lists, price lists, managerial judgment
Brand switching analyses	Scanner panel data, surveys
Analysis of interpurchase times	Scanner panel data
Perceptual maps	Consumer judgment
Forced choice and product deletion	Consumer judgment

Methods Applicable outside the Product Category

Method	Data Source(s)
Perceptual maps	Consumer judgment
Forced choice and product deletion	Consumer judgment
Ansoff's Product-Market Matrix	Managerial judgment
Porter's model	Managerial judgment
Substitution in use analysis	Consumer judgment

highlight new attributes (e.g., caffeine-free colas). On the other hand, they are time-consuming and expensive to collect. Furthermore, if the judgments are elicited from people not interested in the product category, they may not be of use. Secondary data are relatively inexpensive, available essentially immediately, and highly reliable. Unfortunately, they are as they are and cannot be tailored to answer the questions a manager has. Managerial judgment is the easiest, quickest, and least expensive data source around. However, it can be the least reliable.

It is well known that human judgment in general and managerial judgment in particular suffers from systematic flaws and biases.[3] In his Nobel prize-winning work, Herbert Simon argued that managers often find decisions too difficult because they cannot process all the available information. They therefore focus on only a small amount of the information, an amount they can process, and make judgments on the basis of that. These judgments would not necessarily be the correct ones if all the information were correctly used. This decision approach is called "bounded rationality."[4] This simplification of complex problems to simpler ones is what leads to flawed, biased judgments. We return to these issues later in Chapter 7 when we discuss judgmental assessments of strengths and weaknesses.

3　One of the landmark discussions of these biases can be found in Amos Tversky and Daniel Kahneman, "Judgment Under Uncertainty: Heuristics and Biases," *Science* 186 (1974): 1124–1131.

4　Wonderful discussions of this theory are found in Herbert A. Simon, *Models of Man* (New York: Wiley, 1957) and James G. March and Herbert A. Simon, *Organizations* (New York: Wiley, 1958).

IDENTIFYING COMPETITORS INSIDE
THE INDUSTRY OR PRODUCT CATEGORY

The most direct competition a product faces comes from others in the same product category. The most likely firm to be competing against Coca-Cola 10 years from now is Pepsico. The products may not be as we know them today and there might be other firms in the market, but few would deny that the most likely brand that Coke will be trying to stare down in its battle for soft drink supremacy 10 years from now will be Pepsi.

Since competition is a matter of degree, it is likely that all firms within a product category will not be equally competitive with a given brand. Accepting that, the manager must identify those products that are more likely to be more serious competitors of the brand. In this part of the chapter, we discuss one concept that has emerged from the strategy literature (strategic groups), two that employ scanner panel data (brand switching and interpurchase time analysis), and one that requires primary data collection from customers (perceptual maps).

Strategic Groups

Industrial organization economists have long held the view that firms within a given industry are homogeneous, except for differences in market share.[5] Of course, this view is alien to any marketer's thinking. Companies within the same industry employ different strategies. For example, in the hand calculator industry, Texas Instruments seeks competitive advantage in large standard markets based on a long-run, low-cost position; Hewlett-Packard seeks competitive advantage in small markets based on unique, high-value products.[6] This has implication for differences in marketing, manufacturing, and development. TI must aim for rapid growth, must fully utilize their assets, and must design their products to cost. On the other hand, HP must try for controlled growth, must provide quality, and must design their products to performance.

Recognizing the intra-industry variability of firm strategies, Michael Porter proposed that the *strategic group* should be the relevant unit of analysis for corporate strategy. Strategic groups are firms that follow similar "strategies."[7] Economists have had a problem, though, identifying what *similar strategies* really means. They have settled on the logic that a strategic group should be defined in such a way that firms outside a strategic group should not be able to make decisions similar to those within a strategic group without incurring significant costs. It is then natural to conceptualize the key strategic variables as those that affect the heights of these mobility barriers.[8] For example,

5   See M. Hall and L. Weiss, "Firm Size and Profitability," *Review of Economics and Statistics* 49 (August 1967): 319–331 for an explication of this view.

6   This example is discussed more fully in Philip Kotler, *Marketing Management: Analysis, Planning, and Control,* seventh edition (Englewood Cliffs, NJ: Prentice-Hall, 1991): 227.

7   See Michael Porter, *Interbrand Choice, Strategy, and Bilateral Market Power* (Cambridge: Harvard University Press, 1976).

powerful brand names, strong distribution channels, and R&D capabilities represent mobility barriers. Each would incur great cost to establish.

Marketers do not have the same schizophrenia when conceptualizing strategy. As in Chapter 1, the relevant strategic variables relate to market scope and competitive advantage. In fact, using these variables as the basis for strategic group formation makes the concept correspond to our competitive set notion. These firms will be competing for the same customers in the same ways. Firms in the same strategic group can then be said to be in the same competitive set.

Derek Abell proposed three dimensions for the classification of a business that might be useful in defining strategic groups: customer groups served, customer needs served, and technologies employed (ways to satisfy these needs).[9] The first two are essentially product-market selection variables. Customer groups served imply target segments. Firms that compete for customers in the same segment are part of the same strategic group (or competitive set). In a given industry, the manager of one firm can use his or her own judgment to estimate the proportion of each competitor's sales that comes from each target segment. These data, along with hard data on a firm's own segment breakdown, provide a complete profile of segment activity for the industry. If a trade association or another disinterested third party were conducting the study, it could get this type of (hard) data from each firm. One such independent (academic) study of the medical supply industry, using Abell's dimensions, found that most firms can be classified as serving hospitals, serving physicians, or serving both.[10]

Customer needs served can be reflected either by the products a firm offers or the specific benefits those products offer. Firms that offer similar products or products with similar benefits are clearly in the same competitive set (strategic group). In the medical supply industry, firms sell supplies, equipment, or both supplies and equipment. The actual product categories—supplies and equipment—thus form three broad categories of needs that a firm can serve. However, firms that just sell equipment are rare. Furthermore, with respect to benefits, two firms selling similar equipment can provide different benefits. For example, some CT scanners might emphasize scan time. Others might emphasize picture resolution. Lists of the products and/or the benefits they offer (possibly obtained from a manager's judgment) can form a profile of the customer needs served by the firms in the industry.

Firms attain competitive advantage either through low cost or differentiation means (see Porter's Generic Strategies in Chapter 1). Measures of these may be difficult to obtain. Nevertheless, useful surrogates are available.

---

8   The spectrum of variables is described in the review by John McGee and Howard Thomas, "Strategic Groups: Theory, Research, and Taxonomy," *Strategic Management Journal 7* (1986): 141–160.

9   Derek Abell, *Defining the Business* (Englewood Cliffs, NJ: Prentice-Hall, 1980).

10 This study is described by Gary L. Frazier and Roy D. Howell, "Business Definition and Performance," *Journal of Marketing 47* (Spring 1980): 59–67.

Experience curve theory (see Chapter 7) tells us that costs are related to cumulative experience, which is related to market share. Furthermore, low costs tend to lead to low prices. Therefore, price and market share are two variables that potentially lend insight into costs. Differentiation is also difficult to measure. However, highly differentiated products usually must advertise greatly in order to communicate the relevant differentiation. Thus, the ratio of advertising to sales can reflect differentiation.

In sum, the following variables can reflect a firm's strategy: percentage of sales from each segment, specific products offered, specific benefits offered, price, market share, advertising to sales ratio. Each firm can be described on these variables. A cluster analysis can then be performed on these variables, that yields the industry's strategic groups and consequently tells us which companies compete with which others. Computer programs that perform cluster analyses are commonly available in all major statistical packages (e.g., SAS, SPSS, BMDP, Systat, STATA, etc.). If such programs are not available, clusters can be formed by the manager based on a visual inspection of the relevant data. The medical supply industry study revealed six strategic groups: Hospital-Supply, Hospital-Supply and Equipment, Physician-Supply, Physician-Supply and Equipment, Hospital and Physician-Supply, Hospital and Physician-Supply and Equipment.

Brand-Switching Analyses

Marketers of consumer packaged goods have long known that consumers tend to purchase (and consume) many brands within a product category. In one study on soft drinks, consumers drank the same brand as on the previous usage occasion only 45 percent of the time.[11] The academic literature contains many explanations for this "brand-switching" phenomenon. In particular, if consumers are price sensitive, they may gravitate to whichever brand (if any) is on promotion at any given time.[12] Brand-switching behavior is usually summarized in what is called a *brand-switching matrix*. In such a matrix, the rows and columns represent the brands in the product category of interest. The element in the ith row and j^{th} column reflects the conditional probability that a consumer will buy the brand in the jth column on the purchase occasion following one on which the brand in the ith row was bought. For example, in Table 4.2, 11.4 percent of the people who bought Tide on a given purchase occasion bought Wisk on the next one.[13] The diagonal elements of Table 4.2 are the repeat purchase probabilities, the probabilities that a random consumer follows up a purchase of a given brand with another of the same brand.

11 Frank M. Bass, Edgar A. Pessemier, and Donald R. Lehmann, "An Experimental Study of Relationships between Attitudes, Brand Preference, and Choice," *Behavioral Science* 17 (November 1972): 532–541.

12 Scott A. Neslin and Robert W. Shoemaker, "An Alternative Explanation for Lower Repeat Rates after Promotion Purchases," *Journal of Marketing Research* 26 (May 1989): 205–213, develop an intriguing model of how promotions impact repeat purchase probabilities.

13 This table was taken from Randolph E. Bucklin, Gary J. Russell, and V. Srinivasan, "A Relationship Between Price Elasticities and Brand Switching Probabilities in Heterogeneous Markets," Mimeo, April 1992.

TABLE 4.2

MATRIX OF SWITCHING PROBABILITIES—LIQUID LAUNDRY DETERGENT MARKET

	Tide	Wisk	Era	Surf	Solo	Cheer	All	Bold 3	Fab
Tide	.569	.114	.056	.127	.020	.047	.021	.020	.026
Wisk	.155	.493	.073	.118	.024	.040	.040	.023	.034
Era	.094	.104	.590	.102	.027	.031	.012	.025	.015
Surf	.139	.170	.077	.428	.037	.045	.036	.031	.037
Solo	.081	.080	.057	.148	.507	.019	.014	.069	.025
Cheer	.208	.111	.084	.139	.013	.334	.050	.038	.023
All	.133	.191	.052	.136	.017	.061	.322	.026	.061
Bold 3	.105	.126	.086	.185	.068	.037	.033	.327	.033
Fab	.190	.135	.078	.149	.032	.043	.020	.075	.279

Note: Based on brand switches of 2,224 panelists.

Source: R. E. Bucklin, G. J. Russell, and V. Srinivasan. "A Relationship Between Price Elasticities and Brand Switching Probabilities in Heterogeneous Markets," Mimeo, April 1992. Reprinted with permission of the author.

Note that these are the largest elements in each row. It makes sense that a purchaser of a given brand would be more likely to purchase that brand than any other on the next purchase occasion.

Most brand-switching matrices are compiled from the scanner panel data collected by Nielsen and I.R.I. These data reflect products bought in super-markets (both Nielsen and I.R.I. collect data on these) or drug stores (only I.R.I. collects these data). These data are usually distributed at the level of a product category. Any analysis of competition that is based on these data is constrained by the scanner supplier's definition of that category. For example, one cannot easily form switching matrices that contain both Poland Spring Water and Diet Pepsi.

One property of brand switching illustrated by this table is that it is asymmetric. The probability of switching brands from Tide to Cheer does not equal the probability of switching brands from Cheer to Tide. This asymmet-ricity is well-known with respect to different price tiers of packaged goods. The probability of switching from a moderate or low-priced brand to a premium brand is much lower than the reverse. The reason for this is that typical moderate or low-price buyers (e.g., those who typically buy Bold 3 or Fab) will buy a premium brand (e.g., Tide) when it's on promotion because they can get what they believe to be superior quality for the same price. On the other hand, typical premium buyers will not buy lower-priced brands when they are on promotion because they are unwilling to sacrifice quality.[14]

In any event, it stands to reason that brands consumers tend to switch *to* *from* a given brand are likely to be competitive with the given brand. The

---

14 Robert C. Blattberg and Kenneth J. Wisniewski, "Price Induced Patterns of Competition," *Marketing Science* 8 (Fall 1989): 291–309 develop a very compelling model that explains this.

underlying logic is that if consumers tend to use two brands in a given product category, these brands are likely to be seen as substitutes for each other. Table 4.2 suggests that Tide's most serious competitor is Surf, although Wisk is a close second. Wisk's most serious competitor is Tide; Era's is Wisk; Wisk's is Tide, and so on. This type of analysis is straightforward to perform. However, it is very ad hoc and so does not really provide a formal basis for partitioning the market into competitive sets.

Hierarchical Approaches

One way to accomplish this is to convert the switching data into similarity measures and use cluster analysis to form clusters or competitive sets. Cluster analysis is a multivariate statistical technique that groups together items according to how similar they are.

Cluster analysis software often produces output that is visually represented as a hierarchy or tree diagram such as that in Figure 4.1. The diagram contains paths that link each brand with every other brand. The way to interpret these diagrams is that more switching occurs between pairs of brands that are linked with a path towards the bottom of the diagram than towards the top. For example, in Figure 4.1, there is more switching between Pepsi and Tab than there is between Tab and Diet-Rite; there is also more switching between Tab and Diet-Rite than there is between Tab and Coca Cola. Thus, we infer that these are seen by consumers as more similar; consequently, managers should view these as more competitive with each other than with others.

Figure 4.1 depicts the hierarchical structure of a cluster analysis one of us performed using a soft-drink switching matrix. In particular, national brands (left-hand side of the tree) have a greater degree of competitiveness (i.e., exhibit more intragroup switching) with each other than they do with regional brands (right-hand side), regardless of flavor. Additionally, within regional brands, brand name forms a strong basis of competition (i.e., there is more intrabrand switching than intraflavor switching among regional brands).

The hierarchical or tree nature of this output enables the analyst or manager to ascribe a choice process to the brand-switching matrix. Figure 4.2 provides a summary interpretation of Figure 4.1. National/regional distribution (or perhaps price) is the most important attribute, that which consumers use first. The subtree for the national brands has diet/nondiet as the next important feature, followed by flavor.

A Final Comment

One final comment on brand-switching analyses is in order. The vast majority of brand-switching analyses and switching matrices are created for frequently purchased packaged goods. There are two reasons that switching matrices are used less frequently for durables and industrial products. First, the interpurchase times must be short enough so that repeat purchases and brand switches in particular can be observed. This is more common in pack-

FIGURE 4.1
HIERARCHICAL COMPETITIVE STRUCTURE FOR SOFT DRINKS

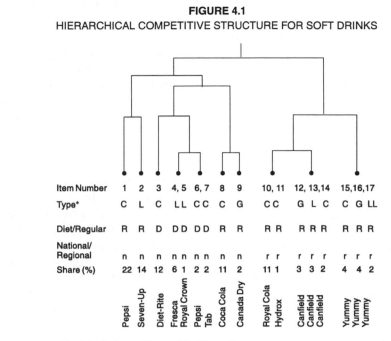

Item Number	1	2	3	4,5	6,7	8	9	10, 11	12, 13,14	15,16,17
Type*	C	L	C	LL	CC	C	G	C C	G L C	C G LL
Diet/Regular	R	R	D	DD	DD	R	R	R R	R R R	R R R
National/Regional	n	n	n	n n	n n	n	n	r r	r r r	r r r
Share (%)	22	14	12	6 1	2 2	11	2	11 1	3 3 2	4 4 2

Pepsi | Seven-Up | Diet-Rite | Fresca Royal Crown | Pepsi Tab | Coca Cola | Canada Dry | Royal Cola Hydrox | Canfield Canfield Canfield | Yummy Yummy Yummy

*C = Cola, L = Lemon/Lime, and G = Ginger Ale.

Source: Vithala R. Rao and Darius J. Sabavala, "Inference of Hierarchical Choice Processes from Panel Data," *Journal of Consumer Research* 8 (June 1981): 85–96. Reprinted with permission, University of Chicago Press.

FIGURE 4.2
SUMMARY INTERPRETATION OF SOFT-DRINK HIERARCHY

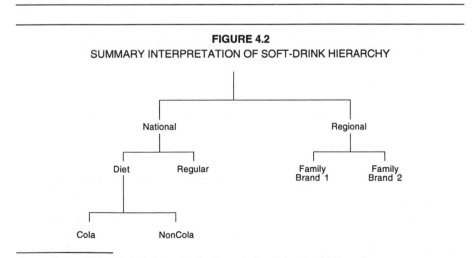

Source: Rao and Sabavala (1981). Reprinted with permission, University of Chicago Press.

aged goods. Second, the major source of data that tracks a consumer's brand choices over time is scanner panel data, which are primarily available only for frequently purchased packaged goods.

Nevertheless, one should not take this to mean that switching matrices cannot be and are not constructed for infrequently purchased consumer durables. Ford Motors used to conduct a survey each year of 20,000 new car buyers. Among the questions asked was what car was traded in for the car just bought. Table 4.3 presents a switching matrix constructed from the data collected in 1960.

Interpurchase Times

Today's scanner panel data contain much more information than simply the sequence of purchases needed to compute a brand-switching matrix. The actual dates and amounts of purchase are available, too. This enables one to compute interpurchase times and the quantities associated with those inter-purchase times. These provide more fuel to identify competitive sets.

Consider a market containing two brands, A and B. Also consider a con-sumer who consumes these two brands at the same rate and who makes a purchase immediately upon running out of the brand previously purchased. Consider the time interval (in days) between two successive purchases of brand A. Brand B may or may not have been bought in the interpurchase interval. In either case, if A and B are being used as substitutes, the interpur-chase time should depend on the amount of A and the amount of B bought during this interval. We can write this in algebraic form as

$$Y_A = \alpha_A \times (Q_A + Q_{BA}),$$

where Y_A is the interpurchase interval, α_A is a parameter that measures the time it takes to consume one unit of A, Q_A is the quantity of brand A purchased on the first purchase occasion, and Q_{BA} is the amount of B purchased in the interpurchase interval.[15]

TABLE 4.3
AUTOMOBILE SWITCHING MATRIX–1960

Previous Car	New Car			
	General Motors	Ford	Other	Chrysler
General Motors	0.68	0.14	0.12	0.06
Ford	0.21	0.60	0.12	0.07
Other	0.15	0.18	0.62	0.05
Chrysler	0.20	0.17	0.16	0.46

Source: Richard A. Colombo and Donald G. Morrison, "A Brand Switching Model with Implications for Market-ing Strategies," *Marketing Science*, 8 (Winter 1989), 80–99: Reprinted with permission, INFORMS.

If, on the other hand, A and B are not substitutes, the interpurchase time should be related to the amount of A bought at the beginning of the time period only. This would be written as

$$Y_A = \alpha_A \, X \, Q_A$$

The question of whether A and B are substitutes (i.e., can be classified into the same competitive set) becomes the question of which of the two above relationships is correct. The analyst can perform a linear regression with the two independent variables, Q_A and Q_{BA}

$$Y_A = \beta_A Q_A + \beta_{BA} Q_{BA}$$

where the regression constant is constrained to be equal to zero. The substitutability of A and B can then be examined by testing the hypothesis that the coefficients of Q_A and Q_{BA} are equal. Standard computer packages allow both this test to be constructed and the constant to be constrained with a couple of simple program instructions.

These ideas can be extended to several brands. The analyst can include a variety of brands in the extended brand regression

$$Y_A = \beta_A Q_A + \Sigma_i \beta_{iA} Q_{iA}$$

where i is taken over all other potential brands in the competitive set of A and Q_{iA} is the amount of the ith brand purchased in the interpurchase interval. The relevant test then is a test that all coefficients are equal.[16]

In principle, these analyses are intended to be performed at the individual level; in other words, a separate analysis is needed for each household. However, if usage rates and the times taken to consume each member of the product category do not vary much across households, data from several households can be pooled and the analysis can be performed at the aggregate level. If the manager believes this is appropriate, the resulting inferences relate to the market as a whole rather than to a particular household.

The foregoing discussion implicitly assumed that A and B were either perfect substitutes or not related at all. This is obviously not the case. While Perrier and Poland Spring Water may not be perfect substitutes (one is carbonated and may be used somewhat differently), it would be silly to assert that they are not related at all. The truth is that these brands, if not most brands in most categories, are *imperfect* substitutes for each other. The manager recognizing this might not want to take the position that either the above

---

15 This relationship can be extended in a straightforward manner if there is a third brand, say C, in the market. The extension becomes $Y_A = \alpha_A \, X \, (Q_A + Q_{BA} + Q_{CA})$, where Q_{CA} is the quantity of C bought in the interpurchase interval. Extensions to larger markets are obvious.

16 Rajiv Grover and Vithala R. Rao, "Inferring Competitive Market Structure Based on a Model of Interpurchase Intervals," *International Journal of Research in Marketing* 5 (1988): 55–72 present a more sophisticated approach, which estimates elasticities of substitution from interpurchase times, allowing for preference heterogeneity and multiple usage occasions. In their framework, brands are perfect substitutes if their elasticity of substitution is equal to 1.

regression coefficients are equal or zero. The β coefficients reflect some degree of substitutability between brand A and the others. For example, if the coefficients of brands A, B, and C in the extended model above are 1, .8, and .2, respectively, the most accurate statement might be that B is fairly competitive with A, and C is not very much so. Recall that competition is a matter of degree.

Perceptual Maps

Perceptual maps, discussed earlier in Chapters 2 and 3, provide another way of assessing competitive sets. Recall that two brands are positioned close together on the map if they are seen as psychologically similar. It follows, then, that if two brands are close together on a perceptual map, they would be seen as substitutes by potential customers and should therefore be part of the same competitive set. For example, in Figure 2.4, one competitive set might be {Mustang, Cougar, Camaro}; another might be {Continental, Imperial}; a third might be {Jaguar, Thunderbird}. These competitive sets could be formed either by visual inspection or a cluster analysis of the map coordinates.

One interesting way of collecting similarities data that is useful for identifying competitors through a perceptual map is the similarity of consideration sets approach. Respondents are asked to pick a subset of brands or products that they would consider buying out of a larger set. The similarity measure is then taken to be the number of times that two products were both included in this "consideration set." The appeal of this approach is twofold. First, the similarity of consideration question is akin to asking a respondent which products have a chance to compete for her or his purchase. Second, since the researcher defines the set of products, she or he can include anything she or he feels appropriate, both Poland Spring Water and Diet Pepsi, for example.

Forced Choice and Product Deletion

In sports, there is a saying that no place is worse than second place. The runner-up in any competition often takes little solace that he or she was the second best player or team in the entire field, that he or she supplied the most competition to the eventual winner. In a consumer's brand choice, the runner-up is never known. If it were, the manager of the runner-up brand would know that the brand was the most competitive to the chosen brand for the consumer in question. This could provide valuable input into the definition of competitive sets.

Consider the following marketing research interview question. Suppose a consumer was asked to make a choice from a prespecified set of brands. Once this is done, the researcher informs the consumer that her or his preferred brand is no longer available. Which one does the consumer choose then? Another way of phrasing this question is What brand benefits most if the preferred brand drops out of the picture? This question captures the essence of what we intuit as competition. The logic behind this research approach very much parallels that of brand-switching analyses. Both ask who affects who types of questions. The major differences lie in the nature of the switch and the data source from which it is measured.

Consider the (hypothetical) data in Table 4.4. The second column of the table lists the distribution of the forced choices of 100 respondents to the choice set comprised of the elements listed in the first column. The remaining columns present the distribution of forced choices that emerge when the product listed in that row is deleted for those who preferred it. For example, six of the 10 respondents that preferred a Peugeot diesel now prefer a Cutlass diesel; eight preferred some type of diesel, and only one stayed with the Peugeot brand and switched to a gasoline engine. Similar statements could be made for those who preferred Cutlass and Jetta diesels. Two possible competitive structures are Diesel vs. Gasoline and Model Name Specific. The data in Table 4.4 seem to suggest that Diesel vs. Gasoline is a more appropriate structure.

Following the logic behind this approach, Glen Urban, Philip Johnson, and John Hauser have formally defined a submarket as a group of products whose choice probabilities are more likely to be affected when one of them is deleted from the overall product category or market. The size of this (positive) effect for a remaining brand is proportional to its market share. Urban and his colleagues developed a formal statistical methodology, using forced choice and product deletion data, to test whether a hypothesized partitioning of products into submarkets satisfies this property.[17]

---

17 Glen L. Urban, Philip L. Johnson, and John R. Hauser, "Testing Competitive Market Structures," *Marketing Science* 3 (Spring 1984): 83–113.

TABLE 4.4
AUTOMOBILE FORCED CHOICE MATRIX

	N of Choices	Diesel			Gasoline			
		Peugeot	Cutlass	Jetta	Cavalier	Peugeot	Cutlass	Jetta
Diesel								
Peugeot	10	—	6	2	1	1	0	0
Cutlass	20	10	—	4	0	2	4	0
Jetta	15	7	2	—	1	1	1	3
Gasoline								
Cavalier	20	0	2	4	—	0	4	10
Peugeot	15	3	1	1	0	—	5	5
Cutlass	10	0	1	0	3	3	—	3
Jetta	10	0	0	2	1	5	2	—

Source: G.L. Urban, P.L. Johnson, and J.R. Hauser, "Testing Competitive Market Structures," *Marketing Science* 3:2 (Spring 1984): 96. Reprinted with permission, INFORMS.

IDENTIFYING COMPETITORS OUTSIDE
THE INDUSTRY OR PRODUCT CATEGORY

In making long-term strategic decisions, management is often concerned not only with current and direct competition from similar brands, but with potential, less-immediate competition from firms that do not compete in the same product market today but may provide threats in the future either as new entrants into the product-market in question or by repositioning their products as substitutes for those of the firm of interest. In packaged goods, Procter & Gamble has such a strong set of relationships with supermarkets, drug, and discount stores and so much experience and marketing know-how that it is a potential entrant in virtually any packaged goods category that can be sold in any of these stores. Arm and Hammer baking soda provides an example of a product that can be positioned as a substitute in other product categories. It has provided competition for toothpastes, household deodorizers, and kitty litters, among other things.

Furthermore, understanding competition in a broader sense allows managers not only to be more keenly aware of potential threats, but to be more likely to spot opportunities as well. The National Basketball Association recognized that if fans were not watching their games, they were likely to be watching other television, going to the movies, and so on. They were competing with entertainment vehicles more than other sports events. The recognition of the entertainment nature of their competition led to a repositioning of the game as entertainment. In the late 1980s, the league actually moved their weeknight cable TV "Game of the Week" from Thursday to Tuesday in order to avoid competing with "The Bill Cosby Show." As another example, cable television and telephone companies are scrambling to set up signposts on the information superhighway, ignoring the electric companies that already have wires running to almost every home in the civilized world. What role these companies play in the highway's eventual route can impact the more visible interested parties.[18]

Many of the research and analysis techniques described in the first part of this chapter can be used to identify competitors outside the product category of interest simply by substituting product categories for brands in the data collection process. For example, consider the perceptual map of breakfast foods in Figure 4.3. This map was based on judged similarities of the different items. Sweet items such as jelly donut, cinnamon bun, and glazed donut all appear on the left side of the map. Nonsweet items such as buttered toast, toast and margarine, and hard roll with butter appear on the right side. There are also many natural groupings of items such as toast pop-up and cinnamon toast, toast with margarine and buttered toast, and so on. These groupings contain items that obviously compete with each other.

---

18 Potential roles are outlined in "Big Hopes Put on Electric Wires," *New York Times* (July 6, 1994): D1.

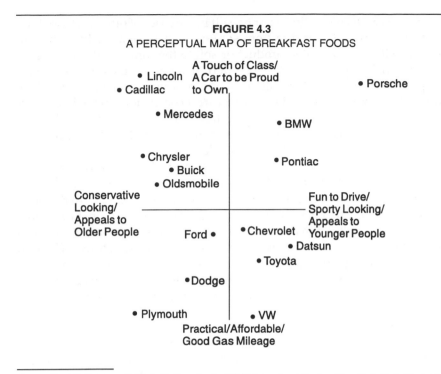

FIGURE 4.3
A PERCEPTUAL MAP OF BREAKFAST FOODS

Source: Paul E. Green and Vithala R. Rao, *Applied Multidimensional Scaling* (New York: Holt, Rinehart, and Winston, 1972): 29. Reprinted with permission from the publisher.

There are other frameworks and techniques that could prove useful in identifying competitors outside the product category. In this section, we discuss two conceptual models of corporate strategy—Ansoff's product-market matrix and Porter's model of five competitive forces—that offer insight into where one might look for (future) competitors from outside the product category. We also discuss one marketing research methodology—substitution in use analysis—the purpose of which is to identify products from different categories that compete with each other.

Ansoff's Product-Market Matrix

Ansoff's product-market matrix, briefly described in Chapter 3, provides a framework with implications for identifying future competitors.

The original purpose of Ansoff's matrix was to structure and identify possible growth paths. A firm can continue with the same products in the same markets (market penetration), sell the same products in different markets (market development), sell different products in the same markets (product development), or sell different products in different markets (diversification). With respect to our purposes, we note that if the matrix structures the strategic growth decision for our firm, it must do the same thing for our competitors.

The manager can then put himself or herself in the place of other firms looking for growth and examine the directions suggested by the matrix. In particular, firms that sell either the same product or sell to the same markets as we do (but not both)[19] are potential future competitors. If one of these firms extends its scope to our markets (if it sells the same product) or our products (if it already sells in our market), it becomes a direct competitor. Indeed, it stands to reason that the most likely future competitors will be firms with some expertise in our arenas. The most obvious candidates are those that know how to make our product or that sell to our markets.

Procter & Gamble mass produces, markets, and sells packaged goods through supermarkets for general consumer use. Any product (i.e., virtually any packaged good) that can be marketed this way is a potential extension for P&G. Any company that makes a packaged good in a category that P&G does not have their own brand in must consider P&G a potential competitor. Scott Paper makes, among other things, paper towels for consumer use. The Fort Howard paper company makes paper towels for institutional and industrial customers. These two companies sell essentially the same product in different markets. Each must be wary of the other as a potential competitor.

Porter's Model

Michael Porter proposed a model that argued that the nature and degree of competition in an industry depends on five "forces": the threat of new entrants, the bargaining power of customers, the bargaining power of suppliers, the threat of substitute products, and the competition among current participants. These are diagrammed in Figure 1.2. His view is that customers, suppliers, potential entrants, and substitute products are all competitors to varying degrees. Some may be more or less active than others, depending on the industry. The firm may have sources of conflict with each. Such conflict inhibits the firm from maximizing its economic welfare. As such, each party with which the firm has a potential conflict is a competitor in a very real sense.

In 1919, the early days of Procter & Gamble, William Cooper Procter decided to eliminate wholesalers and distribute directly to retailers in order to cut down on the number of steps between factory and kitchen cabinets so that he could hold costs down. P&G also dictated that the smallest shipment they would issue was five cases. Small retailers, P&G's customers, who used to be able to buy single cases of P&G products from wholesalers, were no longer able to. They were so angry that they canceled orders. More recently, Wal-Mart, P&G's largest customer at $1.5 billion retail per year, has become dissatisfied because Procter is trying to shift its way of doing business with them away from emphasizing efficient distribution to using its marketing and advertising expertise. Wal-Mart is interested in shortening the path from factory to their shelves. They want to be sure that the customer can always find P&G products available in their stores. Procter is more concerned with

---

19 If the firm being considered does both, it is already a competitor.

building its own brand names. Wal-Mart could not care less about the power of Procter's brand names. In fact, Wal-Mart would probably want Procter's brands to be less strong so that Wal-Mart could maintain the upper hand in negotiations between the two firms. Interests conflict. Competition emerges.[20]

Our viewpoint is somewhat different from Porter's. Instead of the five agents being competitors in an existing environment, we think of the four peripheral forces or agents as potential adversaries that could emerge as direct competitors in a future environment. These should each be scrutinized as potential competitors. For example, potential entrants were discussed in conjunction with Ansoff's product-market matrix in the previous section. A methodology for identifying substitute products will be discussed in the next section. Here, in this section, we discuss suppliers and customers as potential competitors. These are unique to Porter's model.

Suppliers and/or customers can become competitors by vertically integrating. Vertical integration occurs whenever a firm internalizes multiple transactions in the chain that extends from raw materials to final consumer. Suppliers of a given firm can become its competitors by *forward* integrating (i.e., entering the market in which their products are used as ingredients or components); customers can become competitors by *backward* integrating. The decision of whether or not to backward integrate is often called a "make-or-buy" decision. The Polystyrene industry is an example of an industry with firms that vary widely with respect to vertical integration.[21] Polystyrene is a plastic widely used in packaging. It is made from Styrene, which is manufactured from Ethane, which is derived from natural gas. Major producers include Arco Chemical, Dow Chemical, Huntsman, Fina Chemicals, and Polysar. Dow is highly integrated. It produces nearly all of the Styrene needed in its basic chemicals division. It also manufactures the (Styrene) cartons in which fast food hamburgers are often sold. Thus Dow has integrated both forward and backward. On the other hand, Huntsman, the industry leader in terms of capacity, has no end-use markets and buys much of its Styrene from outside vendors.

There are many costs and benefits to vertical integration. The benefits include guaranteed access to supply or demand, elimination of transaction costs, and control of supply and/or end-product quality. The costs include increased operating costs, reduced flexibility as a result of increased investment, and possibility of complacency without the threat of direct competition. Obviously, each firm makes its vertical integration decisions by weighing these costs and benefits. A firm can assess whether a customer or supplier might be a future competitor by subjectively placing itself in the customer's or supplier's head and evaluating these considerations.

---

20 The Procter & Gamble stories are told by Alecia Swasy, *Soap Opera: The Inside Story of Procter & Gamble* (New York: Times Books, 1993).

21 The Polystyrene industry is discussed by Sharon M. Oster, *Modern Competitive Analysis*, second edition (New York: Oxford, 1994): 196–197.

Substitution in Use Analysis

Substitution in use analysis presumes that interproduct competitiveness is largely based on usage situations. Products in different categories can be viewed as competitors if they are used in the same situations. For example, bottled water and soft drinks may both be consumed when a consumer is thirsty. The more similar the usage situations two products are used in, the more competitive they are. Bottled water, soft drinks, and wine may all be used as a beverage accompanying a meal; however, wine is not likely to be used to quench thirst. Beer can be used to quench thirst, as a beverage with meals, and as a beverage at parties. Wine is appropriate for parties. Soft drinks and bottled water may be less so.

The typical substitution by uses task involves giving a sample of consumers a target product and asking them to suggest as many uses for that product as possible. They are then asked for other products that would be appropriate for those same uses. Next, they are asked for additional uses for the products in the expanded list. An independent sample of consumers is then asked whether they would consider using each product in the list for each use previously named. This enables the analyst to create a matrix of products by uses in which the entry in the ith row and j^{th} column is a 1 if the respondent would consider the product in the ith row for the use in the jth column and a 0 otherwise. Products are then determined to be more similar if they have more uses in common; in other words, a similarity measure for two products (matrix rows) is the number of uses (columns) for which the products both have 1's. The overall similarity of a pair of products is then deemed to be the average of the similarity measures for that pair over all consumers in the sample. Finally, a hierarchical clustering can be performed on these similarities. As with the earlier brand-switching analyses, products that are closer together at the base of the hierarchy or that are connected at a lower node in the hierarchy are more competitive with each other.[22]

Figure 4.4 presents the output of such an analysis where the target product was bank credit cards. The result provides a picture of the broad structure of financial services and what competes with what. This analysis produced a couple of insights for the managers of the sponsoring bank. They were exposed to the notion that convenient credit services (credit card account checks, overdraft protection, cash advances on bank cards) were more competitive with checking accounts (a debit instrument) than with other credit instruments such as installment loans. The usual practice (found to be incorrect) was to categorize services into debit or credit instruments. Functional usage was more important to categorizing a service than whether the service was a debit or credit instrument. In addition, the managers found it noteworthy (although quite reasonable in retrospect) that retail installment loans were

---

22 Further understanding of the similarity-in-usage nature of the competitive structure can be gained by examining what uses are appropriate for the products close to each other at the base of the hierarchy.

FIGURE 4.4
STRUCTURING COMPETITION IN FINANCIAL SERVICES

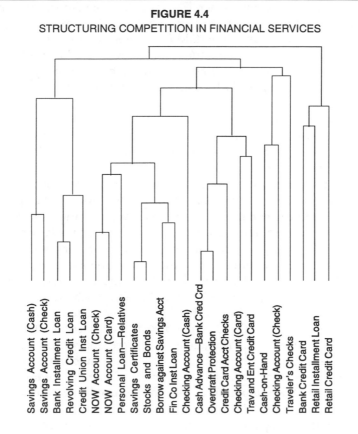

Source: Rajendra K. Srivastava, Robert P. Leone, and Allan D. Shocker, "Market Structure Analysis: Hierarchical Clustering of Products Based on Substitution in Use," *Journal of Marketing* 45 (Summer 1981): 38–48.
Reprinted with permission, American Marketing Association.

more competitive with bank and retail credit cards than with other types of
installment loans. Shopping use was the key.

PREDICTING COMPETITORS' ACTIONS

There are two major components to competitor analyses in marketing plans
at any level: identification and prediction of action. Once competitors have
been identified, firms need to predict their actions. After all, what competitors
do shapes the opportunities (in terms of unmet needs) and threats (in terms
of alternative brands and emerging substitutes) that a firm faces. If E.M.I., the
British music company that pioneered the CT scanner market, had foreseen
the entry of General Electric into the product category, they would have made
very different choices. E.M.I. had a monopoly and became complacent with

their technological position. General Electric developed a superior machine and with their greater marketing expertise in medical electronics buried E.M.I. Without the superior technology, E.M.I. had nothing to offer. If E.M.I. had predicted the entry of GE or some such giant, they would have either licensed the product they developed or tried to advance the technology further at an earlier time so that they could have maintained an advantage.[23] In order to avoid such calamities, firms have three ways to predict competitors' actions: let them tell you, infer from past behavior, or put yourself in their mind.

Firms will often make public announcements about intended actions. For example, they often preannounce new products. They do this for several reasons.[24] Perhaps they are trying to position a product in the most profitable segment. Perhaps they are trying to develop initial levels of support or word of mouth to accelerate the acceptance of the product. Maybe they just want to signal the investment community that they have exciting new products in order to elevate (manipulate?) their stock price. Or perhaps they are trying to associate their company's name with the product in question. Digital Equipment (DEC) recently announced they are working on a little pipe organ that sits on a PC chip and absorbs excess heat.[25] It produces vapors that rise to the top of the machine and are cooled by the PC's fan. With this announcement, DEC has become identified with the device. Any customer worried about excess heat will think of DEC as a potential choice, even if others later duplicate the device. Of course, DEC has made it more likely that others will duplicate the product (and do it more quickly, too) by the preannouncement. In telling potential customers, they also tell competitors. Benefits usually come with costs. In any event, a competitor of DEC didn't need to go any farther than *Business Week* to forecast DEC's new product feature.

Patterns will often appear in a company's behavior. Around the chemical industry, you may hear the phrase "DuPont personality." This refers to DuPont's established pattern of trying to differentiate its products in terms of value. They do this in spite of the fact that much of what they produce can be classified almost as a commodity. The implication of the "DuPont personality" is that DuPont is less likely than other firms in the chemical industry to respond to a price cut with a matching price cut.[26] As another example, Phillip Morris tends to enter businesses in which heavy advertising is a custom.

---

23 The demise of EMI is reported in Cheryll Barron, "What Scarred EMI's Scanner," *Management Today* (February 1979): 67ff.

24 Thomas S. Robertson and Jehoshua Eliashberg, "New Product Preannouncing Behavior: A Market Signalling Study," *Journal of Marketing Research* 25 (August 1988): 282–292, discuss many of these in depth.

25 "Little Fridges for Those Hot PC's," *Busines Week* (July 25, 1994): 82.

26 For more information on how firms react to price cuts, see Vithala R. Rao and Joel H. Steckel, "A Cross-Cultural Analysis of Price Responses to Environmental Changes," *Marketing Letters* 6 (January 1995): 5–14.

Consequently, they purchased General Foods. They would not be likely to purchase a company that makes commoditylike products such as sponges.

Finally, companies can put themselves in their competitors' heads. This requires a thorough understanding of the competitors' strengths, weaknesses, assets, and liabilities (see Chapter 7). A manager can ask the rhetorical question, Given this knowledge of my competitors what would I do? A vehicle for formalizing the answer is to have one's staff write a marketing plan for the competitor. One apocryphal (and probably false) story involves Rolls-Royce and Pratt & Whitney, two competitors in the manufacture of jet engines. A Pratt & Whitney executive was giving a courtesy plant tour to his peer at Rolls-Royce. During his visit, the Rolls-Royce guest saw a loose leaf binder labeled "Rolls-Royce Marketing Plan" on a table. He inquired what it was. The Pratt & Whitney host informed him that his people did competitive analyses by creating hypothetical competitor marketing plans. The guest replied, "Wow! That sounds like a very interesting document. Could I get a copy?"

CONCLUSION

Identifying competitors is not always a straightforward task. Some may even come from outside the industry that a firm operates in. Two principles about competition that give guidance on how to identify it are (1) competition is a matter of degree, and (2) competition is rooted in consumer behavior. Two products are competitors if and only if a consumer only needs one of them on any given occasion. For example, railroads and airlines are competitors. This is not universally true though, since while both are reasonable ways to travel from New York to Boston, they are not equally reasonable ways to travel from New York to Oslo. Thus competition exists only to a degree.

This chapter presented a series of methodologies and frameworks useful in identifying competitors. Some, such as those based on brand-switching matrices, are more useful within the product category of interest. Others, such as substitution in use analysis, are more useful for identifying potential competitors outside the category. In either case, once competitors have been identified, a manager has to try to predict their actions. Indeed, it is these actions that shape the opportunities and threats that a firm faces. Consequently, forecasting competitor action is a prerequisite for long-term success.

BIBLIOGRAPHY

Abell, Derek. *Defining the Business*. Englewood Cliffs, NJ: Prentice-Hall, 1980.

Ansoff, H. Igor. "Strategies for Diversification." *Harvard Business Review* 35 (Sept/Oct 1957): 113–124.

———*The New Corporate Strategy*. New York: Wiley, 1988.

Barron, Cheryll. "What Scarred EMI's Scanner." *Management Today* (February 1979): 67ff.

Bass, Frank M., Edgar A. Pessemier, and Donald R. Lehmann. "An Experimental Study of Relationships between Attitudes, Brand Preference, and Choice." *Behavioral Science* 17 (November 1972): 532–541.

"Big Hopes Put on Electric Wires." *New York Times* (July 6, 1994): D1.

Blattberg, Robert C., and Kenneth J. Wisniewski. "Price Induced Patterns of Competition." *Marketing Science* 8 (Fall 1989): 291–309.

Bucklin, Randolph E., Gary J. Russell, and V. Srinivasan. "A Relationship Between Price Elasticities and Brand Switching Probabilities in Heterogeneous Markets." Mimeo, April 1992.

"Little Fridges for Those Hot PC's." *Business Week* (July 25, 1994): 82.

Colombo, Richard A., and Donald G. Morrison. "A Brand Switching Model with Implications for Marketing Strategies." *Marketing Science* 8 (Winter 1989): 89–99.

Frazier, Gary L., and Roy D. Howell. "Business Definition and Performance." *Journal of Marketing* 47 (Spring 1980): 59–67.

Green, Paul E., and Vithala R. Rao. *Applied Multidimensional Scaling.* New York: Holt, Rinehart, and Winston, 1972.

Grover, Rajiv, and Vithala R. Rao. "Inferring Competitive Market Structure Based on a Model of Interpurchase Intervals." *International Journal of Research in Marketing* 5 (1988): 55–72.

Hall, M., and L. Weiss. "Firm Size and Profitability." *Review of Economics and Statistics* 49 (August 1967): 319–331.

Kotler, Phillip. *Marketing Management: Analysis, Planning, and Control.* 7th ed. Englewood Cliffs, NJ: Prentice-Hall, 1991.

Levitt, Theodore. "Marketing Myopia." *Harvard Business Review* 38 (July–August 1960): 45–56.

March, James G., and Herbert A. Simon. *Organizations.* New York: Wiley, 1958.

McGee, John, and Howard Thomas. "Strategic Groups: Theory, Research, and Taxonomy." *Strategic Management Journal* 7 (1986): 141–160.

Neslin, Scott A., and Robert W. Shoemaker. "An Alternative Explanation for Lower Repeat Rates after Promotion Purchases." *Journal of Marketing Research* 26 (May 1989): 205–213.

Oster, Sharon M. *Modern Competitive Analysis.* 2d ed. New York: Oxford, 1994.

Porter, Michael. *Interbrand Choice, Strategy, and Bilateral Market Power.* Cambridge: Harvard University Press, 1976.

————"How Competitive Forces Shape Strategy." *Harvard Business Review* 57 (March–April 1979): 137–145.

Rao, Vithala R., and Darius J. Sabavala. "Inference of Hierarchical Choice Processes from Panel Data." *Journal of Consumer Research* 8 (June 1981): 85–96.

Rao, Vithala R., and Darius J. Sabavala. "Inference of Hierarchical Choice Processes from Panel Data." *Journal of Consumer Research* 8 (June 1981): 85–96.

Rao, Vithala R., and Joel H. Steckel. "A Cross-Cultural Analysis of Price Responses to Environmental Changes." *Marketing Letters* 6 (January 1995): 5–14.

Robertson, Thomas S., and Jehoshua Eliashberg. "New Product Preannouncing Behavior: A Market Signalling Study." *Journal of Marketing Research* 25 (August 1988): 282–292.

Simon, Herbert A. *Models of Man*. New York: Wiley, 1957.

Srivastava, Rajendra K., Robert P. Leone, and Allan D. Shocker. "Market Structure Analysis: Hierarchical Clustering of Products Based on Substitution-In-Use." *Journal of Marketing* 45 (Summer 1981): 38–48.

Swasy, Alecia. *Soap Opera: The Inside Story of Procter & Gamble*. New York: Times Books, 1993.

Tversky, Amos, and Daniel Kahneman. "Judgment Under Uncertainty: Heuristics and Biases." *Science* 185 (1974): 1124–1131.

Urban, Glen L., Philip L. Johnson, and John R. Hauser. "Testing Competitive Market Structures." *Marketing Science* 3 (Spring 1984): 83–113.

CHAPTER 5

Understanding and Forecasting External Environment—I

INTRODUCTION

Having identified the trends in customer behavior, unmet customer needs, and competitive forces, the analyst has to turn to the other environmental forces affecting the strategies of a business. In general, this analysis will need to be conducted at the level of the industry in which the specific business unit competes. Any given industry's fortunes will naturally depend on the behavior of its customers, competitors, and suppliers. At a macro level, these behaviors are influenced by a variety of environmental factors, which can be categorized into four groups: political, economic, social (e.g., demographic, cultural, and sociological) and technological. The acronyms PEST or STEP or PETS will help one remember these categories. The PEST factors can be instrumental in providing opportunities for and in imposing threats on the firm.

The technological trends in the computer industry offer an interesting illustration. The technological developments in the semiconductor industry leading to the development of the personal computer offered significant business opportunities for several firms (Apple, IBM, Dell, Compaq, etc.) and at the same time contributed significantly to the precipitous decline in the sales of mainframe computers. A firm like IBM faced both an opportunity and threat due to the technological decade of innovations for the personal computer in the 1980s. Moving a few years further, the personal computer industry has been threatened by the technology of miniaturization that led to the introduction of laptop computers in the late 1980s and early 1990s. Interestingly, although this industry is in its bloom period, it may face difficulties due to the advent of even smaller computers, PDAs (or personal digital assistants).[1]

---

1 For details on the PDA industry, see Barbara Kantrowitz, "This is Your Life. Maybe," *Newsweek* (November 15, 1993): 45–46.

The analysis of the environmental factors (PEST) is a major component of the so-called SWOT (Strengths, Weaknesses, Opportunities, and Threats) analysis for any particular business. The results of the analysis of opportunities and threats can be summarized into a number of potential future scenarios and as a set of strategic questions. The strategic questions are What if? type questions that are intended to ascertain the likely impact of a specific environmental trend or a set of related trends. They can be answered when the strategy analyst has developed a forecasting system. While forecasting techniques are at the heart of these analyses, they have come to be grouped under the broad umbrella of "scenario analysis" methods.

The second part of the SWOT analysis relates to the determination of strengths and weaknesses of the business relative to its competition (present or potential). This analysis also involves an assessment of the firm's resources and other capabilities to enable it to compete in the environment of the future.

In this and the next two chapters, we will cover relevant methods for this comprehensive analysis of SWOT. In this chapter, we will describe analytic methods for identifying various factors in the external environment that are most important to the growth of a firm's business. We will also discuss some ways of determining the likely future trends of various environmental factors. In Chapter 6, we will continue this discussion and will cover various analytical methods for forecasting market dynamics. In Chapter 7, we will cover methods for analyzing strengths and weaknesses of a business relative to its competitors.

In the next section of this chapter, we enumerate various factors in the environment to be considered in an opportunities-threats analysis. We will also identify characteristics of strategic situations where environmental understanding is paramount. In the third section, we classify various available techniques for looking at specific aspects of the environment and the various sources of data. In the fourth section, we describe a subset of these techniques in some depth and provide examples. Finally, we conclude with ways of assessing the impact of one or more environmental trends.

SITUATIONS WHERE ENVIRONMENTAL UNDERSTANDING IS CRITICAL

In general, it is necessary for a manager to keep up with the changes in the external environment of his or her business and to adapt the strategies to it. It is also essential for a manager to be proactive and to anticipate the kinds of changes likely to occur in the future so that he or she is well armed with contingent strategies to meet the opportunities and threats posed by any environmental changes. Table 5.1 shows illustrations of trends in various environmental factors categorized into political, economic, social/cultural/demographic, and technological factors; it also shows potential consequences of these trends as opportunities and threats for selected businesses.

TABLE 5.1
SOME ILLUSTRATIONS OF ENVIRONMENTAL TRENDS, OPPORTUNITIES, AND THREATS

Environmental Factors	Opportunities	Threats
Political		
NAFTA	Export possibilities for certain high-technology industries such as computers and software	Potential loss of demand for certain supplier industries in the U.S. due to relocation of their customers
Passage of legislation of taxes on alcohol and cigarettes	Demand for products such as nonalcoholic beer	Potential lowering of demand for alcohol industry products (e.g., wine, whisky, etc.)
Economic		
Economic development in South Asian countries	Potential for certain U.S. companies to form strategic alliances with local firms	Potential for increases in costs of production in those industries that have enjoyed low-cost sources in these countries
Lowering of capital gains taxes	Potential availability of capital for emerging industries	
Social/Cultural/ Demographic		
Increasing participation of women in the workforce	Increasing demand for convenience goods Increasing demand for direct-mail shopping	Potential decline in the demand for certain leisure-oriented industries
Aging of the U.S. population	Increasing demand for various healthcare services	Likely reduction in the school-going population and demand for educational services Potential reduction in the demand for durable goods due to a decrease in the number of households
Increasing diversity of the U.S. population	Several emerging niche markets Increasing opportunities for special media vehicles to appeal to minorities	Potential decrease in the demand for certain well-established industries
Technological		
Developments in genetic engineering	Increasing demand for certain pharmaceutical products	Potential decline in certain well-established pharmaceutical products
Miniaturization of microprocessors	Increasing demand for notebook or palmtop computers and software for such computers	Potential decline in desktop computers and workstations

For example, the creation of NAFTA will offer opportunities for certain high technology industries while at the same time could reduce demand for certain supplier industries in the United States due to possible relocation of their customer companies in Mexico.

The effects of environmental changes may be very small in certain mature industries such as detergent and toothpaste, where the demand trends are essentially governed by the changes in the population size (or customer base). Even here, a firm seeking to focus on a specific market segment may need to understand the changes in the environment as they affect the size of that segment; for example, a toothpaste marketer focusing on selling a brand of toothpaste aimed at cleaning dentures may need to understand the demographic trends in the population that determine the potential market size for such a product.

But understanding and forecasting the effects of environmental changes are essential in nascent industries such as multimedia. Let's assume you are in charge of a business in such an industry and that you wish to direct your staff to monitor various aspects of the external environment that might affect your business. As a manger of this business, you may be called upon to provide direction on the specific environmental trends and facts you will need to make such decisions. The PEST framework described earlier will enable you to reflect upon various factors to be considered in providing direction on the data collection effort involved. Based on the environmental information gathered and your own knowledge of the business, you might consider changing the product positioning or price or adding new products or even deleting some of the existing products.

Figure 5.1 shows the external forces that impinge on any business and that therefore should be systematically monitored.

The task is to obtain relevant data on these various forces on a periodic basis and to interpret them. In addition to collecting current and past information on these factors, it is necessary to gain some insight into the future. This task involves forecasting of trends. Careful interpretation of the results of this process will enable a manager to not only understand the present but to make specific assumptions about the future environment in which the business is expected to be operating in and to make the appropriate strategic adaptations. It is worth pointing out that these adaptations need to be made in a continuous manner. It is almost impossible to stand still in strategy development.

OVERVIEW OF METHODS FOR UNDERSTANDING AND PREDICTING ENVIRONMENTAL FACTORS

Factors to Be Considered

The particular factors to be considered will depend upon the characteristics of the industry in which the business is located. For a multiproduct corporation, different factors may affect individual businesses; for example, the factors that

FIGURE 5.1
EXTERNAL FORCES AFFECTING ANY BUSINESS

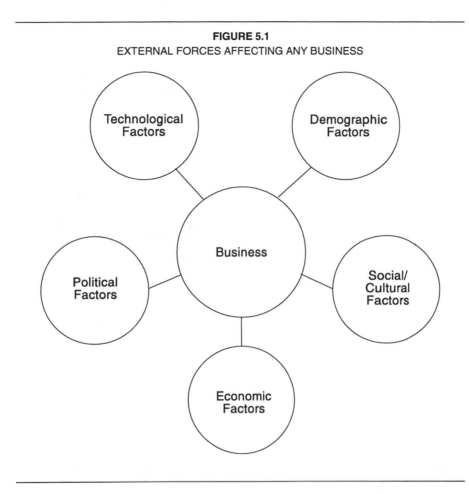

affect the mainframe computer business of the IBM corporation are not the same as those that affect their laptop computer business. Whereas the need for various organizations to maintain and process large volumes of data could affect the mainframe business, the technological trends toward miniaturization and larger computing power in portable computers may reduce the prospects for mainframes. The same trends when combined with the customer desires for convenience of portability will enhance the demand for laptop computers.

Overview of Methods

Table 5.2 lists several illustrative questions specific to each environmental dimension of interest to managers. Selected methods of analysis specific to each environmental dimension are also indicated. For example, social and cultural dimension of the environment affects not only the size of the market in the future but also the demand for specific products. Similarly, regulation

TABLE 5.2
DIMENSIONS AND METHODS OF ENVIRONMENTAL ANALYSIS

Environmental Dimension		Illustrative Managerial Questions	Suitable Methods of Analysis
Political/Government	(a)	What changes in the regulation are possible? How will they affect the business demand?	Analysis of regulations Environmental monitoring Public opinion polls
	(b)	What political risks exist in countries the firm wishes to expand to?	
Social/Cultural/ Demographic	(a)	What trends are emerging in the sociological, cultural, and lifestyle areas in the markets (countries) where the firm is operating?	Content analysis of popular press Lifestyle analysis General purpose Consumer surveys
	(b)	How would these trends affect the demand for existing products or help create new products?	
	(c)	What trends of population growth and population movement are emerging in the next few years?	
	(d)	What are some opportunities and threats due to these trends?	
Economic	(a)	What are the economic prospects in the markets (countries) where the firm currently operates or plans to operate in the future?	Macroeconomic forecasting models
	(b)	How would they affect the business?	
Technological	(a)	What are some emerging technologies that will affect the current products or their production processes?	Technological forecasting methods
	(b)	What are the life-cycle trends of the current technologies?	Life-cycle analysis
All Aspects	(a)	Given various trends, what future environmental scenarios are likely to emerge?	Scenario analysis
	(b)	How should the firm adapt to these changes?	Cross-impact analysis

will affect the ability of a firm to market certain products (e.g., environmentally unsafe products). Various methods are needed—from those used in demographic analysis to sophisticated methods for forecasting technology—in order to perform a full-fledged analysis of environmental factors. It should be clear from this table that because of the importance of a variety of environmental dimensions, a combination of methods is always called for in this phase of strategic analysis.

Sources of Data

The strategic analyst has to consult several sources of data—both public and private—to be confident that he or she has analyzed the trends in a comprehensive manner. In addition to public sources such as the publications of the

U.S. Government's Department of Commerce (e.g., census publications and reports of the economic surveys), the analyst may consult reports of surveys conducted by private organizations such as the Roper, Gallup Poll, and Yankelovich. It is particularly important to include private sources in any information search because they tend to focus on a limited array of topics and produce reports that are often timely. On the other hand, governmental surveys and censuses cover a broad range of topics and generally take a much longer time to become available; nevertheless, they are quite useful to determine general trends in the environment.

In the Appendix to this chapter, we list various sources of interest to a marketing strategist. These sources include corporate annual reports, publications by such organizations as Standard and Poor and Dow Jones, and publications based on media and consumption surveys of Simmons Market Research Bureau, SRDS, and the like. In addition, there is an increase in the number of companies that compile data from several sources and make them accessible to marketing strategists; these include the Gale Research Reports, Claritas, and Equifax. *American Demographics*, a monthly magazine, also synthesizes various types of data (e.g., census, private, and public surveys) and publishes articles on various trends and projections of population.

Role of Experts

While various published data generally refer to past trends and give some direction for the future, strategy analysts may consult experts in various fields to ascertain the import of specific trends and how the technologies of certain industries are likely to develop. Such consultation is particularly necessary in fast-moving technology-intensive industries such as biotechnology, genetic engineering, multimedia, and microprocessors.

METHODS FOR ANALYZING DEMOGRAPHIC FACTORS

Owing to the considerable importance of the demographic data in strategic analysis, we will discuss methods for demographic analysis separately from the other variables in the social dimension of the environment.

Demographic Analysis

Analysis of demographic data is a highly established field. In addition to understanding the trends evidenced in the decennial census, the Census Bureau of the U.S. Department of Commerce conducts periodic surveys of the population to gauge various population trends such as overall growth and movement among different geographic areas.

Understanding Census Data

The 1990 U.S. Census of Population contains a rich set of data on population and housing characteristics highly valuable for marketing analysis. In addition to reports on the decennial census, the U.S. Census Bureau publishes periodic reports that provide projections and estimates on the size and characteristics of the population. Some items in the census are collected on the whole population while others are collected on a sample basis. Among the items collected on complete count are: number of persons in household, relationship among household members, sex, race, age, year of birth, marital status, and national origin of each person in the household and such housing characteristics as number of units in the structure, number of rooms in the unit, tenure (owned or rented), and value of home or monthly rent. Information on social characteristics (e.g., education, place of birth, citizenship, language), economic characteristics (e.g., labor force status, occupation, work experience), and housing characteristics (e.g., number of bedrooms, telephone, house heating fuel, and number of vehicles available) are collected on the sample basis.

Census data are also available at the level of smaller geographic areas such as the census block and at higher levels of aggregation (e.g., county, city, state). Several cross-tabulations of the population characteristics can be made. For marketing purposes, housing characteristics such as number of bedrooms and possession of a telephone are often as useful as demographic characteristics.

Forecasts of Population Trends

Based on the census data and other information, demographers develop periodic forecasts of the entire population or subgroups. A marketing analyst should keep abreast of such forecasts. A good source is the U.S. Bureau of Census. Occasionally, *American Demographics* magazine publishes forecasts of various facets of the population trends, that are either direct compilations or based on additional analyses.

A Method for Population Forecasting Methods

All methods for forecasting population of any geographic area (e.g., a country) use the fundamental equation:

Population at time t+1 = Population at time t + Number of births during the period (t, t+1) − Number of deaths during the period (t, t+1) + Immigration during (t, t+1) − Emigration during (t, t+1).

Population forecasters forecast each component on the right-hand side of this equation and combine them to come up with a forecast. They use the age distribution of the population and age-specific rates of births and deaths to predict the numbers of births and deaths. (The distribution of female population and age-specific fertility rates are used in the forecasts of the number of births. Also, prediction of sex ratio at birth is used to obtain separate estimates of babies born of each sex.) The immigration forecasts are made from legal limits, if they exist, set by the geographic area (e.g., country) or by forecasting past trends. A similar procedure is used for emigration. In either case, forecasts are made by age group.

The Census Bureau estimates birth and death rates for subgroups defined on a larger number of characteristics (e.g., age, sex, occupation, education, and so on), forecasts the numbers of births and deaths for each subgroup defined, and aggregates the forecasts for the population as a whole. This procedure will yield not only a forecast of the total population, but forecasts by age and perhaps sex. The forecasts of population by age and sex can subsequently be used in developing forecasts for the next and subsequent years using a similar procedure. Usually, such projections are made for five-year intervals because much of the population data are grouped into five-year age intervals. This procedure uses knowledge of age-specific birth and death rates, which in turn are dependent on developments in medicine and social and cultural norms, among others.

While the above procedure is suitable for predicting the population of a country, it is much more difficult to use for predicting the future population for smaller geographic areas such as states, cities, and towns. The problem is due to the difficulty in forecasting the component of migration; typically data on internal movements are hard to come by.

We show two forecasts in Tables 5.3 and 5.4 respectively for the projections of households for the years 1990–2000 and for African Americans during the next two decades, 1990–2010.

Two implications of the forecasts in Tables 5.3 and 5.4 are:

1. The number of households in the United States should exceed 100 million by the end of the century. Household population growth is also slowing down. Further, the trend is toward smaller households. These trends have significant consequences for various consumer packaged goods marketers such as the need to develop smaller package sizes, for example.

2. African Americans are the largest ethnic market, with over 30 million people. The number of African Americans between 25 and 34 will actually decline, while those between 45 and 54 and between 55 and 64 will increase at a rate faster than the national average. Thus, middle-aging baby boomers will dominate the population of African Americans to the year 2010.

Other forecasts of population show that Hispanics and Asian Americans are quickly increasing their numbers in the United States. In the year 1990 there were 22.4 million Hispanics and 7.3 million Asian Americans. The rate of growth for Hispanics during the decade 1980 to 1990 was 53 percent as compared to over 100 percent for Asians. These trends offer exciting opportunities for developing niche markets in various industries.

The Standardization Technique—A Method for Comparing Two Areas

Situations often arise in marketing when one needs to make comparisons between the sales performance of two geographic areas, such as states, countries, or market areas. It becomes particularly important to understand the

TABLE 5.3
HOUSEHOLD PROJECTIONS: 1990–2000
(Number of family and nonfamily households by age of householder, 1990–2000, with percent distributions; households in thousands)

	1990	Percent	1995	Percent	2000	Percent	Percent Change 1990–2000
Total Households	91,951	100%	98,265	100%	103,828	100%	13%
Under 35	25,138	27	24,274	25	23,072	22	–8
35 to 54	35,059	38	40,921	41	45,441	44	30
55 and Older	31,754	35	33,070	34	35,315	34	11
Family Households	65,336	100%	70,073	100%	74,174	100%	14
Under 35	17,370	27	16,807	24	15,905	21	–8
35 to 54	28,399	43	33,147	47	36,810	50	30
55 and Older	19,567	30	21,119	29	21,459	29	10
Nonfamily Households	26,615	100%	28,192	100%	29,654	100%	11
Under 35	7,768	29	7,467	26	7,167	24	–8
35 to 54	6,660	25	7,774	28	8,631	29	30
55 and Older	12,187	46	12,951	46	13,856	47	14

Source: Thomas E. Dexter, "Middle-Aging Households," American Demographics (July 1992). Reproduced with permission of the publisher.

TABLE 5.4
AFRICAN AMERICANS: 1990–2010
Middle-aging baby boomers will dominate black population change to 2010.

	1990		2010		Percent Change 1990–2010	
	Men	Women	Men	Women	Men	Women
All Ages	14,204	15,782	17,841	19,558	26%	24%
Under age 5	1,297	1,272	1,366	1,312	5%	3%
5 to 14	2,499	2,497	2,931	2,822	17	13
15 to 24	2,581	2,658	2,888	2,826	12	6
25 to 34	2,840	2,984	2,617	2,666	–8	–11
35 to 44	1,978	2,290	2,595	2,778	31	21
45 to 54	1,162	1,484	2,620	2,933	125	98
55 to 64	895	1,181	1,628	2,084	82	76
65 to 74	636	884	741	1,171	17	33
75 and older	316	532	454	964	44	81

Source: Thomas E. Dexter, "Blacks to 2010," American Demographics (December 1992). Reproduced with permission of the publisher.

reasons why two areas are performing differently. This understanding can assist in forecasting the future sales performance of one area if it attains the same levels of age-specific consumption rates as the other area.

For example, one might wish to understand why the sales rate (i.e., sales of a particular product per 1,000 persons) in one area differs from the corresponding measure for another area. The standardization technique, used in demographic analysis, is useful for this purpose. We illustrate it with hypothetical data shown in Table 5.5 for sales of a consumer product (e.g., shampoo) in two areas, A and B, that differ in population size. Further, we assume we have sales data broken down by the age of the head of household. The relevant data then will be sales in A and B broken down by age and number of households with corresponding age. These data can be collected through a consumer survey or through scanner panels.

The respective populations in the two areas A and B are 1,400,000 and 551,000. The respective sales volumes are 5,040 and 1,613 thousands of units. Because they differ, one way to compare the sales in A and B is by using per capita sales, shown in Table 5.5 at the bottom of the Sales Rate columns. The rate of sales per thousand people in A is 3.6 versus 2.92 in B. On the face of it, this difference is 0.68. The observed difference could be due to various factors. In particular, it could be due to the differences in the population structure by age and to age-specific sales rates. The age-specific sales rates are shown in the Sales Rate columns. Standardization enables one to determine whether the difference is mainly due to population structure or to rate differences. There are two ways of standardizing for comparing A with B: by using the population structure of A with B's age-specific sales rates or by using the population structure of B with A's age-specific sales rates. These standardized rates are shown below along with observed sales rates

	Use of Age-Specific Sales Rates of	
Population Structure of	**A**	**B**
A	3.60*	3.31
B	3.21	2.92*

* Observed sales rates

The standardized rate of A is 3.31 computed using the age-specific rates of B when compared with the unstandardized rate for A of 3.6, indicates that the age-specific rates of A and B are quite different. A direct comparison of 3.6 with 2.92 masks this difference in the age-specific rates. Further, when B's population structure is used with A's age-specific rates, we get a standardized rate of 3.21. Again, when compared with 2.92 (sales rate of B), it points to the fact that the difference between the sales rates of A and B is due both to the factors of the population structures and to age-specific rates.

The formulas used in standardization can be generalized as follows:

TABLE 5.5
ILLUSTRATION OF STANDARDIZATION

	Area A				Area B			
	Population				Population			
Age Group	Number (000s)	Percent Population	Sales (000s)	Sales Rate	Number (000s)	Percent Population	Sales (000s)	Sales Rate
		(w_{ia})		(R_{ia})		(w_{ia})		(R_{ib})
Under 25 Years	462	33	340	0.74	209	38	100	0.48
25–34 Years	280	20	2,520	9.00	105	19	756	7.20
35–44 Years	210	15	1,750	8.33	72	13	570	7.92
45–54 Years	168	12	315	1.875	44	8	110	2.50
55 Years and Older	280	20	115	0.41	121	22	77	0.64
Total	1,400	100	5,040	3.6	551	100	1,613	2.92

Let R_a and R_b be the sales rates of the areas A and B, and w_{ia} and w_{ib} be the percentages of the populations in the age group i for A and B. Further, let the age-specific sales rates for A and B be R_{ia} and R_{ib} respectively. Then, the sales rate of A $= R_a = \Sigma w_{ia} \times R_{ia}$. Similarly, $R_b = \Sigma w_{ia} \times R_{ib}$.

The standardized sales rate of A using the age-specific sales rates of B is $\Sigma w_{ia} * R_{ib}$, while the standardized sales rate of A using the population structure of is $\Sigma w_{ib} \times R_{ia}$. These can be used in identifying the sources of the differences and in interpreting them.

To determine the contributions of the factors of two population structures and age-specific rates in the difference between R_a and R_b, the following formula is often used:

$$R_a - R_b = \Sigma(w_{ia} + w_{ib}) \times (R_{ia} - R_{ib})/2 + \Sigma(R_{ia} + R_{ib}) \times (w_{ia} - w_{ib})/2$$

The first component is a measure of the contribution due to the age-specific rate differences, and the second term is the contribution of the population structure differences. Now, returning to our example in Table 5.5, these two components are 0.39 and 0.29 respectively, making up the total difference of 0.68. This decomposition indicates that the contribution due to the age-specific rate differences is much larger than that due to the difference in the population structures.

Although we have shown the method of standardization with one variable—age—it can be applied to classifications using multiple variables—age, sex, occupation, length of residence.[2] It will help pinpoint the sources of the difference in the sales behavior of any two entities. The technique can be particularly helpful in making international comparisons.

Cohort Analysis

Description

Cohort analysis is a technique that helps in understanding whether or not existing patterns of consumption will persist in the future. A cohort is a generation of people who are born in the same period of time (e.g., five years). Because they are born in the same period, one can expect that they are subjected to the same set of trends in the environment (e.g., same set of events in the society). These common experiences can manifest themselves as a common set of values. In particular, we may expect that they may adopt the same patterns of consumption behavior. For example, people in their 20s (i.e., born about 20 years ago around 1970) were raised on television and require intense but brief stimulation to catch their attention. As time passes, this generation will tend to hold onto these behavior patterns (or more generally a set of values). Thus, if one understands the value systems of people belonging to various cohorts, it is possible to make some extrapolations of the trends that may emerge in the future.

Cohort analysis is distinct from analysis of segments defined by age in two ways. Cohort analysis requires data on consumption (e.g., rates of consumption) for at least two periods of data; age-wise segmentation requires data for point in time. Cohort analysis considers the trends in the consumption data not just across time periods, but tracks the behavior of a cohort of people through time. Naturally, this feature is not available in age-wise segmentation analysis.

An industry view of cohorts is shown in Table 5.6. Perkins, a VP-account manager for an advertising agency, has identified four possible cohorts based on more than two years of research using focus groups (with emphasis on younger generations), expert testimony culled from published articles, and field research.

Use in Analysis of Consumption

The data on consumption of a product at a point time can be divided by age group to understand how consumption differs by age. Consider the following data on consumption of soft drinks per person per year in the year 1979 (some of these data are hypothetical; consumption data are adapted from Rentz and Reynolds).[3]

---

2   For details, see Prithwa Das Gupta, "A General Method of Decomposing a Difference Between Two Rates into Several Components," *Demography* 15 (February 1978): 99–112.

TABLE 5.6
ONE VIEW OF COHORTS IN CURRENT SOCIETY

Cohort	Born During	Core Values	Implications for Marketer
Traditionalists	1920s or earlier	Patriotic, seek financial security, strong religious ethics, respect authority, etc.	Quality and value oriented Use wisdom and experience in making decisions
Transitionists	1930s and 1940s	Protective and sentimental, desire choices, mistrust other nations	Brand-loyal, value-oriented, not impulsive in decision making Influenced by celebrity endorsements
Challengers	1950s and 1960s	Individualism and self-fulfillment concerns, "me"-focused, idealistic, moralistic, short-term thinkers, still believe in having it all, self-indulgent lifestyle	Seek information before purchase Constantly fight the aging process No longer trendsetters
Space-Agers	1970s or later	Skeptical, concerned about the future, economically liberal, politically conservative, show the "just do it" attitude	Street-smart consumers, value products developed for them, look for lasting values, intangible benefits and instant gratification

Source: Adapted from Natalie Perkins, "Zeroing in on Consumer Values: Cohort Analysis Reveals Some Key Differences Among the Generations," *Advertising Age* (March 22, 1993): 23 (with permission).

of these data are hypothetical; consumption data are adapted from Rentz and Reynolds).[4]

Age group (years)	Per Capita Consumption (1979) (gallons)	Population Percent (1979)
10–19	48.6	16.6
20–29	48.3	18.3
30–39	42.1	21.5
40–49	34.8	17.9
50+	23.5	25.7

Based on these data, the per capita consumption of soft drinks is 38.23 gallons. It is also clear from these data that the per capita consumption varies dramatically by age: younger people drink soft drinks much more than the older people. If we are interested in projecting (forecasting) the rate of consumption for a future year, we could obtain population forecasts for the year and use the per capita rates shown above to calculate the average rate of consumption for the future. (Note that population forecasts are available from the Census Bureau.) Such a procedure assumes that the rate of consumption for the age

4   Joseph O. Rentz, Fred O. Reynolds, and Roy G. Stoudt, "Analyzing Changing Consumption Patterns with Cohort Analysis," *Journal of Marketing Research* 20 (1983): 12–20.

a lower forecast for the consumption of soft drinks. This method uses cross-sectional data on rates of consumption without invoking any trends. However, this cross-sectional analysis can be wrong because it does not consider the fact that consumption habits once established for a person at an early age tend to persist over his or her lifetime.

Cohort analysis explicitly considers the possibility of such persistence. In this method, the future rate of consumption for the age groups 30–39 10 years later (1989) is taken as that of the age group 20–29 in 1979; that is to say that the consumption habits of the 20-29 age group will persist through their life stages as they age. In fact, these rates are forecasted using historical data on the rates of consumption by age for several time periods. Usually, such data are compiled from longitudinal panel or cross-sectional surveys conducted at periodic intervals. Such cohort tables are illustrated here:

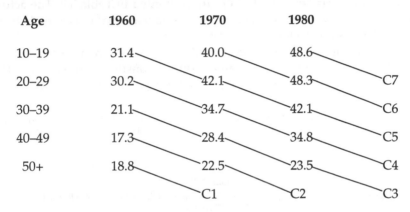

Age	1960	1970	1980	
10–19	31.4	40.0	48.6	
20–29	30.2	42.1	48.3	C7
30–39	21.1	34.7	42.1	C6
40–49	17.3	28.4	34.8	C5
50+	18.8	22.5	23.5	C4
	C1	C2	C3	

This cohort table contains information on seven cohorts, C1 through C7. C1 is the cohort of people born prior to 1910 (who were 50 years or older in 1960), C2 is the cohort of people born between 1911 and 1920, who were in the age group of 40–49 in 1960 and in the age group 50+ in 1970. Similarly, the cohort C4 consists of people aged 20–29 in 1960, 30–39 in 1970, and 40–49 in 1980. Their rates of consumption of soft drinks are 30.2 in 1960, 34.7 in 1970, and 34.8 in 1980. The trend in these three data points can be used to project what their consumption would be in 1990. In a like manner, we can look at the cohort C5, aged 40–49 in 1980 whose rates of consumption were 31.4 in 1960, 42.1 in 1970, and 42.1 in 1980 and project their future rate of consumption in 1990 and later years.

We show below the forecasted rate of consumption in 1990 by age group, assuming no specific trends in the rates for the purposes of illustration. Of course, one will have to make a guess for the first age group in 1990. For completeness, we assume that the rate in 1990 for age group 10–19 is the same as that in 1980. These rates are shown below along with the consumption rates for 1990, assuming that they would be the same as in 1980 (as noted above, these are obtained from cross-sectional analysis without using any trend information).

	Projected Rate in 1990	
Age	Cohort Analysis	Cross-sectional Analysis
10–19	48.6	48.6
20–29	48.6	48.3
30–39	48.3	42.1
40–49	42.1	34.8
50+	34.8	23.5

Based on these rates and expected population distribution of 1990, we can estimate the rate of consumption of soft drinks for the year 1990 to be 37.63 gallons when data on cross-sectional rates are used and 43.40 when estimates from cohort analysis are used. Details are presented in Table 5.7. The actual consumption rate for 1990 was 42.5 gallons. It appears that the estimate from cohort analysis is much closer to the actual rate.

Cohort analysis has yielded forecasts closer to actual than those of cross-sectional rates for coffee (soluble and ground) consumption as well.[4] The method was applied to predict three variables: penetration (proportion of

4 Joseph O. Rentz and Fred D. Reynolds, "Forecasting the Effects of an Aging Population on Product Consumption: An Age-Period Cohort Framework," *Journal of Marketing Research* 28 (August 1991): 355–60.

TABLE 5.7
ILLUSTRATION OF COHORT ANALYSIS FOR ESTIMATING CONSUMPTION
OF SOFT DRINKS

	Population		Age-Specific Rate of Consumption According to	
	Percent			
Age Group	1980	1990	Cohort Analysis	Cross-Sectional Analysis
10–19 years	17.3	13.8	48.6	48.6
20–29 years	18.1	16.2	48.6	48.3
30–39 years	14.0	16.0	48.3	42.1
40–49 years	10.0	12.6	42.1	34.7
50+ years	26.0	25.4	34.8	23.5
Total (10 years +)	85.4	84		
Per Capita Consumption	35.0	42.5	43.40	37.63
		(Actual)	(Estimated)	

persons over 10 years drinking coffee), cups per drinker of coffee and cups per person (both coffee drinkers and nondrinkers). The first two multiplied together produce the third. Thus, forecasts of the first two are sufficient for a forecast of the third. The results are shown below. Cross-sectional forecasts predicted an increase in penetration as a result of an aging population despite a decreasing penetration rate for younger cohorts (people born during the period since 1950). While the cross-sectional forecast was closer for cups per drinker indicator, the cohort forecast was closer for cups per person. This is probably due to the higher accuracy of the cohort forecast.

	Penetration	Cups per Drinker	Cups per Person
1980 Actual	.566	3.57	2.02
1989 Cross-Sectional Forecast	.595	3.35	2.14
1989 Cohort Forecast	.519	3.39	2.07
1989 Actual	.525	3.34	1.75

In practice, cohort analysis uses regression methods to forecast the age-specific rates into the future. For this purpose, data on age-specific consumption rates for a number of years are regressed against three predictors: year for which data are applicable (trend variable), age group, and cohort membership. These regressions capture not only the trends over time, but also the effects of age and cohort membership. They can then be used to predict the future consumption rates of different age groups. It is worth pointing out that ad hoc methods will be necessary to estimate the consumption rate for the new cohort—members born recently and for whom there is no historical information.

METHODS FOR ANALYZING SOCIAL/CULTURAL FACTORS

One might argue that the 1992 decision by the Ralph Lauren company to use a 12-year old girl in their ads for Polo for Boys, a product line that has always sold well with girls, was an adaptation to the changes in the country's cultural attitudes.[5] It appears the firm has embarked on a 25-year project to broaden its image by deemphasizing the icon of the white male in its advertisements. Such changes in strategy require a careful analysis of various social and cultural trends.

Understanding of changes in social values and cultural norms can be gained by a thorough content analysis of various human interest and other stories reported in the media (e.g., newspapers, magazines, and television shows). Given the importance of this kind of analysis, some firms have chosen to analyze these reports and speculate on the evolving trends. We will describe

---

5   See William Grimes, "Ralph Lauren's Revised Guest," *New York Times* (September 13, 1992).

two such content analysis efforts, namely Popcorn Report and Megatrends. In addition, we will review three other ways to assess the impact of social/cultural trends. These are: description of future shock, lifestyle analysis, and general purpose consumer surveys. The last two approaches are based on information gathered through survey research methods, while the first two are assessments based on methods of content analysis and creative assessment and speculation.

Content Analysis of Popular Press

Content analysis of the popular press has become an accepted way to understand social and cultural trends and to predict future trends in a broad sense. These predictions are at a highly aggregated level and are not generally useful for the design of a marketing strategy for a specific product, but they do provide a social context to interpret the sales trends of existing products and to glean new product opportunities. To gain maximum advantage from such predictions, one may have to be creative and forego insisting on a quantitative basis for predictions made. It must be underscored that the knowledge of the broader trends will provide a context in which a specific marketing strategy can be crafted and evaluated. The particulars of any strategy will naturally depend on the specific demand and competitive situation encountered by the business in question.

The task of collecting the necessary information and interpreting the social and cultural trends in the society is quite involved and requires constant vigilance. In light of the importance of this activity and its ensuing difficulties, several consulting firms have emerged to help industrial clients follow various trends. This information helps a firm in the process of designing and changing marketing strategies. We describe two specific trend analysis approaches here. These are the Popcorn Report and the Megatrends Analysis.

Popcorn Report

The Popcorn Report, published periodically by Faith Popcorn (a recent one was published in 1991) describes nine trends which are called BrainReserve Trends. These are:

1. Cashing Out: Working women and men, questioning personal/career satisfaction and goals, opt for simple living.
2. Cocooning: One feels the need to protect oneself from the harsh, unpredictable realities of the outside world.
3. Down-Aging: Nostalgic for their carefree childhood, baby boomers find comfort in familiar pursuits and products of their youth.
4. Egonomics: The sterile computer era breeds the desire to make a personal statement.
5. Fantasy Adventure: Modern age whets our desire for roads untaken.

4. Egonomics: The sterile computer era breeds the desire to make a personal statement.

5. Fantasy Adventure: Modern age whets our desire for roads untaken.

6. 99 Lives: Too fast a pace, too little time, causes societal schizophrenia and forces us to assume multiple roles and adapt easily.

7. Small Indulgences: Stressed-out consumers want to indulge in affordable luxuries and seek ways to reward themselves.

8. Staying Alive: Awareness that good health extends longevity leads to a new way of life.

9. The Vigilante Consumer: The consumer manipulates marketers and the marketplace through pressure, protest, and politics.

While these assessments are essentially the judgments and opinions of the members of the Popcorn group, they may contain an element of truth. They are based on an extensive analysis of several sources of information. Their reading list—the BrainReserve Reading List—consists of some 130 magazines, newspapers, newsletters, and trade publications covering the various subjects shown in Table 5.8. Trends reported in these sources are culled out and then

TABLE 5.8
SOURCES CONSULTED BY THE BRAINRESERVE GROUP

Topic	Number of Publications	Examples
General Interest/Information	21	Newsweek, Working Mother
Men	5	Men's Health, Esquire
News	7	The Wall Street Journal, New York Times
Science	5	Science Digest, Omni
Health	7	American Health, Self
Food/liquor	5	Gourmet, Vegetarian Times
Home	3	Architecture Digest, HG
Travel/International	9	Travel & Leisure, Tokyo Journal
Entertainment/Gossip	10	National Enquirer, Entertainment Weekly
Literary/Art	9	The New Yorker, Atlantic
Business	6	Business Week, Business Ethics
Economics	2	Economist, Japan Economic Journal
Politics	8	New Republic, Washington Spectator
Environment	8	Greenpeace, Ecosource
Newsletters and trade publications	22	Research Alert, Advertising Age, John Naisbitt's Trend Letter
New Age	6	Whole Earth Review, Yoga Journal
Offbeat	5	Utne Reader, Paper

Source: Compiled from Faith Popcorn, The Popcorn Report (New York: Doubleday Currency, 1991).

incorporated into the company's TrendBank. They also interview various executives and other thinkers in the society to look for additional information and assess the emerging trends. The BrainReserve is a trademark for the consulting activity of the Popcorn group.

The methodology the BrainReserve group uses for analyzing the impact of various trends for a particular situation (e.g., an industry or a specific firm) consists of project definition, gathering input, idea development, refinement/presentation, and implementation or action plan. To assess the impact of various trends they use a technique called *discontinuity trend analysis*, which simply involves measuring the specific target (e.g., an industry, business, service, or product) against the more universal trends assessed by the firm. As an example, let us look at the implications of nine trends uncovered by the BrainReserve Group for the supermarket industry. Popcorn asserts that the supermarket industry is not keeping up with any of the trends, except perhaps down-aging. She argues that the supermarket industry is heading for calamity. Her recommendation for correcting the trend in the supermarket industry is through extensive use of electronic media (e.g., Virtual Reality), which can result in maximal consumer shopping satisfaction because they can appreciate where the products are coming from, can get detailed nutrition information on various products, and so on.

Megatrends

John Naisbitt and Patricia Aburdene have updated their 1982 analysis of social trends and published *Megatrends 2000* which identifies 10 major societal trends that they deem to be gateways to the twenty-first century. They content analyze newspapers, magazines, and the like. Table 5.9 shows these new trends in comparison to those identified earlier.

One important aspect of their analysis is the effect of the Cold War ending and the consequent reduction in the arms race. Undoubtedly, this has some interesting consequences for emerging businesses in the countries of the former Soviet Union. Further, they identify the privatization of the welfare state as a megatrend. This trend has already occurred in countries such as India, which have opened their economies for private foreign investment even in such important sectors as power generation. This trend opens up great opportunities for various US firms to do business abroad.

A further trend indicated is that of the "age of biology," which involves the development of biotechnologies including genetic engineering. These technological developments will create opportunities for new products and processes in the future. A success story in this regard is that of Calgene Inc., which marketed its Flavr Savr tomato seeds, which were genetically engineered to retard rotting.[7] The ultimate success of this new tomato will naturally depend upon consumer and channel acceptance.

---

7   Joan O. Hamilton, "A Storm Is Breaking Down on the Farm," *Business Week* (December 14, 1992): 98–101.

TABLE 5.9
MEGATRENDS IDENTIFIED BY NAISBITT AND ABURDENE

1982 List	1990 List
1. Industrial Society → to Information Society	1. The Booming Global Economy of the 1990s
2. Forced Technology → to High Tech/High Touch	2. A Renaissance in the Arts
3. National Economy → to World Economy	3. The Emergence of Free-Market Socialism
4. Short Term → to Long Term	4. Global Lifestyles and Cultural Nationalism
5. Centralization → to Decentralization	5. The Privatization of the Welfare State
6. Institutional Help → to Self-Help	6. The Rise of the Pacific Rim
7. Representative Democracy → to Participatory Democracy	7. The Decade of Women in Leadership
8. Hierarchies → to Networking	8. The Age of Biology
9. North → to South	9. The Religious Revival of the New Millennium
10. Either/Or → to Multiple Option	10. The Triumph of the Individual

Source: Compiled from John Naisbitt and Patricia Aburdene, *Megatrends 2000* (New York: Avon Books, 1990).

Naisbitt's Trend Letter, a biweekly newsletter published by the Global Network, is intended to keep people up to date on emerging trends.

Consumer Trends for the Twenty-First Century

Based on an analysis of a variety of survey and other information, Judith Waldrop, research editor of the *American Demographics* magazine, compiled a list of 21 trends for the twenty-first century.[7] While several of these trends relate to the workplace, some of these have implications for marketing strategies of U.S. businesses. We present below a sample of these trends and briefly comment on their strategy analysis implications.

Trend 1

Everyone belongs to a minority group. The current trends are that by 2020, immigration will play an important role in the growth of the U.S. population and consequently the population will be highly diversified. This diversity will offer great opportunities and challenges for businesses to cater to a diversity of consumer needs and wants. Niche marketing may become even more important to a range of consumer product marketers.

---

7 See Judith Waldrop, "You Will Know It's the 21st Century when . . . ," *American Demographics* (December 1990): 22–27.

Trend 2

Family must be redefined. The current trends in marriage and divorce imply that more than half of all children will spend part of their lives in single parent families by 2000. Further, one in three married couples with children will have a stepchild or an adopted child by 2010. More children will never know a time when their mothers did not work outside home. These trends will need to be carefully integrated by advertisers in the design and execution of advertising strategies.

Trend 9

The retirement population explodes. By July 2009, there will be 37 percent more people aged 62 or older then in the previous year and 63 percent more than in 1990. Combined with economic incentives for early retirement this boom will continue for several decades to come. The growth in this population will offer a significant increase in the demand for travel and related products and services.

Trend 10

Life becomes leisurely. There is a distinct trend toward Americans feeling that leisure time is more important than the time they spend at work. Further the population seeking activities to fill this leisure time will be affluent. Thus, they will be willing to spend more relaxation products and services.

Trend 13

Cooking from scratch means pushing the right buttons. Even if the population gets older, people would not turn into better cooks. The dependence on fast foods and ready-to-serve foods will be in great demand. The microwave oven will become an important cooking appliance in America.

Future Shock

As far back as 1970, Alvin Toffler speculated on several societal changes that will affect our products, communities, and organizations.[8] He labeled the change phenomenon "future shock" and may have essentially shocked various business executives with his predictions. Some of his predictions—such as the death of technocracy (implicitly arguing for the decline of planned economies like the former Soviet Union); acceleration of changes in scientific discovery; and transience in society on such crucial matters as marriage, diversity of lifestyles, multiple choices in product varieties, and the like—have in fact come true. He forcefully argues that any corporation that has not adapted to changes will not survive. The case in point was his assessment of the situation of American Telegraph and Telephone Company (AT&T) in 1972. In his report to the AT&T Board, he identified several environmental problems

---

8   Alvin Toffler, *Future Shock* (New York: Bantam Books, 1970).

they faced including competitive pressures from companies like MCI, Cater-fone, and CATV; the emergence of IBM and other major communications-minded companies; mounting consumerist pressures; the demand that the AT&T system hire more African Americans and hard-core unemployed; pressure to prevent pollution and recycle waste; and rising community resistance to new service installations. He argued that the firm faced the enormous task of defining and becoming a superindustrial enterprise based on more advanced technology and radically different organizational styles, among other features. The controversial strategy he recommended for the firm to adapt to changes in technology and other environmental trends was to divest several of its operations into several Baby Bell Companies and a long distance company in the name of AT&T. His 1972 report, published in 1985, shows the need for a firm to be flexible, resilient, and responsive to changes in the environment.[9] Management can respond to potential changes by being fully informed of any and all potential trends in the society.

As an example, consider the technological changes that are likely to affect one aspect of a corporation, the sales function. Changes in communication, data storage, and retrieval can affect how salespeople carry out their day-to-day activities. Scofield and Shaw predict that the following trends may alter the current ways of doing things and caution managers not to commit to any technology too rigidly:[10]

- Computing tools that enable easy transfer of data and software between various computers people use, such as desktop, laptop, and palmtop computers will become standardized. Such standardization will help easy transfer of sales reports by electronic mail and electronic data interchange.

- Artificial intelligence software technologies will help the sales force identify prospects more effectively than ever before.

- Pad and tablet computers that recognize handwriting will appear on the market and will enable easy data entry. This trend is likely to become a major hardware platform for automating some functions of a sales force such as placing orders.

- The continuing reduction of the price of cellular telephones (hand-held and other) will facilitate effective communication between field sales force and their customers and home office personnel.

- The development of object-oriented software systems, which are easier to understand, learn, and modify, are likely to have a tremendous impact on the way the sales process can be automated. The effects will be felt in the way sales records are maintained and retrieved.

---

9   Alvin Toffler, *The Adaptive Corporation* (McGraw-Hill, 1985).

10 Todd Scofield and Donald R. Shaw, "Avoiding the Future Shock," *Sales & Marketing Management* (January 1993): 16.

- The emerging multimedia trends that involve a blending of several technologies, including voice, sound, video, still pictures, monochrome, and color graphics, will have applications in sales training, visual product demonstrations, order entry systems (with pictures), and the like.

Interestingly, these types of predictions will have an effect on the future demand of the technologies being marketed.

The essential message to a marketing strategy analyst is to compile and analyze any trends that are even remotely applicable to one's business and to evaluate their potential impact.

Lifestyle Analysis

Clearly, many social and cultural trends will manifest themselves in the lifestyles pursued by its members. Thus, one of the methods of understanding and even forecasting the impact of social and cultural trends is through lifestyle or psychographic analysis. We have described these methods in Chapter 2.

In order to implement any marketing strategy at a local level, it may be useful to combine the lifestyle data with the demographic data on the population at the level of smaller geographic areas. SRDS is one firm that publishes such data. Their most recent publication is the 1995 Lifestyle Market Analyst. SRDS divides the United States as a whole into 211 designated market areas (DMAs), each consisting of a few counties. The Lifestyle Market Analyst is a joint venture of SRDS and NDL (National Demographics & Lifestyles, Inc., a part of R.L. Polk & Co.). The demographic and lifestyle profiles of various DMAs are updated annually by SRDS. These data can be used to identify geographic areas where the lifestyle activity rates are too different from the nation's average.

Lifestyle data are collected from households by inserting consumer information questionnaires into packages of a variety of consumer goods, including electronic equipment, appliances, apparel, sporting and camping goods, and other products. These questionnaires solicit demographic and lifestyle information, which National Demographics and Lifestyles (NDL) analyzes for its client companies. The information is based on some 30 million questionnaires. The county level profiles are based on a sample of 19.3 million households, representing questionnaires received over a one-year period, from November 1993 to November 1994. NDL adjusts its raw data in order to extrapolate results from those sampled to the population at large and to compensate for possible flaws in the collection process. NDL follows standard statistical procedures in making these adjustments, and these results are checked against updated figures computed from U.S. census counts. Therefore, the demographic statistics reported by NDL can be deemed reliable and reflect the entire U.S. adult population.

To give a flavor of these data, we present data from the 1995 Lifestyle Market Analyst for the Binghamton DMA, covering the counties of Broome,

Chenango, Delaware, and Tioga in New York State. NDL divides the lifestyle activities into seven major groups: home life activities such as book reading, good-life activities such as attending cultural/arts events, investing and money activities such as casino gambling, great outdoors activities such as camping/hiking, hobbies and interests such as automotive work or sewing, sports/leisure activities such as bicycling or running/jogging, and high-tech activities such as using electronics or photography. Table 5.10 shows these data for the Binghamton area relative to the U.S. population. The table also shows the projected number of households who participate in each of these activities. We find that the average number of activities per household in the United States is 14.1. (A household is considered to be participating in an activity if one or more adult members participates in it.) The numbers of households participating in the range of activities vary considerably. From a marketing perspective, participation in any activity translates immediately to demand for the products that will be used or needed for that activity. (As an example, the development and marketing of walking shoes by Reebok can be attributed to the trend in walking for health by a large number of people; over 33 million households in the United States participate in this activity, according to NDL.)

The participation rates for Binghamton area are compared to those of the United States as a whole by computing an index for the area. Further, the rank of the Binghamton area relative to other DMAs in the United States is shown for each activity. These are shown in the last two columns of Table 5.10. These data show that the participation rates by households in the Binghamton area are lower than the U.S. average in some activities and higher in others. For example, the rates are generally lower for the so-called good-life activities but higher for the great outdoors activities. Further, Binghamton's rank relative to other DMAs also varies across different activities. The top ten lifestyles in Binghamton relative to the United States are shown in the bottom part of the table; these include hunting/shooting, needlework/knitting, and so on.

Let us consider the two activities of photography and home workshop for which the indexes for Binghamton DMA are 104 and 111 relative to 100 for the United States as a whole. If a marketer that produces products for these activities wishes to develop a program to get a higher share for its business, the firm may design strategies such as intensifying its distribution among existing outlets, locating its own retail outlets, and even creating a direct marketing campaign. For a direct marketing campaign, the marketer may look for a suitable mailing list.

General Purpose Consumer Surveys

Various survey organizations such as the Roper Organization, and Yankelovich, Clancey and Schulman conduct periodic surveys to keep track of consumer confidence and sentiment as well as attitudes toward social and cultural trends. These provide a further understanding of how the social and

TABLE 5.10

LIFESTYLE ACTIVITIES OF BINGHAMTON DMA COMPARED TO THE U.S.

	U.S.		Binghamton DMA			
Lifestyle Group and Activity	House-holds (000s)	Partici-pation Rate (%)	House-holds	Partici-pation Rate (%)	Index	Rank
Home Life						
Avid Book Reading	36,802	38.1	55,818	40.0	105	46
Bible/Devotional Reading	18,063	18.7	20,653	14.8	79	186
Flower Gardening	31,490	32.6	50,934	36.5	112	61
Grandchildren	22,023	22.8	35,724	25.6	112	95
Home Furnishing/Decorating	19,415	20.1	25,816	18.5	92	167
House Plants	31,779	32.9	50,097	35.9	109	67
Own a Cat	25,307	26.2	44,654	32.0	122	32
Own a Dog	32,649	33.8	50,376	36.1	107	145
Subscribe to Cable TV	61,724	63.9	99,914	71.6	112	27
Vegetable Gardening	21,734	22.5	38,375	27.5	122	82
Good Life						
Attend Cultural/Arts Events	13,137	13.6	15,489	11.1	82	103
Fashion Clothing	12,944	13.4	15,210	10.9	81	158
Fine Art/Antiques	9,853	10.2	13,396	9.6	94	105
Foreign Travel	13,716	14.2	13,815	9.9	70	107
Frequent Flyer	20,188	20.9	24,141	17.3	83	78
Gourmet Cooking/Fine Foods	16,421	17.0	21,211	15.2	89	77
Own a Vacation Home/Property	10,625	11.0	16,048	11.5	105	62
Travel for Business	18,739	19.4	25,397	18.2	94	79
Travel for Pleasure/Vacation	36,223	37.5	49,957	35.8	95	95
Travel in USA	33,711	34.9	47,027	33.7	97	86
Wines	11,398	11.8	16,885	12.1	103	42
Investing & Money						
Casino Gambling	10,915	11.3	12,140	8.7	77	121
Entering Sweepstakes	13,620	14.1	18,280	13.1	93	174
Moneymaking Opportunities	11,398	11.8	13,396	9.6	81	199
Real Estate Investments	6,085	6.3	6,977	5.0	79	143
Stock/Bond Investments	15,262	15.8	19,676	14.1	89	112
Great Outdoors						
Boating/Sailing	10,336	10.7	14,234	10.2	95	89
Camping/Hiking	21,830	22.6	34,886	25.0	111	81
Fishing Frequently	22,989	23.8	32,654	23.4	98	172
Hunting/Shooting	14,875	15.4	30,421	21.8	142	89
Motorcycles	7,245	7.5	11,582	8.3	111	94
Recreational Vehicles	7,824	8.1	12,838	9.2	114	89
Wildlife/Environmental	15,841	16.4	26,374	18.9	115	26

TABLE 5.10
(Continued)

	U.S.		Binghamton DMA			
Lifestyle Group and Activity	House-holds (000s)	Partici-pation Rate (%)	House-holds	Partici-pation Rate (%)	Index	Rank
Sports, Fitness & Health						
Bicycling Frequently	16,518	17.1	18,280	13.1	77	147
Dieting/Weight Control	19,802	20.5	26,514	19.0	93	182
Golf	19,126	19.8	32,514	23.3	118	36
Health/Natural Foods	14,489	15.0	18,839	13.5	90	113
Improving Your Health	22,796	23.6	30,979	22.2	94	146
Physical Fitness/Exercise	32,842	34.0	42,143	30.2	89	132
Running/Jogging	11,012	11.4	11,443	8.2	72	169
Snow Skiing Frequently	7,148	7.4	12,559	9.0	122	55
Tennis Frequently	5,602	5.8	6,977	5.0	86	85
Walking for Health	33,132	34.3	49,120	35.2	103	78
Watching Sports on TV	37,479	38.8	53,306	38.2	98	125
Hobbies & Interests						
Automotive Work	14,779	15.3	23,164	16.6	108	110
Buy Prerecorded Videos	15,455	16.0	22,188	15.9	99	105
Career-Oriented Activities	8,887	9.2	11,024	7.9	86	128
Coin/Stamp Collecting	6,762	7.0	10,466	7.5	107	50
Collectibles/Collections	10,819	11.2	17,443	12.5	112	39
Crafts	26,757	27.7	45,771	32.8	118	38
Current Affairs/Politics	15,455	16.0	19,955	14.3	89	141
Home Workshop	24,149	25.0	38,794	27.8	111	36
Military Veteran in Household	24,149	25.0	35,305	25.3	101	131
Needlework/Knitting	16,807	17.4	30,142	21.6	124	34
Our Nation's Heritage	4,733	4.9	7,396	5.3	108	57
Self-Improvement	17,967	18.6	23,025	16.5	89	174
Sewing	18,353	19.0	27,769	19.9	105	138
Supports Health Charities	15,552	16.1	24,839	17.8	111	23
High-Tech Activities						
Electronics	10,432	10.8	14,234	10.2	94	99
Home Video Games	11,398	11.8	16,606	11.9	101	116
Listen to Records/Tapes/CDs	47,814	49.5	67,261	48.2	97	92
Own a CD Player	48,683	50.4	64,051	45.9	91	106
Photography	18,063	18.7	27,211	19.5	104	43
Science Fiction	8,500	8.8	12,280	8.8	100	73
Science/New Technology	8,404	8.7	11,582	8.3	95	75
Use a Personal Computer	35,257	36.5	48,003	34.4	94	76
Use an Apple/Macintosh	8,597	8.9	7,675	5.5	62	160
Use an IBM/Compatible	29,365	30.4	42,422	30.4	100	58

TABLE 5.10
Continued

	U.S.		Binghamton DMA			
Lifestyle Group and Activity	House- holds (000s)	Partici- pation Rate (%)	House- holds	Partici- pation Rate (%)	Index	Rank
Mean Number of Interests	14.1					
Total Number of Households	96,594,092		139,545			

The Top Ten Lifestyles Ranked by Index for Binghamton DMA

Hunting/Shooting	142	Golf	118
Needlework/Knitting	124	Crafts	118
Own a Cat	122	Wildlife/Environmental	115
Vegetable Gardening	122	Recreational Vehicles	114
Snow Skiing Frequently	122	Flower Gardening	112

Source: The Lifestyle Market Analyst 1995, SRDS, L.P., Des Plaines, IL, and National Demographics & Life-styles, 1995. Extracted from pages 81 and A-35. Reproduced with permission of the publisher.

cultural factors influence the opportunities and threats for a given business. For example, the attitude of the public toward smoking in public will naturally affect the demand for cigarettes. Similarly, the attitudes toward lobbying by such groups as MADD (Mothers against Drunk Driving) will have an influence on the general demand for alcoholic beverages consumed outside the home.

METHODS FOR ANALYZING ECONOMIC FACTORS

We now turn to a discussion of how economic factors affect a business. The general economic environment is measured by various indicators such as the total gross national product, degree of unemployment, industrial production, and the rate of inflation. The Bureau of Census and the Bureau of Labor Statistics routinely compile various statistics and report them to various Congressional bodies and to the president. These are published in various forms. The most accessible is the Statistical Abstract of the United States. (Similar abstracts exist for other countries as well.) This abstract contains a wealth of statistical information on economic factors relevant to any business.

Economic Statistics

Analysis of economic statistics enables a marketing strategy analyst to understand the broader economic climate in which the business operates. There are firms that specialize in publishing historical data on various economic indicators.[11] The analyst should correct historical series of economic data in nominal terms for inflation before interpreting inherent trends. In general, overall economic trends may not be uniform across all sectors of the economy. For example, slow growth of the U.S. economy in 1990 was largely due to low consumer expenditures for durable goods although there has been a steady growth in the service sector.

A look at the future economic trend can be gleaned from the composite index of leading economic indicators. It is a composite of 11 indicators: average weekly hours in manufacturing, average weekly initial claims for unemployment insurance, manufacturers' new orders, the Standard & Poor's index of stock prices of 500 common stocks, contract and orders for plant and equipment, index of new private housing units, vendor performance (slow deliveries), consumer expectations, change in manufacturers' unfilled orders, change in sensitive material prices, and money supply M2 (which includes all currency, checking accounts, and other types of checkable deposits as well as other liquid assets including money market funds, money market deposit accounts, savings accounts, and small time deposits). This composite index tends to signal the onset of a recession or recovery some months before the economy actually registers the change. It is generally held that a change in the direction of the indicator must be sustained for at least three months before the indicator is an accurate predictor of a change in the economy. Thus, it is useful for a strategy analyst to monitor the changes in this index on a monthly basis.

Implementation of a marketing strategy necessarily involves an understanding of the potential of each geographic area. This aspect requires compilation of economic and demographic data at various disaggregated geographic levels in the country. Several economic and demographic data at the county and city level are routinely compiled from a variety of sources and published for use by marketing analysts. As an illustration, Table 5.11 presents such data for Ithaca, a small city in New York State. It is instructive to reflect on the potential uses of these data for a number of business firms. For example, a firm involved in selling building materials will be interested in the level and changes in the value of construction authorized by building permits in the city. Similarly, a firm marketing scanning equipment for retail operations will be interested in any changes in the number of establishments engaged in retail trade.

Economic Surveys

In order to evaluate how well a business is faring in the marketplace, it is necessary to compare its sales volume with the size of the total market or the size of the corresponding industry by computing a measure of market share. The data published by the Bureau of the Census (described in the Appendix) are useful in estimating the denominator. In addition, the data collected by the

---

11 See, for example, Arsen J. Darnay, ed. *Economic Indicators Handbook*, first edition (Detroit: Gale Research Inc., 1992) and Cheryl Russell and Margaret Ambry. *The Official Guide to American Incomes*, first edition. (Ithaca, NY: New Strategist Publications & Consulting, 1993).

TABLE 5.11
ILLUSTRATION OF COMPILATION OF DATA FROM SEVERAL SOURCES: PROFILE OF ITHACA, NEW YORK

Land Area (1990)	14.1 sq. km.	Persons in institutions	235
POPULATION		Persons identified as homeless	13

Population in 1990			
Total persons	29,441	**CRIMES**	
Density (per sq. km.)	2,095	Serious crimes known to police, 1991	2,178
Population in 1980	28,732	Violent crimes	82
% Change in population,		Rate per 100,000 inhabitants	7,345
1980–1990	2.8		

EDUCATION, 1990

POPULATION CHARACTERISTICS

School enrollment

a. **By race**

Race	Percent

Public	5,648
Private	12,862

Race	Percent
White	81.8
Black	6.5
Am. Indian, Eskimo, Aleut	0.3
Asian and Pacific Islander	10.0
Other races	1.4
Percent Hispanic	3.6
Percent foreign-born	11.5

Educational attainment

Percent completing 12 years or more	86.7
Percent completing 16 years or more	50.2

MONEY INCOME, 1989

b. **By age**

Age group	Percent
Under 5 years	3.0
5 to 14 years	5.4
15 to 24 years	52.7
25 to 34 years	14.8
35 to 44 years	8.6
45 to 54 years	4.1
55 to 64 years	3.7
64 to 74 years	3.7
75 years and older	4.0

Per capita ($)	9,213
Median household income ($)	17,738
Percent change in household Income 1979–89 (constant $)	2.8
Percent households with $100,000 or more	2.5
Percent below poverty, 1989	
Persons	39.4
Households	22.0

HOUSING UNITS, 1990

c. **Sex**

Percent female	48.3

HOUSEHOLDS

Number in 1990	9,617
Percent change 1980–1990	4.9
Persons per household in 1990	2.26
Percent female family householder	8.3
Percent families with one person	36.5
Persons in group quarters	7,649

Total	10,075
Percent change, 1980–1990	5.8
Vacant units for sale or rent	322
Owner-occupied units	
Number	9,617
Percent	28.9
Median value ($)	95,300
Owner cost as percent of income with mortgage	22.2
Owner cost as percent of income without mortgage	13.8
Renter-occupied units	
Number	493
Rent as percent of income	35.1
Substandard units (percent)	2.0

TABLE 5.11
(Continued)

LABOR FORCE

Civilian labor force, 1991 (persons 16 years and older)

Total	17,584
Percent change, 1990–1991	−1.4

Unemployment

Total	665
Percent	3.8

Civilian employment, 1990 (persons 16 years and older)

Total	13,066

Rate per 1,000 employees

Professional, managerial, and technical	47.4
Precision, production, craft, and repair	3.4

DISABILITY, 1990

Work-disabled persons (percent)	3.7

VALUE OF CONSTRUCTION, AUTHORIZED BY BUILDING PERMITS

Total ($1,000)	7,698

Nonresidential

Total ($1,000)	244

Residential

New construction ($1,000)	1,960
Number of units	18
Percent single family	5.6
Alterations and additions	1,085

MANUFACTURES, 1987

Establishments

Total	74
Percent with 2 or more employees	24.3

All employees

Number ($1,000)	2.0
Percent change, 1982–87	−23.1
Annual payroll (mil dollars)	45.5

Production workers

Number (1,000)	1.2
Work hours (millions)	2.4
Wages	
Total (mil dollars)	20.4
Average per production worker (dollars)	17,000
Value added by manufacture (mil dollars)	97.3
Value of shipments (mil dollars)	180.0
New capital expenditures (mil dollars)	5.3

WHOLESALE TRADE, 1987

Establishments	53
Sales (mil dollars)	100.2
Paid employees	488
Annual payroll (mil dollars)	10.1

RETAIL TRADE

All establishments, 1987

Number	596
Sales (mil dollars):	
Total	388.7
General merchandise group	D
Food stores	74.4
Apparel and accessory stores	22.6
Eating and drinking places	38.6

Establishments with payroll, 1987

Number of paid employees	5,007
Percent change, 1982–1987	18.5
Annual payroll (mil dollars)	46.4

TAXABLE SERVICE INDUSTRIES

Establishments with payroll

Number	366

Receipts (mil dollars)

Total	111.7
Selected business types:	
Hotels, motels, and other lodging types	D
Health services	32.3
Legal services	8.3

TABLE 5.11
(Continued)

TAXABLE SERVICE INDUSTRIES (Continued)	
Paid employees	2,564
Annual payroll (mil dollars)	38.0

SELECTED FEDERAL FUNDS, FISCAL 1991 ($1,000)

Procurement contracts

Defense	35,513
Other	5,398

Grant awards

Total	137,645
Health and family welfare	28,290
Energy and environment	6,244
Education	4,127
Housing and community development	753

Direct payments for individuals

Educational assistance	11,828
Housing assistance	2,006
Form of government	Mayor-council

CITY GOVERNMENT FINANCES, 1990

General revenue

Total (mil dollars)	23.4
Intergovernmental total (mil dollars)	5.8
Percent from state government	67.0

Taxes

Total (mil dollars)	11.6
Per capita (dol)	
Total	393
Property	195
Sales and gross receipts	182

General expenditure

Total (mil dollars)	24.9
Per capita (dol)	
Total	843
Capital outlays	152

Percent of total for:

Public welfare	0.0
Highways	12.8
Parking facilities	1.1
Transit subsidies	0.0
Education	0.0
Health and hospitals	0.0
Police protection	12.2
Sewerage and sanitation	7.7
Parks and recreation	9.5
Housing and community development	3.8
Interest on debt	5.4

Debt outstanding

Total (mil dollars)	26.2
Per capita (dol)	882
Percent utility	4.0

CLIMATE

Average daily temperature (degrees fahrenheit)

Mean:	
January	22.2
July	68.8
Average daily minimum for January	13.8
Average daily maximum for July	80.3
Annual precipitation (in inches)	35.27
Heating degree days	7,177
Cooling degree days	328

Source: Courtney M. Slater and George E. Hall, eds., *1993 County and City Extra: Annual Metro, City and County Data Book,* second edition (Lanham, MD: Bernam Press, 1993). Reprinted with permission.

U.S. Bureau of Economic Analysis Survey of Current Business are useful in determining the total expenditure on broader categories (e.g., clothing, shoes, and telephone and telegraph) by all consumers in the market. Other sources for obtaining data on consumer expenditures include the Survey of Consumer Finances conducted annually by the Survey Research Center of the University of Michigan and the surveys done by the Conference Board. The Survey of Consumer Finances also measures the confidence of consumers in their future well-being. Thus, it offers an insight about the tendencies of consumers to purchase various high-ticket items. It behooves the strategy analyst to consult these sources to understand the general environment for his or her industry.

Economic Forecasts

It is not a surprise that forecasting the trends in an economy is in great demand by both business and government. This demand is met by several firms whose main activity is to develop and publish such forecasts of various economic indicators. The methods they use range from formal macroeconomic demand systems to informal back-of-the-envelope judgmental forecasts. (We will describe several forecasting techniques in the next chapter.) Given the difficulty of forecasting any turning points in an economy, forecasters will often miss declines in the output.

METHODS FOR ANALYZING POLITICAL FACTORS

Analysis of Regulatory Data

One of the ways in which political factors manifest themselves as influences on a business is through regulation. Another is through movements such as the green movement or through action groups for protecting the environment and so on. Several laws exist in the U.S. that affect marketing activities.[12] A strategic analyst should keep abreast of the existing laws and pending legislation as they affect the businesses of interest.

The events occurring in the cigarette industry illustrate the importance of a marketing strategist keeping up with legal developments affecting business. In March 1994, Philip Morris Co., the largest tobacco company in the nation, sued the ABC TV network for $10 billion, accusing the network of libel for reporting that cigarette makers artificially spike their products with nicotine.[13] The issue is whether the government should regulate tobacco products as drugs for which congressional hearings were being held. The heart of the story is the Food and Drug Administration's consideration of designating nicotine a drug, a move that Commissioner David Kessler told Congress would probably take most tobacco products off the market. The immediate consequence would be on the sales of cigarettes and the fortunes of various tobacco firms like Philip Morris. A further complication is a report by ABC that tobacco companies add nicotine in order to hook smokers.

---

12 See P. Kotler, *Marketing Management: Analysis, Planning and Control,* seventh edition (Englewood Cliffs, NJ: Prentice-Hall, 1995): Table 5-2 for a compilation of these laws.

13 See the news story "Cigarette firm sues ABC," *Ithaca Journal* (March 25, 1994).

Green Marketing Trends

One specific political trend of note concerns protecting the environment. This trend manifests itself in several forms, such as protecting water, soil, and air. Its main concern is to reduce pollution and ensure the appropriate disposal of both industrial and domestic waste. Businesses are becoming more responsible in dealing with these problems. Their approaches have been labeled "Green Marketing." These strategies include the development and production of products with biodegradable packages, substitution of selected materials with recycled materials, and the design and marketing of products that are environmentally safe to produce and use and that reduce air pollution. Frankel notes that 1993 was a year of steady progress in the worlds of corporate environmentalism and green business. He notes that environmental responsibility is being institutionalized in product development and R&D.[14] For example, the Mobil Corporation spends over 1.3 billion dollars and employs over 700 people simply to deal with various environmental issues that relate to the firm all over the world.[15] In a different vein, the Sun Company of Philadelphia, the 12th-largest oil company in the United States, became the first Fortune 500 company to endorse the Valdez Principles, a code of environmental conduct devised after the 1989 Alaskan oil spill.[16]

It is fair to assume that business will in general face increasingly stricter environmental laws. It is therefore essential for a marketing strategist to develop internal procedures to monitor these laws and to institute and implement appropriate policies. Several "green marketing" legal actions have been taken in 1993, for example. The types of claims at issue in these actions include the following (some companies have multiple claims challenged):[17]

- Compostability and Recyclability: Mr. Coffee, White Castle Systems
- Degradability: Archer Daniels Midland, North American Plastics Corp.
- Energy Savings: Osram Sylvania
- Environmental Friendly/Safe: BPI Environmental, de Mert & Dougherty, Mr. Coffee, Nationwide Industries, Orkin Exterminating
- Ozone Friendly: G. C. Thorsen, Perfect Data, Redmond Products, Texwipe Company

Two companies that are finding strategic environmental management a powerful competitive tool are Bristol-Myers Squibb (New York, NY) and IBM

---

14 Carl Frankel, "1993 in Review: Steady as She Goes," *Green Marketing Alert* 4 (December 1993):1–2.

15 Based on a speech given by Lucio A. Noto, Chairman and CEO of Mobil Corporation at Cornell University, April 4, 1994.

16 "Sun Oil Takes Environmental Pledge," *New York Times* (February 11, 1993).

17 *Green Marketing Alert* 4 :12 (Bethlehem, CT, December 1993).

Corporation (Armonk, NY). Among the strategies implemented by these firms are the following:

Bristol-Myers Squibb analyzed the environmental performance of all existing and new products of the firm. This analysis led to the replacement of methylene chloride, a regular toxic chemical, with water in the company's Bio/Chemical Division by a major product reformulation, development of the first alcohol-free hair spray by Clairol in response to pressure from California calling for reduced volatile organic compounds in consumer products, and a product life-cycle assessment for the company's Ban roll-on deodorant leading to reduction of chemical usage and manufacturing cycle time. All this results in lower costs.

IBM Corporation created an engineering Center for Environmentally Conscious Products. The Center contributed extensively to the development of the IBM PS/2E personal computer, which combines breakthrough performance with superb environmental performance. The environmental features of PS/2E include design for disassembly by reducing number of parts and fasteners, some reusable parts, increased content of recycled materials, potential for recycling the case, energy efficiency, and the use of PCMIA technology, which increases transferability from PCs to a laptop computer. These environmental features bode well for the long term.

Companies can be proactive in the general area of environment by recognizing the importance of various environmental laws that affect their business and by implementing appropriate policies. Such actions will enable them to deal with any potential threats likely in this area of growing importance. According to the Roper Organization surveys, Americans are becoming more concerned about the environment and are willing to pay 5 to 20 percent more for environmentally safe products; also, the share of Americans who take actions that benefit the environment almost doubled from 11 to 20 percent. A productive way to deal with environmental issues is to undertake an "environmental audit" on lines similar to that of a marketing audit.

Public Opinion Polls

Tens of thousands of public opinion polls or surveys are undertaken in the United States and elsewhere every year. A variety of topics of interest to a marketing strategist are explored in these surveys. These include attitude toward big business, attitude toward product safety, consumer confidence and sentiment, general intentions to purchase products, concern for the environment, attitude toward privacy, and information technology. It is essential that a marketing strategy analyst understand which organization is conducting the survey, the time period of the survey, how the questions are worded, consistency in the results of the various survey organizations, and where (in which medium) the results are reported to the public. Results from public opinion polls and surveys provide a good sense of the general public's tone and of the broader environment in which a business has to operate.

A partial list of survey organizations that conduct public opinion polls and surveys includes: Gordon S. Black Corporation, Louis Harris and Associates, National Opinion and Research Center, Opinion Research Corporation, Princeton Survey Research Associates, Survey Research Center of the University of Michigan, The Cambridge Reports, Inc., the Gallup Poll Organization, The Roper Organization for Surveys, and Yankelovich, Clancy and Schulman. It is advisable for a marketing strategy analyst to find out through an appropriate bibliographic search whether there is a recent survey on an environmental trend or potential environmental threat.

As an example, consider the public opinion trends on the issue of privacy and information technology as collected in different public opinion surveys by such survey organizations as Cambridge Reports, The Gallup Organization, Maritz Marketing Research Inc., National Opinion Research Center, and Roper Center for Public Opinion Research. They indicate, for example, that Americans believe that privacy loss will be a larger concern in the future than it is today and the public believes that governmental actions to protect privacy have decreased. These results are quite significant for companies in such industries as credit cards, telecommunications, direct marketing, electronic communication networks like Internet, as well as the U.S. Government. Both business and government have to keep up with trends of this nature in order to be able to design defensive or proactive strategies to contend with public concerns.

SUMMARY

In this chapter, we have identified analysis methods for understanding and forecasting the influence on a business of various factors in the external environment. Five sets of factors—demographic, social/cultural, economic, political, and technological—are identified along with methods for analyzing their impact on the demand. In addition, we have looked at various sources of data that a marketing strategist should keep up with in order to monitor various trends.

We will continue with this discussion in the next chapter, which focuses on the technological factors. We will also discuss various methods for forecasting technological trends and sales of existing and new products. We will further consider methods for evaluating the joint influence of several factors via scenario analysis and cross-impact analysis.

APPENDIX: A GUIDE TO INFORMATION SOURCES FOR MARKETING STRATEGY ANALYSIS

I.   Company Information

Annual reports to stockholders. Financial disclosure statements filed annually with shareholders. *10-K* reports are detailed statements filed annually with the Securities and Exchange Commission. Besides financial reporting, these statements provide insight into new corporate initiatives, research and development, and product lines.

Compustat PC Plus (Standard & Poor's Compustat Services). CD/ROM product providing 20 years of financial data on public companies and industries. Company data include segment level information. Comparative company and industry data, and market share information are also provided.

Dow Jones News/Retrieval (Dow Jones & Company, Inc.). Online service providing access to a variety of business databases. Full-text articles from *The Wall Street Journal, Barron's,* business wire services, and the general business press. Includes information from the Securities Exchange Commission disclosure filings and industry reports.

Moody's Manuals (Moody's Investors Service). Bound annual volumes with current loose-leaf updates. Include corporate histories and basic financials.

Bank and Finance	OTC Industrial
Industrial	OTC Unlisted
International	Public Utility
Municipal and Government	Transportation

OneSource™ U.S. Public Companies (OneSource). Current and historical financial data on companies and industries, full-text investment reports, annual and weekly stock trade data; article abstracts for companies and industries.

Standard & Poor's Stock Reports. Brief overviews of stock performance, updated quarterly.

Value Line Investment Survey. Investment recommendation service tracking current performance of firms and industries.

II.   Industry Information

Predicasts Forecasts. Quarterly analysis of industries by SIC (standard industrial classification code). Annual growth data, sales, production data, and consumption data are routinely reported. Short- and long-term forecasts are included.

---

* Compiled by Lynn Brown, Librarian, Johnson Graduate School of Management Library, Cornell University, Ithaca, NY, 1995.

Standard & Poor's Industry Surveys. Detailed reports on industries, products, and major competitors. Industry trends and the regulatory environment are often discussed.

Standard Industrial Classification Manual. Detailed description of SIC codes and the industries, products, and services represented by this numerical classification system.

U.S. Industrial Outlook. Annual analysis of industries, current and anticipated trends, and statistical analyses.

III. Economic and Demographic Statistical Data Sources

County Business Patterns (U.S. Bureau of the Census). Annual series with a separate report for each state, the District of Columbia, Puerto Rico, and a U.S. summary. Contains employment and payroll data, and number of establishments by employment size. Only series that provides annual sub national data by two, three, and four digit SIC codes.

Current Population Reports (U.S. Bureau of the Census). Detailed statistical series on the population of the United States. Provides information on specific population characteristics and projected population trends.

Consumer Income (Series P-60)
Household Economic Studies (Series P-70)
Local Population Estimates (Series P-26)
Population Characteristics (Series P-20)
Population Estimates and Projections (Series P-25)

Economic Census Reports (U.S. Bureau of the Census). Economic censuses are run every five years. Annual surveys are also conducted to update the data. Data elements include value of shipments, capital expenditures, number of employees, payroll data, and number of establishments. Data are arranged by SIC code and by geographic area.

Census of Construction Industries
Census of Finance, Insurance, and Real Estate
Census of Manufactures
Census of Mineral Industries
Census of Retail Trade
Census of Service Industries
Census of Transportation, Communication, and Utilities
Census of Wholesale Trade

MEI Marketing Economics Guide (Marketing Economics Institute). Ranks metropolitan areas by population, disposable income, and total retail sales. Also includes estimates for population, households, and household income. Provides retail sales estimates for nine retail groups.

The Sourcebook of County Demographics (CACI Marketing Systems). Statistics on income and purchasing power available at the county level. Measures potential demand for products and services. Companion volume, *The Sourcebook of Zip Code Demographics*, provides similar data at the zip code level.

Survey of Current Business (U.S. Bureau of Economic Analysis). Monthly periodical tracking economic indicators, industry data, and import/export data. Special issue in July, "National Income and Product Accounts," includes "Personal Consumption Expenditures by Type of Product."

IV. Consumer Markets

Almanac of Consumer Markets (American Demographics Press). Provides demographic statistics, arranged by age cohorts, to help marketers identify potential consumer markets.

Consumer Expenditure Survey (U.S. Bureau of Labor). Nationwide ongoing study of household spending.

Consumer Power: How Americans Spend Their Money (Margaret Ambry). Consumer market survey tracking household expenditures. Original data source for this work is the *Consumer Expenditure Survey*.

Handbook of Demographics for Marketing and Advertising: New Trends in the American Marketplace, 2nd ed. (William Lazer). Discusses the impact of changing demographics on markets. Highlights significant trends and developments, and familiarizes readers with the vast array of government data relevant to marketers.

Lifestyle Market Analyst (SRDS). Provides profiles of consumers by bringing together demographic, geographic, and lifestyle information for each DMA market.

Study of Media and Markets (Simmons Market Research Bureau). Profiles customers by identifying their socioeconomic characteristics and purchasing behavior.

Survey of Buying Power (Special issue of *Sales & Marketing Management*). Tracks retail sales and population trends and provides an "effective buying income" index for all metros, counties, and major U.S. cities. Ranks metros by their sales and by specific socioeconomic characteristics. Companion volume, *Survey of Media Markets*, provides similar data plus five-year metro market projections and current merchandise line sales statistics.

V. Advertising and Brand Data

Ad$Summary (Leading National Advertisers). Identifies brands and their respective media expenditures across 10 media dimensions. Ranks industries and companies by total media expenditures.

Mediaweek (A/S/M Communications). Publishes regular feature, "Market Trends," which tracks media spending for a variety of brand categories.

SRDS (formerly Standard Rate and Data Service). Multivolume set tracks circulation statistics and advertising costs for consumer and business magazines, and newspapers, and tracks advertising costs for television and radio spots.

Superbrands (A/S/M Communications). Detailed analysis of the top 2,000 U.S. brands.

VI.   Indexing, Abstracting, and Full-Text Services

ABI/INFORM (UMI). Online and cd/rom database providing article abstracts from the general business press and scholarly business journals.

Dialog's Business Connection (Dialog Information Services, Inc.). Full-text articles covering company and industry information. General market information from the trade press can be found for most industries.

Market Research Abstracts (The Market Research Society). Indexes articles primarily in the scholarly journals with emphasis on research methodologies.

NEXIS (LEXIS/NEXIS, Mead Data Central). Online service providing access to full-text articles from regional, national, and international news sources. The "Market Library" includes most of the major marketing publications.

Predicasts F&S Index. Indexes articles by company name and industry, uses "Predicasts codes," based on the SIC code classification of industries, to provide indexing at specific product levels. Excellent source for tracking articles from the industry trade press and for locating product marketing information.

PTS PROMT (Predicasts). PROMT, Predicasts Overview of Markets and Technology, is an online database providing coverage of products, markets, and applied technologies for all industries. Scope is both national and international in its coverage.

VII.   General Information Sources and Bibliographies

Business Information: How to Find It, How to Use It, 2d ed. (Michael Lavin). Provides in-depth descriptions of major business publications and databases with explanations of business terms and concepts. Serves as both a handbook for business information research, as well as being an extensive, annotated bibliography of business sources.

Data Sources for Business and Market Analysis (John Ganly). Annotated bibliography of business and marketing information sources. Extensive coverage of government produced data and reports relevant to marketers.

Encyclopedia of Business Information Sources (Gale Research Co.). Broad-based business bibliography covering over 1,100 subjects of interest to businesses. Each subject entry identifies basic handbooks and background materials, relevant indexing and abstracting sources, trade associations, yearbooks and almanacs, periodicals, and online databases.

BIBLIOGRAPHY

Aaker, David A. *Strategic Market Management*. New York: John Wiley & Sons, 1992.

Aaker, David A., and George S. Day. *Marketing Research*. 4th ed. New York: Wiley, 1990.

Ansoff, Igor, and Edward McDonnell. *Implanting Strategic Management*. Englewood Cliffs, NJ: Prentice-Hall, 1990.

Clancy, Kevin J., and Robert S. Shulman. *The Marketing Revolution: A Radical Manifesto for Dominating the Marketplace*. New York: Harper Business, 1991.

Larreche, Jean-Claude, and Reza Moinpour. "Management Judgment in Marketing: The Concept of Expertise." *Journal of Marketing Research* 20 (May 1983): 110–121.

Little, John D.C., and Leonard M. Lodish. "Commentary on 'Judgment-Based Marketing Decision Models.'" *Journal of Marketing* 45 (Fall 1981): 24–29.

Naisbitt, John. *Megatrends*. New York: Warner Books, 1982.

Naisbitt, John, and Patricia Aburdene. *Megatrends 2000: Ten New Directions for the 1990's*. New York: Avon, 1990.

Newson-Smith, Nigel. "Desk Research." *Consumer Market Research Handbook*, Robert Worcester and John Downham, eds. Amsterdam: North-Holland, 1986: 7–28.

Popcorn, Faith. *The Popcorn Report*. New York: Harper, 1992.

Neubaven, F. Friedrich, and Norman B. Solomon. "A Managerial Approach to Environmental Assessment." *Long Range Planning* 10 (April 1977): 13–26.

Porter, Michael E. *Competitive Strategy*. New York: Free Press, 1980.

Rentz, Joseph O., Fred O. Reynolds, and Roy G. Stoudt. "Analyzing Changing Consumption Patterns with Cohort Analysis." *Journal of Marketing Research* 20 (February 1983): 12–20.

Reynolds, Fred D., and Joseph O. Rentz. "Cohort Analysis: An Aid to Strategic Planning." *Journal of Marketing* 45 (Summer 1981): 62–70.

Sigford, J. V., and R. H. Parvin. "Project PATTERN: A Methodology for Determining Relevance in Complex Decision Making." *IEEE Transactions on Engineering Management* 12 (March 1965): 9–13.

Wheelwright, Steven C., and Spyros G. Makridakis. "Technological Forecasting." *Corporate Strategy and Product Innovation*. Second edition. Robert R. Rothberg, ed. New York: Free Press, 1981: 290–299.

———*Forecasting Methods for Management*. 3d ed. New York: John Wiley, 1980: 267–288.

CHAPTER 6

Understanding and Forecasting Market Environment—II

FORECASTING AND DESIGN OF STRATEGIES

We have seen in the previous chapter how changes in environmental forces—as reflected in demographic, social, cultural, political, and economic factors—will influence the choice of business strategy. In this chapter, we will continue this discussion by focusing on the need to understand changes in the techno-logical aspects of the environment. In addition to understanding the external environmental forces, choosing a specific business strategy will involve an assessment of its impact on the future of the business. This assessment also requires that the firm understand the potential impact of the strategy on competitors in order to identify an appropriate response. This strategy choice involves forecasting not only customer and distributor responses to the new strategy but also competitors' response behavior and potential effects on the firm's business due to competitors' moves.

Managers can utilize their experience and judgment to forecast (or specu-late about) relevant environmental responses. As we have seen earlier, such speculation is subject to biases of judgment. In situations with limited past data, firms will not be able to avoid judgmental forecasts. However, when the firm has data on sales, it can use regression methods to forecast competitor responses; in the same vein, it can use regression methods to identify suitable strategic decisions. Use of regression assumes, however, that the future envi-ronment is not likely to change dramatically from the conditions that prevailed for the data used in the estimation of the regression function.

The business press reports examples of technological developments on a regular basis. For example, consider the following two developments that might revolutionize the health sector and the entertainment industry.

1. A gene therapy treatment that unclogs the arteries damaged by cholesterol was implemented by Dr. James Wilson of the University of Pennsylvania's Institute for Gene Therapy (*USA Today*, April 1, 1994). Gene therapy experiments are also reported under way for a variety of diseases, includ-

ing cystic fibrosis and cancers such as melanoma and brain tumors. Such developments can have a significant effect on the demand for various drugs and health services in the future.

2. Developments in multimedia technology will give people an opportunity to interactively control various household electronic devices. There is a clear need to develop products that will enable such connectivity and control in a household; some authors have compared a household to a mainframe computer, to which various electrical/electronic units can be connected for performing various functions.

UNCERTAINTY AND THE ROLE OF JUDGMENT

Typically, historical data can be used to develop forecasts by using statistical methods. But, in some cases, historical data are not available, and gauging the future essentially is based on judgment. Even when forecasts are developed from the past, it becomes necessary to revise them using various qualitative information not easily incorporated in the forecasting model. Such revisions are also accomplished by managerial judgment.

Managerial judgment is also called for in dealing with various sources of uncertainties in strategic decision making; these uncertainties include assessing future actions of competitors, assessing the trends in technology, and assessing changes in political environment. Managers will need to identify these uncertainties and the risks involved. Such judgments become an important input to the design of appropriate strategies.

Psychologists studying decision making have documented that people's biases affect their judgments.[1] Two biases that are particularly relevant in the context of forecasting are imputing illusory correlations to two variables when in fact they are not and optimism or wishful thinking about the future. Strategic analysts and strategic decision makers need to recognize human limitations and biases and take steps to minimize their impact on forecasts.

FORECASTING TECHNOLOGY

Technology is essential to the success of any firm. We, therefore, focus on the ways in which a strategic analyst can forecast technological trends to provide input into the formulation of a business strategy. The forecasting techniques described in this chapter, however, are also generally applicable to forecasting other aspects of a business, such as sales or costs; therefore, the reader should not exclusively identify the techniques with the task of forecasting technology.

---

1 See S. Makridakis, *Forecasting, Planning and Strategy for the 21st Century* (New York: The Free Press, 1990): 36–37 for a comprehensive compilation of these biases.

Alternatives to Formal Forecasting

Some alternative methods to undertaking a formal forecasting process for technological developments are open to managers.[2] These methods include no forecast, anything can happen, the glorious past, window-blind forecasting, crisis action, and genius forecasting.

- No forecast. This forecasting alternative means a firm is facing the future blindfolded. In most cases, this would mean the firm thinks the future is constant or will only change negligibly.

- Anything can happen. This option implicitly assumes that the future is a gamble. This attitude can create serious trouble and the business can be short-lived.

- Relying on the glorious past. This attitude assumes that the future will be as glorious as the past because the firm has survived well with the decisions of the past. But this approach to dealing with the future uncertainties can lead to disaster.

- Window-blind forecasting. This approach assumes that technology moves on a fixed track, like an old-fashioned roller window blind, and that the only direction is up. Thus, forecasting on this basis assumes that technology will only get better in the future. This view can lead an organization into surprise owing to unanticipated changes in the future.

- Crisis action. This approach to dealing with technological developments involves waiting until a significant change has occurred. An organization following this method of managing technology will probably not make any progress toward its goals. A firm can avoid crisis action by anticipating the future in a systematic manner.

- Genius forecasting. This method consists of asking a genius (or an expert) to find out what the future technological developments will be. In a sense, it is a forecasting method. But, there is no rational way to examine the assumptions behind such a forecast and to seek corroboration for such a forecast.

Clearly there are disadvantages to not using a formal method for forecasting future possibilities. These disadvantages are particularly relevant to forecasting technological developments, owing to the opportunities (and fortunes) that could be lost when a firm selects a specific path of technology. Even large firms such as Sony have lost out in the VCR market by banking on Betamax technology rather than focusing on VHS technology. In the same manner, Zenith lost out in the video storage and transmission market by focusing on videodiscs when the success was clearly in videocassettes. Another example is Apple, which developed the MacIntosh platform when the growth was in the DOS platform for microcomputers. Our view is that a firm will have a

---

2 This material is drawn from Joseph P. Martino, *Technological Forecasting for Decision Making*, 3rd ed. (New York: McGraw-Hill, 1993): 5–8.

significant advantage by developing forecasts systematically and making technological choices with as much information about the future as possible. The advantages of developing such forecasts far outweigh the costs. We must, however, point out that mere availability of technological forecasts does not guarantee that a firm will make the right choices. But we do believe that a firm is better off employing a formal forecasting technique and supplementing its results with managerial judgment wherever necessary. Even with the availability of forecasts, a firm has to make choices regarding specific technologies to be employed for its businesses. The remainder of this section will briefly review a few formal techniques for forecasting technological trends. The reader may note that these techniques are but a subset of techniques generally used for forecasting. We will elaborate on most of these techniques as applied to sales forecasting in the next section.

Measuring Technology

When forecasting technological trends, the first step is to define and measure technology using one or two critical parameters. Two types of measure are available for measuring technology: functional and technical parameters. Functional parameters measure the utility to the user of the technology or a product developed from that technology. Technical parameters can be manipulated by the technology developer to yield the desired utility to the user. For example, a functional parameter for an incandescent electric bulb would be light output measured in lumens; while a technical parameter would be filament temperature, which a product designer may vary to yield the desired lumens. In the case of a personal computer, a functional parameter would be the speed with which the computer would execute a command, while a corresponding technical parameter would be the speed of the chip used in the microprocessor (88, 286, 386, 486, or a pentium).

The measure selected for forecasting a technology should satisfy some criteria. First the measure itself must actually be measurable. Next, the measure should represent state-of-the-art of technology and should be applicable to all the different technologies that may be considered in the forecasting process. (For example, when one considers aircraft speed as a technical measure for the technology of aircrafts, it enables comparison of both propeller-driven and jet-propelled aircrafts, while the weight of an aircraft would not allow such a comparison.) Of course, appropriate data should be available for the measure selected, and the measure should be consistent with respect to the stage of innovation being represented in the data. It would be inappropriate to compare technologies in their early stages of development with technologies in much later stages. This point is well illustrated when one wishes to forecast the technology of computers from the early stages onward; the speed of processing has significantly improved in addition to the size of the processing unit included in the computer. Thus, it would be inappropriate to compare the physical size of a computer of an earlier generation with the size of the current generation of laptop computers.

Once the data for the selected measures are collected, the analyst may adopt any one of several techniques for forecasting.[3] These methods include trend extrapolation methods and fitting growth curves. (Trend extrapolation methods are a subset of various time-series techniques.) Further, the method of analogy may also be appropriate to forecast the impact of a new technology. The analogy technique involves identifying a trend that was exhibited in one or more existing technologies that are quite similar to the one under consideration and applying the observed trend(s) to the technology being forecasted.

An Illustration of Forecasting Technology

To make the technological forecasting problem concrete, assume that the Intel Corporation is interested in assessing when the next microprocessor chip will be introduced and what its spread would be. Undoubtedly, this is a complicated forecasting task. We will suggest some methods.

First, one will be interested in finding out the historical data on the introduction of microprocessor chips by Intel. Fortunately, some details on Intel's introductions in the recent past were reported in *The Wall Street Journal*, December 7, 1994. The data below can be extracted from this article.

Date of Introduction	Intel Corporations Chip	Chip Speed (MIPS)	No. of Months Elapsed since June 1979	Number of Months from Previous Chip
June 1979	8088	0.5	0	0
February 1982	80286	1.1	23	23
October 1985	80386	1.5	67	44
April 1989	80486	20.0	109	42
March 1993	Pentium-60MHZ	100.0	156	47
March 1994	Pentium-100MHZ	200.0	168	12

Methods for Forecasting Technology

Various methods are available to develop forecasts of *when* and *what* in connection with Intel's chip introductions. One method is to fit a mathematical function to go through various data points of time of introduction (when) and MIPS (what) and use the curve to forecast when the next processing chip will be introduced and with what speed. Various functions such as the trend lines (e.g., linear or exponential) and growth curves (e.g., S-shaped curves) can be

---

3   The techniques for forecasting technology are often described as "exploratory" or "normative." The essential distinction is whether the forecast depends upon some knowledge currently available to the forecaster. Thus, the techniques such as trend extrapolation, regression, and the like will be called "exploratory." Normative techniques include methods of relevance trees and morphological analysis. The reader will recall the description of morphological connections for finding solutions in Chapter 3, a "normative" method. We will not delve into normative techniques in this book.

used. This method belongs to a broad class of curve-fitting methods. In particular, the S-shaped curve when fitted to the data on MIPS can reveal how fast a speed is feasible for a microprocessor chip. These techniques do not call for any more information than shown here.

Hence, they suffer from the disadvantage of not being able to incorporate any knowledge on the technological developments in the microprocessor chip industry. Another method that utilizes such knowledge is called the Delphi technique and involves eliciting opinions of experts in one or more rounds (we will describe the details later in this chapter).

A third method, the method of analogy, involves using the developments in an analogous industry and applying those trends to the chip industry. We will elaborate on this later in the chapter.

Accuracy of Technology Forecasts

Wise (1976) analyzed the accuracy of predictions about technological changes and their effects in the United States between 1890 and 1940 and found that fewer than half the predictions (40 percent) have been either fulfilled or are in the process of being fulfilled.[4] His analysis was based on 1,556 predictions in 18 specified areas of technology covering topics such as energy sources, communications, new materials, heating and cooling, computers, and weapons. He also found that the batting average of experts (44.4 percent) was significantly better than that of nonexperts (33.6 percent). Further, the study showed that the effects of technology were more difficult to predict than the technological changes themselves. This finding suggests that social and economic changes evolve in response to an array of technological changes rather than a single technological innovation.

These findings are quite consistent with those of Schnaars and Berenson, who looked at market growth forecasts published in the business press over the 20-year period from 1960–1979.[5] Out of a total of 90 market growth forecasts, 48 (53 percent) failed to materialize. As summarized below, the reasons attributed to failures and successes indicate the need for careful analysis of a multitude of factors when making forecasts for an innovation in the marketplace.

Reasons for Failure	Reasons for Success
Overevaluation of technological wonders.	Demographic forecasts.
No relative advantage for the consumer.	Focus on fundamental market factors.
Shift in the relative advantage demanded by the consumer.	Consistent advances in product and market.

---

4   See George Wise, "The Accuracy of Technological Forecasts, 1890–1940,") *Futures* (October 1976): 411–419.

5   See Steven P. Schnaars and Conrad Berenson. "Growth Market Forecasting Revisited: A Look Back at a Look Forward." *California Management Review* 28 (Summer 1986): 71–88.

Reasons for Failure	Reasons for Success

Reasons for Failure

Changes in social and demographic
  trends.
Technical problems.
Undue pessimism.
Politics.

For these reasons, a strategic analyst has to conduct appropriate analyses of customer and competitive behavior as well as the external environment. The various methods described in earlier chapters and the methods described in this chapter will undoubtedly assist in developing a realistic forecast.

SELECTED FORMAL FORECASTING METHODS[6]

Methods[7] of forecasting sales can be organized in several ways. One classification, shown in Figure 6.1, is based on four variables: (1) whether or not historical sales data are available, (2) whether or not historical data on sales correlates are available, (3) whether or not data on analogous situations are available, and (4) the type of cross-sectional survey data available. As the flow-chart indicates, various combinations of these variables will lead to six categories of forecasting techniques:

1. Trend extrapolation and growth curves.

2. Regression.

3. Analogy.

4. Delphi technique.

5. Methods based upon intentions.

6. Conjoint analysis.

Trend extrapolation and fitting growth curves do not utilize any external data, while regression requires the analyst to obtain data on some correlates of the sales or technology being forecasted. Multiple regression is the most versatile for developing forecasts when data on correlates are available. Analogy and the Delphi technique require using data from a number of sources to build up a forecast. In the case of analogy, historical data on a number of related or analogous situations are analyzed to forecast the sales under question. The Delphi technique involves a series of surveys among a panel of experts; after each round, the participants are provided feedback of their opinions before the next round. Thus, the analogy and Delphi techniques call for a lot of external data in developing a forecast. The last two categories of methods (5

---

6   We thank Rahul Bhalla, Cornell MBA 1995, for his assistance in developing various analyses used in this
    section.

7   See J. Scott Armstrong, *Long-Range Forecasting* (New York: Wiley, 1985) for a comprehensive treatment
    of forecasting techniques.

FIGURE 6.1

A DATA-BASED TAXONOMY OF MAJOR SALES FORECASTING METHODS

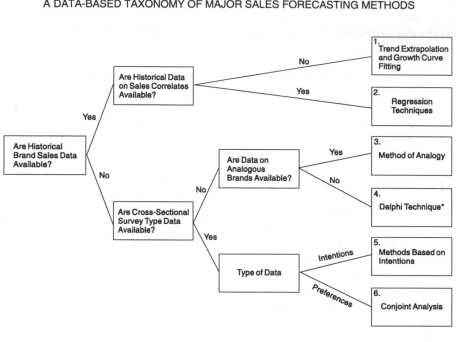

*Not exhaustive.

Source: Adapted from Vithala R. Rao and James E. Cox, *Sales Forecasting: A review of Recent Developments* (Cambridge, MA: Marketing Science Institute, 1978). Reproduced with permission.

and 6) involve data obtained in surveys on purchase intentions and evaluations of hypothetical products.[8]

Advantages and disadvantages of various techniques of forecasting are described in the Appendix to this chapter.

Industry Use of Forecasting Methods

In a survey of 500 U.S. corporations, Sanders and Manrodt (1994) found that responding managers are more familiar with the quantitative forecasting methods than in the past, but the level of usage has not increased. The data are based on usable responses from 96 (19.2 percent of the contacted) executives with the job title vice-president of sales and marketing, director of

---

8   We will limit our discussion to methods under the groups 1 through 4. The techniques based on surveys and purchase intentions are beyond the scope of this book because they deal mainly with short-term forecasting. The technique of conjoint analysis described in Chapter 2 can also be employed for forecasting sales of a new product.

marketing, or director of corporate planning. Although over 90 percent of the executives are familiar with the regression technique (slightly less than the judgmental techniques), they continue to rely largely on the judgmental forecasting methods. The major obstacles to the use of formal quantitative forecasting methods such as multiple regression are lack of relevant data and low organizational support. Executives also adjust data judgmentally, while using quantitative techniques to reflect their knowledge of special conditions of the data.

Techniques Using No External Data

When the analyst has access to a series of data over time, a forecast can be developed using any one of the trend extrapolation methods or by fitting a growth curve. Growth curves are based on a "loose" analogy between the growth in sales and the growth of a living organism. Typically, there will be slow growth in the early period, followed by rapid growth. Later on, the growth tapers off, reaching a plateau. The general shape is an S-curve.

Trend Extrapolation

Essentially, this process of extrapolating a trend involves visually identifying a pattern in the growth of the sales or a measure of technology over time and fitting an appropriate mathematical function to the observed pattern. While any mathematical function can be fitted to describe a time trend, linear and exponential trend functions are usually appropriate and sufficient for consideration. These two patterns are shown in Figure 6.2.

Once a trend pattern has been selected, the analyst fits the trend to the observed data using the method of least squares. Usually, one or two data points at the end are not used in the fitting of the trend. The fitted trend is then used to forecast the data for the points withheld. The prediction is then compared with the observed data to check how well the trend line fits the data. If the fit is good enough, the trend line may then be reestimated using all data points, and the updated trend line is used to forecast the future patterns. Given the ease with which linear functions can be fitted using the method of least squares, exponential trend function is linearized by taking logarithms on either side.

Growth Curves

Among the several curves that can be employed to forecast growth, the Pearl curve and the Gompertz curve are most suitable. The procedure for fitting them is the same as for trend extrapolation. The growth curve is transformed to yield a linear function while fitting the curve.

Figure 6.3 illustrates the patterns for the two growth curves along with their equations.

Illustration of Trend and Growth Curves: Cellular Telephone Sales. We illustrate this process of extrapolating trend and fitting growth curves using the sales

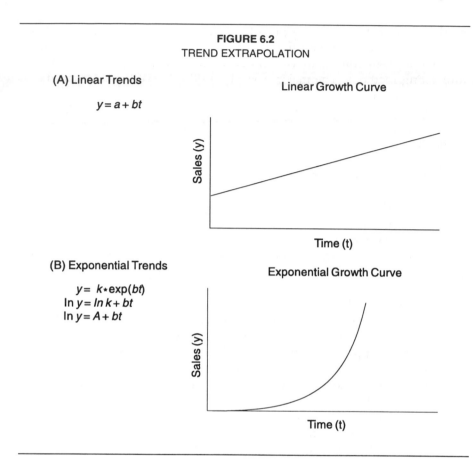

FIGURE 6.2
TREND EXTRAPOLATION

(A) Linear Trends

$y = a + bt$

Linear Growth Curve

Sales (y)

Time (t)

(B) Exponential Trends

$y = k*\exp(bt)$
$\ln y = \ln k + bt$
$\ln y = A + bt$

Exponential Growth Curve

Sales (y)

Time (t)

data of the cellular telephones during the period 1983–1992, shown in Table 6.1. A visual examination of these data shows a phenomenal growth of sales during this period.

We fitted both the linear and exponential trends to these sales data for the years 1983–1990 and used the estimated trends to forecast the sales for 1991 and 1992. We then compared the forecasts with the actual sales. The results are shown in the top part of Table 6.2. As can be seen, the errors in these forecasts are very large.

The bottom part of Table 6.2 shows the results of the fit of growth curves—Pearl and Gompertz—to the same data. In this estimation, one needs to assume a value for the upper limit (L) of the growth-curve equation; we estimated these curves with a value of 5,000 for L. We tested the sensitivity of the results for different values of the upper limit, L. The estimates of parameters, of course, vary with the value of L. In general, the forecasts increase as L increases. This should be expected because the whole growth curve is pushed

FIGURE 6.3
GROWTH CURVES

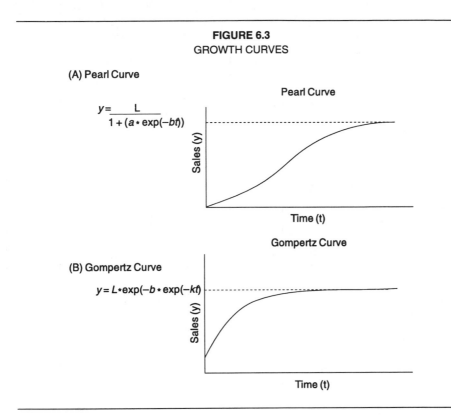

(A) Pearl Curve

$$y = \frac{L}{1 + (a * \exp(-bt))}$$

Pearl Curve

Sales (y)

Time (t)

Gompertz Curve

(B) Gompertz Curve

$$y = L * \exp(-b * \exp(-kt))$$

Sales (y)

Time (t)

TABLE 6.1
SALES OF U.S. CELLULAR PHONES: 1983–1992

Year	t	Sales (thousands of units)
1983	0	5[*]
1984	1	25
1985	2	75
1986	3	280
1987	4	300
1988	5	500
1989	6	870
1990	7	2,100
1991	8	3,100
1992	9	3,750

[*] This number is actually shown as not available (N/A). We use 5 as an approximation.
Source: 1993 Electronic Market Data Book, p. 33. Reproduced with permission.

TABLE 6.2

FIT AND PREDICTIONS FROM DIFFERENT TREND AND GROWTH CURVES FOR CELLULAR PHONE SALES DATA (1983–1990)

Trend or Growth Curve	Mathematical Equation	Parameter	Estimate	Standard Error	Degree of Fit (R-Square)	1991 Actual	1991 Predicted	1992 Actual	1992 Predicted
TREND									
Linear Trend	$y = a + bt$	a	−1,761.62		0.71	3,100	1,600	3,750	1,840
		b	240.13	63.30					
Exponential Trend	$y = ae^{bt}$ or	ln a	1.314		0.95	3,100	5,324	3,750	11,329
	$\ln y = \ln a + bt$	b	0.755	0.071					
GROWTH CURVES									
Pearl Curve	$y = \dfrac{L}{1 + ae^{-bt}}$	a			0.96	3,100	3,057	3,750	3,902
	(L is set at 5,000)	b	0.8148	0.067					
Gompertz Curve	$y = Le^{-be^{-Kt}}$	b	15.002		0.94	3,100	2,047	3,750	2,505
	(L is set at 5,000)	K	0.2565	0.0259					

upwards as L increases. Once L is known, the growth-curve equation can be linearized and estimated by the method of least squares.

The fit measures are all very high for each of these curves. Nevertheless, the forecasts show varying numbers of errors. The forecasts from all of these methods may be summarized by the following values of the absolute percentage errors in the forecasts (computed as the percentage of absolute error in the forecast as a percent of the actual value). The results indicate that the Pearl growth curve not only yielded a better fit, but that forecasts for the years 1991 and 1992 were much more accurate.

Year	1991	1992
Linear trend	48.4	40.6
Exponential trend	42.0	202.1
Pearl curve	1.4	25.9
Gompertz curve	45.4	33.2

The Pearl growth curve yielded the best forecast for the year 1991, although it was subject to a large error for the year 1992. The Pearl growth curve, along with the actual data and predictions, is shown in Figure 6.4.

The Gompertz growth curve gave poor predictions for both 1991 and 1992.

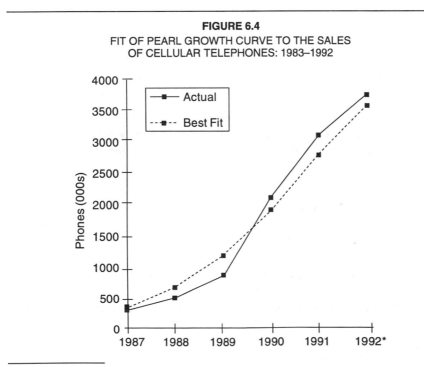

FIGURE 6.4
FIT OF PEARL GROWTH CURVE TO THE SALES
OF CELLULAR TELEPHONES: 1983–1992

*Extrapolated

The exponential trend perhaps is not appropriate for these data; it showed worse errors than the linear trend for the year 1992, although the magnitude of error from the exponential trend is less than the linear trend for the year 1991.

Regression Techniques

The method of regression is highly suitable for forecasting the sales of established products (or brands). In developing a regression model for sales of an established product, the analyst needs first to develop a conceptually defensible framework to describe the process for the sales formation (a similar framework is necessary for using regression method to forecast the development of a technology). This framework should enable the analyst to determine which predictors to include in the regression model for forecasting sales. For example, consider the problem of forecasting the sales of new cars. The relevant conceptual framework may be derived from an economic theory of consumption; variables such as disposable income, credit conditions, prices, and stock of automobiles of different ages may be important predictors. Similarly, the variables of population size, age distribution, and disposable income may be relevant predictors for sales of pharmaceutical products.

Regression Procedure

The procedure for building a regression model for forecasting involves the following nine steps:

Step 1.   Identify an appropriate conceptual model for sales.

Step 2.   Identify predictor variables that affect sales and predictor variables; let Y be the sales variable and n be the predictors affecting sales.

Step 3.   Collect historical data on sales (Y) and on the predictor variables.

Step 4.   Make the series comparable in units used over time; for example, ensure that any dollar measures are in constant terms over time.

Step 5.   Create new variables using dummy variables to account for any sudden changes in the conditions over the period of series of data.

Step 6.   Estimate the postulated regression equation between sales and the X-variables (including any additional dummy variables); test the goodness of fit and interpret the equation.

Step 7.   Develop estimates for the future values of the X-variables in the equation, using external information. It may be useful at this stage to consider multiple sets of future values for the X-variables. (Each of the sets of future values will define a scenario that could occur in the future.)

Step 8.   Assuming that the regression model is acceptable, use it to forecast Y for each of the scenarios.

Step 9. Test for the sensitivity of assumptions made either in the model or in the future values of the predictors that were used in forecasting the future sales.

We will illustrate this approach with two examples. In the first example, we will estimate a forecasting equation for the subscriptions of cable television in the United States using the time-series data for the period 1963–1990 and then make a forecast for the year 1991. In the second example, we will develop a forecasting equation to predict the penetration of telephones in a country using cross-sectional data across various countries.

Example 1: Forecasting CATV Penetration. Because the number of cable television subscribers will be highly related to the population size, we will use the number of CATV subscribers per 100,000 households as the dependent variable in the regression equation. Once a regression model is developed for this measure, it can be forecasted into the future. We can multiply this forecast by the projected number of households to obtain a forecast of the total number of CATV subscribers. This procedure will enable us to forecast an underlying behavior (i.e., rate of CATV subscription) rather than forecast a total that would naturally be affected by population size. (The reader may note that this procedure is essential to distinguish between the reasons for an increase in sales in terms of a change in underlying behavior versus those simply due to population growth with no change in the underlying consumption behavior.) We conjectured that two variables—monthly rate for the cable television and disposable income per household—are useful in predicting the penetration of CATV for this illustration.

We collected relevant data for the period 1975–1989 and estimated a regression equation. The predictor variables were monthly rate for CATV, adjusted for inflation, and disposable income per household measured in 1987 constant dollars. The monthly rate variable reflects the managerial decisions of the CATV systems, while the disposable income variable measures a household's economic status (or its ability to pay). This forecasting model does not include any differences among households. This is because data are at the aggregate level.

The results are shown in panels A, B, and C of Table 6.3. Panel A shows data compiled and identifies the manipulation of data before running the regression. Panel B shows the results of regression analysis R-square, measuring the degree of fit of the regression, the intercept of the regression, the two regression coefficients, their standard errors, and t-values. Panel C shows the forecasts made for the years 1991–1993, using the regression model along with actual values and forecasting errors.

The R-square for this regression is 0.94, indicating the strong ability of this model to predict CATV penetration. The two regression coefficients are statistically significant. They are negative for the monthly rate and positive for disposable income, as one would expect. According to this regression, one unit decrease in the adjusted monthly rate would increase the penetration rate of

TABLE 6.3

ILLUSTRATION OF FORECASTING WITH REGRESSION: CATV DATA

Panel A: *Data Used*

Year	No Subscribers (000s)	Subscription Rate per Month (Current $)	Price Index (Value of a 1982–84 Dollar)	Adjusted Monthly Rate (Constant $)	Disposable Income (1987 $)	Number of Households (000s)	Penetration Rate (per 100 Households)	Predicted Rate of Penetration
1975	9,800	7.85	1.859	14.593	10,906	71,120	13.78	6.56
1976	11,000	7.87	1.757	13.828	11,912	72,867	15.10	18.13
1977	12,200	7.92	1.649	13.060	11,406	74,142	16.45	14.73
1978	13,400	8.09	1.532	12.394	11,851	76,030	17.62	20.54
1979	15,000	8.44	1.380	11.647	12,039	88,330	16.98	23.97
1980	17,500	8.80	1.215	10.692	12,005	80,776	21.66	25.64
1981	21,500	9.02	1.098	9.904	12,156	82,368	26.10	28.79
1982	25,400	9.57	1.035	9.905	12,146	83,527	30.41	28.69
1983	29,450	9.84	1.003	9.870	12,349	83,198	35.40	30.77
1984	32,850	10.08	0.961	9.687	13,029	85,407	38.46	37.88
1985	35,430	10.42	0.928	9.670	13,258	86,789	40.82	40.18
1986	38,740	10.31	0.913	9.413	13,552	88,458	43.79	43.63
1987	41,200	10.15	0.880	8.932	13,545	89,479	46.04	44.58
1988	44,200	10.18	0.846	8.612	13,890	91,124	48.51	48.66
1989	47,390	10.21	0.807	8.240	14,030	92,830	51.05	50.83
1990	50,455	10.38	0.766	7.951	14,154	93,347	54.05	52.67

TABLE 6.3
(Continued)

Panel B: *Regression Results*

R-Square=0.94; Adjusted R-Square=0.93

ANOVA

	df	Sum of Squares	Mean Square	F	P-Value
Regression	2	2,849.90	1,424.95	106.59	<.00001
Residual	13	173.79	13.37		
Total	15	3,023.68			

	Coefficients	Standard Error	t-Stat	P-Value
Intercept	−70.69	36.23	−1.95	0.073
Monthly Rate	−2.10	1.03	−2.04	0.0625
Disposable Income	0.0099	0.0021	4.77	0.0004

Panel C: *Forecasts*

Year	Acutal Number of Subscribers (000s)	Monthly Rate (Current $)	Price Index	Adjusted Monthly Rate (Constant $)	Disposable Income (1987 $)	Number of Households (000s)	Actual Penetration Rate (per 100 Households)	Predicted Penetration Rate (per 100 Households)	% Error = (Actual – Predicted) / Actual * 100
									Actual
1991	52,600	10.27	0.734	7.538	13,990	94,312	55.77	51.91	6.9
1992	54,300	10.06	0.713	7.173	14,219	95,669	56.76	54.94	3.2
1993	56,300	9.11	0.692	6.304	14,330	96,391	58.41	57.87	0.9

CATV by 2.10 units, while a $100 increase in disposable income would increase the rate of penetration by 0.99 units.

We then used the model to see how well it predicted for the year 1991–1993. The forecasts for the three-year period were very close to the actual data. The forecast errors were 6.9 percent for 1991, 3.2 percent for 1992, and 0.9 percent for 1993. The regression model underpredicts the actual rate of penetration of cable TV for all of these years. The actual versus predicted rates of penetration are shown in Figure 6.5.

Example 2: Forecasting Telephone Penetration in Countries. This example involves developing a regression model to predict the penetration of telephones across 29 countries on all continents for the year 1988. Given that these countries are at various stages of development, the data can be thought of as a time series even though they correspond to one year.

We compiled data on number of telephones per 100 people and two predictor variables: percent urban population and railway passenger-kilometers per 100 people in each country. While the first predictor variable obviously contributes to greater telephone usage, the second predictor is a measure of the infrastructure of a country. These two variables combined will measure the extent of industrialization of a country and are therefore important determinants of the telephone penetration. We developed a regression model for predicting telephone penetration using these two predictors. Considering the fact that some countries are highly industrialized, we estimated a multiple

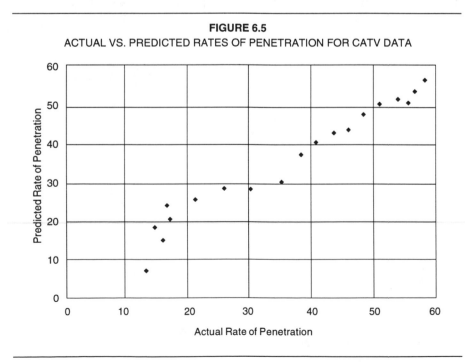

FIGURE 6.5
ACTUAL VS. PREDICTED RATES OF PENETRATION FOR CATV DATA

TABLE 6.4
FORECASTING OF TELEPHONE PENETRATION IN VARIOUS COUNTRIES

Panel A: *Data Used*

Country	Population Thousands in 1988	Telephones per 100 People in 1988 Y	Adjusted % Urban (1988) X1	Railway Passenger–Km Millions (1988)	Passenger–Km per 100 People X2
Austria	7,651	54.30	57.6	7,994	104,488
Belgium	9,845	49.90	95.7	6,348	64,479
Bolivia	7,002	2.80	50.0	369	5,270
Brazil	144,246	9.60	73.7	13,891	9,630
Canada	25,999	51.30	76.6	2,989	11,496
Chile	12,736	6.80	84.1	1,013	7,954
Cuba	10,400	5.20	72.6	2,627	25,260
Czechoslovakia	15,600	25.50	75.3	19,408	124,414
Denmark	5,130	88.20	84.6	4,850	94,547
Finland	4,956	49.90	59.7	3,147	63,496
France	55,880	45.20	72.8	63,290	113,261
Germany	62,356	68.20	85.0	41,760	66,970
Greece	10,008	43.10	61.3	1,963	19,614
India	796,502	0.60	25.0	263,731	33,111
Indonesia	173,356	0.50	27.3	7,863	4,536
Ireland	3,517	23.80	54.7	1,180	33,551
Kenya	23,290	1.50	22.0	2,608	11,198
Malaysia	16,967	9.70	41.3	1,518	8,947
Netherlands	14,765	65.90	88.4	9,664	65,451
Peru	21,132	2.30	69.8	596	2,820
Spain	38,726	28.00	77.5	15,716	40,582
Sweden	8,474	66.20	83.8	6,081	71,760
Switzerland	6,619	88.20	60.5	12,391	187,203
Tanzania	24,023	0.60	19.5	855	3,559
Thailand	54,975	1.80	21.4	10,301	18,738
Turkey	55,211	11.70	58.6	6,708	12,150
Unitod Kingdom	67,000	46.50	88.9	34,112	60,363
United States	245,535	49.60	74.9	9,156	3,729
Venezuela	18,747	9.30	89.6	29	155

· These figures are estimated using 1990 data and growth rates during 1985–90.
Source: UN Statistical Yearbook, 1992.

Table continues

TABLE 6.4

(Continued)

Panel B: *Regression Results for the Exponential Model* (Regression of [ln Y on ln X_1 and ln X_2)

R-Square=0.77; Adjusted R-Square=0.75

Analysis of Variance

	df	Sum of Squares	Mean Square	F	Significance of F
Regression	2	58.14	29.07	43.37	< .0005
Residual	26	17.43	0.67		
Total	28	75.57			

	Coefficients	Standard Error	t-Statistic	P-Value
Intercept	−11.40	1.51	−7.52	<.0001
ln X_1	2.39	0.33	7.21	<.0001
ln X_2	0.44	0.10	4.22	0.0002

Panel C: *Forecasts*

Country	X_1	X_2	Y	ln X_1	ln X_2	Predicted ln Y	Actual ln Y	% Error
Argentina	85.6	32,609	11.50	4.45	10.39	3.745	2.442	53.34
Japan	76.9	290,865	40.20	4.34	12.58	4.441	3.694	20.23
Sri Lanka	21.3	11,248	1.10	3.06	9.32	−0.0359	0.0953	−137.6
Norway	74.1	62,187	47.80	4.31	11.03	3.682	3.867	−4.78
South Africa	48.6	63,391	14.60	3.88	11.05	2.685	2.681	0.14

exponential model to describe a growth pattern across countries. We linearized the model by transforming the variables into logarithms. Such transformation will yield estimates of elasticities.

The results of this analysis are shown in Table 6.4. The data used in the regression are shown in the top panel, and the results are shown in the middle panel. The forecasts are shown in the bottom panel. We made the data comparable across all countries by estimating any data missing in the original source.

The regression coefficients for the two variables—percent urbanization and infrastructure—are highly significant. The respective coefficients are both positive (as could be expected); the elasticity (or the regression coefficient in the multiple exponential model) for the urbanization variable is 2.38, indicating a 2.38 percent change in the number telephones per 100 people for each percent change in the degree of urbanization. Similarly, the elasticity for the infrastructure measure is 0.44. The R-square of the model is 0.77, indicating a good fit.

We used the model to predict the telephone penetration for five countries—Argentina, Japan, Sri Lanka, Norway, and South Africa—with mixed results. The forecasting errors are very large for the less developed countries and quite low for developed countries. In particular, the model forecasts the telephone penetration for Norway and South Africa very well. These results indicate that the model has not captured all of the essential aspects of the process of telephone penetration in a country.

Precautions in Using Regression Technique

Some precautions in using multiple regression model for forecasting should be pointed out. First, it is important to have a theoretically sound basis to identify the predictor variables to be included in the regression model and to develop suitable measures for them. This problem is quite evident in the second example; although we believe that infrastructure is an important construct in predicting telephone penetration in any country, we did not capture it well by the measure of railway passenger-kilometers. This was due to lack of suitable data. A related issue is that the analyst should include those variables for which forecasts are available so that the fitted regression model can be used to forecast the dependent variable. Next, it is important to choose a suitable functional form for the regression equation that describes the structure of the data and the underlying demand-formation process. We have used two different forms—linear and exponential—in the two illustrations. Choice of a functional form is a complicated subject; discussion of this topic is beyond the scope of this book.[9] Further, the analyst has to ensure that the fitted model has face validity so that the regression coefficients can be suitably interpreted. The two examples developed above satisfy this consideration. It is also important that the model fits the data well; this is seen by the large value of the R-squared measure. Another concern in using the regression model for forecasting is that the model predicts well for the data points withheld from the estimation stage of the analysis. While the first example did better on this criterion, there is room for improvement in the second example. Another way to judge the forecasting ability of the model is by examining whether it predicts the turning points in the data. (We did not encounter this problem in our examples.) A final problem is due to high correlation between the included predictors in the model. This problem is called multicollinearity. While high multicollinearity is not detrimental for using the model for forecasting, it causes the estimated coefficients to be unstable and hard to interpret. Further discussion of this issue is beyond the scope of this book.

---

9 See any text on econometrics, such as J. Johnston, *Econometric Methods*, 3d ed. (New York: McGraw Hill, 1984). See also, Dick R. Wittink, *The Application of Regression Analysis* (Boston: Allyn and Bacon, 1988).

Method of Analogy

In cases when the new product or technology has no history whatsoever, the task of forecasting its growth is monumental. Researchers have developed creative ways to arrive at a reasonable forecast in such situations. They tend to look for past similar situations for which historical data now exist or seek the advice of knowledgeable people (experts). The corresponding methods are called "analogy" and the "Delphi" technique. We will discuss these in some detail.

When a new technology appears, it is possible to compare it to an existing technology and try to forecast the growth of the new technology from the experience accumulated with the existing technology. This approach is essentially qualitative in that only general trends can be forecasted. However, when one can utilize the experience of several existing technologies, it is possible to relate the growth rate of each existing technology to a set of characteristics that describe them. When a relationship between the growth rate of a technology (using a measure such as rate of penetration 10 years since the introduction of the technology) and its characteristics (such as speed and cost) is developed, it can be used to forecast the future growth of the new technology using information on its characteristics. Generally, the method of multiple regression can be employed for this purpose.

Illustration of Forecasting HDTV Diffusion

As an illustration, consider the potential diffusion among U.S. households of high-definition television (HDTV), based on a new technology under development. The manner in which the HDTV will be diffused can be forecast using the experience with television and related innovations.

These growth curves can be used to compute the penetration of color TV and VCRs whose technology *may* be analogous to that of HDTV. Further, because the price of HDTV is likely to be substantially higher than either of these two innovations, one may forecast that the diffusion of HDTV would be lower (perhaps much lower) than that of these two products. In fact, the projections made by the FCC's Working Group shown in Figure 6.6 seem to be consistent with this view.

Bayus has assessed the viability of existing forecasts for the HDTV using the method of analogy.[10] For this purpose, he first identified some 27 technologies (or products) that had been introduced at various times during the last 70 years or so, such as black and white television, color television, room air conditioner, lawn mower, turntable, and VCR. Utilizing data on the growth patterns of these products and the path of their prices over time, he estimated three parameters to describe the technology for each product: coefficient of innovation, coefficient of imitation, and a learning coefficient that depicts the decrease in costs due to experience. (The innovation and imitation parameters

---

10 See Barry L. Bayus, "High Definition Television: Demand Forecasts for Next Generation Consumer Durable," *Management Science* 39 (November 1993): 1319–1333.

FIGURE 6.6

FCC WP5 ESTIMATE OF U.S. HDTV PENETRATION RATES

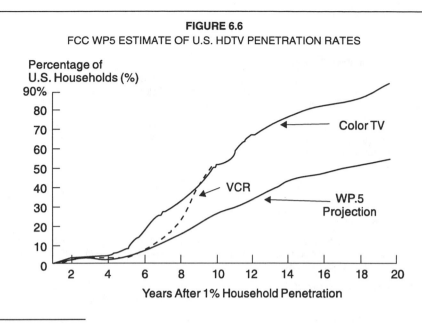

Years After 1% Household Penetration

Source: Extracted from the Harvard Business School Case, "Zenith: Marketing Research for High Definition Television (HDTV)," #9-591-025, Exhibit 10.

describe the way a new product gets diffused in the market; we will describe them in a later section of this chapter.) The 27 products were then grouped into five appliance segments. Table 6.5 shows the characteristics of these segments.

Bayus then analyzed the estimates of demand for HDTV for 1996–2007 published by the American Electronics Association (AEA), Electronics Industries Association (EIA), and National Telecommunications Information Administration (NTIA). He used their sales estimates to infer the coefficients of innovation and imitation for HDTV. He also analyzed the assumed price paths to determine the coefficient of the learning curve for price for each set of sales estimates. The parameter estimates obtained from this analysis of published demand estimates for HDTV were then combined with the grouping information of the 27 products in order to obtain revised estimates of the way the diffusion of HDTV will occur in the United States. Bayus then used these revised parameters to judge the reasonableness of each of the published demand estimates for HDTV. These revised estimates are also shown in Table 6.6. Given the high initial price for a HDTV, he concluded that the market potential of 50 million households was more reasonable for HDTV in the United States. He further concluded that the estimate published by the AEA for the period 1996–2007 is consistent with the prior sales histories of the 27 products he analyzed.

TABLE 6.5
USE OF ANALOGY FOR FORECASTING HDTV DEMAND

Panel A: Segment Mean Characteristics

Segment	Products	Coeff. of Innovation $(x\ 10^{-2})$	Coeff. of Imitation	Market Potential $(x\ 10^3)$	Price	Price Trend	Learning Coefficient
1	Electric toothbrush, fire extinguisher, hair setter, slow cooker, styling dryer, trash compactor, turntable	8.30 (0.91)	0.22 (0.03)	38903.8 (8379.5)	108 (53.5)	0.051 (0.01)	0.216 (0.04)
2	Can opener, cassette tape deck, curling iron, electric blanket, heating pad, knife sharpener, lawn mower, waffle iron	2.32 (0.74)	0.32 (0.04)	36323.6 (12781.0)	151 (53.7)	0.086 (0.01)	0.279 (0.02)
3	B&W TV, blender, deep fryer, electric dryer, food processor, microwave oven, room A/C	1.41 (0.46)	0.48 (0.05)	38231.7 (14328.1)	623 (208.0)	0.054 (0.01)	0.119 (0.02)
4	Color TV, refrigerator, VCR	0.20 (0.14)	0.54 (0.07)	42646.1 (23566.5)	2109 (338.7)	0.090 (0.03)	0.158 (0.05)
5	Calculator, digital watch	2.49 (0.45)	0.27 (0.15)	382722.7 (194664.2)	140 (33.0)	0.182 (0.05)	0.472 (0.11)

Standard error in parentheses.

Panel B: HDTV Parameter Estimates and Market Potential for the Three Forecasting Schemes

	AEA	EIA	NTIA
Coefficient of Innovation $(x\ 10^{-2})$	0.20	0.20	1.85
Coefficient of Imitation	0.54	0.54	0.46
Market Potential $(x\ 10^3)$	42,646	42,630	38,261

Source: B.L. Bayus, *Management Science* 39 (November 1993).

To use the method of analogy for forecasting, the analyst has to be able to identify appropriate analogous situations. Analogies may be identified on several dimensions. In addition to technological criteria, these dimensions include economic, managerial, political, and social criteria. For example, when forecasting the diffusion of VCR, the fact that its function is complementary to color television can be used; such an analogy will be based on technological dimensions. One may also use economic criteria such as price and use the diffusion paths of products with comparable prices (e.g., medium-priced cameras or medium-priced stereo systems). Because product diffusions don't just happen without appropriate managerial actions, one may look at the diffusion paths of products marketed by the same firm (or similar firms) as the one under consideration and use that experience in developing a forecast. Similar arguments can be made for other criteria. The basic idea is to identify products that have similar characteristics and to use their experience in the process of analogy forecasting.

Delphi Technique

The Delphi technique combines the expertise of several individuals who are knowledgeable in the technology of interest. The technique has been successfully used by the RAND Corporation for forecasting various technologies. In a survey on past applications of the Delphi technique among individuals who either conducted Delphi studies or participated in such studies, Brockhaus and Mickleson found that about one-fourth of the Delphi studies were conducted for tackling business and economics forecasting problems.[11] The respondents felt that topics such as material shortages, the energy crisis, pollution control, and long-range forecasting for various types of industries and product types are better handled by the Delphi technique. The respondents also noted that the Delphi technique was chosen over other methodologies due to its low cost.

The technique involves selecting a panel of experts in the technology of interest, such as research scientists, engineers, or university professors. The panel then considers various developments in the technology of interest and speculates on the specific technological developments likely to occur in the future (e.g., during five years). For each development identified, the panel members will also provide their best estimate of the probability of its occurrence. Usually, but not always, they will also guess the date in the future (e.g., year) when they believe the development is likely to occur. (In cases of complicated technologies, the experts may be asked to indicate the specific reasons why they believe the developments will occur; such information may be valuable in ascertaining various trends that may contribute to the growth of a particular technology.) The anonymous responses are collected by an independent moderator who collates the suggested developments and summarizes the data using the median and interquartile range of the probabilities assigned by the experts. The median date and interquartile range of the date is fed back to the panel so that they may modify their previous predictions. This process is iterated a few times until the experts reach consensus. Various studies have revealed that three or four iterations are sufficient for reaching consensus. The features of this technique are anonymity and iteration with controlled feedback and statistical inference, with responses fed back to the participants of the panel.

Advantages

The Delphi technique eliminates the disadvantages of using a committee to develop a composite forecast: the social pressure a group places on its members, the tendency on the part of the group to be swayed by any misinformation of any single member, and the undue influence of dominant members of

---

11 See William L. Brockhaus and John F. Mickelsen, "An Analysis of Prior Delphi Applications and Some Observations on Its Future Applicability," *Technological and Social Change* 10 (1977): 103–110.

the group. It also retains the specific advantages of a group approach, such as the feasibility of considering a diversity of views and the ability to preserve the total amount of information displayed by its members.

Disadvantages

Nevertheless, the Delphi technique has been criticized for its nonscientific nature, in that survey research procedures are not rigorously followed. Accordingly, a few variations are adopted in practice to ensure the rigor of the Delphi exercise. These variations include providing a better description of the context for developing the forecast, providing initial descriptions of potential future events, eliciting confidence bands for the predictions made by the panelists, and conducting the Delphi study for large number of rounds until a consensus is achieved.

Studies assessing the validity of the Delphi method of forecasting point to the significant role that expertise of the panel member plays in the accuracy of the forecast obtained. Thus, it is essential to ensure that high a degree of expertise is represented on the panel.

Applications of Delphi

We will now describe two applications of the Delphi technique. The first application dealt with a 10-year forecast of the electronics industry developed for Corning Glass Works and the second with a 40-year forecast developed for the Alaskan economy for the year 2000 and beyond.

Application 1: The Corning Electronics Delphi Study. The standard Delphi process was modified by researchers at Corning Glass works in their attempt to forecast component sales in the electronics industry for a 10-year period.[12] While actual results were not available, this study described the various steps Corning followed in adapting the Delphi technique to business forecasting purposes. In a standard Delphi study, experts are asked to predict the date by which a specific event will occur. Corning researchers modified this procedure by first selecting a date and asking experts to predict the extent to which a specific change would have taken place by that time. This variation was found to be much more useful for business forecasting because the business environment changes rather gradually. In fact, predictions were sought for two specific points in time, making it possible to look at trends over time.

Given that outside experts were needed in this study and that the electronics industry was very diversified, Corning researchers found it difficult to find individuals with detailed knowledge to qualify as experts. The problem was compounded by the need to protect confidentiality so that the results were of some use to Corning. These considerations led the researchers to develop three different panels: one for consumer-oriented businesses, one for industrial businesses, and one for government businesses; the respective sizes in these

---

12 See Jeffrey L. Johnson, "A Ten Year Delphi Forecast in the Electronics Industry," *Industrial Marketing Management* 5 (February 1976): 45–52.

panels were 15, 19, and 12. By the end of the third round, the number of responses had been reduced to 14 for consumer-oriented businesses, 17 for industrial businesses, and 9 for government businesses; thus, there was a high degree of commitment on the part of panel members. The researchers found a high degree of consensus in these diverse panels in over 80 percent of the questions either at the beginning or by the end of the third round. The biggest problem experienced was the amount of time the study took—nine months rather than the original estimate of six.

Application 2: Forecasting the Economy of Alaska. An interesting application of the Delphi technique was the forecast of the Alaskan economy for the year 2000 and beyond.[13] This forecast was developed by a 91-member panel drawn from several categories of decision makers, technical experts, and advocates. The large size was used in part to ensure balance of the group in expertise, in advocacy orientation, in responsibility areas represented, and in geographic affiliation. By deliberately including opposing viewpoints, the research group achieved not only appearance but also substance of objectivity. The panel developed forecasts of policies, trends, and events suitable for forecasting the dynamics of the changing Alaskan economy.

In addition to the use of a large panel, the basic Delphi technique was modified in two other ways: by conducting parallel interviews to obtain input from Alaskan natives and by designing several scenarios and using cross-impact analysis to ascertain the likelihood of future events. The research design attempted to resolve some of the problems with the Delphi method described earlier.

The innovations in this research design proved valuable. The study yielded probabilities and timing of key events in the growth of the Alaskan economy. For example, the Delphi study predicted that the population of Alaska will reach 633,000 by the year 2000. It seemed very consistent with an independent projection by the U.S. Census Bureau of 630,000. Given the insights obtained from this study, two other Delphi projects were undertaken by the Alaskan state agencies. Further, the report of this Delphi study continued to be in so much demand by both private and public sectors even a year and a half after its completion, that it had to go into a fourth printing.

SCENARIO ANALYSIS METHODS

It is quite clear that strategy analysts need to incorporate the effects of different factors when considering future strategies. If only a few factors (e.g., three to five) need to be considered, judgmental approaches may be satisfactory in any given situation; but more systematic methods are usually called for in any realistic case of environmental analysis. Scenario analysis has been developed specifically to handle such a complex situation in strategic planning. The

---

13 See Ted G. Eschienbach and George A. Geistatus, "A Delphi Forecast for Alaska," *Interfaces* 15:6 (November–December 1985): 100–109.

method involves identifying several factors that may influence the outcome of a particular strategy and considering combinations of them as a scenario. The analyst selects a few of the many possible scenarios for analysis and attempts to predict their potential.

As an example, assume that General Motors Corporation is evaluating alternative strategies for the design of its automobiles, including electric vehicles, for the next century. Naturally, this problem would call for making assumptions about the future of road transport in the country. Several factors such as the public policies toward encouraging privately owned low pollution internal-combustion-engined cars versus privately owned electric cars versus public transport, technological developments in the technology of a high-energy/high-power-density battery or an efficient low-pollution combustion engine, assumptions about the resource availability (oil and other fuels), political climate which may determine the flow of oil from the Middle East, economic growth, public attitudes toward environment and public transport, and so on. Scenario analysis is a technique that would assist in synthesizing several of these factors, taking their interdependencies into account.

More traditional methods (e.g., quantitative forecasting methods) try to extrapolate from the knowledge and experience of the past to make predictions about the future. They assume that the frameworks of the past are applicable to the future. Such an assumption is not tenable when the future world is likely to change dramatically. One way to make the forecasts more realistic is to include qualitative knowledge of current trends with the help of people directly involved with the marketplace (e.g., local managers). Even then, extrapolation can overlook new trends, risks, and opportunities that a business faces, particularly when conditions change more rapidly. Under these situations, the strategic analyst needs a method that supplements the traditional techniques. Scenario analysis serves this purpose well.

There is no single accepted procedure for implementing scenario analysis. The term *scenario* has become somewhat of a management buzzword with several meanings. In general, it is not a forecast, but a description of the possible future environment. Depending upon the forecasting task, scenarios may be quite general or very specific. For example, if the strategic task is to forecast the demand for energy in a country and the particular strategy the country may need to pursue, scenarios will be defined in terms of the world political situation and the technological development of energy sources such as solar energy; but such scenarios need not contain descriptions of specific corporate activities regarding technological investments. On the other hand, when the task is to develop forecasts for the potential sales of a significant product and to choose an appropriate strategy for the company, scenarios need to be defined not only in general terms of economic and political conditions, but also in terms of competitive situations and managerial actions. Whether general or more specific, a scenario is a written description of a

TABLE 6.6

SELECTED RESULTS FROM A SURVEY OF SCENARIO USE

All Respondents Long-range planning horizon	Fortune 1000 Industrials n=215	Fortune 500 Non- Industrials n=85	Fortune Foreign 500 Industrials n=105
3–4 years	14%	20%	5%
5 years	63%	53%	61%
6–9 years	2%	3%	3%
10 years	15%	12%	21%
Over 10 years	6%	12%	10%
Have a formal environmental unit or department	20%*	24%	44%
Users of Scenarios			
Firms that use multiple scenarios in the strategic planning process and/or for evaluating major investments, such as building a new facility, an acquisition, or a new business area.	50%**	58%	53%
Length of time that firms have been using scenarios			
• 1 to 2 years	36%	33%	21%
• 3 to 4 years	26%	22%	52%
• 5 years or over	38%	45%	27%
The extent of use for multiple scenarios in arriving at strategic decisions			
• Multiple scenarios are used on an experimental basis.	6%	7%	14%
• Multiple scenarios are used, but not regularly.	35%	37%	23%
• Multiple scenarios are used often, but are not fully integrated into the formal planning process.	34%	37%	42%
• Multiple scenarios are fully integrated into the formal planning process and are used regularly.	25%	17%	20%
• Other.	—	2%	1%
How multiple scenarios are used in arriving at strategic decisions			
• Scenarios are used to indicate new potential areas of business/product/market activity.	67%	66%	68%
• Scenarios are used to design and/or to evaluate the flexibility/adaptability/robustness of strategies.	76%	75%	79%
• Scenarios are used to evaluate the feasibility of major investments (such as building a new plant).	85%	70%	76%
All Respondents			
Planned extent of future use of multiple scenarios in the strategic planning process			
• Multiple scenarios will not be used.	11%	8%	8%
• Multiple scenarios will be attempted on an experimental basis.	20%	9%	23%
• Multiple scenarios will be used, but not regularly.	24%	30%	24%
• Multiple scenarios will be used often, but will not be fully integrated into the formal planning process.	21%	22%	20%
• Multiple scenarios will be fully integrated into the formal planning process and will be used regularly.	24%	28%	25%
• Other.	—	3%	—

*Adjusted for nonrespondent bias: 10%.

**Adjusted for nonrespondent bias: 35.

Source: Robert E. Linneman and Harold E. Klein, "Using Scenarios in Strategic Decision Making," *Business Horizons* (January–February 1985): 64–74. Reproduced with permission.

possible future environment facing the particular entity. In this sense, scenario analysis is a qualitative forecasting technique.

Industry Utilization

Table 6.6 presents some data on the degree of utilization of scenario analysis among large corporations in the United States. The typical long-range planning horizon for a majority of the Fortune 100 companies was five years, according to this survey. About one-half of the companies have used the technique in the strategic planning process and/or for evaluating major investments, such as building a new facility, acquisition, and a new business area. Among 25 percent of the companies, multiple scenarios are fully integrated into the formal planning process and are used regularly, while over a third of the companies use multiple scenarios but not on a regular basis, and over a third of the firms use multiple scenarios often although they are not fully integrated into the formal planning process. Three major uses of multiple scenarios are identification of the potential for new business opportunities; evaluation of flexibility, adaptability, or robustness of strategies; and evaluation of major investments. About one-fifth of the firms intend to use multiple scenarios on an experimental basis, while a similar number intend to use the technique less regularly. About one-quarter of the firms plan to fully integrate multiple scenarios into their formal planning process.

Methodology of Scenario Analysis

The methodology of scenario analysis consists of three phases: (1) Phase One consists of identifying the problem and relevant external influences; (2) Phase Two, called development path analysis, involves identifying paths of devel-

---

TABLE 6.7
PHASES OF SCENARIO ANALYSIS AND RELEVANT METHODS

Phase	Objective	Suitable Methods
Phase One	Analysis Phase: Problem definition Identification of relevant external influences	Brainstorming Brainwriting Delphi technique Morphological analysis
Phase Two	Development path analysis: Identification of paths for development of relevant external influences	Cross-impact analysis Battelle method (using various methods ranging from literature interpretation to formal analytical models)
Phase Three	Synthesis of influences: Selection of alternative future scenarios using various interdependencies uncovered	Cross-impact analysis and algorithms such as those employed in the Battelle method

Source: Adapted from Jutta Brauers and Martin Weber, "A New Method of Scenario Analysis for Strategic Planning," *Journal of Forecasting* 7 (January–March 1988): 31–47.

---

opment for various relevant external influences; and (3) Phase Three consists of synthesizing various influences. Suitable methods for each of these phases are shown in Table 6.7. The methods used in Phase One include brainstorming and its variations. The objective in this phase is to develop a list of external factors that are relevant to the specific forecasting problem. The second and third phases involve determination of the relative impact of the various factors on each other and synthesizing their influences; different quantitative techniques are used in these two phases. The general objective is to identify a few plausible scenarios using the data collected in Phase Two and synthesized in Phase Three. While the technique of cross-impact analysis is used in the second and third phases of scenario analysis, it can also form the core of a scenario analysis by itself.

Alternate Methods for Scenario Analysis

The various methods of scenario analysis in application can be divided into three classes: cross-impact analysis, the Battelle method, and the method developed by Brauers and Weber.[14] These methods differ in the specific techniques used in the three phases of scenario analysis, particularly in synthesizing various interdependencies between factors. There are differences in the way a scenario is defined in three methods. While cross-impact analysis defines a scenario as a combination of the presence or absence of identified events (each defined by only two outcomes), the other two methods allow for several outcomes for a factor (see Table 6.8).

Cross-impact analysis requires marginal and conditional probabilities as input for the pairs of events. Data collection for eliciting these probabilities is very demanding on the decision maker. Also, the estimates may not satisfy probability theory axioms, and consistency tests and corrections are often required. The output from this analysis is a ranking of the scenarios in terms of their likelihood of occurring in the future. Because the likelihoods for several scenarios are extremely small, individual scenarios are often grouped to represent composite scenarios.

The Battelle method, on the other hand, requires much simpler input: the compatibility estimates for every possible pair of factor outcomes. The interdependence between the individual outcomes are evaluated by experts using a five-point scale of compatibility, taking values from one to five. If two outcomes are incompatible, they are assigned a value of one. A compatibility rating of five indicates they are very compatible. The intermediate values of two, three, and four represent increasing degree of compatibility between factor outcomes. The resulting matrix of compatibility ratings (k_{ij}) is symmetric. The matrix is used to generate a number of compatible scenarios, and their average compatibility values or weights are used to represent their occurrence in the future. In this process, only a few scenarios are used for further

14 See Jutta Brauers and Martin Weber, "A New Method of Scenario Analysis for Strategic Planning," *Journal of Forecasting* 7 (January–March 1988): 31–47.

TABLE 6.8
A COMPARISON OF THREE SCENARIO ANALYSIS METHODS

Method Details	Cross-Impact Analysis	Battelle Method	Brauers and Weber Method
Identification of relevant factors	Brainstorming and similar techniques to generate a set of future events.	Same; but each factor is defined in terms of a set of possible future outcomes.	Same as the Battelle method.
Definition of a scenario	A combination of presence or absence of the identified events.	A combination of possible future outcomes of the identified factors.	Same as the Battelle method.
Data input for analysis	Marginal and conditional probabilities for the pairs of events.	Compatibility estimates for all pairs of factor outcomes.	Compatibility estimates for all pairs of factor outcomes and estimated probabilities for each outcome by factor.
Selection of scenarios	Based on the highly probable scenarios, using the estimated probabilities according to a model.	Scenarios are selected for which compatibility scores are very high based on the matrix of compatibility values for all pairs of factor outcomes.	A bounded enumeration of all possible factor outcomes is examined to check for compatibility of the scenario.
Computation of scenario probabilities	Computed according to a formal linear programming model (e.g., Sarin's or De Kluyver-Moskowitz's models).	No probabilities are computed for the scenarios.	Procedure is similar to De Kluyver-Moskowitz LP model.
Determination of some main scenarios	Selected on the basis of ranking of the scenario probabilities defined as combinations of events.	A few disparate and compatible scenarios are chosen.	Done through cluster analysis based on characteristics of scenarios in terms of factor outcomes.

investigation. Because the Battelle method does not use probabilities, the selected scenarios may in fact have very small probabilities of occurrence. The selected scenarios may not be the basis for a meaningful planning effort.

The method proposed by Brauers and Weber is generally similar to the Battelle method but differs in the way scenarios are selected and their probabilities are computed. Further, main scenarios are identified using cluster analysis, while the Battelle method chooses a few disparate and compatible scenarios as the main ones to consider for strategic purposes.

A Case History of the Use of Scenario Analysis

Battelle's method of scenario analysis was applied to the Goodyear Aerospace Corporation in forecasting the international environment and the U.S. defense expenditures to 1995.[15] The procedure involved identifying 16 key factors and trends, which Battelle calls "descriptors." These descriptors included Soviet–American strategic balance, arms control, international conflict, defense technologies, and U.S. defense expenditures in their international context. As we described earlier, the Battelle researchers prepared a five-page essay on each descriptor that explained why it was important, gave data on past trends, and projected alternative states for the descriptor for 1995, with assigned prior probabilities of their occurrence based on trend analysis and expert opinion. The alternative states are mutually exclusive and exhaustive of all reasonable possible outcomes. The prior probabilities add to 1.0 for each descriptor. In all, there were 49 possible alternative states across the 16 descriptors.

The Battelle researchers then applied the method of cross-impact analysis to determine the relative impact of each alternate state of any descriptor on those of other descriptors. The 49 × 49 matrix of cross-impacts are filled in with numbers ranging from −3 (greatly decreases) to +3 (greatly increases); each entry describes the impact of the column state on the row state of the descriptors. A section of the large cross-impact matrix is shown in Table 6.9 for two descriptors of U.S. strategic nuclear delivery vehicles and U.S. defense expenditures.

---

15 See Stephen M. Millett and Fred Randles, "Scenarios for Strategic Business Planning: A Case of History for Aerospace and Defense Companies," *Interfaces* 16:6 (November–December 1986): 64–72.

TABLE 6.9
ILLUSTRATION OF CROSS-IMPACT MATRIX

		U.S. Defense Expenditures		
		9–13% GNP	6–9% GNP	3–6% GNP
US SNDV's	2400+ (0.10)	2	−1	−2
	2000–2400 (0.30)	1	0	−1
	1700–2000 (0.40)	−1	0	1
	<1700 (0.20)	−2	−1	2

Note: This 3 × 4 matrix is a block of a larger 49 × 49 matrix. Each cell denotes the cross-impact of the column on the row.

Source: S. M. Millett and F. Randles, "Scenarios for Strategic Business Planning: A Case History for Aerospace and Defense Companies," *Interfaces* 16: 6 (November–December 1986): 64–72.

The researchers used the BASICS program to calculate all possible cross-impact index values and to adjust the prior probabilities of the alternate states of the 16 descriptors. The program ran several simulations to identify scenarios, which are combinations of the alternate states of the descriptors. The combinations occurring frequently in the simulations are deemed to be likely scenarios in the future. Based on these scenarios, the Battelle researchers can design future plans for the defense contractor firm.

The most likely future uncovered by this analysis was a combination of the following: the size of the U.S. and Soviet strategic arsenal would remain stable, the Strategic Arms Limitation Talks (SALT) regime would continue, and strategic doctrine (deterrence with a triad of strategic forces) would endure. The mainline forecast prepared in 1984 proved to be entirely correct during the first year of its 10-year period, much to the delight of the forecasters. Further, U.S. defense expenditures were forecasted to be between 3 and 6 percent of the GNP by 1995. Goodyear managers were able to incorporate the results from the scenario analysis in their yearly strategic planning. This involved their identifying the implications of the mainline forecast for market conditions and for each of their products in a systematic manner. The "This is what needs to be done" approach followed directly from an interpretation of the scenarios' answers to the question, "What are the future prospects for our products?"

Although somewhat detailed, the above description illustrates the mechanics and use of scenario planning. The reader may note that cross-impact analysis is just one part of the whole process of scenario analysis.

Illustration of Brauers-Weber Method

Brauers and Weber applied their method to a forecasting problem by considering three environmental subsystems. These subsystems are: Society, Technology, and Economy defined respectively by four, one, and two factors. Their definitions and levels for each are as follows:

Subsystem	Factor	Levels
Society	S1: Dominant political opinion	Socialist, liberal, or conservative
	S2: Government influence on the economy and society	Strong or weak
	S3: Consumer spending	Strong or weak
	S4: Environmental protection	Strong or weak
Technology	T1: Rate of technological innovation	High or low
Economy	E1: Economic growth	Rising or stagnating
	E2: Unemployment	Rising, no change or failing

TABLE 6.10

DESCRIPTION OF CENTER OF SCENARIO CLUSTER (BRAUERS AND WEBER) METHOD

Factor	Description	Minimum	Center	Maximum
S1	Political opinion	2 (liberal)	2.6	3 (conservative)
S2	Influence of government	1 (strong)	2.4	3 (weak)
S3	Consumer spending	1 (strong)	1.0	1 (strong)
S4	Environmental protection	3 (weak)	3.0	3 (weak)
T1	Rate of technological innovation	1 (high)	1.0	1 (high)
E1	Economic growth	1 (rising)	1.8	3 (stagnating)
E2	Unemployment	1 (rising)	2.2	3 (falling)

Source: Adapted from J. Brauers and M. Weber, "A New Method of Scenario Analysis for Strategic Planning," *Journal of Forecasting* (January–March 1988): 31–47 (with permission).

These factors when combined yield a total of 16 outcomes, labeled e1–e16. The analysis then consists of obtaining compatibility ratings for all pairs of the 16 factor outcomes, along with probabilities for the outcomes of each factor.

Given these data, Brauers and Weber identified 32 scenarios as compatible out of the possible 288 ($= 3 \times 2 \times 2 \times 2 \times 2 \times 2 \times 3$) scenarios of the future defined by the seven factors. The 32 scenarios are grouped into three clusters of 10, 15, and 7 scenarios. The center of the first cluster represented by the factor outcomes is shown in Table 6.10. This cluster represents the future as having conservative public opinion, relatively weak influence of government on the economy, strong consumer spending, weak protection for the environment, a high rate of technological innovation, relatively neutral economic growth, and essentially no change in unemployment. The other two clusters will yield different scenarios. The strategic analysts can utilize these three scenarios in preparing business plans.

Illustration of the Battelle Scenario Analysis

The Battelle Consulting firm has been performing scenario analysis since 1980 with an approach called BASICS (Battelle Scenario Inputs to Corporate Strategy). The method is an adaptation of the cross-impact techniques developed at the Rand Corporation and the University of Southern California. It was coupled with Battelle's computer-based algorithm developed in Geneva, Switzerland. An expert judgment methodology is also an element of the Battelle system.

This procedure was applied in 1988–1989 to the problem of evaluating the changes in the European market for an information technology company with a disguised name, REM Inc. Battelle employed three essential steps of BASICS for tackling this problem: (1) identifying the issues, (2) trend analysis, and (3) cross-impact analysis. [16]

In the first step, Battelle researchers interviewed the REM managers most familiar with the marketplace and conducted three group dynamics sessions using the Nominal Group technique (a procedure that solicits the professional judgment of experts that is similar to a focus group method). These group sessions were conducted both in Europe and the United States. The participants were drawn from REM's managers and technologists, and economists and market analysts employed at Battelle. The first step produced a list of most important factors that would determine the extent of EC single market cohesion by end of 1992.

The second step involved writing an essay on each of the 20 factors identified in the first step. These essays showing the alternative outcomes possible for each of the factors were composed by Battelle researches and other knowledgeable individuals. The outcome possibilities—equivalent to the attribute levels in conjoint analysis—were reviewed by peers in the consulting firm. A total of two to four possible outcomes were developed for each factor. Prior probabilities of occurrence of the possible outcomes by 1992 for each factor were assigned by the researchers.

The third step in the procedure was to elicit cross-impacts of change in the outcome of a factor on the outcomes of other factors. These data were elicited with the help of a computer program of the BASICS system. These judgments were made by a few individuals, and any differences were discussed and reconciled. The BASICS algorithm used these cross-impact indexes to evaluate the likely conditions for a variety of initial probabilities of factor outcomes. It also organized outcomes with high probabilities into sets that were internally consistent. Having examined the patterns, the analysts prepared a report outlining four possible principal scenarios for 1992 Europe to be used in the REM company's strategic planning. The four scenarios were as follows:

Scenario 1: EC 1992 Works. In this scenario, a single market will emerge in Europe, but it will possibly lack monetary unification. In this scenario, the information technology market in Europe will experience medium to high growth.

Scenario 2: EC 1992 Disappoints. This scenario identified a much slower emergence of a single market than Scenario 1. The information technology market was expected to grow moderately despite the slower unification.

Scenario 3: The EC Fails. This scenario painted a gloomier picture for a common market. The information technology market was expected to grow very slowly.

Scenario 4: The U.S. of Europe. This scenario showed the emergence of a common market that exceeded the expectations of Scenario 1. In addition to a common

---

16 See Stephen M. Millett, "Battelle's Scenario Analysis for a European High-Tech Market," *Planning Review* (March–April 1992): 20–24.

currency, it predicted a more unified governmental structure. The information technology market growth was expected to be high under this scenario.

This scenario analysis led the REM company management to undertake several strategic actions, such as increasing local presence in every EC country by expanding marketing and service networks, committing to expansion of its office in Brussels in order to monitor changes in the policies of the EC commission, making plans to expand capacity within one particular EC country, and the like. The firm used this procedure to do long-term planning in 1992 for EC activities in 1995.

Practical Issues in Scenario Analysis

Below, are three practical questions that arise when conducting scenario analysis, along with

1. How many scenarios should one use in the final analysis?

   The consensus with regard to this question is that three final scenarios is best; identifying more than three is not practical in a forecasting task.

2. How should the scenarios be ranked?

   The final scenarios should be ranked against each other using one of four criteria: favorability to the sponsor of the project in question, probability of occurrence of the scenarios according to a single dominant factor (such as the potential involvement of the government by regulation), or themes of the environment. The themes for arraying the scenarios could include economic expansion, technological domination, economic contraction, and the like.

   When using the criterion of favorability to the sponsor, it is useful to include an optimistic and pessimistic prediction along with a surprise-free (or base line) scenario. Various techniques are used to estimate the probability of outcome of a scenario using the methods described above.

3. How should one select scenarios?

   In the early development of the methodology of scenario analysis, highly qualitative or intuitive methods were employed in selecting the three or four scenarios to consider. But quantitative methods such as cross-impact analysis and models for estimating probabilities are now available. In general, an eclectic approach that combines both methods is highly recommended. Table 6.11 compares selected scenario-generating procedures that had been employed in various situations.

METHODS FOR FORECASTING SALES OF DURABLE PRODUCTS

The demand for durable products in any year comes from three sources: initial purchases, replacements, and additions. The contribution from the third source is usually small for most products. In the early stages of introduction,

TABLE 6.11

A COMPARISON OF SELECTED SCENARIO-GENERATING PROCEDURES

	Becker (1983)	DeKluyver (1980)	Linneman and Klein (1977)	MacNulty (1977)	Vanston et al. (1977)	Wilson (1978)	Zenter (1975)
Number of scenarios	3	3	3 or 4	3 or 4	3–6	3 or 4	3
Length of scenarios	—	—	1 or 2 paragraphs	—	7–10 pages	—	< 50 pages in all
Base scenario	Most likely	Most likely	None	Surprise-free	Most likely	Surprise-free	None
Alternative scenarios	Opt./pess.	Opt./pess.	Themed	Themed	Themed	Opt./pess.	Themed
Are probabilities assigned?	No	Yes	No	—	No	No	No
Does it use cross-impact analysis?	No	No	No	Yes	No	Yes	No
How is the number of factors reduced?	Considers only key factors.	Considers only key factors.	Considers only key factors.	They are not.	Considers many factors.	Scoring by probability and importance.	—
How are the scenarios selected?	Selects plausible combinations of key factors.	Judgmental translation into opt./pess. and most likely.	Selects plausible combinations of key factors.	Judgmental integration of trends and intuition.	To conform to the themes.	Scenario writing and cross-impact analysis.	—

Source: Adapted from Steven P. Schnaars, "How to Develop and Use Scenarios," *Long Range Planning* 20:1 (February 1987): 105–114 and Brauers and Weber, "A New Method for Scenario Analysis for Strategic Planning," *Journal of Forecasting* (January–March 1988): 31–47 (with permission).

growth, and maturity, initial (or first-time) purchases are a major component. In the later stages of life cycle (maturity and decline), replacements will become significant.

Forecasting Initial Purchases

An approach that has proven valuable in estimating initial purchases is the diffusion model of new product acceptance developed by Bass.[17] We will describe it as a major method for forecasting first-time purchases of durable goods. We will describe a procedure to estimate replacement demand using additional survey data on failure rates.

The Bass model of diffusion is essentially a model of timing of initial purchases of *new* consumer durable goods. New, generic classes of products (not new brands) are covered by this model. The model is useful in making long-range planning decisions (plant capacity expansion, etc.) for a new product. A typical pattern of first-time sales of a new durable product over time is shown in Figure 6.7. Sales grow to a peak and then level off at some magnitude lower than the peak. Stability occurs owing to relative growth replacement purchases and decline of initial purchases.

In this model, first-time sales of a new product are the result of two forces on the part of consumers: innovation and imitation. Thus, an individual's probability of buying the new product for the first time is a sum of two components: an inherent ability to innovate and an inherent ability to imitate others who bought it.

---

17 See Frank M. Bass, "A New Product Growth Model for Consumer Durables," *Management Science* 15 (January 1969): 215–227.

FIGURE 6.7

TYPICAL PATTERN FOR FIRST-TIME SALES OF NEW DURABLE PRODUCT

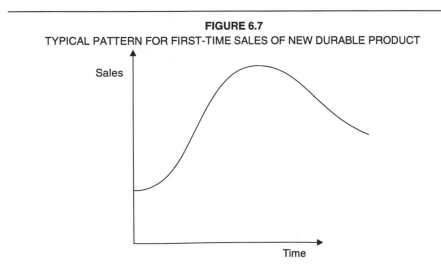

Assuming there will be a maximum of m initial purchases of the new product over the life of the product, the Bass model derives an equation for the first purchasers at any time as

$$S_T = pm + (q-p)Y_{T-1} - \left(\frac{q}{m}\right)Y_{T-1}^2$$

where:

p = coefficient of innovation for the population of consumers.
q = coefficient of imitation for the population of consumers.
Y_{T-1} = cumulative number of initial purchases up to T.
S_T = sales during the period T.

The sales curve over time will increase, reach a peak, and then decline when the imitation coefficient (q) is larger than the innovation coefficient. It will decrease continuously from the beginning, when the imitation coefficient is smaller than the innovation coefficient. These cases are shown in Figure 6.8.

The model can be estimated by a regression of S_T on Y_{T-1} and y_{T-1}^2:

$$S_T = a + bY_{T-1} + cY_{T-1}^2; \qquad T = 2,3,\ldots$$

The estimated values of a, b, and c in this regression are used to solve the parameters p, q, and m. The equations used are $a = pm$; $b = q - p$; and $c = \dfrac{-q}{m}$.

Solving for m using: $b = q - p = -cm - \dfrac{a}{m}$, we get:

$$m = \frac{b \pm \sqrt{b^2 - 4ca}}{2c}$$

FIGURE 6.8

TWO CASES OF THE FIRST-TIME SALES OF A NEW DURABLE PRODUCT
ACCORDING TO THE BASS MODEL

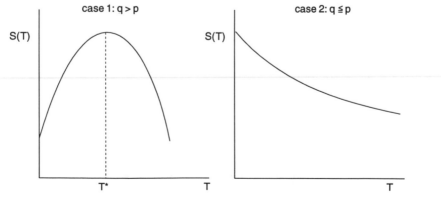

The values of parameters a, b, and c can be employed in making sequential predictions of sales.

The model can be used to predict when the sales are likely to reach a maximum. This information is useful in building up adequate capacity in the industry. For $q \leq p$, sales will decline over time; maximum occurs in the initial period. For $q > p$, maximum occurs when the cumulative sales reach the level of $m\left(\dfrac{q-p}{2q}\right)$ (approximately $\dfrac{m}{2}$ for most products since $q > p$). The peak value of $S(T)$ occurs when $T = T^* = \dfrac{q}{q}\ln\left(\dfrac{q+p}{p}\right)$ and the sales level at the peak is $S(T^*) = \dfrac{m(q+p)^2}{4q}$. Figure 6.9 graphically estimates peak time. Several estimates were made of the model for various products and services with good results. Our previous discussion of forecasting HDTV sales utilizes this model.

Estimating Replacements

Using a survey of ownership of durable goods, one can estimate the age distribution of existing durable goods. These data can be used to estimate the failure rate of the durable good at each age. If necessary, technical sources can also be utilized.

The data would look like the table below for a durable good in year 4.

Age	Failure Rate	# with Age
1	0.1	100
2	0.2	90

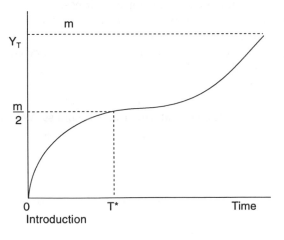

FIGURE 6.9

CUMULATIVE FIRST-TIME SALES OF NEW DURABLE PRODUCT
(BASS MODEL FOR q >P)

Age	Failure Rate	# with Age
3	0.4	72
4	1.0	43
Total		305
Population		

Estimate of number of units replaced next year (year 5) = $100 \times 0.1 + 90 \times .2 + 72 \times .4 + 43 \times 1.0 = 90.8$.

Final Forecast

The final forecast for any given year is obtained by adding the estimates of first-time purchases and replacements of the durable product.

SUMMARY

This chapter covered a variety of techniques for developing forecasts useful for strategic planning. The methods described include formal quantitative techniques such as trend extrapolation and regression as well as methods of analogy and Delphi. These methods are equally applicable for forecasting sales of a product and technological trends. We developed a taxonomy of various forecasting techniques that span the criteria of the availability of historical data, type of data available, and the availability of data on analogous situations.

We then described a set of methods known as scenario analysis applicable to combining expectations of the impact of several factors. These judgmental methods involve identifying various factors relevant to any complex forecasting situation and determining their impacts on each other. The data on their relative impact are synthesized to develop a small number of scenarios that are more plausible in the future. These scenarios then become the basis for developing any contingent strategies for a business.

The problem of forecasting the sales of durable products requires special attention due to the inherent diffusion processes involved in the adoption of a new durable good. We described methods useful in forecasting the diffusion of a new durable good as well as in forecasting sales due to replacement.

The discussion in this chapter and the previous chapter covers an array of methods available to a strategic analyst in understanding and forecasting the various environmental forces that affect any business. We now turn to the methods for determining the strengths and weaknesses of competitors to a business.

APPENDIX: DESCRIPTIONS, ADVANTAGES, AND DISADVANTAGES OF SELECTED METHODS OF FORECASTING

Technique	Description	Main Advantages	Main Disadvantages
A. Trend Extrapolation			
Linear Trend Fitting	A line is fitted to the data by minimizing the squared error between the estimated curve and actual observations.	Logically reproducible. Can apply to most series.	Poor turning point indication.
Exponential Trend Fitting	An exponential curve is fitted to the data.	The curve has known properties.	Projections may be much higher than actual, given the exponential growth.
B. Regression			
Simple Regression	Functionally relates sales to one explanatory variable (economic, competitive, etc.).	Statistical estimates of confidence can be developed.	May not be possible to forecast explanatory variables with adequate accuracy.
		True causal relationships should be more stable and lead to more accurate forecasts.	High degree of statistical competence needed.
Multiple Regression	Functionally relates sales to more than one explanatory variable and takes into account the explanatory variable's intercorrelations.	Allows more than one explanatory variable.	May not be possible to forecast explanatory variables.
		Same as simple regression.	High degree of statistical expertise required.
C. Analogy			
Method of Analogy	Attempts to find relationships in past known situations and uses them in forecasting for a new product or technology.	Uses past information even when the product/technology is new.	Difficult to find analogous situations.
		Offers some basis for developing forecasts.	Conditions relevant to past products may not apply to current situation.
D. Delphi			
Conventional Delphi	Attempts to elicit expert opinion in a systematic manner by use of questionnaire; feeds back iteratively until convergence of opinion or point of diminishing returns.	Eliminates relationship interactions.	Forecasts cannot be made rapidly.
		May take into account factors difficult to quantify.	May be difficult to obtain cooperation.
Panel Consensus	Group forecast by experts who have defended their thinking to each other.	Check and balance of several opinions.	Relationship interactions may give poor forecast.
		May take into account factors difficult to quantify.	Rapid forecast may not be possible.

BIBLIOGRAPHY

Armstrong, J. Scott. *Long-Range Forecasting from Crystal Ball to Computer.* 2d ed. New York: Wiley, 1985.

Bayus, Barry L. "High-Definition Television: Demand Forecasts for Next Generation Consumer Durable." *Management Science* 39 (November 1993): 1319–1333.

Becker, Harold S. "A Tool of Growing Importance to Policy Analysis." *Technological Forecasting and Social Change* 23 (May 1983): 95–120.

Brauers, Jutta, and Martin Weber. "A New Method of Scenario Analysis for Strategic Planning." *Journal of Forecasting* 7 (January–March 1988): 31–47.

Cazes, Bernard. "The Future of Work: An Outline of a Method for Scenario Construction." *Futures* (October 1976): 405–410.

Dalkey, Norman. "An Elementary Cross-Impact Model." *Technological Forecasting and Social Change* 3:3 (1972): 341–351.

Duperin, J.C., and M. Godet. "SMIC 74—A Method for Constructing and Ranking Scenarios." *Futures* (August 1975): 302–312.

Gershuny, J. "The Choice of Scenarios." *Futures* (December 1976): 496–508.

Gordon, T.J., and H. Hayward. "Initial Experiments with the Cross-Impact Matrix Method of Forecasting." *Futures* 1 (December 1968): 100–116.

Helmer, Olaf. "Reassessment of Cross-Impact Analysis." *Futures* 13 (October 1981): 389–400.

Huss, William R. "A Move Toward Scenario Analysis." *International Journal of Forecasting* 4:3 (1988): 377–388.

Jackson, J. Edward, and William H. Lawton. "Some Probability Problems Associated with Cross-Impact Analysis." *Technological Forecasting and Social Change* 8:3 (1976): 263–273.

Johnson, Jeffrey L. "A Ten-Year Delphi Forecast in the Electronics Industry." *Industrial Marketing Management* 5 (February 1976): 45–52.

Linneman, Robert E., and Harold E. Klein. "The Use of Multiple Scenarios by U.S. Industrial Companies: A Comparison Study, 1977–1981." *Long Range Planning* 16:6 (December 1983): 94–101.

————"Using Scenarios in Strategic Decision Making." *Business Horizons* (January–February 1985): 64–74.

Lootsma, F.A., P.G.M. Boonekamp, R. M. Cooke, and F. Van Oostvoorn. "Choice of a Long-Term Strategy for the National Electricity Supply via Scenario Analysis and Multicriteria Analysis." *European Journal of Operational Research* 48 (September 1990): 189–203.

Mahajan, Vijay, Eitan Mueller, and Frank M. Bass. "New Product Diffusion Models in Marketing: A Review and Directions for Research." *Journal of Marketing* 54 (January 1990): 1–26.

Martino, Joseph P., and Kuei-Lin Chen. "Cluster Analysis of Cross-Impact Model Scenarios." *Technological Forecasting and Social Change* 12 (June 1978): 61–71.

Millett, Stephen M. "Battelle's Scenario Analysis of a European High-Tech Market." *Planning Review* (March–April 1992): 20–24.

Millett, Steven M., and Fred Randles. "Scenarios for Strategic Business Planning: A Case History for Aerospace and Defense Companies." *Interfaces* 16 (November–December 1986): 64–72.

Mitchell, R.B., and J. Tydeman. "Subjective Conditional Probability Modeling." *Technological Forecasting and Social Change* 11: 2 (1978): 133–152.

Mitchell, Robert B., John Tydeman, and John Georgiades. "Structuring the Future Application of a Scenario-Generation Procedure." *Technological Forecasting and Social Change* 14 (September 1979): 409–428.

Rao, T.R. "Scenarios for the Indian Iron and Steel Industry." *Long Range Planning* 17:4 (August 1984): 91–101.

Sanders, Nada R., and Karl B. Mandrot. "Forecasting Practices in U.S. Corporations: Survey Results." *Interfaces* 24 (March–April 1994): 92–100.

Sarin, Rakesh K. "A Sequential Approach to Cross-Impact Analysis." *Futures* 10 (February 1978): 53–62.

Schnaars, Steven P. "How to Develop and Use Scenarios." *Long Range Planning* 20:1 (February 1987): 105–114.

Schnaars, Steven P., and Conrad Berenson. "Growth Market Forecasting Revisited: A Look Back at a Look Forward." *California Management Review* 27 (Summer 1986): 71–88.

Turoff, Murray. "An Alternative Approach to Cross-Impact Analysis." *Technological Forecasting and Social Change* 3:3 (1972): 309–339.

Wise, George. "The Accuracy of Technological Forecasts, 1890–1940." *Futures* (October 1976): 411–419.

CHAPTER 7

Analyzing Strengths and Weaknesses: How Will We Compete?

INTRODUCTION

A successful marketing strategy involves identifying a sustainable competitive advantage and implementing programs to accomplish it. In pursuit of such advantage, businesses utilize certain assets, skills, and resources in carrying out policies to reach their goals. Once a firm has analyzed its skills and resources relative to those of its competitors, it can identify relative strengths (areas in which its skills and resources exceed those of its competitors) and weaknesses (areas in which the competitors' skills and resources exceed those of the firm). The firm must then apply its strengths and minimize the impact of its weaknesses in order to deliver its products and services at lower cost or to provide superior customer value by differentiating them in a meaningful way. For example, Toshiba is an expert in miniaturization technology. This enables them to produce small, light, notebook computers that work efficiently.

Whatever advantages a company employs will produce marketplace results. The profits derived from the marketplace results are used to sustain or improve the business's strengths and lessen its weaknesses in a cyclical manner (see the framework in Figure 7.1).

The skills and resources useful in this process can range from things as tangible and concrete as money and superior technology to things as procedural and attitudinal as how a company serves and generally relates to its customers and employees. For example, if a company involves its customers in its design process, it has a better chance of producing winning products. Products such as Gillette's Sensor razor, Reebok's Pump sneaker, Motorola's MicroTac cellular phone, and IBM's ThinkPad computer have all been developed with the use of ethnographic techniques such as videotaping human behavior and observing the work environment.[1] Furthermore, the early suc-

FIGURE 7.1
THE ELEMENTS OF COMPETITIVE ADVANTAGE

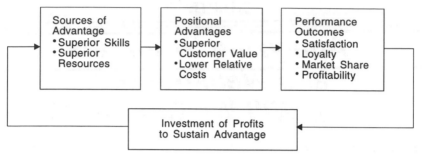

Source: George S. Day and Robin Wensley, "Assessing Advantage: A Framework for Diagnosing Competitive Strategy," *Journal of Marketing* 92 (April 1988). Reprinted with permission, American Marketing Association.

cess of the Saturn automobile was attributed to the degree of control employees had in running the company. They were involved in selecting suppliers, future products, and advertising campaigns. Employee enthusiasm enabled Saturn to become one of the highest quality cars made in the United States.[2]

Competitors always strive to erode a firm's competitive advantage. Therefore, profits derived from the application of skills and resources and the attainment of superior cost or differentiation positions must be reinvested to reaffirm the skills and resources that led to the profits in the first place (or perhaps to develop new ones). Consider the contrasting experiences of Honda and EMI, a Japanese and a British company, in the American market.[3] In the face of a stagnant market dominated by American and British producers of large motorcycles used largely for primary transportation, Honda produced smaller bikes that appealed to the middle class as secondary, recreational vehicles. They mass-produced, lowered costs, employed heavy advertising and extensive distribution, and consequently produced superior customer value. The profits generated from initial success were reinvested to cut costs further and to develop new models for specialized use (e.g., dirt bikes). Honda was always a step ahead on the differentiation treadmill.

EMI, on the other hand, developed the CT scanner for a welcoming and waiting market. Being the technology pioneer, they concentrated on sales and production. But before long, companies like General Electric leapfrogged EMI in technology, and their competitive advantage was gone. There was no reason

1   "Hot Products," *Business Week* (June 7, 1993): 54–57.

2   "Saturn: Labor's Love Lost?" *Business Week* (February 8, 1993): 122–123.

3   See Note on the Motorcycle Industry—1975, Intercollegiate Case Clearing House, Boston, MA: Harvard Business School, and EMI and the CT Scanner (B), Intercollegiate Case Clearing House 9-383-195, Boston, MA: Harvard Business School, 1978.

for anyone to buy an EMI CT scanner. The moral of the Honda and EMI stories is that if a skill or resource is to become a sustainable advantage, it must be nurtured, not neglected.

According to Howard Stevenson, skills and resources can take any of three forms of an attribute, all of which begin with E: *Existence, Efficiency,* and *Effectiveness.*[4] Consider a personal computer manufacturer. An example of a resource of the existence type is whether or not the company offers 24-hour technical support. How many support calls that same technical staff can handle in an hour is an example of an efficiency skill. Finally, the overall quality of support service (perhaps reflected as proportion of problems solved) is an example of an effectiveness skill.

Firms must try to participate in those segments in which its skills and resources can produce competitive advantages. Figure 7.1 suggests some key questions for management to consider in the pursuit of this endeavor. Corresponding to each of the three major boxes in the figure, these questions include What skills and resources are necessary to compete successfully in a given segment? How can we assess our cost and customer value positions? and How can we assess our major performance outcomes? The focus of this chapter is on approaches that can provide answers to these questions. Table 7.1 lists the methods that will be discussed along with the appropriate data sources for each approach.

SKILLS AND RESOURCES ON WHAT DIMENSIONS?

The number of assets, skills, or resources that can be used to assess potential strengths and weaknesses is as large as the number of dimensions on which firms differ. Because of the vast number of dimensions on which firms may differ, the literature contains a myriad of checklist models, such as the one in Table 7.2. Some of the better known ones include Ansoff's Grid of Competencies[5] and The Marketing Audit.[6] Each of these checklists provides a framework useful for searching out competitive advantages.

Does a firm need to be superior to its competitors on all (or even most) of these dimensions in order to gain competitive advantage? The answer is clearly no. Firms with different competitive advantages coexist in a variety of industries. Consider the laptop (notebook) computer industry. Japanese and American firms divide this market almost in half. The Japanese firms have much greater expertise in design and manufacturing than the American firms. Producing small computers would be next to impossible without the miniaturization techniques that the Japanese electronic firms mastered in calcula-

4   Howard H. Stevenson, "Defining Corporate Strengths and Weaknesses," *Sloan Management Review* (Spring 1976): 51–68.

5   H. Igor Ansoff, *The New Corporate Strategy* (New York: Wiley, 1988).

6   Philip Kotler, William Gregor, and William Rogers, "The Marketing Audit Comes of Age," *Sloan Management Review* (Winter 1977): 25–43.

TABLE 7.1

METHODS FOR ASSESSING STRENGTHS AND WEAKNESSES

Method	Data Source
IDENTIFYING CRITICAL SKILLS AND RESOURCES	
Judgmental comparison of successful and unsuccessful competitors	Managerial judgment
Value-chain analysis	Managerial judgment
CSF Method	Structured interviews
Sensitivity analysis	Managerial judgment
Elasticity analysis	Internal historical data
PIMS analysis	Surveys collected from participating companies
Project NEWPROD	Surveys collected from participating companies
Conjoint analysis	Primary consumer data
Perceptual mapping	Primary consumer data
ASSESSING STRENGTHS AND WEAKNESSES IN COMPETITIVE POSITION	
Judgmental evaluation of positional advantage	Managerial judgment
Market share	Secondary data
Order of entry	Secondary data
Dollarmetric measurement of brand equity	Primary consumer data
Extension-based measurement of brand equity	Primary consumer data
Brand-specific constants (conjoint analysis)	Primary consumer data
Experience curve	Historical cost data
ASSESSING STRENGTHS AND WEAKNESSES IN PERFORMANCE OUTCOMES	
Customer satisfaction surveys	Primary customer data

tors, camcorders, and watches. Furthermore, the Japanese possess the ability to produce better LCD screens. On the other hand, the American firms possess superior technology in producing miniature disk drives. In addition, spearheaded by Apple and IBM, the American firms are light-years ahead of the Japanese in marketing. Finally, Intel remains the world's major source of microprocessor chips. The coexistence of all these firms would not be possible if any one had to dominate on all dimensions.[7]

---

7   "Laptops Take Off," *Business Week* (March 18, 1991): 118–124.

TABLE 7.2
A CHECKLIST OF ASSETS AND SKILLS

Research and Development (Innovation)	Production (Manufacturing)	Finance	Organization (Management)	Marketing Skills	Relations with External Entities
Technical Resources	Cost Structure Experience Process efficiency	Access to Capital From operations	Organizational Synergies	Customer Orientation	Customers Loyalty
Technological ability	Scale	From parent	Key people Loyalty	Segment Choice	Retailers
Patents	economies Access to raw material	From net short-term assets	Knowledge of business	New Product Development	Distributors
Key People			Quality of	Marketing	Banks
Financial Resources Internally generated Government supplied	Product Quality Flexibility Workforce Attitudes and Motivation Capacity	Ability to use both debt and equity	Planning Process Speed of Response Culture Entrepreneurial thrust	Research Reputations Brand-name Quality Advertising Sales Force Size Customer Service Product Line Breadth	Political Figures

Source: Adapted from Donald R. Lehmann and Russell S. Winer, *Analysis for Marketing Planning,* 3d ed. (Homewood, IL: Irwin, 1994).

In contrast, a single dimension of superiority may not be quite enough. In one study, David A. Aaker found that firms tend to use between four and five assets on average in attempting to create competitive advantage.[8] IBM has several strengths that enable it to continue, even in times of trouble. These include a huge software business (over $11 billion in revenue), semiconductor technology (IBM is still the world's largest chip maker), research labs (employing three Nobel Prize winners), the brand name (none carries more weight in the computer industry), and unmatched global marketing and service.[9]

So we are left with the question of which dimensions are most relevant in creating competitive advantage in any given industry. These *critical* or *key success factors* represent the dimensions on which measuring strengths and weaknesses is most critical.

8　David A. Aaker, "Managing Assets and Skills: The Key to a Sustainable Competitive Advantage," *California Management Review* (Winter 1989): 91–106.

9　"The Hunt for Mr. X: Who Can Run IBM?" *Fortune* (February 22, 1993): 68–71.

Critical or key success factors have been defined as:

the limited number of areas in which results, if they are satisfactory, will ensure successful competitive performance for the organization. They are the few key areas where "things must go right" for the business to flourish. If results in these areas are not adequate, the organization's efforts will be less than desired.[10]

the handful of skills and resources that will exert the most leverage on positional advantage and performance outcomes. These . . . must be managed obsessively to ensure success. Poor performance on these factors will almost certainly mean failure.[11]

Judgmental Identification of Critical Success Factors

Some authors contend that critical success factors are obvious to the firms participating in an industry.[12] This is a dangerous view. The judgment involved in assessing one of these "obvious" factors may well be flawed. Indeed, the behavioral sciences have long established that human judgment exhibits systematic errors that result in known biases.[13] One of those biases most relevant to identifying critical success factors stems from the excessive weight managers may give to vivid information.

The importance of the vividness of information can be illustrated in a study one of us performed with Rashi Glazer and Russ Winer.[14] The researchers supplied half of the decision makers in a simulated environment with a perceptual map, vivid in its pictorial nature. The other half did not have access to it. Those that had access to the map made decisions consistent with its implications. However, they did not perform as well in the market. The reason for this was that the market was extremely sensitive to sales force expenditures, decisions that the map had no information about. But decision makers with the vivid information did not do as well in the market because it distracted them from what was really important. On the other hand, decision makers without the map paid more attention to other aspects of the decisions that were more important.

The prevalence of such biases suggests that methods for determining which of those success factors are critical or key, other than unstructured judgment,

---

10 John F. Rockart, "Chief Executives Define Their Own Data Needs," *Harvard Business Review* 57 (March–April 1979): 85.

11 George S. Day, *Market Driven Strategy: Processes for Creating Value* (New York: Free Press, 1990): 136.

12 See, for example, Charles W. Hofer and Dan Schendel, *Strategy Formulation: Analytical Concepts* (St. Paul, MN: West Publishing, 1977).

13 Extensive discussions of biases can be found in Daniel Kahnemann, Paul Slovic, and Amos Tversky, *Judgment Under Uncertainty: Heuristics and Biases* (Cambridge, England: Cambridge University Press, 1982) and Amos Tversky and Daniel Kahnemann, "Judgment Under Uncertainty: Heuristics and Biases," *Science* 185 (1974): 1124–1131.

14 Rashi Glazer, Joel H. Steckel, and Russell S. Winer, "Locally Rational Decision Making: The Distracting Effect of Information on Managerial Performance," *Management Science* 38 (February 1992): 212–226.

could be very useful. Aaker suggests that a way to frame the analysis (or structure judgment) is simply to compare the successful firms in an industry with the unsuccessful ones and see how they differ.[15] These differences can suggest what the critical or key success factors are. While this is a very powerful idea, additional structured approaches and frameworks can help implement it more successfully. In the next sections, we present a theoretical framework (the Value Chain), two ways to elicit managerial judgment (the Critical Success Factor Method and Sensitivity Analysis), a more empirical approach (Elasticity Analysis), and the results of two large-scale empirical investigations (the PIMS project and Project NewProd), all of which are potentially useful in isolating critical or key success factors.

The Value Chain

Michael Porter describes a firm as "a collection of activities that are performed to design, produce, market, deliver, and support its product."[16] The value chain, depicted in Figure 7.2, represents the interrelationships of these activities. Porter argues that, if a firm is to gain competitive advantage, it must perform one or more of these activities either better or at a lower cost than its competitors.

As Figure 7.2 suggests, the activities of the value chain can be divided into two major categories: primary and support activities. Primary activities are those performed in the physical creation and transfer of the product to the consumer in usable form. Inbound logistics involve the collection of inputs to the product; operations represent the transformation of the inputs to output which is delivered via outbound logistics. Consumers are made aware of the product through marketing, and sales and service ensures that the product reaches the consumer in workable form. Each of these primary value-producing activities requires purchased materials, some form of technology, and people to implement it. Thus, these are the support activities. The vertical dotted lines suggest that each support activity can be associated with each primary activity as well as the chain as a whole. For example, technology can be developed to both produce (operations) and deliver (outbound logistics) the product. Omaha Steaks International sells premium quality meats through the mail. They had to develop ways to nourish their cattle as well as get their steaks to the public fresh.

The value chain activities can be analyzed as to whether they are critical or key success factors. Do they provide opportunities for differentiation or cost reduction?

For example, in the late 1970s, Savin went from a minor plain paper copier company, in an industry dominated by Xerox, to a major force with $200 million in annual sales (up from $63 million) within two years.[17] Their leading

---

15 David A. Aaker, "Managing Assets and Skills: The Key to a Sustainable Competitive Advantage," *California Management Review* (Winter 1989): 91–106.

16 Michael E. Porter, *Competitive Advantage* (New York: Free Press, 1985): 36.

FIGURE 7.2
THE GENERIC VALUE CHAIN

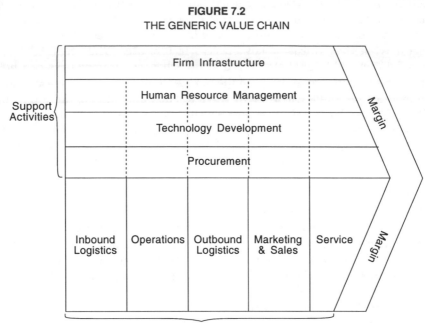

Source: Michael E. Porter, *Competitive Advangage* (New York: Free Press, 1985):37. Reprinted with permission.

products used a liquid toner technology that the industry had avoided until that time because of uneven copy quality. This technology change, coupled with changes in manufacturing, distribution, and service approaches, enabled Savin to offer its machines at a much lower price. Savin took a different approach from Xerox at almost every stage of the value chain. Not only did it change technology, Savin also emphasized low-cost standardized parts (inbound logistics), low-cost foreign assembly (operations), independent distributors (outbound logistics), and equipment sale (marketing and sales). In contrast, Xerox emphasized customized parts, domestic assembly, a direct sales force, and equipment leasing. Customers placed less of a value on the copy quality than they did on price. By 1978, Xerox's market share in the low end shrank to 10 percent.

In any event, thoughtful examination of the value chain should lead to an identification of the assets and skills that are critical for success.

---

17 This example is drawn from Roberto Buaron, "How to Win the Market-Share Game? Try Changing the Rules," *Management Review* 70 (January 1981): 8–19.

The Critical Success Factor (CSF) Method

What has come to be called *the* Critical Success Factor Method (but is actually only one of many techniques that can be used to uncover critical success factors) grew out of a cooperative program by an MIT research team during the mid-1970s. The program was directed at establishing managerial information needs to structure an information system.[18]

The CSF method involves a series of structured dialogues or interviews between a skilled interviewer and the key managers in a business. The interviews are conducted in two or three separate sessions. In the first, the manager's goals are recorded, and those CSFs that relate to the achievement of those goals are discussed. The discussion proceeds in depth so that the CSFs are clarified, combined, restated, or eliminated. The second session is used to review the results of the first. It is an opportunity to refine the set of CSFs after the analyst has had a chance to think about them.

Rockart reports on the application of the CSF method to a major electronics company. He cites seven critical factors: (1) strong field sales force, (2) good customer relations, (3) improved productivity, (4) government R&D support, (5) new products, (6) new technological capabilities, and (7) improved facilities.[19]

The CSF method has several advantages and disadvantages.[20] It is efficient in terms of time required (three to six hours). Foremost among the advantages, however, is that it is usually received enthusiastically by management. The major weakness appears to be that managers who may not be involved with the totality of the business can find it difficult to deal with the conceptual nature of CSFs.

Sensitivity Analysis

Sensitivity analysis uses financial or performance statements (such as the income statement, balance sheet, market share analyses, etc.) as a point of departure. The manager examines each component of the statement and asks What If? for each. In other words, the manager's job is to imagine how a certain change in each component would impact all the remaining components of the statement. Those that have the greatest impact on the performance measure are candidates for critical or key success factors.

Sensitivity analysis suffers from several major limitations. First, it is limited to those factors that are quantifiable and can be arithmetically related to performance in some formal reporting mechanism. Second, being judgmentally based, sensitivity analysis is vulnerable to any of the many documented judgmental biases. Third, it essentially examines only one variable at a time.

---

18 See John F. Rockart, "Chief Executives Define Their Own Data Needs," *Harvard Business Review* 57 (March–April 1979): 81–93, for a discussion of the method and its background.

19 *Ibid.*

20 These are discussed by Andrew C. Boynton and Robert W. Zmud, "An Assessment of Critical Success Factors," *Sloan Management Review* 25 (Summer 1984): 17–27.

Fourth, since sensitivity analysis focuses on one income statement, it is very difficult to see how a company compares to its competitors. The next technique, elasticity analysis, attempts to formalize the spirit of sensitivity analysis while alleviating the second limitation.

Elasticity Analysis

Elasticity analysis depends on the existence of sufficient historical data on performance measures and the factors that might influence them. It stems from a regression model of the form

(% change in performance measure)=e_0+e_1(% change in potential success factor 1)+e_2(% change in potential success factor 2) +......+e_k(% change in potential success factor k).

The coefficients, the e's, reflect the percent change in the performance measure resulting from a 1 percent change in each of the potential success factors. This conforms to the economic definition of elasticity, hence the name of the technique. Of course, the most critical success factors are those for which the e's are highest in absolute value.

For example, if one were to perform an elasticity analysis of the notebook computer market, one might regress percent change in profit or market share against percent change in production costs, percent change in R&D expenditures, percent change in advertising, percent change in price, and so on. The variables with the highest coefficients would warrant special attention.

PIMS Analyses

While critical or key success factors certainly vary from industry to industry, or even firm to firm, it stands to reason that there are some things that are necessary (or perhaps sufficient) for *any* business to succeed. The PIMS (Profit Impact of Market Strategy) project database allows one to investigate these factors. Researchers affiliated with the Strategic Planning Institute have built regression models that analyze data from over 3,000 strategic business units (in approximately 500 companies covering a wide variety of industries) in an attempt to determine those factors that explain differences in profitability among various kinds of businesses. Buzzell and Gale[21] and Kerin, Mahajan, and Varadarajan[22] review the spectrum of factors that seem to govern profitability. It seems that profitability is positively related to market share, product quality, degree of vertical integration (in mature markets only), market growth rate, R&D (in mature markets), and breadth of product line (in growing markets). Profitability is negatively related to costs, vertical integration (in growing markets), and investment intensity (net assets per dollar value added).

---

21 Robert D. Buzzell and Bradley T. Gale, *The PIMS Principles: Linking Strategy to Performance* (New York: Free Press, 1987).

22 Roger A. Kerin, Vijay Mahajan, and P. Rajan Varadarajan, *Contemporary Perspectives on Strategic Market Planning* (Boston: Allyn and Bacon, 1990).

The PIMS project can only provide a starting point for any analysis of success factors. Its results are very general. Any specific firm or industry will face requirements that include some of those implied by PIMS and others that are not. Furthermore, PIMS suffers from a number of limitations;[23] it uses the SBU as a level of analysis and ignores any synergies that SBUs within a firm may have; it treats a set of extremely diverse firms as being of the same population without the appropriate statistical tests; the data are based on single time periods; and there are statistical problems (e.g., multicollinearity) in the regressions.

Do these limitations render the PIMS results useless? Absolutely not! They merely highlight the proper role of PIMS in assessing critical success factors. It provides a starting point, no more, no less.

Project NewProd

Project NewProd, conducted by Robert G. Cooper, is offered in the same spirit as the PIMS project. Like PIMS, it is essentially an empirical multifirm, multi-industry investigation into what separates successful and unsuccessful products.[24] As such, it is very general and may not apply to any given firm or industry. Nevertheless, like PIMS, it can provide a starting point.

The most recent results of the project are summarized in Table 7.3.[25] It appears that the single most critical success factor is product superiority and quality: the competitive advantage the product has by virtue of its features, benefits, quality, uniqueness, and so on. Cooper suggests that this is often so obvious it tends to be overlooked. Project/company fit (i.e., synergies with existing business) also plays a critical role as does the economic advantage the product affords the customer.

An Important Limitation

The methods for isolating critical success factors described to this point suffer from an important limitation. They all focus on the way business *has been* done. In particular, Sensitivity Analysis, PIMS, and Project NewProd focus on historical data. The CSF method emphasizes information needs for the company as it is operating at the time the analysis is being performed. None of these methods lend themselves to answering the question What factors are critical in the acceptance of a really innovative offering?

If in the plain paper copier example, Savin had focused on historical business or "current" information needs, they never would have been able to isolate the critical success factors for success of their new strategy. In terms of the methods we have already discussed, their only hope would have been a

---

23 *Ibid*, pp. 168–173 for further discussion.

24 See Robert G. Cooper, "The Dimensions of Industrial New Product Success and Failure," *Journal of Marketing* 43 (Summer 1979): 93–103 for full details.

25 See Robert G. Cooper, "The NewProd System: The Industry Experience," *Journal of Product Innovation Management* 9 (June 1992): 113–127.

TABLE 7.3
PROJECT NEWPROD SUMMARY

Factor Name and Description	Relative Value of the Factor
Product Superiority/Quality. The competitive advantage the product has by virtue of features, benefits, quality, uniqueness, etc.	1.48
Overall Company/Project Fit. The product's synergy with the company—marketing, managerial, business fit.	1.19
Economic Advantage to the User. The product's value for money for the customer.	0.86
Market Need, Growth, and Size. The magnitude of the market opportunity.	0.70
Familiarity to the Company. How familiar or "close to home" the project is to the company (as opposed to new or "step out").	0.49
Defined Opportunity. Whether the product has a well-defined category and established market (as opposed to a true innovation and new category of products).	0.30
Competitive Situation. How easy the market is to penetrate from a competitive standpoint (as opposed to a tough and competitive market).	0.25
Project Definition. How well defined the product and project are.	0.23
Technological Compatibility. The technological synergy with the company—R&D, engineering, production fit.	0.23

Note: Factors not discriminating between success and failure include technical complexity and magnitude, product customness, product determinateness, existence of a dominant competitor, proficiency of production start-up, proficiency of precommercialization activities, and product uniqueness/first to market.

Source: Adapted from Robert G. Cooper, "The Dimensions of Industrial New Product Success and Failure," *Journal of Marketing* 43 (Summer 1979) and Robert G. Cooper, "The NewProd System: The Industry Experience," *Journal of Product Innovation Management* 9 (June 1992).

value chain analysis. There, they could have asked the questions How can we provide value to our customers? and What do we need to be able to do to provide this value? Greater insight about these questions can be gained from an intensive study of consumer preferences.

Consumer Preference Models

Consumer input can be essential in determining the skills and assets that a business needs to develop. This input usually comes in the form of a "market-back" approach where the analyst begins with analyses of customer motivations within given market segments and works backward to the company to identify those benefits the company needs to deliver and the assets needed to deliver them. For example, if the major buying criterion for a snack food is freshness, companies participating in that category will need to develop packaging and preservatives that can keep the product fresh as well as distribution channels that get the product from factory to shelf as quickly as possible.

Given the role customer motivations play in determining the assets or skills the company needs to possess, any method that helps diagnose these motivations can be valuable in assessing a firm's strengths and weaknesses. The methods for assessing consumer preferences described in Chapter 2 certainly fall into this category. In particular, conjoint analysis and perceptual mapping give insight into how a customer would choose from among alternative offerings.

ASSESSING STRENGTHS AND WEAKNESSES IN COMPETITIVE POSITION

Once critical success factors have been identified, the manager must then assess how his or her firm and its competitors compare with respect to these factors. This comparison will hopefully reveal a positional advantage for the firm in question: something it does that either provides superior customer value or enables it to sell the product at a lower price. Not surprisingly, this assessment and comparison is most often judgmentally based. However, there are other concepts and analytic tools that can reveal advantage as a natural consequence of market evolution (market share, order of entry); as a consequence of greater brand equity; or as a consequence of lower costs, as modeled by the experience curve. After discussing the problems endemic to using judgment in this task, we discuss these other tools and concepts.

Judgmental Evaluation of Positional Advantages

It stands to reason that if management's judgment in identifying critical success factors is limited, it should be limited in the process of evaluating firms on the critical success factors as well. Consequently, errors and biases can affect the assessment of relative strengths and weaknesses of a firm and its competitors. One of the biases most relevant to this part of the strategic planning process is the *self-serving bias*,[26] the tendency for individuals to take credit for their successes but to deny responsibility for their failures. Such a tendency necessarily clouds a manager's judgment about what factors lead to successful performance.[27]

Howard H. Stevenson performed a study demonstrating that managers' perceptions of strengths and weaknesses of their firms are strongly biased by factors associated with the individual.[28] In particular, he showed that an individual's position in the organization, perceived role, and type of responsibility have a huge impact on the factors he or she presumes are critical for

---

26 The self-serving bias is discussed extensively in Susan T. Fiske and Shelley E. Taylor, *Social Cognition*, second ed. (New York: McGraw-Hill, 1991).

27 The self-serving bias is demonstrated for marketing decision making by Mary T. Curren, Valerie S. Folkes, and Joel H. Steckel, "Explanations for Successful and Unsuccessful Marketing Decisions: The Decision Maker's Perspective," *Journal of Marketing* 56 (April 1992): 8–31.

28 Howard H. Stevenson, "Defining Corporate Strengths and Weaknesses," *Sloan Management Review* (Spring 1976): 51–68.

success. For example, upper level managers are biased towards organizational and personnel factors; middle managers are biased more towards marketing and technical factors; and entry level managers are biased towards financial factors.

Understanding the biases relevant to evaluating competitors on given dimensions stems from answers to two questions: (1) What information becomes salient or vivid to the manager? and (2) How can it be interpreted in such a manner that it confirms the manager's prior expectations or is consistent with the manager's experience or views? The relevance of these questions stems from the notions that people pay a disproportionate amount of attention to vivid information and like to have control over their environments.

Information can be vivid for a variety of reasons. It could be visual, as was the case with the perceptual map. It could relate directly to a manager's personal experiences. It could be concrete. Such is the case with the well-known *ignoring of base rate bias.*[29] Suppose that a manager in an automobile company casually reads a comprehensive statistical study of accident rates on various cars including a competitor's. The study implies that the competitor's car is in the lowest quartile of fatal accidents. Later, a coworker tells him he had a friend who died in an accident while driving the competitor's car. This information becomes vivid to the manager; he bases his judgment on it rather than the more valid, but less vivid, statistical study.

One final place a manager can find vivid information is his or her memory. The *availability bias* refers to the ease with which specific instances can be recalled from memory. The easier something can be recalled from memory, the more a decision maker will think that it is a general phenomenon.[30] Suppose that another manager in the same automobile company saw one of his or her competitor's cars disabled on the side of the road one morning. From that, the manager (perhaps mistakenly) concludes that the competitor's car breaks down frequently.

With respect to how managers interpret information, it is important to keep in mind that they tend to avoid evidence that would disconfirm any of their experiences, expectations, or theories.[31] Decision makers tend to focus on a single conclusion, a single interpretation, and a single hypothesis. Not only will managers avoid information that might disconfirm their ideas, they will interpret information that does not confirm their ideas as actually doing so. This type of information is sometimes called *pseudodiagnostic.*[32] For example,

---

29 See, for example E. Borgida and Richard Nisbett, "The Differential Impact of Concrete vs. Concrete Information on Decisions," *Journal of Applied Social Psychology* 7 (1977): 258–271.

30 The availability bias was first discussed by Amos Tversky, "Availability: A Heuristic for Judging Frequency and Probability," *Cognitive Psychology* 5 (1973): 207–232.

31 For example, see Norman H. Anderson and A. Jacobson, "Effect of Stimulus Inconsistency and Discounting Instructions in Personality Impression Formation," *Journal of Personality and Social Psychology* 2 (1965): 531–539.

32 For more information see Stephen J. Hoch and John Deighton, "Managing What Consumers Learn from Experience," *Journal of Marketing* 53 (April 1989): 1–20.

the nineteenth century British physicist Lord Kelvin, after trying to design one, concluded that heavier than air flying machines were impossible.

Market Share

Market share is unique with respect to Figure 7.1 in that it is both a positional advantage and a measure of performance.[33] As a source of strength or competitive advantage, market share carries a lot of perks. It makes it easier to get shelf space and makes it easier to get a consumer new to the product category to pay attention to the brand. The power that market share exerts on the consumer's mind is illustrated in the battery market. Eveready's Energizer battery and the pink bunny that dominated its television commercials was responsible for one of America's favorite advertising campaigns in recent years; yet Duracell, the market leader, watched its share continue to grow while Eveready's declined! The solution to this paradox lies in the results of Video Storyboard Tests Inc.'s survey of television viewers. Energizer was America's second favorite ad campaign in the first quarter of 1990. Duracell broke into the top ten at number seven. The interesting aspect of Duracell's ranking was that no new major campaign was instituted in the first quarter of 1990. Forty percent of the people who cited the bunny commercial as being the most outstanding said that it was a Duracell commercial! They associated the bunny with a battery, did not remember the brand, and just assumed it was the one that they and their friends used most often: the market leader, Duracell.[34]

Consider another example. In the early nineties, Toshiba has been the share leader in the notebook computer market. Because of the advantages it accrues as a consequence, Toshiba can command a price premium over most of its competitors for a comparably equipped machine. Indeed, a casual visit to a local computer store will show that Toshiba is one of the higher priced machines on display.

Order of Entry

The order of market entry is thought to be critical to a firm's welfare. Pioneering a new market may have a big payoff, but it is usually very expensive and risky. If pioneers do gain advantage in access to supply, cost, consumers' attention, R&D, or distribution, then firms should pioneer when they have the opportunity. On the other hand, if later entrants can surpass pioneers by learning from their mistakes, producing superior technology, or taking up better product positions, then waiting until technological and market uncertainty is resolved is the best move.[35]

---

33 Aneel Karnani, "Equilibrium Market Share—A Measure of Competitive Strength," *Strategic Management Journal* 3 (1982): 43–51 presents a theoretical justification of market share as a measure of competitive strength.

34 "Too Many Think the Bunny is Duracell's, Not Eveready's," *The Wall Street Journal* (July 31, 1990): B1.

35 Marvin B. Lieberman and David B. Montgomery, "First-Mover Advantages," *Strategic Management*

Studies on the PIMS data demonstrate that there is indeed a positive relationship between a brand's order of entry and its market share.[36] These studies show that a first mover tends to have higher quality and more differentiated products as well as broader product lines. However, the evidence is far from unequivocal. The relationship between order of entry and market share is moderated by industry type, purchase transaction size, and breadth of served markets. Furthermore, it is acknowledged that a pioneer may not have an advantage when it is challenged by a firm established in a related market. Finally, it is thought that strategy and organizational structure are at least as important as order of entry in determining market share.

Whether or not there is an enduring advantage of early entry is unclear. Researchers in the discipline disagree.[37] The laptop (notebook) market shows mixed evidence as well. The first laptop computer was a 10-pound machine introduced in 1982 by Grid, a company that remains a minor player today. The first notebook, however, appeared in October 1988 under the NEC UltraLite brand name. Compaq followed a year later. Experts report that today the Compaq and NEC lines are two of the most successfully differentiated lines available.

What is clear though, despite the confusion, are the trade-offs of early vs. late entry. Furthermore, order of entry is an unambiguous piece of information. Any firm can put the potential assets and liabilities of early entry on opposite sides of the ledger as strengths and weaknesses and act accordingly.

Measuring Brand Equity

A brand is a name and/or symbol that distinguishes a product from its competitors. It provides a signal of the product's origin and protects the customer as well as the firm from competitors who would attempt to duplicate it. One of marketers' primary activities these days is to build strong brands. As George J. Bull, the chief executive of Grand Metropolitan, the food and beverage conglomerate, has said, "If you can convince consumers that your product tastes better than your competitor's, that it is made with superior ingredients, then you can command a premium price for it."[38] Hopefully, the brand name conveys the appropriate information to customers. Grand Met practices what its CEO preaches. American consumers pay 15 to 20 percent more for premium brands like J&B Scotch, Smirnoff's Vodka, and Haagen-Dazs ice cream, all Grand Met brands.

Journal 9 (1988): 41–58 fully explore the trade-offs between early and late entry.

36 Roger A. Kerin, P. Rajan Varadarajan, and Robert A. Peterson, "First-Mover Advantage: A Synthesis, Conceptual Framework, and Research Propositions," *Journal of Marketing* 56 (October 1992): 33–52 review these studies.

37 Peter N. Golder and Gerard J. Tellis, "Pioneer Advantage: Marketing Logic or Marketing Legend?" *Journal of Marketing Research* 30 (May 1993): 158–170.

38 "Grand Met's New CEO Emphasizes Premium Brands," *The Wall Street Journal* (October 7, 1993): B4.

Kevin Keller defines brand equity as "the differential effect of brand knowledge on consumer response to the marketing of the brand."[39] In other words, consumers will react differently to an element of the marketing mix for different brands. That reaction will be more favorable for brands with higher brand equity. He goes on to suggest that the consumer knowledge from which brand equity is derived is made up of two major components: brand awareness and brand image. Brand awareness is often measured in terms of brand recall and brand recognition. Brand image is measured in terms of the associations a consumer makes with a brand. These associations can be with respect to attributes, benefits, user category, price, and so on, anything that comes to a consumer's mind when prompted by the brand.

Brand awareness and strong, favorable, unique brand associations present the company with a variety of benefits. These come from three sources:[40]

1. Enhanced performance (e.g., increase in market share or increase in revenues due to the firm's ability to charge a premium price) and/or marketing efficiency (e.g., reduced advertising and promotional expenditures) associated with the brand.

2. Longevity of a brand due to its loyal customer base and distribution relationships.

3. Carryover (e.g., brand extension) potential to other brands and markets.

See Figure 7.3 for a graphical representation of those benefits. Indeed, in one study of the hotel industry, researchers found that the brand equity of a prospective acquisition accounted for as much as 30 percent of the explained variance in its desirability.[41]

The last of the three benefits above may be the most beneficial for fostering growth. Fewer and fewer products exist as stand-alone brands these days. Consider the example of detergents in the United Kingdom.[42] Before Lever introduced the first liquid, Wisk, the market was shared by Persil, a Lever (powdered) brand and Aeriel, a P&G (powdered) brand. Wisk's launch resulted in a 4 percent share. Aeriel responded with Aeriel liquid and gained nearly 10 percent of the market. Consumers hesitant to try a new product form were less so when there was a recognized name. Lever gained another 7 percent by responding with Persil liquid (which was really the same product as Wisk except for the container).

It is worth pointing out as an aside that although brand equity is usually thought of as a strength, it can be a weakness as well. For example, Air Canada

---

39 Kevin Lane Keller, "Conceptualizing, Measuring, and Managing Customer-Based Brand Equity," *Journal of Marketing* 57 (January 1993): 2.

40 These are taken from Vijay Mahajan, Vithala R. Rao, and Rajendra K. Srivastiva, "An Approach to Assess the Importance of Brand Equity in Acquisition Decisions," *Journal of Product Innovation Management* (1993).

41 *Ibid.*

42 This example is taken from "Brand Equity," *Brandweek* (June 28, 1993): 20–24.

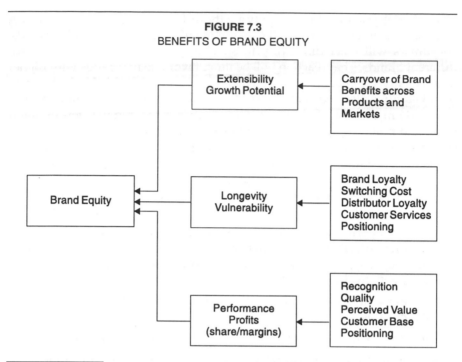

FIGURE 7.3
BENEFITS OF BRAND EQUITY

Source: Vijay Mahajan, Vithala R. Rao, and Rajendra K. Srivastiva, "An Approach to Assess the Importance of Brand Equity in Acquisition Decisions," *Journal of Product Innovation Management* (June 11, 1994). Reprinted with permission of the publisher.

can be thought of as having negative brand equity.[43] Customers associate the airline with the Canadian government. A recent survey showed that 49 percent of Canadians are "very dissatisfied" with their government. Given the association, this feeling translates to negative brand equity for Air Canada. This association would be bad enough if Air Canada were indeed state owned, but it isn't! It's as private as American or United Airlines.

Various marketing research firms have either adapted their existing products or designed newer methods to measure brand equity. Most of these involve implementing measures of one of the components of Keller's awareness-image classification scheme. For example, DDB Needham Worldwide and Landor Associates measure "share of mind," a variable they conceptualized that reflects brand awareness. "Share of mind" can be measured by asking a sample of consumers to list the brands of a certain product category in the order that they come to mind.

Another straightforward method involves simply getting consumers to provide bipolar ratings of overall brand evaluation, quality (poor-excellent),

43 "Ah Canada," *Forbes* (January 3, 1994): 74.

or value for money (poor-excellent) scales. While this is exceedingly simple and it gives the analyst an idea about how consumers see the brand, it does not really address the value of the brand name apart from other company assets.

It has become popular recently to disparage the power of brands. A recent Roper Organization survey found that 37 percent of shoppers judged name brands in premium categories worth paying more for.[44] In 1988 the figure was 45 percent. Consumers are simply becoming more price conscious. In 1992, Kraft charged 45 percent more than private label brands. Its market share fell three points. They then cut prices 8 percent, and sales volume rose five points.[45] Stephen J. Liguori, vice-president for marketing at Frito-Lay, says, "Brand equity is being challenged like never before."[46]

We do not believe that this phenomenon signals the decreasing importance of brand equity. We believe that it is signaling just the opposite. Phil Dusenberry, vice-chairman of BBDO Worldwide, says, "The brands that will succeed are the No. 1 and No. 2 in a category, plus a private label. Anything below that will get squeezed right off the shelf."[47] If this is true, that will only make a brand-equity based competitive advantage more difficult to achieve and sustain. Therefore, firms trying to build such an advantage will need an even greater understanding of the concept than before.

In the remainder of this section, we will address three more sophisticated approaches to measuring brand equity: the dollarmetric approach, an extension-based approach, and brand-specific constants in choice models.

Dollarmetric Approach

The dollarmetric method is appropriately named. Its objective is to create a metric (measure) of brand value in dollars.[48] Consider the following experiment: A subject is offered the choice between two brands of chocolate chip cookies, each marked with its "regular" price. After choosing, the subject is asked to indicate the price to which the preferred brand must rise before the subject would switch his or her original preference. The difference between that price and the price of the original brand contains information about how much the subject values the brand.

McKinsey & Co. and Intelliquest Inc. used a variation of the dollarmetric approach to assess the brand values of personal computers.[49] These values

---

44 "Brands on the Run," *Business Week* (April 19, 1993): 26–29.

45 *Ibid.*

46 *Ibid.*

47 "Brands: It's Thrive or Die," *Fortune* (August 23, 1993): 52–56.

48 This concept was introduced into the marketing literature by Edgar Pessemier, Philip Burger, Richard Teach, and Douglas Tigert, "Using Laboratory Brand Preference Scales to Predict Consumer Brand Purchases," *Management Science* 17 (February 1971): B371–B385.

49 "Computers: They're No Commodity," *The Wall Street Journal* (October 15, 1993): B1.

ranged from $295 for IBM, $232 for Compaq, and $195 for Apple to –$44 for NEC, –$47 for Everex, and –$69 for Packard Bell.

Research International uses a variant of the dollarmetric approach in their BETA (Brand Equity Trade-Off Analysis) procedure.[50] They use an experiment similar to the one we are about to describe for cookies. Subjects are shown up to five brands of cookies, each priced at average supermarket prices, and are asked which one they would buy. The price of the chosen brand is increased a few cents, and the subjects are asked to reconsider. They can either stay with the (more expensive) preferred brand or switch. Whichever brand they decide on, its price is increased by the same amount, and the process is repeated. These trade-off choices provide a complete map of the subject's brand preferences. Research International derives a price elasticity curve for any brand by using the trade-off data to predict the market shares for that brand at a range of different prices.

Extension-Based Approach

If one of the benefits of brand equity is the ability to extend the brand successfully, it stands to reason that brand extensions should provide a suitable context in which to measure brand equity. If a brand is strong, there should be a high likelihood of consumers trying an extension they deem appropriate. Researchers have used seven-point bipolar perceived quality (Inferior–Superior) and likelihood of trying (Not at all likely–Very likely) scales to evaluate extensions.[51] One of us has used this method to evaluate the brand equity in several brands of candy bars.[52]

In applying this approach, one must be careful in interpreting negative results. Even when a potential extension is evaluated poorly, it does not necessarily mean that the brand has low equity or value. It could simply mean that the extension is simply a bad one. For example, consumers are likely to evaluate Levi's business suits negatively despite the fact that the Levi's brand name is well thought of. Therefore, it is important to make sure that the extensions are reasonable. In the course of the candy bar study, we determined that the best way to do this was to use an extension that is a substitute for the original product. For example, Milky Way ice cream bars are a substitute for the candy bar.

Brand-Specific Constants

Imagine you were performing a conjoint analysis for notebook computers. Conjoint analysis allows you to examine the contribution that each of several attributes made to consumer preference. One of those attributes may be brand

---

50 For a more complete description, see "Brand Equity," *Brandweek* (June 28, 1993): 20–24.

51 See, for example, David A. Aaker and Kevin L. Keller, "Consumer Evaluations of Brand Extensions," *Journal of Marketing* 54 (January 1990): 27–41.

52 See Manoj K. Agarwal and Vithala R. Rao, "An Empirical Comparison of Consumer-Based Measures of Brand Strength," Working Paper, Johnson Graduate School of Management, Cornell University, 1992.

name! Indeed, the part-worth of brand name indicates how much utility is provided by the brand name beyond that provided by the other attributes (processor speed, screen quality, hard disk size, warranty, service policy, etc.). That is certainly a measure of brand value or brand equity. The rank order of the magnitudes of the brand name part-worths would correspond to the order of brand values. Furthermore, since the range of part-worths for an attribute represents the importance of that attribute, we can compute the importance of brand name in the consumer's decision by computing the ratio of the range of brand name part-worths to the sum of the ranges for all the attributes.

Consider the following spot remover conjoint analysis example.[53] Spot removers can be thought of as possessing five attributes with the corresponding levels:

Package design (Spray, Brush Applicator, Plain Plastic Container)
Brand names (K2R, Glory, Bissell)
Price ($1.19, $1.39, $1.59)
Good Housekeeping Seal (Yes, No)
Money back guarantee (Yes, No).

Suppose further that a conjoint analysis of these attributes produced the following part-worths:

Package design (Spray=0, Brush Applicator=0.9, Plain Plastic Container=0.5)
Brand names (K2R=0.1, Glory=0, Bissell=0.3)
Price ($1.19=0.9, $1.39=0.6, $1.59=0)
Good Housekeeping Seal (Yes=0.1, No=0)
Money back guarantee (Yes=0.5, No=0).

Bissell has the highest brand equity followed by K2R and Glory. Furthermore, the relative importance of brand name in the decision can be seen to be $0.3/(0.9+0.3+0.9+0.1+0.5)=3/26$, much less than those of package design and price.

Cost and Experience

In any competitive context, two large classes of competitive advantage stand out: differentiation and low cost. Porter has argued that all successful strategies involve at least one of these.[54] In pursuing a low-cost strategy, a firm strives to achieve a cost advantage in producing or distributing some element of the product or service. This can be accomplished through experience gained from a high-market share, favorable access to raw materials, or state-of-the-art production equipment. A low-cost strategy can either be associated with a lower price (thereby providing customer value) or enhanced profits that could potentially be reinvested. Indeed, the prices of laptops and notebooks are

---

53 This example is drawn from Paul E. Green and Yoram Wind, "New Ways to Measure Consumer Judgments," *Harvard Business Review* 53 (July–August 1975): 107–117.

54 Michael E. Porter, *Competitive Strategy* (New York: Free Press, 1980).

constantly falling. The price premiums that notebooks command over comparably equipped desktops are also vanishing.

Given the importance that cost has as a source of advantage and given that every market has a cost leader, a tool that could help managers understand and predict costs would obviously be helpful in assessing strengths and weaknesses. The experience curve, developed by the Boston Consulting Group in the 1960s, is such a tool.

The experience curve refers to the empirical generalization that (value-added) costs (net of inflation) decline systematically with increases in accumulated production. In particular, costs tend to decline by a constant fraction, r, each time accumulated production doubles. We call such a relationship a $(1-r)$ experience curve.[55]

This type of relationship is described by the following model:

$$C_q = C_n \left(\frac{q}{n}\right)^{-b}$$

where q = accumulated production to date, n = accumulated production at a particular (perhaps earlier) time, C_n = the cost of the nth unit (net of inflation), C_q = the cost of the qth unit (net of inflation), and b = a learning constant (which reflects how costs decline).

This model can be simplified by letting n be equal to 1 and C_1 be the *initial* cost of production. In that case, the cost of the qth unit is equal to

$$C_q = C_1 q^{-b}$$

Either form can be used, depending on the user's preference or whether an initial ($n=1$) cost is available. Either model can be graphed as a curvilinear function directly or as a linear function on log-log graph paper, as in Figure 7.4. The learning constant, b, is uniquely related to the cost reduction fraction, r, by the following expressions:

$$r = 100 \, (2^{-b})$$

and

$$b = \frac{\ln 100 - \ln r}{\ln 2}$$

where $\ln$ is the natural log.

In order to apply the experience curve, one needs to calculate b. Then C_q can be computed for any value q. The ingredients for calculating b are the costs at at least two different levels of accumulated experience. The appropriate calculation is demonstrated as follows:

---

55 See George S. Day and David B. Montgomery, "Diagnosing the Experience Curve," *Journal of Marketing* 47 (Spring 1983): 44–58 for a more thorough discussion of the theoretical structure behind and the empirical evidence for the experience curve as well as its strategic implications.

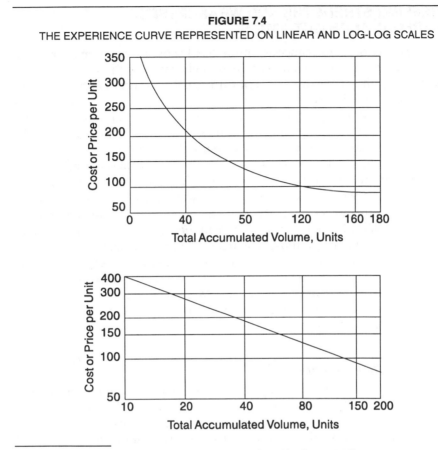

FIGURE 7.4

THE EXPERIENCE CURVE REPRESENTED ON LINEAR AND LOG-LOG SCALES

Source: *Perspectives on Experience* (Boston: The Boston Consulting Group, 1972).

We begin with the basic expression

$$C_q = C_n \left(\frac{q}{n}\right)^{-b}.$$

Taking the logarithm of both sides, we obtain:

$$\log C_q = \log C_n - b\,(\log q - \log n)$$

which is a straight line in $\log C_q$ and q with slope $-b$. That is why the graph of an experience curve is a straight line on log-log graph paper. If we know the costs for two levels of accumulated production, we can simply plug them in the above expression for c, n, C_q, and C_n. Solving for b then becomes an easy task. If we know more than two values, we run a regression on the logs. The negative of the slope of that regression line is then b.

ASSESSING STRENGTHS AND WEAKNESSES
IN PERFORMANCE OUTCOMES

Many measures of performance are immediately obvious from financial data: profits, market share, and so on. While extremely valuable, these measures are limited in that they measure past, not future, performance. Future performance depends on whether current customers will continue to patronize the company, the ability of the company to attract new customers, and the ability of the company to introduce new products that respond to unmet needs. Customer satisfaction surveys can provide insight to all three.

That customer satisfaction surveys yield information about whether current customers will be future customers is self-evident. The value of such studies to the other two is not as obvious. However, as discussed in Chapter 3, customer motivations exist that are often not met by any existing offering in the marketplace. These represent opportunities for firms not competing in the industry and threats for those that are. Customer satisfaction surveys can help uncover whether any such opportunities or threats exist, especially if the surveys are done with respect to a category as a whole and not just one brand in that category. For example, the Apple MacIntosh was developed in response to a need for a user-friendly system. This technology has proved to be an important strength for Apple.[56]

We turn now to a discussion of survey structure.

Customer Satisfaction Surveys

Some companies periodically sample their customers in order to evaluate the quality of their products, the efficiency of their delivery, the friendliness of their service, and so on. The Lord & Taylor department store mails the postcard in Figure 7.5 to all credit card customers who have shopped at their stores.

Usually, customer satisfaction surveys elicit responses to questions on a five to ten point bipolar (very dissatisfied–very satisfied) scale. For example, Figure 7.6A presents a questionnaire that McDonald's uses to get information on customer satisfaction. It is given to customers as they leave the restaurant. Customers are asked to fill it out at home and return it. Figure 7.6B shows how McDonald's motivates their customers to actually return the questionnaire. The questionnaire is printed on the back of a one dollar check. All the customer has to do is complete the questionnaire and deposit the check in his or her account. McDonald's gets the consumer's responses when the check is returned to them.

Other approaches do not directly ask whether the customer is satisfied. Rather, they employ the conceptual foundation of satisfaction (dissatisfaction) as expectations that are (are not) met. Questions are then framed in terms of

---

56 This is discussed by David A. Aaker, "Managing Assets and Skills: The Key to a Sustainable Competitive Advantage," *California Management Review* (Winter 1989): 91–106.

FIGURE 7.5

LORD & TAYLOR'S SATISFACTION POSTCARD

Dear Customer:
All of us at Lord & Taylor want you to be served properly. Our records show you recently shopped in our Fifth Avenue store. As part of our continuing efforts to see how we are doing, would you please tell us if the service you received at _Fifth Avenue_ was:

(Check ONE Box)

Below Expectations	☐	☐	☐	☐	Above Expectations
	1	2	3	4	

←──────────────────────→

We would also be pleased to have any comments you may wish to make:

_____

_____

_____

_____

Detach this card and drop in
any mail box. Postage free.
21-01-64471-1

Thank you,
Ron Tanler
President, Lord & Taylor

Reprinted with permission, Lord & Taylor.

expectations and performance. Such is the case in the Lord & Taylor postcard. However, if the customer checks "Above Expectations" on this postcard, it is not clear if the reason was that expectations were very low or that performance was very high. Both pieces of information are necessary. For example, suppose you were interested in the sound quality of a stereo system. You could begin by asking What kind of sound quality did you expect before listening to the system? Responses might be on a (say) seven-point bipolar (Good sound–Poor sound) scale. Next, you could use the same scale to ask how good the sound actually was. The difference between performance and expectation can then be taken as a measure of satisfaction. Alternatively, one could simply ask one judgment on a bipolar "much better than expected–much worse than expected" scale. In this mode, no need for a difference score exists.

ASSESSING STRENGTHS AND WEAKNESSES WITH MANAGERIAL JUDGMENT

With all the techniques discussed in the previous sections, one can often reduce the process of assessing strengths and weaknesses to objective analyses of concrete data and the quantitative processing of customer judgment and

FIGURE 7.6A
McDONALD'S CUSTOMER SATISFACTION QUESTIONNAIRE

Please tell us how satisfied you were with McDonald's today by writing numbers from 1 to 10 in the spaces to the right of the perforation. If you were extremely satisfied, use a high number. If you were not at all satisfied, use a low number ... like this:

Not at all Satisfied Today   Extremely Satisfied Today

1 2 3 4 5 6 7 8 9 10

Answer Here

Overall:
With the service you got during your visit
With the value we provided for the money you spent
With the food you ate
With how comfortable our restaurant was

About today's service:
Being able to order quickly
Getting your food promptly after you order
Getting your order right the first time
Welcoming special requests
Providing salt, pepper, ketchup, sauces, straws and utensils

About the Interior of the restaurant:
Providing a neat and clean dining area
Keeping the restrooms clean and well stocked
Having a menu board that is easy to read
Having plenty of seating available
Providing a friendly, fun place for children

About the food today:
Serving you fresh tasting food
Serving hot things hot and cold things cold
Offering enough variety for you to visit often
Offering food choices for everyone's tastes

About the employees today:
Being friendly and courteous
Being clean and neatly dressed
Being available to handle customers' problems or complaints

About prices:
Having competitive prices every day

Please tell us a few thing about you and your visit to McDonald's today:
How many times have you visited this McDonald's in the past month?   D M N
Would you visit this McDonald's again? (Please circle Definitely, Maybe or No)
How much money did you spend at McDonald's today? $ _____
Who came with you to McDonald's today? (Please circle No one, Family, Friends or Other)   N Fa Fr O
Did your party include any children under age 10? (Please circle Yes or No)   Y N
If this McDonald's had been closed, which ONE of the following would you have been most likely
to visit, instead?: (Please circle only one: Burger King, Wendy's, Hardee's, Taco Bell or Other)   B W H T O
What ONE thing do you like best about that restaurant? (Please circle only one: Price, Service,
Employees, Taste or Convenient locations)   P S E T C
Overall, how satisfied have you been with your visits to that restaurant? (Please use a scale of 1 to 10)

May we contact you in the future?

Name: _____

Phone: (_____) – _____ – _____

Sign Here

FIGURE 7.6B
McDONALD'S CUSTOMER SATISFACTION QUESTIONNAIRE

Here's $1.00
For You
To
Check
Us Out

It's Easy:

1. Complete the survey by writing your answers on the back of the check.

2. Remove the check. You may cash it at this McDonald's or wherever you usually cash or deposit checks.

3. After you cash or deposit your check, the bank will return your answers to us.

We Want To
Make Your Visit
Even Better At

McDonald's
Campus Office Building
Kroc Drive
Oak Brook, IL 60521

Dear Customer,

Your feedback will help make this McDonald's even better.

We want to know how satisfied you were with your visit today. And we want to offer you $1.00 as a "Thank You" for taking the time to tell us.

If you have any questions, please don't hesitate to ask one of our employees.

Thank you again for taking the time to participate in our survey.

For distribution on:

Friday
Lunch (10:30 am - 2:00 pm)
at the Counter

- - - - - - - - - - - - - DETACH BEFORE CASHING - - - - - - - - - - - - -

320-0510

CheckMetrix
CheckMetrix
CheckMetrix
CheckMetrix
CheckMetrix

1512-10799

CheckMetrix, Inc.
500 North Michigan Ave.
Chicago, IL 60611

"Thank You"
Check

0010521649

May 10, 1993
(Void after June 25, 1993)
2-52/710

Pay to the order of **BEARER** _____ **$1.00**

One and 00/100 .... *Dollars*

Boulevard Bank
Member Boulevard Bancorp
Chicago, IL 60611–4181

_____
Stephen Turner, CheckMetrix

⑈071000521⑈ ⑈706204 4⑈

behavior. However, we should not lose sight of the fact that managerial judgment is still a major, if not the predominant, component of the process.

Two ways of alleviating the problems endemic to the use of managerial judgment are to provide management with the most complete relevant information available for the task at hand and to train managers about the limitations of their judgments. Awareness of biases is the first (but not final) step in minimizing their potential negative impact on organizations. In this section, we discuss sources of information useful in forming judgments about a firm and its competitors. We follow this with a discussion of how one might reduce the effect of some biases.

Collecting Information

Useful data for assessing strengths and weaknesses are available from a wide variety of sources. Some of these are internal to the firm. Others are external to it. Information sources are often classified as being either primary or secondary. Primary sources are those the marketer collects the information from directly. Secondary sources are those in which the relevant information has been collected by someone else.

Primary and secondary data have clear and obvious trade-offs. Primary sources are more tailored to increase a firm's understanding of the aspects of consumer behavior most critical for developing strategy, assessing customer motivations, and uncovering unmet needs in the marketplace. On the other hand, they are more expensive to collect and more likely to be biased in some way.

Of course, the choice among data sources must first and foremost depend on the particular strength or weakness being assessed. If primary data are better suited to understanding consumer behavior, secondary data collected via scanner panels may be better suited to understanding the extent of a competitor's distribution.

It stands to reason, though, that two of the most important sources of information related to assessing competitive advantage is the firm itself and its competitors. The keys to tapping a firm's internal resources in acquiring relevant information is sensitizing its executives, sales force, engineers, and scientists to the need for assembling such information and training them to recognize and transmit it. One way to accomplish this is to have managers visit the point of transaction often, as a customer or customer representative. Managers should take regular shopping trips and buy the company's (and competitors') products for their own use. They should also spend time as a customer-service representative. They could even interview customers, perhaps using a predesigned survey instrument. This will enable them to appreciate how customers perceive their products. Indeed, every McDonald's marketing executive must go to a branch and take customers' orders several times a year.[57]

---

57 "Customer Conversations: The Benefits of Being a Good Listener," *Brandweek* (February 15, 1993): 30–31.

Ironically, while getting your employees to do what McDonald's does may often be like pulling teeth, competitors will often give you a great deal of information without your even asking for it! Speeches and public announcements will often reveal management philosophy, priority, and company skills (as they perceive them). For example, the cover of Xerox's 1987 annual report says "We achieve customer satisfaction through dedication to quality in everything we do;" the 1988 report cover says "In ... our businesses, customer satisfaction is the key to our success." Xerox makes no secret of its strategy. While these are often made for the benefit of either the investment community or trade associations, these communications enter the public domain. Inferences made from these can be confirmed by reverse engineering competitors' products. Are they well made? What are their essential features?

Consulting firms specializing in collecting information from which to assess strengths and weaknesses are emerging. Furthermore, there is a professional association in the area, the Society of Competitive Intelligence Professionals, located in suburban Virginia.

Judgmental Biases

One of the recurring themes of this book in general, and this chapter in particular, is that managers, like humans in general, are limited to their abilities to make judgments and decisions. Jay Russo and Paul Schoemaker enumerate common "decision traps" that occur frequently in a wide variety of decisions.[58]

Russo and Schoemaker propose that decision traps essentially occur because people and managers plunge right in and worry more about making the decision than *how* to make the decision. For example, in his autobiography, John Scully describes an example of how worrying about *how* to make a decision helped Pepsi in the 1970s. Pepsi had long felt that Coke's hourglass bottle was one of its biggest advantages. It made Coke recognizable, easier to stack, and more comfortable to grip. Pepsi's swirl bottle, introduced in 1958, became its standard for 20 years but never achieved the recognition of the Coke bottle. Scully recognized that Pepsi was studying new bottle designs haphazardly and never realized what consumers wanted in a bottle. Without that knowledge, how could Pepsi improve its bottle design? Pepsi undertook a study of household soft-drink consumption patterns and found that people always consumed the entire bottle, no matter how large it was. The implication is that larger bottles lead to increased consumption. Scully realized that Pepsi needed to develop a bottle that enabled people to get more soda into their homes. Pepsi began to produce larger, more varied sizes. Coke's hourglass shape would not allow it to respond quickly. Stepping back and asking how the bottle design decision should be made led Pepsi to more fully understand

---

58 See Edward J. Russo and Paul J.H. Schoemaker, *Decision Traps: The Ten Barriers to Brilliant Decision-Making and How to Overcome Them* (New York: Simon and Schuster, 1989).

one of their relative weaknesses, combat one of Coke's strengths, and achieve a stronger market share position.

Unfortunately, simply making someone aware of a judgmental bias or decision trap does not guarantee it will no longer be a problem. Research has shown that explicitly describing a bias to people does not prevent them from falling prey to it.[59] The major hope lies in providing intensive personalized feedback to immunize the individual to the bias and in constantly questioning each decision so that it is less vulnerable to bias.

Max Bazerman advocates an immunization approach where an individual is given a series of quiz questions designed to elicit a particular bias.[60] The individual will get many of these wrong and will want to know why and how he or she can do better. A pure text format or lecture is not likely to achieve as much success as this interactive approach. For example, the quiz can consist of questions like "Which is riskier, flying 400 miles or driving 400 miles?" and "Do more Americans die each year from lung cancer or stomach cancer?" In both cases most people will choose the first option. However, in both cases, the second option is correct. The key here is for people to get frustrated and realize that they are basing their answers on stories eminating from the news (plane crashes and smoking controversies). They would be better off placing these stories in a more proper perspective.

SUMMARY

Marketing strategy is concerned with the search for and application of competitive advantage. Competitive advantage begins with certain skills and/or resources that the firm can use to create a superior competitive position. This usually entails either the creation of superior customer value or lower costs than competitors. Both advantages lead to superior company performance and profitability. In order for companies to sustain their competitive position, they must reinvest their profits in enhancing old or in building new skills and/or resources.

Assessing competitive advantage, then, entails three separate tasks: (1) identifying those skill and/or resource factors that are most critical for success in a given market, (2) evaluating each competitor (including the firm itself) on these critical success factors, and (3) evaluating the performance the positional advantage has produced. There are a variety of approaches to performing these tasks. Some involve internal historical data, others involve externally available secondary data, and still others require primary data collection from customers.

However, the ingredient most often used in this process is human judgment. Given the variety of flaws and biases in human (managerial) judgment,

---

59 This is demonstrated by Baruch Fischoff, "Cognitive Liabilities and Product Liability," *Journal of Products Liability* 1 (1977): 207–220.

60 Max Bazerman, *Judgment in Managerial Decision Making*, 2d ed. (New York: Wiley, 1990).

it is important for managers to have the best information available and to know how to avoid these biases.

BIBLIOGRAPHY

Aaker, David A. "Managing Assets and Skills: The Key to a Sustainable Competitive Advantage." *California Management Review* (Winter 1989): 91–106.

Aaker, David A., and Kevin L. Keller. "Consumer Evaluations of Brand Extensions." *Journal of Marketing* 54 (January 1990): 27–41.

Agarwal, Manoj K., and Vithala R. Rao. "An Empirical Comparison of Consumer-Based Measures of Brand Strength." Working Paper. Johnson Graduate School of Management, Cornell University, 1992.

"Ah Canada." *Forbes* (January 3, 1994): 74.

Anderson, Norman H., and A. Jacobson. "Effect of Stimulus Inconsistency and Discounting Instructions in Personality Impression Formation." *Journal of Personality and Social Psychology* 2 (1965): 531–539.

Ansoff, H. Igor. *The New Corporate Strategy.* New York: Wiley, 1988.

Bazerman, Max. *Judgment in Managerial Decision Making.* 2d ed. New York: Wiley, 1990.

Borgida, E., and Richard Nisbett. "The Differential Impact of Concrete vs. Concrete Information on Decisions." *Journal of Applied Social Psychology* 7 (1977): 258–271.

Boynton, Andrew C., and Robert W. Zmud. "An Assessment of Critical Success Factors." *Sloan Management Review* 25 (Summer 1984): 17–27.

"Brand Equity." *Brandweek* (June 28, 1993): 20–24.

"Brands: It's Thrive or Die." *Fortune* (August 23, 1993): 52–56.

"Brands on the Run." *Business Week* (April 19, 1993): 26–29.

Buaron, Roberto. "How to Win the Market-Share Game? Try Changing the Rules." *Management Review* 70 (January 1981): 8–19.

Buzzell, Robert D., and Bradley T. Gale. *The PIMS Principles: Linking Strategy to Performance.* New York: Free Press, 1987.

"Computers: They're No Commodity." *The Wall Street Journal* (October 15, 1993): B1.

Cooper, Robert G. "The Dimensions of Industrial New Product Success and Failure." *Journal of Marketing* 43 (Summer 1979): 93–103.

———"The NewProd System: The Industry Experience." *Journal of Product Innovation Management* 9 (June 1992): 113–127.

Curren, Mary T., Valerie S. Folkes, and Joel H. Steckel. "Explanations for Successful and Unsuccessful Marketing Decisions: The Decision Maker's Perspective." *Journal of Marketing* 56 (April 1992): 18–31.

"Customer Conversations: The Benefits of Being a Good Listener." *Brandweek* (February 15, 1993): 30–31.

Day, George S. *Market Driven Strategy: Processes for Creating Value.* New York: Free Press, 1990.

Day, George S., and David B. Montgomery. "Diagnosing the Experience Curve." *Journal of Marketing* 47 (Spring 1983): 44–58.

Day, George S., and Robin Wensley. "Assessing Advantage: A Framework for Diagnosing Competitive Strategy." *Journal of Marketing* 92 (April 1988): 1–20.

EMI and the CT Scanner (B). Intercollegiate Case Clearing House 9-383-195. Boston, MA: Harvard Business School, 1983.

Fischoff, Baruch. "Cognitive Liabilities and Product Liability." *Journal of Products Liability* 1 (1977): 207–220.

Fiske, Susan T., and Shelley E. Taylor. *Social Cognition.* 2d ed. New York: McGraw-Hill, 1991.

Glazer, Rashi, Joel H. Steckel, and Russell S. Winer. "Locally Rational Decision Making: The Distracting Effect of Information on Managerial Performance." *Management Science* 38 (February 1992): 212–226.

Green, Paul E., and Yoram Wind. "New Ways to Measure Consumer Judgments." *Harvard Business Review* 53 (July–August 1975): 107–117.

Golder, Peter N., and Gerard J. Tellis. "Pioneer Advantage: Marketing Logic or Marketing Legend?" *Journal of Marketing Research* 30 (May 1993): 158–170.

"Grand Met's New CEO Emphasizes Premium Brands." *The Wall Street Journal* (October 7, 1993): B4.

Guadagni, Peter M., and John D.C. Little. "A Logit Model of Brand Choice Calibrated on Scanner Data." *Marketing Science* 2 (Summer 1983): 203–238.

Hoch, Stephen J., and John Deighton. "Managing What Consumers Learn from Experience." *Journal of Marketing* 53 (April 1989): 1–20.

Hofer, Charles W., and Dan Schendel. *Strategy Formulation: Analytical Concepts.* St. Paul, MN: West Publishing, 1977.

"Hot Products." *Business Week* (June 7, 1993): 54–57.

Kahneman, Daniel, Paul Slovic, and Amos Tversky. *Judgment Under Uncertainty: Heuristics and Biases.* Cambridge, England: Cambridge University Press, 1982.

Karnani, Aneel. "Equilibrium Market Share—A Measure of Competitive Strength." *Strategic Management Journal* 3 (1992): 43–51.

Keller, Kevin Lane. "Conceptualizing, Measuring, and Managing Customer-Based Brand Equity." *Journal of Marketing* 57 (January 1993): 1–22.

Kerin, Roger A., P. Rajan Varadarajan, and Robert A. Peterson. "First-Mover Advantage: A Synthesis, Conceptual Framework, and Research Propositions." *Journal of Marketing* 56 (October 1992): 33–52.

Kerin, Roger A., Vijay Mahajan, and P. Rajan Varadarajan. *Contemporary Perspectives on Strategic Market Planning*. Boston: Allyn and Bacon, 1990.

Kotler, Philip, William Gregor, and William Rogers. "The Marketing Audit Comes of Age." *Sloan Management Review* (Winter 1977): 25–43.

"Laptops Take Off." *Business Week* (March 18, 1991): 118–124.

Lehmann, Donald R., and Russell S. Winer. *Analysis for Marketing Planning*. Third edition. Homewood, IL: Irwin, 1994.

Lieberman, Marvin B., and David B. Montgomery. "First-Mover Advantages." *Strategic Management Journal* 9 (1988): 41–58.

Mahajan, Vijay, Vithala R. Rao, and Rajendra K. Srivastiva. "An Approach to Assess the Importance of Brand Equity in Acquisition Decisions." *Journal of Product Innovation Management* (June 11, 1994): 221–235.

McFadden, Daniel. "Conditional Logit Analysis of Qualitative Choice Behavior." *Frontiers in Econometrics*, P. Zarembka, ed. New York: Academic Press, 1974: 105–142.

Note on the Motorcycle Industry—1975. Intercollegiate Case Clearing House 9-578-210. Boston, MA: Harvard Business School, 1978.

Perspectives on Experience. Boston, MA: Boston Consulting Group, Inc., 1968.

Pessemier, Edgar, Philip Burger, Richard Trach, and Douglas Tigert. "Using Laboratory Brand Preference Scales to Predict Consumer Brand Purchases." *Management Science* 17 (February 1971): B371–B385.

Porter, Michael E. *Competitive Strategy*. New York: Free Press, 1980.

———*Competitive Advantage*. New York: Free Press, 1985.

Rockart, John F. "Chief Executives Define Their Own Data Needs." *Harvard Business Review* 57 (March–April 1979): 81–93.

Russo, J. Edward, and Paul J.H. Schoemaker. *Decision Traps: The Ten Barriers to Brilliant Decision-Making and How to Overcome Them*. New York: Simon and Schuster, 1989.

"Saturn: Labor's Love Lost?" *Business Week* (February 8, 1993): 122–123.

Stevenson, Howard H. "Defining Corporate Strengths and Weaknesses." *Sloan Management Review* (Spring 1976): 51–68.

"The Hunt for Mr. X: Who Can Run IBM?" *Fortune* (February 22, 1993): 68–71.

"Too Many Think the Bunny is Duracell's, Not Eveready's." *The Wall Street Journal* (July 31, 1990): B1.

Tversky, Amos. "Availability: A Heuristic for Judging Frequency and Probability." *Cognitive Psychology* 5 (1973): 207–232.

Tversky, Amos, and Daniel Kahneman. "Judgment Under Uncertainty: Heuristics and Biases." *Science* 185 (1974): 1124–1131.

CHAPTER 8

Resource Allocation

INTRODUCTION

The implementation of almost any marketing strategy involves determining the magnitude of the resource commitment and its allocation to competing means of accomplishing the strategy. For example, when a firm decides to extend an existing brand to a new product category, it needs to decide on the level of marketing budget for implementing that decision as well as how the expenditure will be allocated to various marketing mix elements such as product design, advertising, and trade support. In a general sense, one may view the task of strategic decision making to be one of allocation of resources to various tasks.

To streamline the problem of allocating resources, we consider each brand marketed by the firm as the basic unit at which resources are allocated. Typically, a corporation markets several brands, some of which may compete with each other because they are intended to serve customers' needs similarly. Such brands may be grouped into a product category.[1] In general, such aggregations are called *strategic business units* (SBUs).[2] A corporation can be thought of as a collection of a number of product categories or strategic business units. Thus, the resource allocation problem generally involves allocating resources between various SBUs of a company and between various brands within each SBU. Further, the problem also involves determining resources for existing versus new projects (that may lead to either new SBUs or new brands within existing SBUs).

For purposes of appreciating the complexities involved in resource allocation, consider a hypothetical firm that markets four brands in two product categories, P and Q. We call these brands A and B for the category P, and C and D for Q. We also assume that the two product categories are managed as two divisions within the firm. Given this structure, four decision-making levels

---

1 In the case of Chevrolet division, for example, the product categories may be vans, sedans, coupes, and hatchbacks. Further within each product category, the division may market multiple makes of automobiles such as Corsica and Beretta.

2 We use the term *Strategic Business Unit* interchangeably with *product category*, although there are some differences between the two. We discuss the concept of SBU more formally in the next section.

will be of interest to us in the management of these brands within the corporation: top management level, divisional level, middle level (or product category level), and brand level.[3] Their major responsibilities are shown below:

Level	Resource Allocation Responsibility
Top Level	Determination of the level of resources between existing product categories as a group and research and development for possible new products.
Division Level	Allocation of the funds for the existing product categories between the two divisions.
Category Level	Allocation of the funds for the division between the brands within it.
Brand Level	Allocation of the predetermined resources among the elements of marketing mix for a given brand.

This example illustrates the fact that unit of analysis (e.g., product category or brand) chosen for determining resource allocation will naturally depend on the managerial level at which such decisions are made. While product category is the unit at the division level, the unit is a brand at the category level of management in the above management structure.

At the firm-wide level, strategic decisions are made about the specific product/markets the firm wishes to enter, wishes to support in the future, and wishes to reduce its support of or even withdraw from entirely. The decisions at this level define the general constraints within which mid-level marketing managers make their resource allocation decisions for both the long and short term. Decisions at this level of the firm may also enhance the level of aggregate support for an individual product/market. As an example, one may view PepsiCo's decision to acquire Frito-Lay as enabling PepsiCo to expand its resource base, which helped build its other businesses, such as restaurants.

Once a general decision on the level of total marketing resources for a particular business (e.g., product/market) has been made, the allocation problem is essentially one of deciding on the amounts to be spent on each of the competing elements in the marketing mix. These include not only the set of elements such as advertising, sales force, trade support, and consumer promotion, but also the expenditures necessary to maintain and improve the product (and service) quality associated with the business. Specifically, three significant factors will need to be included in this allocation task: (1) the interdependence between one product/market and another; (2) the interdependence of the effects of any expenditures over time, and (3) the interdepend-

---

3   The procedure may be more complex in a large multidivisional corporation such as General Motors. The top management at GM may essentially deal with determining the level of resources for each division of the corporation (e.g., Chevrolet, Buick, Cadillac, Saturn, and Pontiac), leaving the responsibility of allocating them within the division to the general manager of each division. At the level of the division, the allocation will be in terms of existing and new businesses, following the procedure identified above.

ence of expenditures among the elements of the marketing mix. Consideration of these interdependencies is extremely critical for the successful maintenance of the strategic advantage of each business of the firm.

Further, the decisions concerning resource allocation must explicitly take into account the nature and degree of competition to the respective business (product/market) of the firm. Intensive competition is likely to erode the benefits of marketing expenditures. First, the firm ought to consider the overall environment in which the business is likely to operate in the future—an understanding achieved by a careful analysis of the threats and opportunities faced. If the threats are likely to be serious, the firm may wish to devote a portion of the allocated resource to deal with the emerging threats from such entities as future entrants, technological developments, and potential supplier and intermediary behavior. For example, Procter and Gamble (P&G) may need to increase the advertising expenditures in the detergent category (with several major brands such as Tide and Cheer) if the competition from Lever Brothers becomes more intense due to either introduction of a new brand of detergent or an expanded advertising campaign for its existing brands (e.g., Surf or Wisk). P&G may also need to allocate more resources to its detergents if new private label brands are likely to appear on the market.

Even if the external environment is favorable to the growth of the business, the firm needs to consider the intensity of competition within the industry as well as within various submarkets in which the business in question competes. When Condé Nast acquired the magazine *Architectural Digest* in 1993, it needed to close down its publication of *House and Garden* due to the significant overlap in competing for advertisers.[4] This example is an illustration of competition within a submarket and its effects on overall resource allocation.

The actual decision-making process may involve negotiations at various levels within the organization. The process is usually iterative. Plans drawn at a lower level (say at the brand level) may be aggregated to arrive at the total level of resources called for. After consideration of various constraints, adjustments may be made. Alternatively, the decision-making process may be totally hierarchical, and the unit at the lower level may be given a level of resources to be allocated among the competing demands at that level. In general, either procedure may be suboptimal for the firm because it may ignore the conditions of response at the market level. Further, the decision-making process at each level will need to consider any potential synergistic effects associated with any allocation between competing demands.

Resource allocation decisions are also made among existing products and new opportunities within various product markets (not currently served by the firm). Furthermore, new opportunities may reside within existing strategic business units or lead to the creation of new SBUs. The procedures for such an allocation are not as precise as those for allocating a given marketing resource among different elements of the marketing mix; this is due to the inherent

---

4 See Deirdre Carmody, "In a Reversal, Condé Nast Closes HG," *New York Times* (April 21, 1993): D1.

uncertainties involved in predicting the success of research and development activities.

A streamlined procedure for a firm to allocate its marketing resources consists of the following steps:

1. The firm needs to determine the total amount of resources that could be expended on all of its current and future businesses in a given time period (e.g., a year).

2. The total resources need to be allocated among existing businesses and future businesses that are under development.

3. The resources determined for the existing businesses need to be allocated to each of the existing businesses.

4. The expenditure on an existing business needs to be allocated to various marketing mix elements (if the business consists of multiple brands, resources should first be allocated among the brands).

We believe that it is important to explicitly consider the allocation to future businesses (e.g., via research and development) owing to the enormous importance of new products for the continued success of any firm. The magnitude of the total resource and its particular allocation will determine the overall profit for the firm. The objective will be to determine both magnitude and allocation so as to maximize the overall profit to the firm. This procedure requires a clear knowledge of the market response functions at all levels of the firm.

Against this background, this chapter will describe several methods of analysis for allocating marketing resources. First, we discuss some general principles of resource allocation. Second, we will discuss methods for allocating resources among various product categories (or SBUs) of a firm. These include five different approaches: graphical product portfolio approaches; mathematical portfolio method of STRATPORT; methods based on pooled business experience (e.g., PIMS, ADVISOR); methods using the analytical hierarchy process (AHP); and methods that use elasticities computed from market response functions. Following this, we will consider methods for allocating resources among mix elements for a brand. These methods include the use of elasticities computed from the marketing response function for a brand, techniques based on pooled business experience, and AHP. Finally, we will describe approaches for allocating resources among geographic territories for a brand, a product category, or the firm as a whole.

In principle, the methods for allocating resources among different brands within an SBU are similar to those for allocating resources among different SBUs. However, in some product categories, the interdependence among brands may be very significant and cannot be ignored. The problem of interdependence is not likely to be critical when allocation is considered among different product categories.

PRINCIPLES OF RESOURCE ALLOCATION

The general principle of allocating any resource to competing means is quite simple. The resource allocation to each competing element should be such that the marginal benefits expected are equal for all. In general, marginal benefits associated with any resource will diminish as more of that resource is invested. Therefore, if the marginal benefits are not equal, the firm may increase or decrease the expenditures on those elements with lower marginal benefits to increase overall benefit. When the allocation across competing elements results in equal marginal benefits, any departure will necessarily decrease the total benefit, rendering the new allocation suboptimal. The major task is to determine the marginal benefit after taking into account various factors identified above. When one considers the resource allocation problem at the level of a particular business (say, a brand), the determination of the marginal benefits for each means is essentially determined by the market response function for that brand.

Figure 8.1 shows various determinants of market response to a set of marketing mix decisions (which are effectively the result of allocation of resources) for one brand. The relationship between market response and its determinants (e.g., marketing mix decisions for the brand and brands compet-

FIGURE 8.1

DETERMINANTS OF MARKET RESPONSE FOR ONE PRODUCT

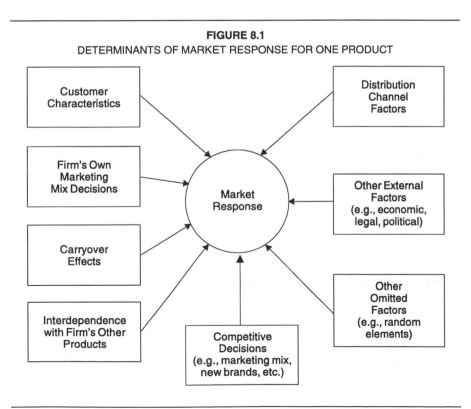

ing with it, customer characteristics, other environmental factors, and so on) is called the market response function. Such a response function can be conceptualized at three levels of aggregation: for a single brand in a product category, for all brands marketed by the firm in a particular category, and for all product categories marketed by the firm. The reader may note that the specific response for a brand a firm could expect from a market would depend not only on the firm's actions, but also on the competitors', and the conditions in the environment. Optimal allocations of marketing resources and the magnitude of total resources will thus be contingent on the firm's expectations with respect to competitive behavior and assumptions made with respect to other determinants of market response.

The foregoing discussion should indicate that the task of determining the optimal resource level and optimal resource allocations is quite intricate, particularly when the firm has no specific knowledge of market response functions. The methods discussed in this chapter range from the use of market response functions where the firm has them to heuristic methods that provide approximate solutions to the resource allocation problem. These include a range of methods called product portfolio models. Other methods pool past experience of several businesses to develop rules for allocating resources for the business under question. Further, the analytic hierarchy process (AHP) methodology that seeks to tackle large-scale decision problems using judgmental data collected from decision makers can also be adapted to this problem. We offer a taxonomy of these methods in Figure 8.2. The methods fall into five broad categories:

- Optimal methods that use elasticities[5] calculated from market response functions.

- Several graphical product portfolio methods that attempt to simplify the problem usually to two composite dimensions.

- Mathematical portfolio methods of STRATPORT that use market response functions and mathematical programming techniques.

- Methods that use the Analytic Hierarchy Process methodology, which attempts to decompose and synthesize executive judgments on various relevant dimensions of the allocation problem.

- Methods that use estimation techniques of conjoint analysis of selected judgmental data.

Further, we have identified in Figure 8.2 four major tasks in the allocation problem: allocating resources at the firm level among different product cate-

---

5 When one marketing mix variable, x (e.g., price) affects the market response, y (e.g., sales in units), price elasticity of sales measures the percent change in sales for 1 percent change in price; it is usually negative. Similarly, advertising elasticity of sales measures the percent change in sales for 1 percent change in advertising expenditures. Because elasticity is a ratio of 2 percent changes, elasticity is a "unit free" measure. It can be used to compare responses of expenditures of two different marketing mix variables, such as advertising and sales force expenditures.

FIGURE 8.2
A TAXONOMY OF DIFFERENT METHODS FOR ALLOCATING MARKETING RESOURCES

	Market Response Functions Are	
Task of Allocation of	**Not Used**	**Used**
I. Resources among different product categories	• Several graphical product portfolio methods • AHP	• Methods based on elasticities • Mathematical portfolio method of STRATPORT
II. Resources among multiple brands of a product category	• AHP • Conjoint analysis	• Methods based on elasticities
III. Resources among marketing mix elements for one brand	• AHP • Conjoint analysis	• Methods based on elasticities • Based on pooled business experience
IV. Resources among different geographical territories for a brand		• Methods based on elasticities

---

gories; allocating resources among multiple brands of a product category; allocating resources among marketing mix elements for one brand; and allocating resources among different geographic territories for a brand, a product category, or a number of categories. We have indicated how suitable these methods are for each of these tasks depending upon the use or nonuse of market response functions. We must also note that even the optimal methods that use elasticities may require some adjustments to accommodate additional (usually conjectural) information available on competitive behavior.

Another observation worth noting is that these methods do not yield any specific guidance on the level of resources to be devoted to a particular situation. But the allocation process can be repeated for various levels of total resources, and the level for which the corporate objective (e.g., profit) is the highest can be deemed the appropriate level for consideration. Of course, financial and other constraints on the firm will have a major influence on the ultimate level of resources to be devoted to a brand or a product category.

METHODS FOR ALLOCATING RESOURCES AMONG SBUs

In this section, our focus will be on techniques of allocating resources among a firm's various SBUs. These methods can also be used for allocating resources for both existing and new opportunities. The general premise is that a firm is better off seeking a balance among the competing demands on its resources.

At the outset, we should note that the problem of allocating resources among various SBUs can also be handled using finance-oriented models such as the risk-return model.[6] But this approach requires additional data on discount rates and market indexes and requires calculation of financial return for each SBU. These details are not easy to compile and are also not normally accessible to a marketing member of a corporation. It is also not clear whether the assumptions required for diversification of stocks in an individual's portfolio are satisfied when the risk-return model is applied to the case of SBUs of a particular firm. Given these considerations, we will not delve into this set of methods for resource allocation.

As noted earlier, there are four sets of methods for allocating resources among the various SBUs of a corporation: graphical portfolio methods, mathematical portfolio methods, methods based on pooled business experience, and the method based on the analytic hierarchy process methodology. (It is worth recalling that the firm does not have knowledge of the market response functions for each SBU or product category and that this lack of knowledge calls for the use of graphical portfolio methods to yield approximate answers.)

While portfolio methods attempt to compare the demands on resources of one SBU versus another in the same firm, the methods based on pooled business experience try to compare an SBU of a firm against all other corresponding SBUs in a large number of firms. The attempt here is to see how the firm's SBU is performing versus a standard or PAR developed from the experience of other companies. This approach does not assume that the behavior of the various firms whose experience is pooled is optimal. Also, both types of method try to use objective data on sales and costs.

The method based on the AHP methodology is relevant to one firm. It is a method for determining relative attractiveness of competing resources from judgmental data provided by key managers of the firm; these judgments relate to the general objective of maximizing overall profitability of the firm. The portfolio methods covered below can be thought of as standardized approaches, while the use of AHP can be thought of as a customized approach to the problem of resource allocation.

Criteria for Defining SBUs

It should be quite clear that the methods of portfolio analysis require a clear definition of a strategic business unit (SBU). The following criteria are relevant for defining an SBU:

- An SBU must serve an *external* rather than internal market.

---

6 See, for example, Stuart Myers, "Finance Theory and Financial Strategy," *Interfaces* (January–February 1984): 126–137; Alfred Rappaport, *Creating Shareholder Value* (New York: Free Press, 1986); and Thomas H. Naylor and Francis Tapon, "The Capital Asset Pricing Model: An Evaluation of its Potential as a Strategic Tool," *Management Science* (October 1982): 1166–1173.

- An SBU should serve distinct groups of *customers* that are different from those serviced by other SBUs and should have a distinct set of external competitors it is trying to equal or surpass.

- The management of an SBU should have control over the key factors that determine success in their served market (can utilize shared resources).

- An SBU should be *strategically autonomous*. (One SBU's strategy should be independent of others.)

- The profitability of the SBU can be measured in real income rather than in artificial dollars posted as transfer payments (which enables evaluation of the management's performance).

Graphical Portfolio Methods

The problem of allocating resources among several SBUs of a firm has received the attention of managers for several years.[7] Several consulting companies have developed techniques for accomplishing this task and have systematically dispensed their advice to various firms. Whether these methods will stand the scrutiny of rigorous analysis is debatable; but the methods seem to have significant face value and appear to give general direction to management for thinking about the various factors involved. Fundamentally, these methods are based on two criteria: market attractiveness of the industry in which a SBU is located and relative market position of the SBU in the industry. The premise is that those SBUs in more attractive industries and weaker market positions should receive higher allocation of resources, while the SBUs operating in less attractive industries with stronger market positions should get allocation no more than the level required to maintain the existing market position. Recommendations are also made to withdraw or reduce support for those SBUs with weaker market position in less attractive industries. Two empirical phenomena are used to generally support these guidelines: the product life cycle for a given industry or SBU and the experience curve for cost reduction over time due to accumulated production. These ideas were initially formulated by the Boston Consulting Group (BCG) using simpler operationalizations of the two constructs: market attractiveness was measured by growth rate and market position by relative market share in the BCG approach. Refinements to this simpler approach have been made over the years, resulting in several paradigms for allocating resources. We delve into these in this section.

Assumptions

Graphical portfolio methods are based on the following critical assumptions. In reality, all of these assumptions may not be satisfied in a specific situation:

---

7 For a comprehensive discussion of portfolio methods, see Roger A. Kerin, Vijay Mahajan, and P. Rajan Varadarajan, *Contemporary Perspectives on Strategic Market Planning* (Needham Heights, MA: Allyn and Bacon, 1990).

- All managers of various products/divisions share the same corporate goals. In fact, any manager is willing to make his or her business goals subservient to the overall corporate goals.

- All managers agree that opportunities in various product markets vary at any one point in time and over time.

- There is sufficient information on the major competitors to each business, and the respective market structures have been clearly identified. Presumably, various methods we described in the previous chapters have been utilized to obtain a clear picture of competition and market structure.

- It is also assumed that the production cost functions for the products are known. One also assumes that the fixed costs have been allocated in an amicable manner across the various products.

Several approaches have evolved over the years which are more or less standardized approaches to the portfolio problem.[8] Our focus here will be on four of these, which are representative of these approaches: Growth/Share Matrix (BCG); Business Assessment Array—also called GE-Business Screen (Industry Attractiveness/Competitive Business Position Matrix); Directional Policy Matrix, also called Competitive Capabilities/Profit Prospects Matrix; and Life Cycle Portfolio Matrix, also called Competitive Position/Industry Maturity Matrix. We now turn to a brief description of these approaches.

Measuring Market Share

A significant question in using the portfolio methods is how market share for the SBU in question is defined. The measurement of market share is almost invariably elusive because it depends critically on the definition of the particular market or segment in which the SBU competes. Actual measure will vary according to the units of measurement, definition of product used, particular market or segment, and nature of denominator and time period used.

As an example, consider the following data[9] on market shares of brands of soft drinks in the United States during 1986, ranked from high to low:

Rank	Brand	Market Share (Based on Quantity Consumed)
1	Coke Classic	18.9%
2	Pepsi	18.5
3	Diet Coke	7.1
4	Diet Pepsi	4.3
5	Dr. Pepper	4.1

8 See Yoram Wind and Vijay Mahajan, "Designing Product and Business Portfolios," *Harvard Business Review* 59 (January–February 1981): 155–165.

9 See Betsy Morris, "Coke vs. Pepsi: Cola War Marches on," *The Wall Street Journal* (June 3, 1987): 31.

Rank	Brand	Market Share (Based on Quantity Consumed)
6	Sprite	3.6
7	7 UP	3.5
8	Mountain Dew	2.6
9	Coke	2.3
10A	RC	1.7
10B	Cherry Coke	1.7
	Other brands	

From these data, it is clear that the total share of all brands marketed by the Coca-Cola company in the soft drink market is 33.6 percent (= 18.9 + 7.1 + 3.6 + 2.3 + 1.7), the share of the cola submarket is 54.5 percent (18.9 + 18.5 + 7.1 + 4.3 + 2.3 + 1.7 + 1.7) and the share of Coke brand in the cola submarket is 55 percent (= 30.0 ÷ 54.5). Similarly, the share of Coca-Cola in the direct segment of the market is 62 percent (= 7.1 ÷ (7.1 + 4.3)). Thus, the actual value of market share depends on the base used.

The BCG Business Portfolio Matrix

This approach is relevant for a firm with multiple brand/products. It involves computing two indices for each SBU: its relative market share and the growth rate of its market.

The SBUs can be classified into one of the four cells: stars—high-market growth and high-relative share, question marks—high-market growth and low-relative market share, cash cows—low-market growth and high-market share, and dogs—low-market growth and low-market share. Given this classification, some prescriptions are given as to the allocation of resources; for example, injection of new resources, withdrawal of support, or even withdrawal of the SBU itself from the market. *Our* view of these prescriptions is shown in Figure 8.3.

From the firm's perspective, all the SBUs are plotted in a graph that looks like the two panels shown in Figure 8.4. The portfolio of products for the firm depicted in the first panel is more balanced than that in the second panel. Although both of these firms have 10 products each, the firm in the top panel has four products—A, B, C, and D—in the star category compared with two products—a and b—of the second firm. Also, each of the four products of the first firm seems to offer greater potential than the two corresponding products for the second firm. Further, the second firm has more products (four versus two) in the cash cow category, which implies that it could generate cash to improve its position in the two question mark products—g and h. But the possibility of improving the position of the question mark products of the first firm—G and H—is greater because they are in relatively more attractive (higher-growth) markets. Also, the second firm may find it more difficult to divest its two dogs because of the less attractive market growth rates. All of

FIGURE 8.3

CLASSIFICATION OF PRODUCTS AND RECOMMENDATIONS
ACCORDING TO THE BCG MATRIX

	Relative Market Share	
	High	Low
High	Stars: Maintain share by reinvesting earnings in price reductions, product refinement, advertising, and personal selling to discourage competitive entry. Stars become cash cows as the product matures. *	Question marks: Invest in market-segmentation strategies, thereby reducing competition and increasing share or reduce further marketing investment and let the product drop to the dog category. ?
Market Growth Rate Low	Cash cows: "Milk" the cash out of the product by investing in marketing only enough to maintain market share. The product is now too late in its life cycle for a strong competitive entry. $	Dogs: Move the dogs into the cash cow category if the returns exceed the cost of an effective segmentation strategy or prepare to drop the product. Drop the product. X

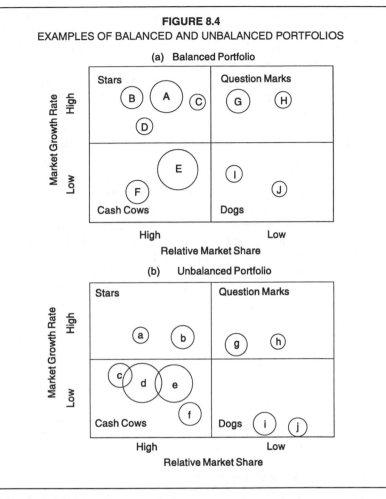

FIGURE 8.4

EXAMPLES OF BALANCED AND UNBALANCED PORTFOLIOS

divest its two dogs because of the less attractive market growth rates. All of these judgments imply that the first firm is likely to have significant growth in the longer term than the second, and one may conclude that the first firm's product portfolio is more balanced than that of the second firm.[10]

Business Assessment Array

This approach is also known as G.E.'s Business Screen. It is also based on two factors: industry attractiveness and competitive business position. The industry attractiveness is an expanded concept of relative market growth of

---

10 This judgmental analysis can be complicated if the firms have unequal numbers of products. One may require a multiattribute model to determine the degree of balance among a set of products; see Peter H. Farquhar and Vithala R. Rao, "A Balance Model for Evaluating Subsets of Multiattributed Items," *Management Science* 22 (May 1976): 528–539.

the BCG approach. In like manner, the competitive business position factor measures the firm's ability to compete in the market, a notion much broader than simple relative market share. The score for each factor is computed using a number of variables. For industry attractiveness, the variables include: market growth, market size, market cyclicity, market concentration, technological maturity, and competitive concentration. For business position, such variables as advantage in technology, advantage in marketing, advantage in production, size, and market share are used. Specific variables to be included in those factors will naturally depend upon the industry context.[11]

The method of applying this matrix is as follows. The analyst computes values of these two factors for each of the firm's products and classifies them into the 3×3 table shown in Figure 8.5. The range of each factor is divided into three equal intervals; these intervals determine the High, Medium, and Low categories for the industry attractiveness factor and the Strong, Medium, and Weak categories for the competitive business position. The products falling into the High/Strong cell are recommended for additional investment and growth of the corresponding businesses. The products in the Medium/Strong or High/Medium cell are considered carefully for growth but with some care in the investments made; therefore, they are called the Selective Growth category. The products in the diagonal cells—High/Weak, Medium/Medium and Low/Strong—are recommended for careful analysis of their market segments, and investments are recommended for strengthening the firm's position in some segments and letting its position be weakened in other segments. It is recommended for the products in the three other cells—Medium/Weak, Low/Medium, and Low/Weak—that the company either harvest the existing business (by withdrawing current investments or not increasing the current rates of investments) or divest them altogether. These resource allocation prescriptions are also shown in Figure 8.5.

The Directional Policy Matrix (Shell)

This approach developed by Shell Chemical Companies is quite similar to the business assessment array.[12] It uses two composite factors: business sector prospects and company's competitive capabilities. In a manner analogous to the business assessment array, these two factors are weighted sums of scores given on several variables. Figure 8.6 shows the components included in each composite factor. The procedure for computing these factor scores is similar to that of the business assessment array. Each variable of the factor is rated using 1–5 point scale (using stars rather than numbers). Some details follow.

11 For complete lists of variables that can be used for computing scores on the two factors, see Derek F. Abel and John S. Hammond, *Strategic Market Planning* (Englewood Cliffs, NJ: Prentice-Hall, 1979).

12 See S.J.Q. Robinson, R.E. Hichens, and D.P. Wade, "The Directional Policy Matrix—Tool for Strategic Planning," *Long Range Planning* 11 (June 1978): 8–15.

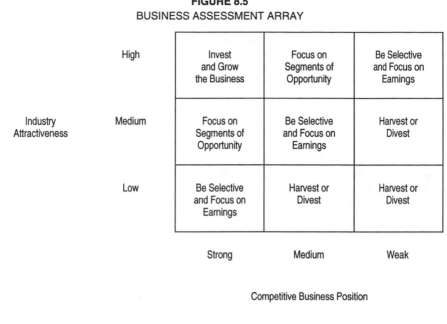

FIGURE 8.5
BUSINESS ASSESSMENT ARRAY

Industry Attractiveness		Strong	Medium	Weak
	High	Invest and Grow the Business	Focus on Segments of Opportunity	Be Selective and Focus on Earnings
	Medium	Focus on Segments of Opportunity	Be Selective and Focus on Earnings	Harvest or Divest
	Low	Be Selective and Focus on Earnings	Harvest or Divest	Harvest or Divest

Competitive Business Position

Business Sector Prospects

- **Market Growth:** This variable is intended to measure the business sector's profit potential in the future. Therefore, high market growth rates are not always regarded as those with high profit growth. Various other criteria that affect profit are included in this measure. The center point or average rating (three stars) is given to a business sector that is average for the broader industry in which the sector is located. The rating is adjusted using this as the benchmark.

- **Market Quality:** The rating on this variable is arrived at using answers to such questions as: Has the sector a record of high, stable profitability? Can the margins be maintained when manufacturing capacity exceeds demand? Is the product resistant to commodity pricing behavior? Is the technology of production freely available or is it restricted to those who developed it? and Is the product free from the risk of substitutes of an alternative synthetic or natural product? There are 10 questions for this variable.

- **Industry Feedstock Situation:** This variable is an attempt to consider whether the supply of raw materials (feedstock) is likely to be stable or whether there are alternative demands from other industries for such a supply. Based on this assessment, a rating is given. In some industries, this variable is not that relevant.

FIGURE 8.6
DIRECTIONAL POLICY MATRIX

Business Sector Prospects

		Unattractive	Average	Attractive
Weak	Disinvest	Phased Withdrawal	Double or Quit
		Custodial	
Average	Phased Withdrawal	Custodial	Try Harder
		Growth	
Strong	Cash Generation	Growth	Leader
		Leader	

Company's Competitive Capabilities

Source: S.J.Q. Robinson, R.E. Hichen, and D.P. Wade, "The Directional Policy Matrix—Tool for Strategic Planning," *Long Range Planning* 11 (June 1978). Reproduced with permission of the publisher.

Variables Included in the Dimensions

Business Sector Prospects

Market growth rate
Market quality
Industry feedstock situation
(supply of raw materials)
Environmental (regulatory) aspects

Company's Competitive Capabilities

Market position (primarily market share)
Production capability
Product research and development

- **Environmental (Regulatory) Aspects:** This variable is an assessment of the extent of restrictions from government on manufacture, transportation, or marketing that will affect the prospects for the business sector.

Company's Competitive Capabilities

- **Market Position:** Leader, five stars; major producer, four stars; strong and viable position, three stars; minor market share, two stars; and one star for negligible market share.

- **Production Capability:** This variable is a combination of process economics, capacity of hardware, location and number of plants, and access to feedstock. Stars are assigned to this variable depending upon the answers to questions such as Does the producer employ a modern economic production process? Is it his own process or licensed? and Has the producer secured access to enough feedstocks to sustain his present market share?

- **Product Research and Development:** This variable is intended to measure how a customer will judge the technical package offered by the business. The five-star rating is given using judgment on whether the company's product R & D is better than, commensurate with, or worse than its position in the market.

After each variable has been rated using the five-star scale, the total score for each factor is computed as a weighted sum of the scores on the variables. The weights determined are specific to the organization. Each factor is divided into three intervals as shown in Figure 8.6. After scores for all the products of the firm have been computed, they are located in the 3×3 matrix. The approach offers prescriptions for resource allocation, as shown in the figure. For example, if a product is classified into the cell of unattractive business prospects and strong competitive capabilities for the firm, the prescription is to use the product to generate cash, some of which may be used to support products in other cells such as those with attractive business prospects and average competitive capabilities of the firm.

Life Cycle Portfolio Matrix

With a view to implement the portfolio approaches more easily, researchers at A. D. Little developed the Life Cycle Portfolio Matrix, which has many of the features of the approaches described above.[13] Their premise is that industries, like products, have life cycles and that the level of maturity of the business unit's industry should be an important factor in a portfolio analysis. Accordingly, this approach reduces different variables into two composite dimensions: industry maturity and competitive position of the business unit. This approach distinguishes between four phases of industry maturity—embryonic, growing, maturing, and aging—and five levels of competitive position—dominant, strong, favorable, tenable, and weak. All business units of a firm are classified on these two factors and positioned into a 4×5 matrix, as shown in Figure 8.7.

Variables included in the industry maturity factor are market growth rate, growth potential, market share distribution among the participants, market

---

13 See Peter Patel and Michael Younger, "A Frame of Reference for Strategy Development," *Long Range Planning* 11 (April 1978): 6–12. See also Roger R. Osel and Robert V.L. Wright, "Allocating Resources: How to Do It in Multi-Industry Corporations," in Kenneth J. Albert, ed., *Handbook of Business Problem Solving* (New York: McGraw-Hill, 1980): 1-89–1-109 for a comprehensive application of this approach.

FIGURE 8.7
THE LIFE CYCLE PORTFOLIO MATRIX

	Stage of Industry Maturity			
Competitive Position	**Embryonic**	**Growth**	**Mature**	**Aging**
Dominant	All out push for share Hold position	Hold position Hold share	Hold position Grow with industry	Hold position
Strong	Attempt to improve position All out push for share	Attempt to improve position Push for share	Hold position Grow with industry	Hold position or Harvest
Favorable	Selective or all out push for share	Attempt to improve position	Custodial or maintenance	Harvest
	Selectively attempt to improve competitive position	Selective push for share	Find niche and attempt to protect	Phased withdrawal
Tenable	Selectively push for position	Find niche and protect it	Find niche and hang on or Phased withdrawal	Phased withdrawal or Abandon
Weak	Up or Out	Turnaround or Abandon	Turnaround or Phased Withdrawal	Abandon

Source: P. Patel and M. Younger, "A Frame of Reference for Strategy Development," *Long Range Planning* 11 (April 1978). Reproduced with permission of the publisher.

share stability of market share distribution, breadth of product line in the industry, number of competitors, customer stability, ease of entry, and technological stability. Each variable is measured, and a weighted score is computed to classify industries into the four categories. While the specific coding scheme is not publicized, the industry maturity and competitive position categories may be described as follows:[14]

Industry Maturity

- **Embryonic Industry:** Rapid growth, changes in technology, vigorous pursuit of new customers, and fragmented and unstable market shares.
- **Growth Industry:** Continues to exhibit rapid growth, established trends in customer purchase patterns, better-known competitors and technology, and difficulties in entering the industry.

---

14 See Arnoldo C. Hax and Nicholas S. Majlaf, *Strategic Management: An Integrative Perspective* (Englewood Cliffs, NJ: Prentice-Hall, 1984).

- **Mature Industry:** Exhibits stability in known customers, technology, and market shares (although the industry may still be highly competitive).
- **Aging Industry:** characterized by falling demand, declining number of competitors, and a narrowing of product line.

Competitive Position

- **Dominant:** This situation is extremely rare. Dominance results from a quasi-monopoly or from a strongly protected technological leadership. (An example is Intel in the microprocessor chip industry.)
- **Strong:** Exhibited by the firm's ability to follow strategies of its choice, irrespective of its competitors. (An example may be Kellogg in the cereal industry.)
- **Favorable:** This category is assigned to a leader in an industry that is quite fragmented, with no significant competitor.
- **Tenable:** This category is applied to a business whose profitability can be maintained through product specialization or a niche strategy.
- **Weak:** A position that cannot be sustained in the long term given the competitive economics of the industry. The business may be suffering from past mistakes or from a critical weakness.

Figure 8.7 also shows the proposed guidelines for resource allocation and strategies for various cells of the product life cycle matrix. For example, if the competitive position is weak in an embryonic industry, the firm has essentially two options: significantly investing to grow or divesting the business. If the position is strong in a growing industry, the strategy of selective push for market share is recommended. The recommendations in general imply changes in the resource allocations to various businesses.

An Empirical Comparison of Portfolio Models

Wind, Mahajan, and Swire compared the correspondence of four standardized portfolio models in classifying 15 SBUs of a large Fortune 500 firm.[15] The models are Growth-Share Matrix (BCG); Business Assessment Array; Directional Policy Matrix (Shell); and Modified A.D. Little (Market Share and Stage of Life Cycle) or what we called the Life Cycle Portfolio Matrix.

The authors operationalized the different constructs in these portfolio approaches using data collected from the company on the 15 businesses. First, four different definitions were used for the market growth variable: (1) Average annual rate of growth of the served market over a four-year period in real terms; (2) Same rate as (1) but in nominal terms; (3) Company's own forecast of average annual growth in real terms over the next four years; and (4) Average of company's forecast of growth in real terms over next four years

---

15 See Yoram Wind, Vijay Mahajan, and Donald J. Swire, "An Empirical Comparison of Standardized Product Portfolio Models," *Journal of Marketing* 47 (Spring 1983): 89–99.

and six years after that (used as an approximation of the outlook for a 10-year period).

Next, four different definitions were used for measuring market share of each business: (1) The ratio of the company's sales to the total sales of the served market; (2) The ratio of company's sales to the total sales of three largest competitors; (3) The ratio of company's sales to the sales of the largest competitor; and (4) A market share index computed as the sum of the two normalized market shares—normalized market share in the served market and the normalized market share of the firm versus three leaders in the market. The result of normalization is that the mean of all market shares in the corresponding set is zero. (In the case of market share in the served market, the average of market shares of all the companies in the served market is adjusted to zero by subtracting each share from the mean. A similar procedure is followed for the second normalization.) The effect of normalization is that a market share index of zero implies that it is pretty much like the industry, and values above zero imply that the firm is doing better than the industry.

Three other issues need to be resolved while making this comparison. First, some approaches are stated in terms of three or four categories on each composite dimension, while the rest are stated in terms of two categories for each. To ensure comparability, the authors used two dimensions for all approaches. The second issue deals with the rule to be used for dividing a dimension (or composite score) into high and low categories. The authors had used two methods for doing this division: (1) the internal rule of classifying businesses as high (or low) on a dimension depending upon whether the business is above (or below) the mean of all the 15 businesses of the company; and (2) an external rule in which the cut point is the mean of all businesses in the PIMS database.[16] The third issue is in deciding upon the weights to be used for computing the composite scores for the dimensions such as industry attractiveness. The authors used two options: no weights at all and the weights determined in a PIMS PAR ROI model (which involves estimating the future ROI for a business according to the characteristics of an average or PAR business in the PIMS database).

Thus, this comparison involved a variety of ways of implementing the four approaches of portfolio analysis: all combinations of the market growth and market share computation, two ways of determining the categories on a dimension, and two options for weights. The authors compared how the 15 businesses would be classified into the four quadrants of the 2×2 matrix for each approach of portfolio analysis.

This study brought out several important concerns of the standardized product portfolio models:

- Classification of an SBU depends upon the operational definition used for market share market growth.

---

16 The PIMS database consists of over 600 businesses that provided periodic data on their characteristics.

FIGURE 8.8
A COMPARISON OF FOUR STANDARDIZED PORTFOLIO MODELS

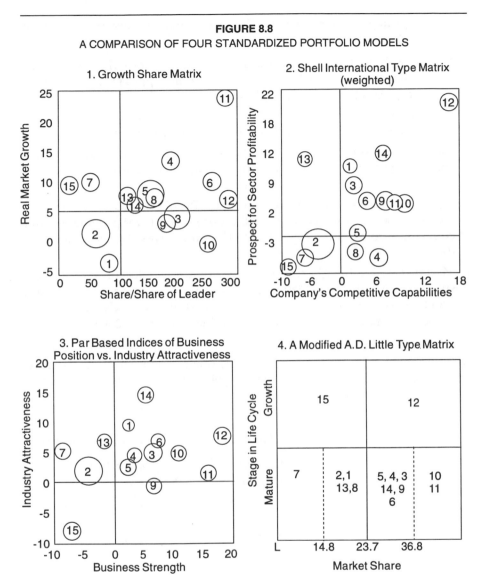

Source: Yoram Wind, Vijay Mahajan, and Donald J. Swire, "An Empirical Comparison of Standardized Portfolio Models," *Journal of Marketing* 47 (Spring 1983): 89–99. Reproduced with permission of the publisher.

- The rule for dividing a dimension into high or low or high, medium, or low is critical.

- The weighting schemes used in building a composite score can change the classification of an SBU.

Figure 8.8 shows the results of classifying the 15 businesses for one particular way of implementing each of these four portfolio approaches. The details used in these classifications are as follows:

- BCG Growth-Share Matrix: Market share versus leading competitor and real growth rate for the market over the last four years.
- Business Assessment Array: Weights from the PIMS PAR ROI model for computing the two composite dimensions and mean for each dimension as the cutoff for classifying into high or low.
- Directional Policy Matrix: Weights from the PIMS PAR ROI model used to compute the two composite dimensions of prospects for profitability and company's competitive capabilities. The cutoff was the mean on each dimension.
- Modified A.D. Little Matrix: Market position was determined by market share (similar to the BCG Matrix) and two stages of life cycle—maturity and growth—were used to describe the life cycle dimension. Using the cutoff of mean for market share, this approach also yielded a 2×2 matrix.

The comparison of the classifications of the 15 businesses based on these four portfolio approaches showed that only one business (#12) was classified consistently across them. Of the remaining 14 businesses, there were different patterns of classification as follows:

Number of Businesses	Patterns	Specific Businesses
7	high/low and high/high	3, 4, 5, 6, 9, 10, 11
3	low/low and low/high	2, 7, 15
2	low/low, high/low, and high/high	8, 14
1	low/low, low/high, and high/high	13
1	low/low and high/high	1

Based on these, the authors concluded that a specific portfolio model yields classifications that are highly specific to it; thus it is almost impossible to replicate the results from any one approach with another approach. Thus, the

FIGURE 8.9

THE PORTFOLIO TRAJECTORY: PRESENT AND PROJECTED POSITONS
OF STRATEGIC BUSINESS UNITS

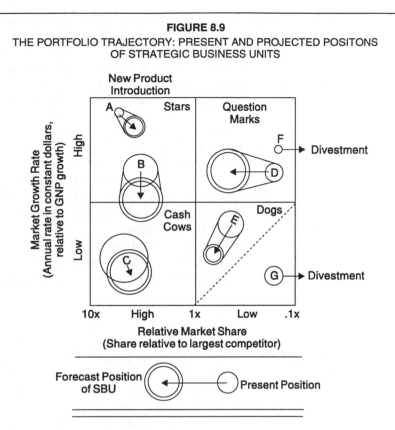

Diameter of circle is proportional to product's contribution to total company sales volume.

Source: George S. Day, "Diagnosing the Product Portfolio," Journal of Marketing 41 (April 1977). Reproduced with permission of the publisher.

recommendations for resource allocation will differ from one approach to another.

Evolution over Time

Suppose that a firm utilizes one portfolio approach consistently over time. In that case, it may be possible to study changes in the positions of businesses due to various resource allocation decisions. A pictorial way to depict the expected impact of specific allocations of resources to various business units is shown in Figure 8.9. In this example, the likely movement of an SBU's position is well illustrated. Note that a log-scale is used for the relative market share.

First, it is important to recognize that this figure represents products (or business) by circles and that the diameter of each circle is proportional to the product's contribution to the total company sales volume. (One way to draw these circles is by first computing the diameter of the circle as proportional to the square root of the area of the circle or the contribution of the product.)

It is interesting to see in this figure that product A, a star, was forecasted to be quite prominent. Similarly, product D, a question mark, is expected to grow much larger, presumably with heavy injections of marketing resources. By withdrawing the investment from product E, the figure forecasts that it will shrink considerably. The released resources are presumably used for developing A and D in the future. The market growth of product B's industry is expected to be slower, which is reflected in it being demoted from the star category to the cash cow, although the investments are such that its market share is expected to remain stable. Product C's industry is also expected to grow slower, indicating that it is better for the firm to milk it in the future. Finally, the figure depicts that the firm is currently better off divesting product G, which is essentially a dog in the firm's portfolio.

In closing this discussion of dynamics of portfolio, we must caution that a considerable amount of data is necessary to develop forecasts. Our discussion of the mathematical portfolio approach will indicate these requirements.

Some Developments in Portfolio Analysis

The foregoing discussion should indicate the problems of consistency of results obtained from a graphical approach to portfolio analysis. This situation could be due to such factors as the reliance on at most two dimensions to describe a product or a business, relatively simple operationalizations of the dimensions chosen and computing them with limited number (in most cases only one) variable, not using appropriate weights in determining the composite dimensions relying upon historical data, and treating each business as a composite unit, not in terms of several submarkets or segments. When historical data are not available, the tendency is to rely on the judgment of one manager in the firm. The aforementioned factors will lead to inconsistency in following the implied recommendations (prescriptions) reached from a graphical analysis for resource allocation decisions; thus, this approach will lead to a high degree of uncertainty for a firm.

To correct these problems, product portfolios can be developed on a situation-by-situation basis. This customized approach supplements existing objective data with judgments from several managers who have some experience with the product. Management's input is solicited to help with the decision about the specific variables to use in describing a product and with deriving appropriate weights for the variables as well. Further, the trend is to think in terms of future situations (e.g., projected data) rather than to use historical data alone. Another trend is to consider resource allocation at multiple levels and at smaller units such as product segments. These customized approaches include the analytic hierarchy process and the use of conjoint analysis, which we discuss in a later section.

The STRATPORT Approach (A Mathematical Portfolio Method)

The standardized product portfolio approaches may be deemed more descriptive in terms of giving recommendations on the actual allocation of resources across various SBUs of a firm. The procedures are quite intuitive and put emphasis on the process of computing factors that go into the pictorial representation of the positions of each SBU on a product portfolio chart. The methods do not involve any optimization of an objective of the firm, and thus the recommended allocations of resources are likely to be suboptimal.

One procedure that attempts to accomplish the optimization process is due to Larreche and Srinivasan.[17] They developed a decision support system that represents an extension and operationalization of the standardized product portfolio approaches. It is designed for managers to evaluate and formulate various business portfolio strategies (i.e., various resource allocation schemes). The system is based on a mathematical model that utilizes existing data on SBUs as well as judgmental data obtained from managers.

The basic structure of the STRATPORT system for a single business unit is shown in Figure 8.9. The system begins with a decision made on the marketing investment for the business unit in the planning period. The STRATPORT system uses six main functional relationships at the level of the business unit (product category) indicated in Figure 8.10. These are: (1) the market response function, (2) the maintenance marketing function, (3) the capacity expenditures function, (4) the working capital function, (5) the cost function, and (6) the price function. These six relationships are identified in Figure 8.10. The authors utilize well-established functional forms and estimate their parameters either from past data or from judgmental data collected from managers.

As can be seen, the STRATPORT system incorporates the relationships between marketing investment (resources devoted to a SBU) and the expected market share at any given time in a planning period; this relationship is marked 1 in the figure. Further, it determines the amount of expenditure needed to maintain the market share beyond the planning period (called post-planning period); this is marked 2 in the figure.

The experience-curve effects on the costs of production are incorporated as shown by the section marked 5. The STRATPORT model assumes that unit costs, expressed in constant dollars, decline as a function of the business unit's cumulative production. In this model, however, unit costs incorporate all costs (including depreciation) with the exception of marketing investments, which are accounted for separately in the system. The model also utilizes a relationship between the total market size of the category that determines the cumulative production of the industry. This variable determines the competitive price level for the firm (as shown by relationship 6). The price function also

17 See Jean-Claude Larréche and V. Srinivasan, "STRATPORT: A Decision Support System for Strategic Planning," *Journal of Marketing* 45 (Fall 1981): 39–52.

FIGURE 8.10

STRUCTURE OF STRATPORT FOR A SINGLE BUSINESS UNIT

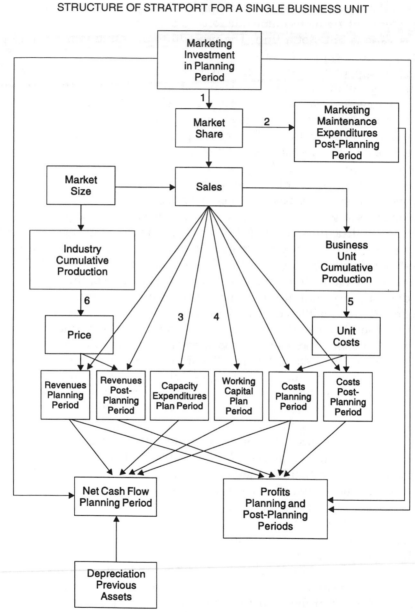

Source: Jean-Claude Larréche and V. Srinivasan, "STRATPORT: A Decision Support System for Strategic Planning," *Journal of Marketing* 45 (Fall 1981): 39–52. Reproduced with permission of the publisher.

assumes that average industry price per unit declines as a function of cumulative production, a behavior similar to that of unit costs.

The cash flows during the planning period for the SBU are computed as the after-tax profits from the business unit (revenues minus costs minus marketing investments, adjusted by the appropriate tax rate) minus the portion of the increase in the working capital not expensed during the planning period, minus the portion of additional capacity investment not depreciated during the planning period, plus the depreciation during the planning period of assets acquired before the beginning of the planning period. (The effects on capacity expansion and working capital are shown by the numbers 3 and 4, respectively, in the figure.) In other words, the computation for the cash flows is made as precise as possible, taking into account all of the relevant factors, including tax and depreciation. (However, there is the problem of allocating various fixed costs of the firm among the several SBUs; the model assumes that this allocation is feasible.) The level of risk associated with any SBU is incorporated into the STRATPORT system by computing the present value of the cash flows using a discount rate higher than the expected rate of return for risk-free assets. The authors propose using a rate of return model using the financial beta coefficients computed for closely related industries.

The results for the different SBUs are then combined to obtain the present value of profits for the firm as a whole. The authors utilize an efficient algorithm to optimize the allocation of resources among the SBUs so as to maximize the present value of the firm subject to a constraint on the discounted cash flow during the planning period. The effects of the allocation can also be evaluated for various levels of the cash constraint of the firm, which represents the firm's ability to borrow or lend during the planning horizon.

Table 8.1 illustrates the use of STRATPORT. This illustration shows the situation of a firm with four existing business units, 1, 2, 3, and 4, which are respectively a cash cow, a star, a dog, and a question mark (in the terminology of the Boston Consulting Group) with current market shares of 20, 30, 5, and 5, respectively. The first portion of the table shows the projections of the model for the planning and post-planning period for the current situation (with no optimization used). These projections show that the four business units require $45 million, $150 million, $40 million, and $30 million, respectively, to maintain their current market shares. Also, the status quo strategy implies that the firm does not make any investments into two new business units, labeled 5 and 6. This status quo strategy would generate cash needs of –297 million or equivalently a net cash flow of 297 million over a three-year planning period and profits of $1,367 (= 665 + 550 + 37 + 115) million over the eight-year time horizon considered in the analysis (planning period plus post-planning period). Further, during the planning period, Business Unit 1 contributes 204 million to the net cash flow of the firm (or about 69 percent to the total profit to the firm). Over the long run, Business Units 1 and 2 contribute over 90 percent of the firm's total profits.

TABLE 8.1

AN ILLUSTRATIVE RUN OF THE STRATPORT MODEL

Indicate Marketing Investment for
    Business Unit 1: 45
    Business Unit 2: 150
    Business Unit 3: 40
    Business Unit 4: 30
    Business Unit 5: 0
    Business Unit 6: 0
Output Saved in File for Off-Line Printing
Do You Want to Proceed (0), or to Display Results (1)? 1

Evaluation of Portfolio Strategy

Cash Needs	−297
Profit Level	1367
Market Share	
BU 1	.202
BU 2	.300
BU 3	.050
BU 4	.050
BU 5	.000
BU 6	.000

Sources and Uses of Funds

Business Unit Number	BU 1	BU 2	BU 3	BU 4	BU 5	BU 6
Cash Needs						
Revenue PL	824	1372	345	190	0	0
Costs PL	551	1082	295	127	0	0
Mktg. IN PL	45	150	40	30	0	0
Capa. IN PL	25	79	−11	23	0	0
Total Profits	−204	−61	−21	−10	0	0
Revenue PL	824	1372	345	190	0	0
Costs PL	551	1082	295	127	0	0
Mktg. IN PL	45	150	40	30	0	0
Revenue PP	1623	3838	623	468	0	0
Costs PP	1089	2969	530	302	0	0
Mktg. IN PP	98	460	67	84	0	0
Total	665	550	37	115	0	0

Input minimum and maximum levels of external cash availability: −600.200
Output saved in file for off-line printing
Do you want to proceed (0), or to display key results (1)
Profit contributions (2), or cash flows (3) 1

Table continues

TABLE 8.1

(Continued)

Key Optimization Results

	Option 1	Option 2	Option 3	Option 4	Option 5	Option 6
Cash Needs	206	195	185	175	165	106
Profit Level	2911	2894	2877	2860	2842	2735
Marg. % Yield	19.53	20.26	21.00	21.73	22.46	23.19
Market Share						
BU 1	.203	.201	.198	.195	.193	.150
BU 2	.394	.393	.391	.390	.389	.387
BU 3	.010	.010	.010	.010	.010	.010
BU 4	.171	.170	.170	.169	.169	.168
BU 5	.360	.358	.355	.353	.351	.349
BU 6	.000	.000	.000	.000	.000	.000

	Option 7	Option 8	Option 9	Option 10	Option 11
Cash Needs	−383	−386	−389	−393	−609
Profit Level	1813	1807	1801	1793	1330
Marg. % Yield	23.92	24.66	25.39	26.12	26.85
Market Share					
BU 1	.150	.150	.150	.150	.150
BU 2	.050	.050	.050	.050	.050
BU 3	.010	.010	.010	.010	.010
BU 4	.168	.167	.167	.166	.166
BU 5	.346	.344	.342	.339	.000
BU 6	.000	.000	.000	.000	.000

PL = Planning Period   BU = Business Unit
PP = Post-Planning Period   IN = Investment

Source: Jean-Claude Larréche and V. Srinivasan, "STRATPORT: A Decision Support System for Strategic Planning," *Journal of Marketing* 45 (Fall 1981). Reproduced with permission of the publisher.

The second part of Table 8.1 shows the optimization results for 11 different portfolio strategies for different cash constraints, ranging from a net cash generation of $609 million to a net cash need of $206 million. These strategies produce widely varying results. At one extreme, option 1 would require a net cash injection of $206 million and would generate a total profit of $2911 million. At the other extreme, option 11 would generate a net cash flow of $609 million (or a cash need of −$609 million) and a total profit of $1330 million. Under each of the options, Business Unit 6 does not appear to be an attractive opportunity. Also, the most appropriate strategy for Business Unit 3 in all options is minimum investment, while Business Unit 4 appears to warrant a substantial marketing investment so as to increase its market share. The optimum business strategies for the remaining three business units appear to differ widely under the eleven options.

Methods Based on AHP

Consider the problem of allocating resources by a firm that seeks to make additional investments in product modification, market development, or new product development as opposed to an existing investment strategy. (These allocation decisions are equivalent to allocating resources across various SBUs of a firm.) The firm may have multiple objectives such as growth of sales, increasing market share, high profitability, and reduction of vulnerability to external forces. Further, the firm needs to make investment decisions without knowing how the environment will be during the planning horizon. The problem here is to judgmentally integrate several factors in some manner and reach a final allocation decision.

The Analytic Hierarchy Process (AHP) methodology developed by Saaty offers a natural tool to facilitate such integration of multiple factors.[18] First, it calls for breaking down the larger problem into smaller problems, each of which is hierarchically organized by the decision maker. Figure 8.11 shows a hierarchical decomposition for this problem of allocation for new product activities. This hierarchy implies that environment is the overriding factor affecting the overall well-being of the firm. It is, therefore, placed at the top of the hierarchy. The next two levels of the hierarchy show various objectives of the firm and the competing strategies to reach them. Various objectives of the firm need to be traded off against each other in order for each environmental scenario to reach the overall objective of corporate well-being. This example considers four objectives: sales growth, increasing market share, increasing productivity, and reducing vulnerability to competitive pressures. The competing alternative strategies are existing product modification, market development, creating new products, and other nonmarketing related activities. Further, one needs to consider all four objectives under each of the scenarios in the process of allocating resources among the four alternatives. The AHP methodology offers a way to accomplish this difficult task using judgmental data obtained from executives. The AHP exercise results in the percentage allocations of a budget to the competing alternatives. As shown in Figure 8.11, the judgments of the executives indicate that 32 percent of the resources should be allocated to modifying products, 22 percent to developing markets, 20 percent to developing new products, and 28 percent to existing plans of the firm. (In fact, these numbers are derived from similar numbers at the previous two levels in the hierarchy.)

For implementing AHP methodology, various factors relevant to the main problem are grouped into subgroups deemed relevant to each subproblem. Thus, the decision problem is hierarchically decomposed into a hierarchy with several layers, each consisting of a subgroup of factors. Using a simple data

---

18 See Thomas L. Saaty, *The Analytic Hierarchy Process* (New York: McGraw-Hill, 1980).

FIGURE 8.11
A HYPOTHETICAL HIERARCHY FOR ALLOCATION DECISIONS
FOR GROWTH STRATEGIES

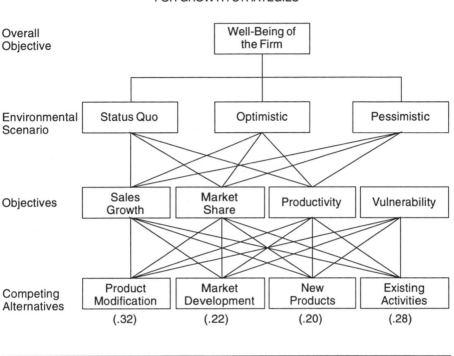

collection procedure and analysis, weights are developed for each factor in any layer. In this process, judgmental data are collected from the decision maker. If the decisions are to be made by a group, this procedure can be repeated for every member of the group. The methodology provides for combining data from each decision maker in a group. We illustrate this methodology for the case of one and multiple decision makers.

An Illustration of AHP with One Decision Maker

The AHP methodology has been applied to the problem of allocating resources for the Colonial Penn Insurance Company, a fast growing firm specializing in developing and marketing auto and homeowner's policies to the over-50 market segment.[19] The AHP helped guide the selection of desired portfolio of products/markets and distribution outlets, and the allocation of resources among the portfolio's components. The hierarchy developed for handling this problem is shown in Figure 8.12.

---

19 See Yoram Wind and Thomas L. Saaty, "Marketing Applications of the Analytic Hierarchy Process," *Management Science* 26 (July 1980): 641–658.

FIGURE 8.12
WEIGHTS ESTIMATED FOR THE ANALYTICAL HIERARCHY OF
COLONIAL PENN INSURANCE COMPANY

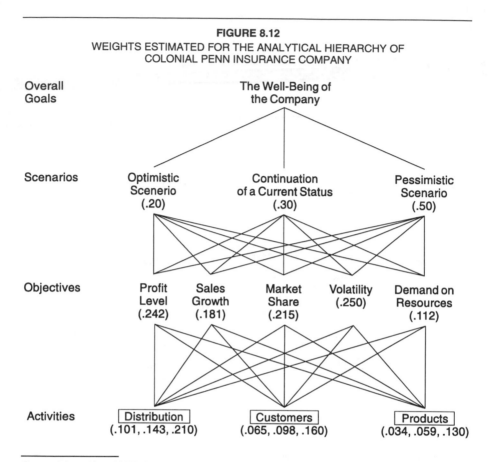

Overall Goals		The Well-Being of the Company
Scenarios	Optimistic Scenerio (.20)	Continuation of a Current Status (.30) Pessimistic Scenario (.50)

Objectives   Profit Level (.242)   Sales Growth (.181)   Market Share (.215)   Volatility (.250)   Demand on Resources (.112)

Activities   Distribution (.101, .143, .210)   Customers (.065, .098, .160)   Products (.034, .059, .130)

Source: Adapted from Y. Wind and T.L. Saaty, "Marketing Applications of the Analytic Hierarchy Process," *Management Science* 26 (July 1980). Reproduced with permission of the publisher.

In this hierarchy, the objective of increasing the well-being of the company is evaluated under three possible environmental scenarios describing the growth of the economy. Five specific objectives are considered relevant to the well-being of the company: profit level, sales growth, market share, volatility, and demand for resources. The three activities highlighted here are distribution, customers, and products. Once the data are obtained on the relative priorities and are combined, the AHP will yield numbers that show the judged allocations of resources for the three activities. In this situation, the chief executive of the company provided the input data. The results are also shown in Figure 8.12.

According to Figure 8.12, the chief executive considers the pessimistic scenario to be more likely (with a weight of 0.5) relative to the optimistic scenario (weight of 0.2) and continuation of current status (weight of 0.3).

Further, the five objectives leading to the well-being of the company differ in their relative importances. For example, volatility is deemed more important, with a relative weight of 0.250 as compared to a profit level objective with a relative weight of 0.242. The final weights for the three activities as estimated by this analysis are as shown for each of the scenarios:

Activity	Optimistic	Continuation	Pessimistic	Total
Distribution	0.101	0.143	0.210	0.454
Customers	0.065	0.098	0.160	0.323
Products	0.034	0.059	0.134	0.223
Total	0.2	0.3	0.5	1.000

According to this analysis, based on the judgments of the chief executive, the firm should allocate 45.4 percent of its resources to the development and maintenance of its distribution outlets. Further, 32.3 percent of its resources should be allocated to identifying and targeting its customers (current and new), and 22.3 percent of its resources should be allocated to the development and maintenance of its products.

The interactive software EXPERT CHOICE can be used to implement AHP.[20] With a set of questions posed to the user, the software develops a hierarchy for the problem and collects necessary judgmental data to compute the weights for the alternatives.

An Illustration of AHP with Multiple Decision Makers

The setting for this application was an industrial manufacturing firm, an internationally known and highly diversified firm with annual sales revenue in excess of $3 billion. It shows how judgments of different decision makers can be integrated via AHP.

In the midst of a severe recession, several of the firm's SBUs were operating at less than half their capacity. Earnings were sharply reduced, and the number of layoffs was substantial.

The transportation equipment SBU was perhaps the hardest hit. The general manager of this SBU was determined to improve the profitability of his products. He believed the key to better profits was "smarter" resource allocation. Consequently, he commissioned an external consulting team to study his SBU and recommend a resource allocation scheme that would improve long-term profitability and gain consensus among his top managers. He was reflecting upon the implications of this study for his unit's strategic planning.

Transportation Equipment Division Market Position

The transportation equipment division manufactures and markets a wide variety of industrial components such as sprockets, industrial timing belts,

---

20 Expert Choice, Inc., EXPERT CHOICE, Version 9.0 (McLean, VA: Decision Support Software, Inc., 1995).

and couplings. Since its formation, this division generally operated with acceptable efficiency, especially in solving short-term problems, but paid almost no attention to long-term planning issues. Product development, market expansion, and facilities expansion were sacrificed in order to maintain current dividends and high employee bonuses. Due to the cyclical nature of the transportation industry, the division had been through some challenging periods, but the then current recession coupled with increased foreign competition had made management eager to implement an effective planning and resource allocation system.

Resource Allocation Study

The consulting team was charged to "get more with less" and assigned to develop a plan for allocating resources between the division's four major products (sprockets, roller bearings, clutches, and couplings) based on the inputs of several key managers. The consulting team conducted the study using the Analytic Hierarchy Process (AHP).

The model addresses the allocation of limited resources within a given product mix. Unlike other portfolio models such as the Boston Consulting Group's growth/share matrix or PIMS, AHP focuses on multiple objectives (in this study, profitability, sales, growth, and productivity).

Research Design

Eight executives from various levels and functional areas of the organization were interviewed. During the interview, a questionnaire was administered to the managers. If a completed questionnaire contained ambiguities, with respect to legibility, completeness, consistency, or accuracy, a second interview was conducted.

Current Allocation Scheme

A recent organizational audit showed that 10 percent of the transportation equipment division's resources were allocated to sprockets, 30 percent to roller bearings, 25 percent to clutches, 25 percent to couplings, and 10 percent to various other products within the division. Thus, the allocation of resources to the four product groups (excluding other products) is 11 percent to sprockets, 33 percent to roller bearings, 28 percent to clutches, and 32 percent to couplings. All eight managers indicated they were not satisfied with the current allocation, feeling that the plan was too "middle-of-the-road" to be anything other than "suboptimal." Based on several interviews, the researchers developed the hierarchy shown in Figure 8.13.

Table 8.2 shows the detailed results for one manager, Manager A, as well as the computed allocations for all eight managers interviewed in this study. An important question to consider in this situation is how to arrive at consen-

FIGURE 8.13

ANALYTICAL HIERARCHY DEVELOPED FROM INTERVIEWS AMONG SEVERAL
DECISION MAKERS FOR AN INDUSTRIAL MANUFACTURING FIRM

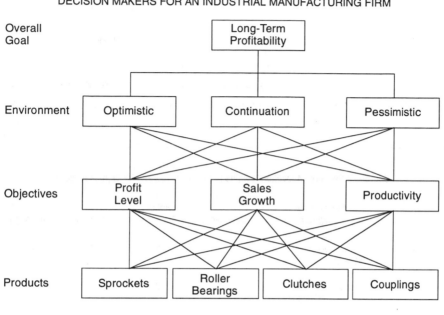

sus for the resource allocation scheme for this unit. The estimated allocations for each manager can be weighted in proportion to their expertise with the various businesses or their experience with the company. Another weighting scheme could be on the basis of the degree of consistency of their judgments with the AHP model. For ease, we simply show the average allocation for the eight managers. Compared to the current allocation of resources to the four product groups, the average scheme based on AHP suggests a reduction in emphasis on couplings in preference to roller bearings.

Methods Based on Conjoint Analysis

Conjoint analysis can be employed to determine the appropriate allocation of resources to a set of businesses. (The essentials of this methodology are described in Chapter 2.) The method runs as follows. The analyst first determines the range of resource allocation feasible for each business and determines a small number of levels for each; for example, the range for any business could be between 10 and 25 million with levels of 10, 15, 20, and 25 million. Using this information, the analyst develops a number of potential resource allocations to the businesses under consideration. In a situation with four businesses—A, B, C, and D—these profiles will be as follows:

TABLE 8.2

ESTIMATED ANP WEIGHTS FOR THE MANAGERS OF THE INDUSTRIAL FIRM

Manager A

Environment		Objectives		Products	
Optimistic	0.101	Profit level	0.46	Sprockets	0.2581
Continuation	0.799	Sales growth	0.055	Roller bearings	0.0916
Pessimistic	0.099	Productivity	0.48	Clutches	0.4508
				Couplings	0.1991

Computed Resource Allocation Weights to the Four Products for Eight Managers

Managers	Position and Background	Sprockets	Roller Bearings	Clutches	Couplings
A	Product Manager, MBA, 7 yrs.	.26	.09	.45	.20
B	Industrial Marketing Manager, BS, 14 yrs.	.05	.49	.31	.15
C	General Manager, BS, 20 yrs.	.04	.54	.30	.12
D	Division Manager, BS, 16 yrs.	.10	.43	.17	.30
E	Marketing Manager, MBA, 6 yrs.	.08	.52	.10	.30
F	Vice-President Operations, BS, 17 yrs.	.03	.28	.28	.41
G	Field Sales Manager, MBA, 10 yrs.	.14	.62	.15	.08
H	Vice-President Marketing and Sales, MBA, 10 yrs.	.03	.14	.45	.38
Average Allocation		.09	.39	.28	.24
Current Allocation		.11	.33	.28	.32

Allocation Profile	A	B	C	D
1	10	15	20	12
2	20	18	15	15
etc.	etc.			

Along with detailed descriptions of the industries and current business situations, the profiles are presented for evaluation by a number of managers. Each resource allocation profile will be judged on such criteria as growth of profits for the firm and feasibility. Using this information, the analyst estimates each respondent's utility functions for allocations to each business. This information is then used to simulate a number of potential allocations plans.

This approach is fully adaptable to the specific situation. The levels of resources used in profiles, the businesses selected, and the criteria of evaluation can be adjusted to the particular needs of the management. Although it is judgmental, it is in the same spirit as the different portfolio approaches described above. It enables one to synthesize managerial experience in resource allocation decisions. The results do not yield optimal allocations, but can be used in a computer simulation to evaluate how a number of suggested allocations will fare on the criteria used in the conjoint study. Only limited applications of this method exist.

Methods Based on Market Response Functions

Rules for optimal allocation of marketing resources among different products or SBUs can be developed using their market response functions. For this purpose, one needs to estimate the elasticity of sales response to changes in the total marketing expenditure for any product or SBU. The optimal allocation for a given product category will depend on its degree of interdependence with other categories; products are interdependent if expenditures in one category influence the sales of another category. We will consider the cases of absence and presence of interdependence separately.

The methods for estimating market response functions[21] include econometric methods, the decision-calculus approach, and experimental methods such as conjoint analysis.

No Interdependence

Once a market response function has been estimated, the rule for optimal allocation across products (assuming no interdependence among products) is as follows:

---

21 These functions are used to compute the elasticity of sales of a product with respect to the marketing expenditures devoted to it. In addition to this self-elasticity, one may also compute a cross-elasticity for one product with respect to the marketing expenditures for another product to determine the cross-effect.

$$X_i^* = \frac{(P_i - c_i)e_{ii}S_i}{\displaystyle\sum_{i=1}^{n} (P_i - c_i)e_{ii}S_i} * B$$

$$i = 1, 2, ..., n.$$

where

B	=	Budget for all n products
n	=	Number of products
S_i	=	Sales (units) for the ith product
X_i^*	=	Optimal allocation for the ith product
P_i	=	Price per unit for the ith product
C_i	=	Cost per unit for the ith product
e_{ii}	=	Self-elasticity of ith product's sales with respect to amount of resources devoted to it

This rule indicates that a product will receive higher optimal allocation of resources if its margins are higher, the market is more responsive to such expenditures (i.e., higher elasticity), and its sales are larger. Such a determination is quite intuitive.

Interdependence

When products interact in their demand functions, the rule for optimal allocation across products is

$$X_i^* = \frac{\displaystyle\sum_{j=1}^{n} \left(P_j - c_j\right)e_{ji}S_j}{\displaystyle\sum_{i=1}^{n}\sum_{j=1}^{n} \left(P_j - c_j\right)e_{ji}S_j} * B$$

where the new term, e_{ji} = cross-elasticity of jth product sales with respect to the amount of resources devoted to ith product; $i,j = 1, 2, ... n$. Other notation terms in this equation are the same as before. If the cross-elasticities are zero, the products do not interact, and this formula reduces to the one above for the case of no demand interdependence.

The impact of demand interdependence among products can be observed in several situations. Examples include the Gillette Sensor and Gillette Sensor Prestige series of men's razors, the American Express Green, Gold, and Platinum credit cards, and various brands of laundry detergents of Procter & Gamble. The effects of interdependence on the optimal allocation of resources depend upon the magnitudes of the cross-elasticities among the products as shown in the above formula. We will illustrate these effects with hypothetical data.

For this purpose, assume that a firm marketing a brand of men's personal use item has developed a more expensive version of the same product (perhaps made with better materials and packaged more elegantly). We call these items "Regular" and "Elite" versions. Also, assume that experience with the promotion of the Elite version indicates that it has a more pronounced effect on the demand for the Regular. But, the Regular version has almost no effect upon the demand for Elite. Essentially, the Regular version is aimed at the mass market. This situation could be due to various factors such as the exclusive distribution achieved for the Elite version and the way it is promoted. As could be expected, the sales of the Regular version are many times larger than those of the Elite version; for the purpose of this illustration, we will assume that the sales of the Regular version are $1,400 million versus a sales level of $30 million for the Elite. A total resource of $250 million is to be allocated between these two products.

Further, assume that the average prices per unit of the Regular and Elite versions were approximately $4.00 and $40.00 with respective margins of 50 percent and 70 percent. Further, we will assume that the judgments of the self- and cross-elasticities of sales with respect to the marketing expenditures on the two versions were as follows:

| | Sales of | |
Expenditure on	Regular	Elite
Regular	0.4	almost zero
Elite	0.05	0.2

Optimal allocations of marketing expenditures to the two products under different assumptions of product interdependence are shown in Table 8.3; these are labeled Cases I, II, and III. Under Case I, the Elite version would receive a budget of 30.7 million, while the Regular version would receive 219.3 million, using the elasticities shown above. However, if the products are deemed independent, the Elite version would receive only 3.7 million, and the lion's share would be spent on the Regular version. Presumably, the image of the Elite version would have a considerable impact on the sales of the less expensive brand.

Cases II and III demonstrate that even if the judgments on self-elasticities were changed, the impact of interdependence is quite dramatic. If both products are judged to have equal self-elasticities, the Elite version would receive higher allocations than Case I. If, on the other hand, the Regular's expenditures are not as effective as the Elite version (compare 0.2 with 0.4), Regular would receive less allocations. But the impact of interdependence continues to be high.

TABLE 8.3
ILLUSTRATIVE ALLOCATION OF BUDGET UNDER DEMAND INTERDEPENDENCE

Product	Price per Unit	Margin (P-C)	Sales ($000s)	Sales Units (000s)
Regular	$ 4.00	$ 2.00	1,400	350
Elite	40.00	28.00	30	0.75

Cross-Elasticity Matrix

		Effect on Sales of	
Expenditure on		Regular	Elite
X1	Regular	e_{11}	$e_{21} = 0$
X2	Elite	e_{12}	e_{22}

Case	Interdependence	Optimal Allocation	
		X_1^* (Regular)	X_2^* (Elite)
Case I			
$e_{11} = 0.4$ $e_{12} = 0.05$	Yes	219.30	30.7
$e_{22} = 0.2$	No	246.30	3.7
Case II			
$e_{11} = 0.4$ $e_{12} = 0.05$	Yes	216.50	33.5
$e_{22} = 0.4$	No	242.72	7.28
Case III			
$e_{11} = 0.2$ $e_{12} = 0.05$	Yes	190.84	59.16
$e_{22} = 0.4$	No	235.85	14.15

ALLOCATION OF RESOURCES ACROSS MULTIPLE BRANDS OF ONE PRODUCT (SBU)

Methods Based on Conjoint Analysis

Given the versatility of the conjoint method, it is not surprising that it can also be applied to the problem of determining appropriate allocation of a given resource for an SBU to various brands. The method is essentially the same as that described for allocation among various SBUs. The difference will be in terms of detailed descriptions of the positions of various brands within the SBU where the allocations will be made. Further, the analyst should design the study to ensure determination of any potential interactions between the allocations to the brands. This issue is important because of the potential synergy (both positive and negative) between the brands of an SBU. The design will accordingly be more complicated.

Methods Based on AHP

The problem of allocating a given resource for a product (or a brand) to different marketing mix elements is no different from that of allocating a resource to various products. The methodology of AHP can be immediately applied to this situation. The relevant hierarchy will be much simplified perhaps with only two layers.

Methods Using the Market Response Function

The procedure based on market response function described in the previous section and illustrated with the Regular and Elite product lines is directly applicable to allocating a given level of marketing resources across multiple brands of a product category. Various brands in a multibrand corporation are likely to be interdependent. Thus, the market response functions for any brand should include self-elasticities as well as cross-elasticities. Once these elasticities are estimated, allocation can be made using the formula shown earlier.

METHODS FOR ALLOCATING MARKETING EXPENDITURES FOR A BRAND

Methods Based on Pooled Business Experience

In this section, we will briefly discuss methods for allocating resources that are based on pooled business experience. Pooled business experience refers to the accumulation of business decisions made and the resulting performance of several businesses in different industries at one or more points in time. It is clear that any one business can yield only a limited number of data points to build a statistical model relating decisions to results. Researchers, therefore, have begun to collect data on pooled business experience for developing such statistical relationships.

The principle involved is that a model can be developed using the historical or cross-sectional experience of several businesses and that it can be used to determine the average performance of a business under various contingent assumptions about the resources and other business characteristics. The idea is that managers dealing with similar problems over a period of time may develop decision rules that appear reasonable. Thus, a model developed using data on several businesses may be applicable to a separate business, once we account for variables that are specific to it.

Relevant data for building these models are obtained through surveys administered in a sample of businesses. One of the major efforts for collecting such data is the PIMS system of the Strategic Planning Institute (SPI), which grew out of an internal project of the General Electric Corporation. The SPI was created in 1975 as a nonprofit, autonomous corporation. The PIMS database has grown steadily over the years and included over 2,600 businesses by mid-1986.[22] It covers various industry categories (durable, nondurable, consumer, industrial, and service and distribution).

The second major effort is the ADVISOR project, which focuses on industrial products and collects more detailed data on products rather than businesses, as in PIMS.[23] Further, the definition used by PIMS for an industrial product is much less stringent than that used in the ADVISOR (e.g., less than 50 percent of the business's sales could be to households). The second phase of this project, ADVISOR 2, involved 22 companies and 131 products.

The PIMS PAR Approach

The PIMS data were used to build a regression model to predict the business's profit performance (as measured by the ROI, return on investment) in terms of various product, market, and customer characteristics. In this regression model, the influence of several variables is statistically significant, as one would expect. Importantly, the variables of market growth and market share (which are the core of the graphical portfolio approaches) are significant and influence the ROI in a positive direction. Other variables included in these models capture various characteristics of the product (e.g., relative quality and percent of new products), the market (e.g., vertical integration), and the customer (e.g., purchase amount and customized products). Business characteristics such as R&D as a percent of sales and marketing as a percent of sales are also included in this model.

The SPI produces several reports using the PIMS analyses; one significant one for the purposes of resource allocation is the PAR Report. The PAR Report specifies the return on investment that is normal (or "par") for a business, given the characteristics of its market, competition, position, technology, and cost structure. The experience of other similar businesses is used in computing the par for a business. The par then refers to an estimate of the normal return of a business that is quite akin to the one under consideration. It also indicates major strengths and major weaknesses (or major positive factors and major negative factors) of the business in realizing the normal rate of return. The business under question is then compared to the par. With the knowledge of the factors influencing the par, the strategist will be in a position to determine which factors should be changed in order to realize higher returns than the par. The PAR report also includes Strategy Sensitive Reports that show how the rate of return for the business would change for assumptions on the environment of the business and for different strategies that could be used for the business (e.g., a strategy to build market share). In addition, the report indicates the "optimum" combination of several strategic moves that promise

22 See Robert D. Buzzell and Bradley T. Gale, *The PIMS Principles: Linking Strategy to Performance* (New York: The Free Press, 1987).

23 See Gary L. Lilien, "ADVISOR 2: Modeling the Marketing Mix Decisions for Industrial Products," *Management Science* 25 (February 1979): 191–204.

to give optimal results for a business. The combination of strategic moves is translated into a specific allocation of resources.

Several aspects of PIMS analysis are worth noting. First, there will be a trade-off between ROI and market share. Second, strategy to optimize discounted net income will be quite distinct from that of seeking increases in market share. Finally, the associated level of investment will vary for different strategies. Once the management decides upon the specific objective to be realized (e.g., a major decrease or a small increase in market share), these analyses will identify the total amount of investment (or resource) called for to achieve that objective.

ADVISOR Approach

In contrast to the PIMS approach, the ADVISOR models are specific to industrial products. They involve estimation of regression models for advertising expenditures, marketing expenditures (defined as advertising, personal selling, and technical service spending), and the proportion of the marketing budget allocated to advertising for a product in the sample.

ADVISOR results can also be used to produce a PAR-type report for a product. A portion of a sample PAR report for a hypothetical product is shown below.

	Actual	Industry Norms	
	Budget	Center	Range
Advertising (K$)	20.00	24.00	19.20 – 28.80
Advertising/Marketing	0.020	0.025	0.020 – 0.030
Marketing (K$)	1,000.00	950.00	760.00 – 1,140.00

In addition to the par report, the ADVISOR results can be used for the determination of spending levels for an existing product or even for a product with no sales history.

The ADVISOR approach is used as follows. First, all measurements are made for all the variables included in the norm model for marketing expenditure (i.e., using the estimated equation for LMKTG or logarithm of marketing expenditures) for the product in question. Using this information, an estimate is made for the norm of marketing expenditure for the product. Because this is a statistical model, we can compute the range for the norm expenditure for the product. Further, the same model is also used to estimate the spending level for an average brand in the database of ADVISOR; this estimate is called the base. A ratio of the norm for the product and base can be decomposed into a number of terms as follows:

Norm = Base   (1 + Effect of Customers/100)X
   (1 + Effect of Special Order/100)X
   (1 + Effect of Life Cycle/100) and etc.

This decomposition takes into account the fact that some variables in the model are continuous while others are zero or one variables. The values of the

TABLE 8.4
ADVISOR PAR REPORT FOR FLOWCLEAN

		Marketing Spending ($000s)	Personal Selling/ Technical Service ($000s)	Advertising Spending ($000s)
Norm		1,813.3	1,712.2	101.1
Range	Low	1,178.6	1,112.9	65.7
	High	2,774.3	2,619.6	154.6
Current Spending		2,900	2,652.0	248.0
Diagnosis				
Spending base		$2,226.2	$1,882.4	$343.8
Number of customers		1.7%	−0.4%	2.3%
Fraction of special orders		−27.6	−25.1	−50.1
Customer concentration		−35.6	−35.1	−46.2
Fraction of direct sales		−0.5	−2.6	
Plans		41.4	51.5	81.9
Customer/prospect attitude		−5.8	−8.8	
Product complexity		59.1	−66.4	
Life cycle		−18.5	−16.2	−41.1

Product Description Variables

Product category:	Fabricated Metal	Product Complexity (1 = machinery or component; 0 = otherwise)	0
Number of customers last year (end users, resellers, and downstream specifiers):	1,049	Stage in product life cycle:	Mature
Fraction of special orders:	1.00	Product sales ($ mil) to users plus independent resellers	
		Last year	24.1
		Year before last	23.5
Customer concentration (fraction of sales by three largest customers)	0.63	Industry Sales ($ mil) to users and independent resellers	
		Last year	48.2
		Year before last	47.0
Fraction of direct sales:	0.55		
Plans:	Maintain market share; improve image; retaliate against competitive action	Customer/prospect attitude, difference of product quality relative to industry average	0 (Prospects not higher than current customers)

Source: Adapted from Convection Corporation Case in Darral G. Clarke, *Marketing Decision Making: Text and Cases with Lotus 1-2-3* (Redwood City, CA: The Scientific Press, 1987). Reproduced with permission of the publisher.

effects coefficients as estimated are used for diagnostic purposes. Each effect coefficient will indicate the percentage change in the spending level due to a unit change in the variable.

An illustration of a PAR report is shown in Table 8.4 for Flowclean Soot-blowers, a brand of the Convection Corporation. (The ADVISOR approach was implemented for three of this firm's brands in 1980.) This brand increased the efficiency and reduced the need for cleaning in a large-scale fossil fuel steam boiler, resulting in less boiler downtime.

The estimated norm spending level for this product was 1.813 million with a range of 1.178 to 2.774. The current spending was 2.9 million. The marketing spending base corresponding to Flowclean was estimated to be 2.226 million. Analysis of diagnostics indicates that the spending norm will be lower for increases in the fraction of concentration of customers with special orders and as the product matures in its life cycle (a change from growth to maturity). Further, the norm will increase if manager's objective was to increase the market for the product.

Table 8.4 also shows norms and ranges for expenditures on personal selling/technical service and advertising spending for Flowclean as well as the corresponding diagnostics.

This example illustrates how the ADVISOR approach can be used in determining marketing expenditures for an industrial product. The analysis yields estimates of norm and diagnostic effects, which become a valuable input into final determination by the managers concerned.

Methods Based on AHP

The AHP methodology is also applicable to the case of allocating marketing resources for a given brand among competing mix elements. The procedures are very similar to those described earlier. The hierarchy relevant to increasing the long-term profitability of a brand will consist of two layers: one describing the subobjectives for the brand such as profitability, market share, and competitive retaliation and the other describing the alternative marketing mix elements such as media advertising, temporary price promotions to consumers, trade promotions, expanding distribution, use of direct marketing, and so on. The procedures described above are immediately applicable to this situation.

Methods Based on Conjoint Analysis

Again, the problem of allocating a given resource to different marketing mix elements can be tackled by conjoint methods. The approach is essentially the same as that described for allocating resources across SBUs. The difference will be in terms of attributes and levels.

Levy, Webster, and Kerin applied conjoint analysis to the problem of determining marketing mix strategies (or marketing mix allocations) for one product.[24] Their objective was to determine the profit function for alternative push strategies for a margarine manufacturer. Each push strategy was described in terms of four marketing mix variables: cooperative advertising, coupons in local newspapers, financial terms of sale, and service level defined in terms of percentage of items shipped that were ordered by the retailer. While costs for a push strategy could be computed from the firm's internal records, sales response could not be estimated from past data. The authors utilized conjoint analysis to determine the retailers' sales response to different push strategies. For this purpose, nine profiles, developed using a partial factorial orthogonal design, were presented to a sample of 68 buyers and merchandising managers. Details of the levels for the four marketing mix variables, profiles developed, and data collection instrument are shown in Table 8.5. It is interesting to note that the response from a retail buyer is essentially conditioned on the level of past buying from the firm; the retail buyers were classified into small, medium, and large buyers with the respective levels of past purchases of 5,000, 15,000, and 30,000 cases. The sales level used in the questionnaires was changed according to the size of past buying by the retail buyer. The part-worth functions were estimated for each segment of retailers (defined by the size of their past purchases). These functions were used to estimate the sales response and profit for each of the 54 possible marketing mixes.

Determining the Profit Function

To determine the total sales response function, the sales response values for the individual variable levels for each segment derived above were combined into 54 unique marketing mixes using the model

$$S_i = N\left[\alpha + \sum_{i=1}^{n} B_{is_{ji}}\right]$$

where
  S_i = the overall sales estimate of the ith marketing mix
  a = the sales constant
  N = the number of customers adjusted for size
  B_i = the value 1 or 0, depending on whether or not a particular marketing mix variable j is included in the ith marketing mix
  s_{ji} = the sales dollar estimate contributed by a particular marketing mix variable level j
  n = the number of different variable levels

The total cost for each of the 54 marketing mixes can be determined by adding the costs for the component variables:

24 See Michael Levy, John Webster, and Roger A. Kerin, "Formulating Push Marketing Strategies: A Method and Application," *Journal of Marketing* 47 (Winter 1983): 25–34.

TABLE 8.5

ILLUSTRATION OF USING CONJOINT ANALYSIS FOR ALLOCATING MARKETING MIX
EXPENDITURES FOR A BRAND

Panel A

Sales Dollar Estimates of Various Levels of Marketing Mix Variables

Marketing Mix Variable Level		Sales
Cooperative Advertising		
(0)	3 times at 15¢/lb.	$2477
(1)	4 times at 10¢/lb.	873
(2)	6 times at 7¢/lb.	0
Coupons in Local Newspapers		
(0)	2 times at 25¢/lb.	0
(1)	4 times at 10¢/lb.	481
(2)	3 times at 15¢/lb.	913
Financial Terms of Sale		
(0)	2%/10 days/net 30	0
(1)	2%/30 days	1366
"Service Level" Percentage of Items Shipped That Were Ordered		
(0)	96%	0
(1)	98%	1283
(2)	99.5%	1173

Panel B

Partial Factorial Orthogonal Design[a]

Package	Cooperative Advertising	Coupons in Local Newspapers	Financial Terms of Sale[b]	Service Level
1	0	2	1	0
2	1	0	0	0
3	2	1	1	0
4	0	0	1	1
5	1	1	1	1
6	2	2	0	1
7	0	1	0	2
8	1	2	1	·2
9	2	0	1	2

[a] Numbers in table correspond to descriptions in Panel B.

[b] Only 2 levels are defined for this variable.

Panel C

Typical Question in the Data Collection Instrument

Profiles: ACTIVITIES

1.	Cooperative advertising:	3 times a year at 15¢
2.	Manufacturers' ROP coupons in newspapers:	3 times a year at 15¢
3.	Financial terms of sale:	2%/30 days
4.	Percent of total cases ordered that were shipped:	96%

24 lb.
Cases   15   18   21   24   27   30   33   36   39   42   45
(000)

%
Change   -50 -40 -30 -20 -10   0   10   20   30   40   50 Scale
                                                                for
                                                                Response

Source: Adapted from Michael Levy, John Webster, and Roger A. Kerin, "Formulating Push Marketing Strategies: A Method and Application," *Journal of Marketing* 47 (Winter 1983). Reproduced with permission of the publisher.

$$C_i = \sum_{j=1}^{n} B_i c_{ji}$$

where

C_i = the overall cost estimate of the ith marketing mix
B_i = 1 or 0, depending on whether or not a particular marketing mix variable is included in the ith marketing mix, respectively
c_{ji} = the cost estimate contributed by a particular marketing mix variable level j
n = the number of different variable levels

Based on this analysis, the authors conclude that the least profitable marketing mix is cooperative advertising offered three times a year at 15 cents per pound, coupons in newspapers offered two times a year at 25 cents per pound, terms of sale 2 percent/10 days/net 30, and 96 percent level of service. The most profitable marketing mix consisted of cooperative advertising six times a year at 7 cents per pound, coupons four times a year at 10 cents per pound, 2 percent/30-day terms and a 98 percent service level. Although the particular results are specific to the situation considered, the application shows how conjoint analysis can be employed to determine the most profitable allocation of a marketing mix budget for a brand.

Methods Using Market Response Function

The rule for optimal allocation across the marketing mix elements for one product is shown below.

$$P* = \frac{e_p}{1 + e_p} \bullet C$$

$$X_j^* = \frac{e_j}{\sum e_j} \bullet B$$

$$j = 1,2, ..., n$$

where

B = Budget allocated to the product
X_j^* = Optimal allocation to the jth mix element for the product
e_j = Partial elasticity of sales of the product with respect to the jth mix element
e_p = Price elasticity for the product
C = Cost per unit for the product per unit
P^* = Optimal price per unit for the product

Montgomery and Silk estimated the market response function for an ethical drug using econometric methods.[25] They used 54 monthly observations of the drug's market share of new prescriptions along with current and lagged expenditures for journal advertising, direct mail, and sampling and literature used for promoting the drug. The dependent variable in this analysis was the drug's market share of the new prescriptions. The estimates for both the short-run and long-run elasticities[26] for these marketing mix elements are shown in Table 8.6. Also shown are actual monthly expenditures and optimal expenditures according to the above rule for both short run and long run.

These estimates indicate that the ethical drug market share was highly responsive to journal advertising and moderately responsive to expenditures on sampling and literature and direct mail. Also, long-run effects are much higher than the short-run effects for each marketing element. The actual monthly expenditures were $1.209, $1.630, and $1.355 for the three methods of journal advertising, direct mail, and sampling and literature (these were coded to preserve the confidential nature of data, while maintaining the actual relative values).

---

25 See David B. Montgomery and Alvin J. Silk, "Estimating Dynamic Effects of Market Communication Expenditures," *Management Science* 18 (June 1972): B-485–B-501.

26 A short-run elasticity measures the influence of a marketing element in the period in which expenditures were incurred. However, because of carryover effects, the short-run elasticities underestimate the influence of marketing expenditures. Long-run elasticities account for these carryover effects and measure the influence of a marketing element on response over a long period.

TABLE 8.6

ACTUAL AND OPTIMAL MARKETING MIX ALLOCATIONS FOR A PRESCRIPTION DRUG

| | | | | | Optimal Expenditures | | | |
| | Estimated Elasticities | | Actual Monthly Expenditures | | Short Run | | Long Run | |
Marketing Element	Short Run	Long Run	%	Amount	%	Amount	%	Amount
Journal advertising	0.157	0.303	29	1.209	90	3.784	76	3.187
Direct mail	0.002	0.019	39	1.630	1	0.048	5	0.210
Sampling and literature	0.015	0.076	32	1.355	9	0.362	19	0.797
Total			100	4.194	100	4.194	100	4.194

Source: Extracted from David B. Montgomery and Alvin J. Silk, "Estimating Dynamic Effects of Market Communication Expenditures," *Management Science* 18 (June 1972): B-485–B-501, Table 3. Reproduced with permission of the publisher.

But when compared to the average monthly expenditures made by the firm for each of the marketing communication methods, it appears that the firm is allocating expenditures in an inverse relation to the estimated elasticities! While the optimal allocation among the three methods of journal advertising, direct mail, and sampling and literature using the short-term elasticities should be 90, 1, and 9 percent, actual allocations were 29, 39, and 32 percent. Also, the allocations based on long-run elasticities are higher for direct mail and sampling and literature than those based on short-run effects; there is a corresponding reduction in the allocation to journal advertising. This example illustrates how one could compute the optimal expenditures using rules based on the market response function and examine how far the current practice in a situation is from the optimal allocation.

METHODS FOR ALLOCATION OF RESOURCES ACROSS GEOGRAPHIC MARKETS

Methods Based on Market Response Function

Once a total budget has been decided for a marketing mix element (e.g., sales force expenditure) for a product, it is necessary to allocate it across the different geographic territories in which the product is marketed. The optimal method for this allocation requires knowledge of the market response functions for each territory. The rule for optimal allocation is essentially the same as that for allocating across different marketing mix elements for a brand. It is to allocate the total budget in proportion to the elasticities for the different areas. A geographic area that is more responsive to the expenditure will receive a higher budget than the less responsive area.

SUMMARY

This chapter covered a number of approaches for allocating resources in a multiproduct firm. Any strategic decision involves determination of the magnitude of resources and their allocation.

We have considered allocation of resources among several SBUs of the firm, among different brands within a particular SBU, among various marketing mix elements for a brand, and across different geographic territories for a product. Methods include product portfolio approaches, methods based on analytic hierarchy process, methods using conjoint analysis, and methods using market response functions. While methods using market response functions are deemed most appropriate (and even optimal), estimation of such functions is quite difficult, particularly for aggregations such as a business (or an SBU). Owing to this, different product portfolio methods have been proposed by various consulting organizations. The objective for these portfolio approaches is to develop composite dimensions from a large number of relevant variables and to classify businesses into matrices of various sizes (e.g.,

2×2, 3×3, or 4×5). Based on such classifications, each portfolio approach makes prescriptions on the direction of allocation of resources. Intensive research on comparisons of these approaches to one situation indicates there is almost no consistency in the way businesses are classified according to the product portfolio methods. This result is perhaps the most disturbing for applying these simplified portfolio approaches to a practical problem.

In order to contend with the problems with portfolio methods, various customized approaches have evolved in the literature. These include methods based on AHP and conjoint analysis. We have described how they can be used for several resource allocation situations.

BIBLIOGRAPHY

Abell, Derek F., and John S. Hammond. *Strategic Market Planning.* Englewood Cliffs, NJ: Prentice-Hall, 1979.

Ansoff, Igor, and Edward McDonnell. *Implanting Strategic Management.* Englewood Cliffs, NJ: Prentice-Hall, 1990.

Buzzell, Robert D., and Bradley T. Gale. *The PIMS Principles: Linking Strategy to Performance.* New York: Free Press, 1987.

Caroll, J. Douglas, Paul E. Green, and Wayne S. DeSarbo. "Optimizing the Allocation of a Fixed Resource: A Simple Model and Its Experimental Test." *Journal of Marketing* 43 (January 1979): 51–57.

Chakravarti, Dipankar, Andrew Mitchell, and Richard Staelin. "Judgment Based Marketing Decision Models: Problems and Possible Solutions." *Journal of Marketing* 45 (Fall 1981): 13–23.

Kerin, Roger A., Vijay Mahajan, and P. Rajan Varadarajan. *Contemporary Perspectives on Strategic Market Planning.* Needham Heights, MA: Allyn and Bacon, 1990.

Larréche, Jean-Claude, and V. Srinivasan. "STRATPORT: A Decision Support System for Strategic Planning." *Journal of Marketing* 45 (Fall 1981): 39–52.

Levy, Michael, John Webster, and Roger A. Kerin. "Formulating Push Marketing Strategies: A Method and Application." *Journal of Marketing* 47 (Winter 1983): 25–34.

Lilien, Gary L. "ADVISOR 2: Modeling the Marketing Mix Decision for Industrial Products." *Management Science* 25 (February 1979): 191–204.

Little, John D.C. "Models and Managers: The Concept of a Decision Calculus." *Management Science* 16 (April 1970), B466–B485.

Lodish, Leonard M. *The Advertising and Promotion Challenge: Vaguely Right or Precisely Wrong?* New York: Oxford, 1986.

Montgomery, David B., and Alvin J. Silk. "Estimating Dynamic Effects of Market Communication Expenditures." *Management Science* 18 (June 1972): B-485–B-501.

Pessemier, Edgar A. *Product Management* 2d ed. New York: Wiley, 1982: Chapter 4.

Rao, Vithala R., and Darius Sabavala. "Measuring and Use of Market Response Functions for Allocating Marketing Resources." Marketing Science Institute Technical Working Paper (July 1986): 86–105.

Rao, Vithala R., Jerry Wind, and Wayne S. DeSarbo. "A Customized Market Response Model: Development, Estimation, and Empirical Testing." *Journal of the Academy of Marketing Science* 16 (Spring 1988): 128–140.

Saaty, Thomas L. *The Analytic Hierarchy Process*. New York: McGraw-Hill, 1980.

Srinivasan, V. "Computer-Aided Decision Making for Strategic Business Portfolio Decisions." *Marketing in an Electronic Age*, R.D. Buzzell, ed. Boston: Harvard Business School Press, 1985: 329–343.

Wind, Yoram, and Vijay Mahajan. "Designing Product and Business Portfolios." *Harvard Business Review* 59 (January–February 1981): 155–165.

Wind, Yoram, Vijay Mahajan, and Donald J. Swire. "An Empirical Comparison of Standardized Portfolio Models." *Journal of Marketing* 47 (Spring 1983): 89–99.

Wind, Yoram, and Thomas L. Saaty. "Marketing Applications of the Analytic Hierarchy Process." *Management Science* 26 (July 1980): 641–658.

CHAPTER 9

Analyses in Action: Case Examples

INTRODUCTION

Marketing strategy is a simple concept. As argued in Chapter 1, it all essentially boils down to where and how to compete. One of the premises of this book, however, is the notion that, despite the simplicity of the concept, *formulating* marketing strategy is a very difficult task. In so doing, firms need to be sensitive to their ever-changing marketplaces. This involves a thorough understanding of customers, competitors, and the various other external forces (e.g., political, economic, social, technological) that affect the behavior of customers and competitors (both present and future). Required information is either unavailable or difficult to interpret. Part of the difficulty lies in the fact that the information required relates more to the future than the present.

This book has presented a cornucopia of techniques for the collection and/or analysis of information (data) to assist in making appropriate decisions. We have presented techniques for identifying market segments, consumer needs, and competitors; analyzing a firm's strengths and weaknesses relative to competitors; forecasting environmental considerations for a business; and allocating resources.

Just reading the text up to this point will not necessarily enable the practicing manager to implement these techniques with total confidence. Consider people learning how to use spreadsheet software such as Microsoft Excel or Lotus 123. How confident would they be just by reading the manual? Similarly, one cannot learn how to do market analyses simply by reading about the methods described in this book. To fully appreciate these tools, the reader has to actually use them. Unfortunately, it is not within the scope of this book to provide the reader with such opportunities. That can only be provided in either the workplace or in a practical component of classroom experience (such as road training in high school driver's education). The closest we can come within these pages is to show how people have applied some of these tools in their workplaces.

Towards that end, we present four, real-life case studies, summarized in Table 9.1. The first, a sports apparel industry study, was sponsored by a trade association. The second, the Victoria Moore activewear line study, was performed for a high-profile fashion designer interested in that same market. The third, the Citibank photocard study, was conducted by Citibank personnel themselves. The fourth, a study performed for Holdzer catering, related to institutional catering facilities in Finland. These studies represent a variety of products, research objectives, and research methodologies.

The sports apparel industry study and the Victoria Moore study concern consumer products; the Citibank photocard study concerns a service; and the Holdzer catering study concerns business-to-business marketing. The sports apparel industry study was conducted to find growth opportunities within an industry for firms participating in that industry; the objective of the Victoria Moore study was to investigate growth opportunities within an industry for a firm outside that industry; the Citibank photocard study was conducted to examine the viability of a specific basis of differentiation in a market that is difficult to differentiate in; and the Holdzer catering study was conducted to

TABLE 9.1
OVERVIEW OF CHAPTER 9 STUDIES

Study	Research Objectives	Relevant Techniques	Chapters with Relevant Material
Sports Apparel	Identify benefit segments	Focus groups; factor analysis; perceptual mapping	2, 4
	Identify competition across conventional product lines		
Victoria Moore	Identify unmet needs	Standard surveys	2, 3, 4, 5, 7
	Identify target customers, assess potential, determine benefits required		
Citibank	Assess solution to unmet need	Focus groups	3, 5, 7
	Evaluate basis for differentiation		
Holdzer Catering	Determine value customers place on the Holdzer brand name	Conjoint analysis	2, 7
	Determine service components customers require		

identify customers most favorably disposed to the company and to provide insight into how to design their service offerings.

With respect to methodologies, the sports apparel study uses many of the sophisticated computer-intensive techniques presented in Chapters 2 and 4; the Victoria Moore study uses much simpler approaches to survey and questionnaire design; the Citibank study uses the focus group approaches described in Chapter 3; and the Holdzer catering study uses a modified form of conjoint analysis.

After digesting these three studies, the reader should have a good feel for the spectrum of market analyses and appreciate their potential contribution to the corporate enterprise.

SPORTS APPAREL INDUSTRY STUDY[1]

The sports apparel industry can be characterized as large, omnipresent, and extremely diverse. Spearheaded by companies such as Nike, Reebok, L. A. Gear, Champion, and Adidas, the industry accounts for close to 50 billion dollars in retail sales annually. It grew about 10 percent from 1991 to 1992. Many of the competitors in this market began as shoe companies. Looking for growth avenues, they followed the prescriptions of Ansoff's product-market matrix (see Chapters 3 and 4) and asked themselves the question "What else can we sell in our markets?" The answer came back sports apparel.

Almost everyone (86 percent of the American population) owns some item of sports apparel. The category has equal penetration among both men and women. Women spend even more on sports apparel than men. The industry produces a wide variety of products (shirts, shorts, socks, sweats, hats, apparel with team logos, etc.[2]) made for an even wider variety of activities (running, walking, tennis, aerobics, biking, swimming, soccer, etc.). The increasing diversity of such activities has helped to fuel recent growth in the industry. Growth has been further fueled by people using sports apparel for activities other than sports. In particular, approximately 92 percent of the people who own sports apparel also commonly use it as casual wear. In fact, over one-third of the people who own sports apparel use it *only* as casual wear.

Despite this rosy picture, dark clouds have begun to appear on the horizon. In 1993, for the first time in a long time, the industry saw essentially no growth at all. Sales to women actually declined. Furthermore, new competitors entered the arena. The importance of casual use has left the industry vulnerable to fashion companies such as Donna Karan, Liz Claiborne, and Pierre Cardin that have not traditionally marketed sports apparel but *have* marketed casual wear. Doubtlessly, this contributed to the decline in women's sales in 1993.

---

1   The authors would like to thank Elliot Savitzky of Directions for Decisions, Inc., 10 Exchange Place, 17th floor, Jersey City, New Jersey 07302, (201) 413–9000 and Maria Stefan of the Sporting Goods Marketing Association, 200 Castlewood Dr., North Palm Beach, FL 33408, (407) 840-1150, for permission to use this research.

2   Nike, for example, has over 5,000 SKUs of sports apparel.

In response to these circumstances, the Sports Apparel Products Council of the Sporting Goods Manufacturers Association, a trade association, recognized the need for new strategies to not only defend the markets of its participating companies, but to establish new directions for the companies to grow in. Towards this end, the council commissioned Directions for Decisions, a New York–New Jersey based survey and market research consulting firm, to perform a study with the following objectives:

1. To uncover whatever benefit segments exist in the marketplace.

2. To examine how consumers perceive the different items in the sports apparel category.

Satisfying the first objective will enable manufacturers to discover exactly what consumers want in their sports apparel and who wants it. This will potentially reveal growth opportunities by either uncovering desired benefits that are not being provided (unmet needs) or suggesting how and to whom manufacturers might promote their products that provide specific benefits. The implications of satisfying the second objective include a customer-oriented understanding of the competitive structure of the industry, thereby leading to an understanding of how potential competitors (either existing firms or new entrants) might compete with current ones.

The study centered on a survey that was developed after a series of focus groups were conducted to refine issues and test preliminary questions. A 36-page interviewer-administered questionnaire was developed and administered to 1,107 consumers in 60 locations during June 1993. The respondents ranged in age from 10–75. The interview took about 45 minutes. During the interview, respondents filled out work sheets and studied photographs of different types of sports apparel. After the interview was completed, respondents completed a leave-behind booklet containing questions about their lifestyles, hobbies, and media habits. This booklet was picked up later the same day.

Benefit Segments

Data Collection and Procedures

In the interview, respondents (both men and women) were asked to rate the importance (on a five-point scale) of several characteristics they might consider in the purchase of sports apparel. These characteristics are listed on the page from the interviewer's script presented in Figure 9.1.[3] The percentage of the sample that responded to the question of how important a given characteristic is when being used for sports activity with the top point of the scale, extremely important, is shown in Figure 9.2. A similar question was asked for casual activity with similar results. The individual respondents' sports and casual use importance ratings were pooled and factor analyzed,

---

3   This page includes only the first 22 of the 29 raw benefit items asked about.

FIGURE 9.1
PAGE FROM SPORTS APPAREL INTERVIEW SCRIPT

DIRECTIONS FOR DECISIONS INC.   –15–   Job #93-41-003

ASK EVERYONE 13-75

20. Let's talk for a few minutes about how you decide to buy your sports apparel.

First, I'd like to know what is important to you when deciding to buy sports apparel. To do this, I'm going to read several characteristics. For each one I read, I'd like you to rate how important you feel that characteristic is in your decision to buy sports apparel. Please use any number from 1 to 5, where 1 means the characteristic is "not important at all" and 5 means the characteristic "is extremely important."

Let's start with (INSERT CIRCLED CHARACTERISTICS). How important is (CHARACTERISTIC) in your decision to buy sports apparel? (RECORD RATING # BELOW)

How important is (INSERT NEXT CHARACTERISTIC)? (CONTINUE FOR ALL CHARACTERISTICS)

	1 **Not At All** **Important**		**5** **Extremely** **Important**
a.	The look or style	_____	(92)
b.	Good value for the money	_____	(93)
c.	Fits comfortably	_____	(94)
d.	Advertising	_____	(95)
e.	It performs the way you want it to .	_____	(96)
f.	Brand name	_____	(97)
g.	Knowledgeable salespeople	_____	(98)
h.	The color	_____	(99)
i.	Can be used for casual use as well as for sports	_____	(100)
j.	The quality	_____	(101)
k.	The fabric it's made of	_____	(102)
l.	Durability	_____	(103)
m.	All your friends have it	_____	(104)
n.	Is in style	_____	(105)
o.	Playing the sport for which it is intended	_____	(106)
p.	Won't shrink	_____	(107)
q.	Being easy to care for	_____	(108)
r.	Being endorsed by a celebrity . . .	_____	(109)
s.	Having good stitching	_____	(110)
t.	Made in USA	_____	(111)
u.	Can be used for a number of different sports	_____	(112)
v.	Having a team logo that you want .	_____	(113)

BE SURE ALL CHARACTERISTICS HAVE BEEN RATED BEFORE PROCEEDING.

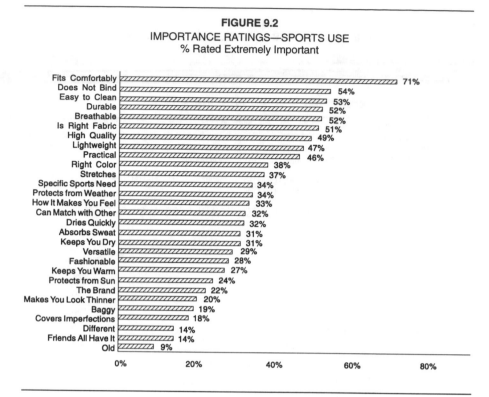

FIGURE 9.2
IMPORTANCE RATINGS—SPORTS USE
% Rated Extremely Important

and the factor scores were clustered into seven groups. The demographics, spending patterns, and media habits of each group (segment) were then summarized.

Figure 9.3 shows the seven benefit segments and their relative sizes. The segment names were chosen by the firm that conducted the research to correspond to the segment's benefits desired, demographics, lifestyles, and media habits. It is noteworthy that these segments were formed to maximize the differences across and similarities within with respect to their benefit importances. This does not guarantee that there will be any differences with respect to demographics, lifestyles, spending patterns, and media habits. Fortunately, in this study there were. Many of these differences are profiled in Table 9.2. The table presents information only that differs from the population as a whole. For example, all segments consider "comfortable fit" to be the most important benefit, so it is not highlighted in the table; however, the young urban trendsetters have a greater-than-average desire to wear clothes that "all their friends are wearing."

The *self-oriented* segment is puzzling in terms of the benefits they consider extremely important, as the only benefit with greater-than-average importance is that the apparel be "old." However, this value is so low on the average (see Figure 9.1) that it is not useful here. Responses to lifestyle questions in the

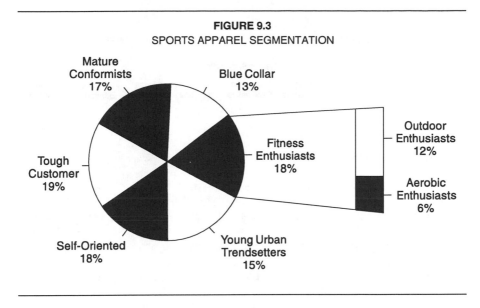

FIGURE 9.3
SPORTS APPAREL SEGMENTATION

leave-behind booklet indicate that their motives for participating in sports were to attract the opposite sex, experience the feeling of competition, improve their skills, and make new friends. Their name comes from the fact that they have a low level of concern for today's social issues.

More than any other segment, the *tough customer* demands an extraordinary number of benefits for sports apparel. Their importance ratings are higher than average on almost every benefit. Their "comfortable fit" rating is even 14 percent higher than the population as a whole. They walk for exercise to control their weight. They are old-fashioned in that they do not believe women with children should work. Finally, they do not like to be in public unless they look their best, probably because they feel you can tell a lot about a person by the way he or she dresses.

The primary benefit desired by the young urban trendsetters segment (relative to the population) is that "all their friends have it." They jog, lift weights, and play basketball more than the average person, and exercise for the competition it provides and to be with their friends. They like to spend money on their appearance and are fashion conscious. They tend to be single and live in urban areas.

Blue collars require sports apparel that is versatile and used for the sport for which it is intended. They own a higher-than-average level of outdoor wear and would like to be able to spend more on clothes. Blue collar jocks lift weights, bowl, fish, and play a lot of football and softball. They have little concern for the politics and place a greater-than-average level of emphasis on sports.

The *mature conformists* segment tends to be a bit older. Their primary activities are exercise and fitness walking. Health is more important than

TABLE 9.2

PROFILES OF SPORTS APPAREL BENEFIT SEGMENTS

Market Segments

	Self-Oriented	Tough Customers	Young Urban Trendsetters	Blue Collar	Mature Conformists	Aerobic Enthusiasts	Outdoor Enthusiasts
Male	X		X	X	X		X
Female	X	X	X		X	X	X
Age (Mean)	35.0	41.0	33.0	35.0	45.0	38.0	40.0
% Married	56%	69%	36%	44%	65%	59%	54%
Income (mean)	$44.0	$43.0	$40.0	$40.0	$36.0	$45.0	$40.0
% of sample	18%	19%	15%	13%	17%	6%	12%
$ spent past year	$76.7	$59.6	$73.0	$71.5	$53.7	$53.7	$75.5

Media

Television

Sports	X		X	X			X
Drama						X	
News					X	X	
Talk Shows		X					
MTV	X		X	X			
Cartoons		X	X				
Sitcoms		X					
Variety							
Documentaries					X		
Soaps		X					

Magazines

General Sports	X		X	X			X
Women's		X					
General interest		X	X				
TV Guide			X				
African American			X				
Teen							
Men's Lifestyle			X				

Benefits Sought	Old	Higher on most	All friends have it	Authentic use	Protects from weather Easy Care	Non-binding Breathable Stretches Practical Need for sport	Nonbinding Durable Protects from weather Breathable

appearance. They tend to be conservative and like to garden, spend time with their spouse, and participate in church and religious activities. They are one of the few segments that do not expect their income to increase.

Members of the *aerobic enthusiasts* segment are primarily homemakers and participate heavily in aerobics. Its members have the highest household income of all the segments and are impulse purchasers. They feel that the way one looks strongly affects the way one feels.

Outdoor enthusiasts are heavy spenders (12 percent of the people, 17 percent of the dollars). More than the average, they desire sports apparel that is nonbinding and durable, provides protection from the weather, and is breathable. They participate in camping, biking, boating, fishing, and weight lifting. They are progressive thinkers who are down to earth. They place a great deal of emphasis on career.

Implications

A comfortable fit is clearly the most important benefit in sports apparel across all segments. Therefore it becomes crucial to communicate fit in advertising.

We have identified a wide variety of market (benefit) segments that could be developed. The decisions related to which segments to pursue would have to involve a trade-off between the magnitude of the opportunity the segment represents and the expenditures necessary to develop programs and/or apparel that will fit the segment's needs.

In assessing the opportunity each segment provides, several factors should be considered. These include segment size, expenditures per customer, and projected growth. Size and expenditures per customer are found in Table 9.2. To get a handle on projected segment growth, the leave-behind booklet included questions directed at expected expenditures as well as current expenditures. The mean values for these as well as the resultant growth are given in Table 9.3.

The three segments with the greatest growth are the self-orienteds, tough customers, and blue collar jocks. The self-orienteds and tough customers are especially attractive because not only do the data indicate that their expenditures increase the most; they are the largest segments, too (see Table 9.1). Thus, the expenditure increase is carried over more people! However, marketing to these groups could be quite competitive. Some companies might be better off choosing a target, like the mature market, that represents a growing group in terms of population size. The mature market of the future will be filled with today's baby boomers, who will probably bring many of their attitudes and habits with them.

Consumer Perceptions

Data Collection and Procedures

A portion of the interview was devoted to a card-sorting task. Respondents were given 62 different photographs of sports apparel items. Different sets

TABLE 9.3
SPORTS APPAREL SEGMENTS
Market Spending

	Total	Self-Oriented	Tough Customers	Inner City Influenced	Blue Collar Jocks	Mature Population	Aerobic Enthusiasts	Outdoor Enthusiasts
Mean amount spent last year	$44.5	$76.7	$59.6	$73.0	$71.5	$53.7	$41.7	$75.5
Mean amount willing to spend next year	68.5	$85.9	$47.1	$76.3	$79.1	$57.8	$44.1	$73.9
Mean % increase/decrease	+6%	+12%	+13%	+5%	+11%	–2%	+6%	–2%

were used for men and women. In each case, respondents were instructed to sort into groups the items that were similar to each other and different from those in other piles. Respondents were free to choose any number of piles up to 62. They could have as many photos in a pile as they wished. The frequency with which two items were put into the same pile across the entire sample served as a measure of similarity between them.

Perceptual maps were created from these data for men and women separately. These are presented in Figures 9.4 and 9.5 respectively.

As is evident from the figures, there are several qualitative similarities to the ways men and women view the market. First, both maps have garments of similar categories (e.g. jackets, shirts, shorts, hats, etc.) positioned closely to each other. Nike shirts appear to compete more with Reebok shirts than they do with Nike shorts. Second, within a category, items associated with the same sport are located in close proximity. Finally, it seems that other distinguishing features (e.g., color, brand, presence of a team license, etc.) determine precise locations.

The category-primary nature of the way consumers view the market suggests that extensions to other categories provide greater opportunities than line extensions within a category. Within a category, line extensions will simply be seen as substitutes and are likely to cannibalize a firm's current offerings to current customers. Recall that the penetration of sports apparel is so high that new (category) customers are rare. The dominant mode of sales increase, then, is likely to be capturing customers from other firms.

Thus, different apparel categories should be added before new styles are added to a currently manufactured category. If L. A. Gear, for example, invested in the design and production of more (say) tennis shirts, they could avoid competing with (and cannibalizing) their tennis shoes. Consistent with this, licensing could be done in several categories. Furthermore, manufacturers trying to attract attention to their entire line should encourage retailers to merchandise and display combinations of separates. This could overcome the

FIGURE 9.4
MEN'S PERCEPTIONS OF THE SPORTS APPAREL MARKET

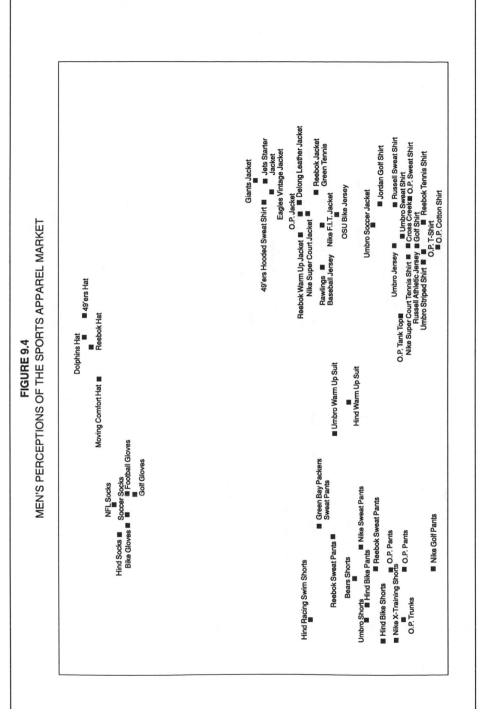

FIGURE 9.5

WOMEN'S PERCEPTIONS OF THE SPORTS APPAREL MARKET

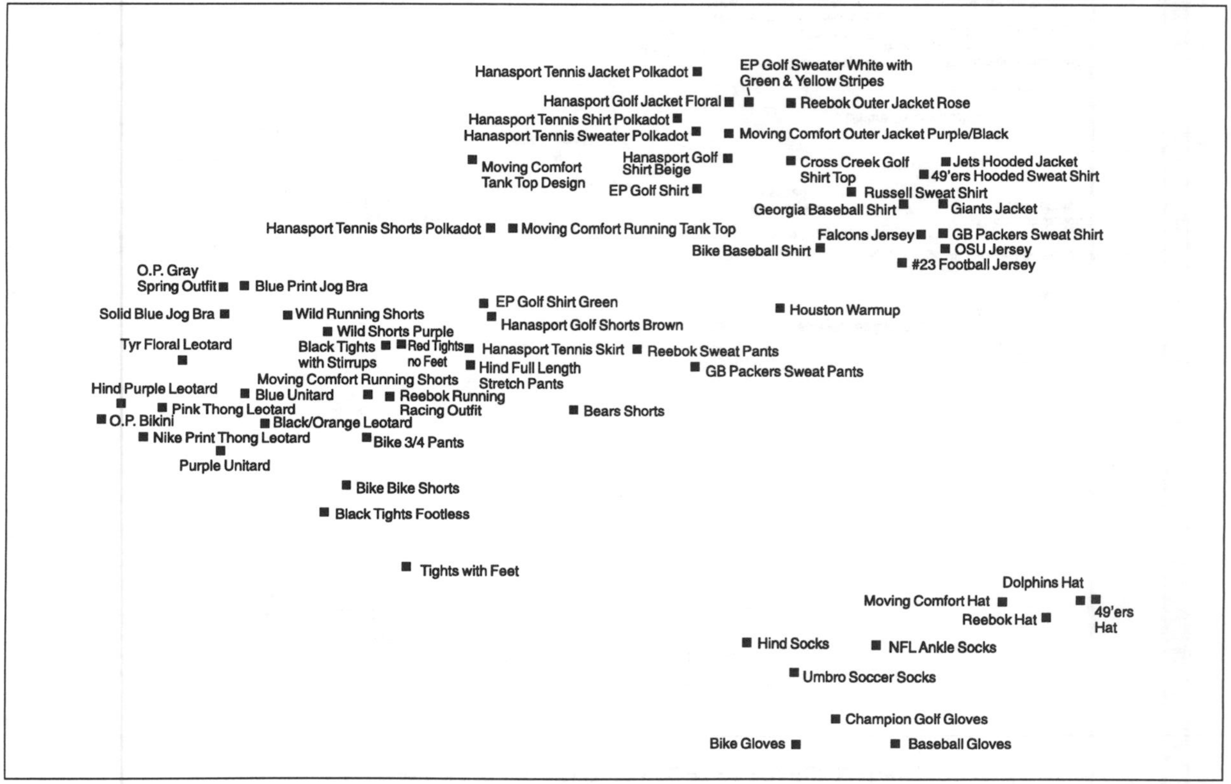

brand primary perception and suggest that someone buying a shirt consider a pair of pants as well.

THE VICTORIA MOORE ACTIVEWEAR LINE[4]

The Victoria Moore Company is a multifaceted upscale clothing designer. It designs and manufactures women's dress and casual clothing, shoes, jeans, accessories, men's wear, and children's wear. The vast majority of their business is in women's clothing, the area in which the company began. One day, while in an airport readying for vacation, the company president saw that a few of her fellow passengers were dressed in warm-up suits and sweatpants. She had the inspiration for the Victoria Moore activewear line. She wondered whether there was a market for another upscale high-fashion prestige line of sports apparel. Other designers have recognized this opportunity. Recent entrants include the Ralph Lauren active line, Evan Picone's EP Sport line, and the Liz (Claiborne) Sport line. However, Victoria Moore had a more upscale image than these designers. In contrast, Ellesse, traditionally an upscale active line, has been contemplating entry into the fashion casual wear segment, further signaling a potential blurring of market boundaries.

The company president needed answers to several questions in her investigation of Victoria Moore Activewear. In particular, she needed to answer these questions:

1. How should she identify her target customers? What is the potential they represent?
2. Who would her competitors most likely be, other fashion designers of casual wear or sports apparel manufacturers?
3. What benefits do potential customers look for in leisure sports apparel: fit, fashion, comfort?
4. Is the Victoria Moore brand name an advantage in this category? And if so, what is the value of it?

In order to answer these questions, the president authorized a mail survey to be conducted by a team of students from New York University's Stern School of Business. The survey questionnaire developed by the team and a summary of the responses received can be found in the Appendix to this chapter. The questionnaire was the result of pretesting an earlier version on 50 women to ensure low levels of difficulty and self-administration. Two thousand questionnaires were mailed, 1,600 to female American Express Gold Card holders and 400 to female NYU business school alumni who had graduated 5–10 years earlier. (The responses of the two subsamples proved indis-

---

4 Victoria Moore is a disguised name. The real company featured in this example preferred to remain anonymous. The authors wish to thank the "Victoria Moore Company" for permission to use this study. They further wish to thank the research team of Kimberly Banks, Gina Lee Plaia, Tracy Pollastri, and Joseph Weglein.

tinguishable.) To increase the response rate, a drawing for Victoria Moore accessories was promised to all who returned the questionnaire in a self-addressed stamped envelope. The eventual response rate was 30 percent.

The sample was clearly skewed towards upper income respondents. This was done because targeting lower income households would likely damage the Victoria Moore image. Furthermore, the company was too unfamiliar with the market to enter into with a brand new product.

Target Customers

Three steps were implemented in the identification of potential customers. First, question 12 provided information on the proportion of the sample that would be interested in buying Victoria Moore activewear. These were identified as potential customers. Second, the demographics of this subgroup were compared with those of the sample at large and those of activewear customers in general (from question 1 on the survey). Third, differences were isolated to identify distinguishing characteristics of this target population.

Consistent with the trade association study described in the last section, 79 percent of the sample indicated that they were activewear buyers; 26 percent of these indicated they would consider buying Victoria Moore activewear.

The largest share of activewear consumers (28 percent) report a household income of less than $50,000 (question 17). However, 30 percent of Victoria Moore's potential customers came from households with incomes in excess of $100,000. Furthermore, 40 percent of all activewear customers with incomes exceeding $100,000 were interested in Victoria Moore activewear. Thus, Victoria Moore's customer base could be characterized as high income.

Eighty percent of all activewear consumers are employed full time, while only 66 percent of those interested in Victoria Moore were. Thus the potential Victoria Moore customer appears to have more time for leisure activity than the average active customer. In addition, it was found that while the overall activewear customer was most likely to be between 35 and 44 years old, the potential Victoria Moore customer was more likely to be between 25 and 34.

Sixty percent of Victoria Moore's potential customers said they spend between $100 and $500 annually on activewear. Given that many customers spend in excess of $1,000 annually, and the distribution of annual expenditures is therefore asymmetric, it was assumed that $350 per year (not $300, the midpoint of the $100–$500 range) was the average amount the Victoria Moore prospect spends. Taking these figures together with the incidence of Victoria Moore prospects in the sample and making the assumption that the target market includes women residing in households with incomes greater than $75,000,[5] we conclude that the maximum market potential for Victoria Moore activewear is in the healthy neighborhood of *one billion dollars!* This is seen as follows:

---

5   There are approximately 15 million U.S. households with income greater than $75,000 according to the *Statistical Abstract of the U.S.: 1992*, Washington: US Dept. of Commerce.

15 million women in target market
×   <u>79% of population who are activewear buyers</u>[6]
   11,850,000 market potential customers
×   <u>26% would consider Victoria Moore</u>[7]
   3,081,000 potential customers for Victoria Moore
×   <u>$350 expenditures per customer</u>
   $1,078,350,000 sales from potential Victoria Moore customers!

Competition

In Chapter 4, we emphasized that the identification of competitors rested on how customers used a product. Question 14 of the survey asked respondents whether they would wear Victoria Moore activewear for sports purposes, leisure activities, or both. *No respondent in the group of potential Victoria Moore customers indicated that they would purchase Victoria Moore for sports alone!* Thirty-six percent of the respondents who were potential Victoria Moore customers did not answer this question; perhaps it was too complicated. Nevertheless, 14 percent said they would use Victoria Moore activewear for leisure alone; 50 percent said that they would use it for both. These results indicate that women expect Victoria Moore activewear to be too nice to use only for exercising. It seems, then, that Victoria Moore could potentially draw from both traditional sports apparel manufacturers and other high-fashion designers. In any event, given the universality of leisure use, the latter certainly cannot be ignored.

Benefits Required

Question 6 of the survey asked respondents to rank six factors in order of importance in the purchase decision for both sports and leisure activities. In both categories, comfort was rated the number one criterion; 69 percent ranked it in the top two for sports activities and 71 percent did so for leisure activities. This is consistent with the results of the sports apparel industry study described in the last section. In this study, fashion ranked a clear second for leisure or casual activities; 46 percent had it in the top two. There was no clear second for sports. Nevertheless, since Victoria Moore's customers are more interested in leisure activities, the comfort first–fashion second benefit priorities seem paramount.

Brand Equity

The amount of equity built into the Victoria Moore name can be determined by the amount customers are willing to pay for the brand relative to other designers. The responses to question 13 on the survey generally indicate that activewear consumers are willing to pay at least as much for Victoria Moore

---

6   Seventy-nine percent of the sample were activewear buyers. This figure was projected to the population.
7   Again, the sample figure was projected to the population.

activewear (or a sweatshirt to be specific) as they are for other designer activewear. They are also willing to pay approximately a 10 percent premium for Victoria Moore over Liz Claiborne and Leslie Fay. This can be seen in the table below.

Sweatshirt Designer	All Activewear Consumers	Victoria Moore Activewear Potential Customers	Current Victoria Moore Customers
Victoria Moore	$48	$51	$53
Leslie Fay	41	46	47
Liz Claiborne	42	45	48

One possible caveat to these findings is that, as the table above shows, current owners of Victoria Moore clothing are willing to pay more for all brands than Victoria Moore potential customers who are not currently Victoria Moore owners![8] This implies that current customers place a higher value on brand name than noncustomers do. Furthermore, Victoria Moore should consider marketing their activewear in distribution outlets that their current customers shop in.

Implications

The implications of this research are quite straightforward. There is a demand for designer activewear, as 75 percent of respondents said they would purchase it. None, however, would buy it for sports alone. Thus it is important that the items be comfortable and fashionable. The Victoria Moore name carries a lot of value, so the company can command its usual price premium. All signs point to Victoria Moore entering this market. The appropriate target seems to be higher income households with the female head being between 25 and 34 years old.

CITIBANK PHOTOCARD FOCUS GROUP PROJECT[9]

The credit card industry is a difficult one to compete in. Market penetration approaches 90 percent. Furthermore, new untraditional competitors are entering the market (e.g., AT&T, Ford, GM). This has led consumers to carry more and more credit cards, with each card already held being used less and less. Most of the major attributes of credit cards are immediately duplicatable (e.g., annual fee, interest rate, length of grace period). Thus, suppliers are compelled to continually search for new and unique ways to differentiate their offerings. If they succeed, they get to keep a decreasing share of the customer's

---

8   The last column in this table as well as the complete table in the appendix to this chapter is universally higher than the next to last column.

9   The authors would like to thank Betty Hoople of Citibank for permission to use this research.

business. Nevertheless, credit cards reflect a very profitable business; so there is no shortage of companies and institutions willing to participate in this extremely competitive arena.

In the early 1990s Citibank has been attempting to differentiate their classic Visa and MasterCard by placing a photograph of the customer on them.[10] The intent behind this is to reinforce Citibank's Bankcard Division's positioning statement, "No other credit card gives you the security and confidence of Citibank MasterCard and Visa because no one is as responsive to your needs." Like their price protection plans, the photo is designed to appeal to security-conscious consumers who might be afraid of fraudulent charges made with a lost card. It also reinforces Citibank's image as a leader in card products and technology, as they pioneered several banking innovations. Among others, they were the first to use ATMs on a large scale, issue a preferred Visa, institute usage incentives (e.g. Citidollar$ and free gifts), and offer emergency credit line increases.

Before the photocard was introduced on a wide scale, Citibank was interested in obtaining customers' reactions to various aspects of obtaining and using their cards. In particular, the bank wanted insight into the relative importance of the photo in terms of acquiring and using the card. As a first step, Citibank conducted three focus groups on October 1, 1990, in the Las Vegas test market where the card was introduced before national rollout. The three groups were made up of recent acquirers of a Citibank Visa photocard who had used it at least once. One group consisted of cardholders who were 55–66 years old, and the other two consisted of cardholders between the ages of 21 and 54. Each group was approximately half male and half female. Reflecting population norms, two-thirds of the participants revolved their balances, while one-third paid their balance off each month. All had at least a high school education and household incomes of $15,000 or more. In the two younger groups, all of the males and at least three-fourths of the females were employed full-time. Several participants in the older group were retired.

It is important to recognize that the results of this study should be considered as qualitative aids for management judgment only and not generalized to the total U.S. population. A copy of the focus group moderator's discussion guide can be found in the Appendix of this chapter.

This small-scale research suggested that the photocard was a promising vehicle for both retaining current customers and increasing their Citibank Visa usage. Members of the focus groups were quite positive about the Citibank photocard. Transcripts of the focus group sessions reflected two categories of reasons: practical and emotional.

---

10 Photocards were available in the early 1980s from some regional banks (e.g. Baybank in Boston). These cards were abandoned because of excessive production costs. In the early 1990s, technology has advanced to a point where cost is no longer an issue.

Practical Reasons

Although older card holders appeared to be more concerned about the practical reasons for owning and using a photocard, these issues surfaced in all groups to some degree. Convenience and positive identification were cited most frequently as reasons for obtaining the card. A photocard was viewed as more convenient in that it saved time in the purchase transaction. Customers no longer had to dig through their wallets for additional identification when using the card. The following are quotes from the transcript:

With this card, a clerk has no reason to ask you any questions.

It's convenient . . . a time saver. It's a positive I.D. so I only have to pull one thing out of my wallet.

I don't get asked for other I.D.'s. It's "no hassles."

It's easy to use because the picture is so good [clear].

They can verify that it's you right away.

Several participants also noted that they could use (and some had already used) their photocard as "proof of identity," which would be useful when cashing a check or when a merchant asked them for identification when they were using another credit card. One respondent said she favored using the photocard as an I.D. over her driver's license because, "People don't have to know personal information about me like how old I am or where I live."

Emotional Reasons

The perceived safety and security that the photocard offers were seen as key reasons for having one. Both older and younger cardholders were greatly concerned about losing their cards or having them stolen. The photo would be a deterrent to anyone else using it. The following are some of the comments made:

I keep this card with me because it's a "sure thing." Even if I lose it, no one else can use it.

Even if someone steals it, they're likely to throw it away.

You don't have to worry if it's stolen because the chances of someone else using it are slim to none.

The focus groups seemed to agree that while they are liable for the first $50 of fraudulent use of their cards, a photocard should even limit this liability because of its difficulty of use. Some also felt that the burden should fall on the merchant if he or she accepts a fraudulent card. Additional comments made included the following:

All cards should have this (photo) on it for safety . . . I feel better having my picture on it. I feel safer.

If my picture's on it, the merchant should be held liable if it's misused.

Furthermore, given the reduced likelihood of fraudulent use, many felt there would be minimal hassles associated with card replacement. There would be few fraudulent charges made, and the consumer would not have the hassle of determining whether or not each charge was legitimate.

In addition, the newness and uniqueness of the photocard led some cardholders to associate the card with status and prestige. The photocard differentiated them from the crowd and made them feel special as illustrated in the following transcript excerpts:

It makes me feel "preferred."

It makes you feel good in a store because you know they noticed you.

I feel superior to the merchant [when I use the card].

Finally, some participants liked the idea that Citibank was "nurturing" them. The photocard communicated that Citibank was taking care of them and looking out for their best interests:

They [Citibank] look at me as a person, not just as a number.

[Citibank is saying] "you're important. That's why we want your picture, not just your signature."

Citibank is working for you, not just for themselves, so that you'll be more secure.

Summary and Implications

The overall findings of the focus groups were overwhelmingly positive. Having their photo on a credit card caused some participants to increase their usage of the Citibank Visa card over other cards. This can be attributed to a combination of convenience, safety, security, and status. The positive image created by the Citibank photocard appears to reflect on Citibank in general. Participants felt that a bank that takes the "extra step" to put photos on credit cards is innovative and caring.

HOLDZER CATERING[11]

Holdzer Catering was the market leader in Finnish employee catering in 1986 with a 10 percent market share. Management essentially decided that their growth, in the terms of Ansoff's Product-Market matrix, would be in the direction of market penetration (i.e., increase share of current products in current markets). Specifically, they issued an objective to increase company market share to 16.5 in 1991. The market was expected to grow only about 5 percent between 1986 and 1991, which made the objective extremely demanding. If all of the new customers went to Holdzer, the objective would still not

---

11 At the request of the company, Holdzer catering is a fictitious name. Other aspects of the study are also disguised. The study reported here was conducted by SCIENMAR: Scientific Marketing Consultants, 318 Blackstone Avenue, Ithaca, NY, 14850.

be reached. The difficulty is further highlighted by the fact that Holdzer's two major competitors grew faster than Holdzer in the years immediately preceding 1986. If Holdzer had any hope of coming close to its objective, it had to truly understand (1) which classes of potential customers perceived the company in its most favorable light and (2) the criteria used by corporate and association executives responsible for selecting employee catering arrangements for their firms and how they traded these criteria off against price.

Holdzer therefore conducted a study with an eye towards answering the following four questions:

1. How do potential customers value the Holdzer name in employee catering?

2. Does this value vary at all with customer requirements?

3. What is the relative importance to the customer of different aspects of the menu Holdzer could offer?

4. What is the relative importance to the customer of different aspects of the price and bid mechanisms?

Pricing mechanisms are very complicated in this market. Potential suppliers submit competitive bids that propose a fixed (one-time) payment. Beyond this payment, is a fee schedule that includes prices for each item sold at normal meals in the standard company facility as well as prices for office catering and banquets. Understanding how customers make the trade-offs implicit in these price components was critical for Holdzer to achieve its objectives in market penetration.

Research Approach and Variables Employed

Given the role that understanding customer preferences played in Holdzer's research objectives, the company commissioned a conjoint analysis study to answer the above questions. Conjoint analysis was discussed in Chapter 2 as a method for uncovering the benefits consumers look for and how they trade them off among each other.

Preliminary qualitative interviews and focus groups revealed that the components of daily and weekly assortment that customers paid attention to were as follows:

- The number of hot entrees available for employees.
- Whether or not an entree was available á la carte.
- Whether or not a salad table was available.
- Whether or not sandwiches were available.
- Whether or not hot cereals were available.
- Whether or not desserts were available.
- Whether or not the weekly menu was repeated.

Table 9.4 presents a set of dummy variables that operationalize these seven assortment components. It also describes four price and five bid variables used in the study.

TABLE 9.4
VARIABLES AND CODING FOR HOLDZER CATERING CONJOINT STUDY

Brand Name

	Z_1
Holdzer	1
Other	0

DAILY ASSORTMENT VARIABLES

Number of Warm Entrees

	Z_2
Two or three	1
One	0

Á La Carte Entree Available

	Z_3
Yes	1
No	0

Salad Table

	Z_4
Yes	1
No	0

Sandwiches

	Z_5
Yes	1
No	0

Hot Cereals

	Z_6
Yes	1
No	0

Dessert

	Z_7
Yes	1
No	0

Weekly Menu Repetition

	Z_8
Yes	1
No	0

PRICE VARIABLES

Lunch Price
Z_9 = actual price in Marks

Company Subsidy
Z_{10} = actual subsidy in Marks

Catering Costs
Z_{11} = costs in 100,000 Marks units

Banquet Costs
Z_{12} = costs in 100,000 Marks units

BID VARIABLES

Z_{13} to Z_{17} = variables reflecting the relative bids of the five major competitors to some reference or expectation: Holdzer, Fazer, Polarkesti, Lounasrengas, and Yrityksen Oma Toiminita. The potential values were 5% increments above or below the reference (up to 20%). The reference price is assumed to be 100. Thus, the potential values for these variables are 80, 85, 90, 95, 100, 105, 110, 115, and 120.

CUSTOMER REQUIREMENT VARIABLES

X_{a1} = Number of employees (in 100s)
X_{a2} = Number of managers and white collar employees (in 100s)
X_{a3} = Percent of women employees
X_{a4} = Preference for dining environment (six-point scale; 1 = cozy, 6 = elegant)
X_{a5} = Preference for service style (six point scale; 1 = effective and neutral, 6 = courteous and high standard)
X_{a6} = Preference for food type (six-point scale; 1 = institutional type, 6 = home-cooked type)

Model Development

We begin with the following model formulated as a regression equation

$$\text{Utility} = b_0 + b_1 Z_1 + b_2 Z_2 + \ldots b_{17} Z_{17}.$$

In this equation, b_0 is an additive constant, the precise value of which does not matter because it is common to all utilities and does not impact the differences between the utilities of any two combinations of attributes; b_1 is the part-worth for the brand name Holdzer; b_2 to b_7 are the part-worths for the higher levels of the daily assortment variables; b_8 is the part-worth for weekly menu repetition; b_9 to b_{12} are the coefficients of price variables (lunch, company subsidy, catering costs, and banquet costs).

Using the actual price variables, Z_9 to Z_{12}, implicitly assumes that response to the price variables is linear—raising the price by two dollars has twice the effect on utility of raising the price by one dollar. Holdzer could have allowed for nonlinear response to price by using multiple dummy variables as in the credit card example in Chapter 2. However, this would have increased the number of independent variables in the above equation, and more independent variables require more data to make any estimation reliable. Data collection for this problem was already thought to be cumbersome enough. The actual bid indices, Z_{13} to Z_{17}, were also used in the model. Similar comments about the trade-offs between data collection and incorporating nonlinearities apply.

The model as presented does not allow for the variation of the value of the name Holdzer with customer requirements as stated in question 1 above. The basic model can be extended to allow for this by modeling b_1 as a function of customer requirements as follows

$$b_1 = b_{a0} + b_{a1} X_{a1} + \ldots + b_{a6} X_{a6}$$

where b_{a0} is an additive constant, X_{a1} to X_{a6} are variables that reflect customer requirements, and b_{a1} to b_{a6} reflect the impact of the associated variable on the part-worth value for Holdzer. The customer requirement variables that management felt important enough to examine are also detailed in Table 9.4.

Substituting b_1 from the previous equation into the one before that leaves us with the final model

$$\text{Utility} = (b_0 + b_{a0}) + b_{a1} X_{a1} Z_1 + B_{a2} X_{a2} Z_1 + \ldots$$
$$+ b_{a6} X_{a6} Z_1 + b_2 Z_2 + b_3 Z_3 + \ldots + b_{17} Z_{17}$$

This approach of modeling variation in part-worths as a function of other characteristics draws its inspiration from the work of Paul Green and Wayne DeSarbo.[12]

---

[12] See Paul E. Green, and Wayne S. DeSarbo, "Componential Segmentation in the Analysis of Consumer Trade-Offs," *Journal of Marketing* 43 (Fall 1978): 83–91.

Data Collection

The seventeen assortment, price, and bid attributes were used to form an appropriate, orthogonal, fractional factorial design. A design large enough to accommodate so many attributes (variables) would be a tremendous burden for any single subject to respond to. Therefore, portions of it (nine profiles) were given to each respondent in the study. All the data were then pooled, and one aggregate model was estimated. This approach treats the population as if it were homogeneous except in that it may vary with respect to the value it places on the Holdzer brand name. That variation is dictated by the customer requirement variables. An alternative approach would have been to reduce the variables to a more manageable number. This would have allowed the researcher to construct a data collection task that would in turn have allowed him or her to derive a utility model for each respondent. There is an obvious trade-off here between accounting for a comprehensive set of decision criteria and accounting for individual variation in how customers weigh those criteria.

A questionnaire designed to collect utility measures for nine hypothetical profiles and the customer requirement variables in Table 9.4 was administered to 207 respondents: 123 from manufacturing firms, 34 from retail companies, 25 from financial services, and 25 engaged in business-to-business marketing.[13] Utility was measured through a seven-point "likely to consider" scale. Of course, each respondent reacted to a different set of nine profiles. This enabled the analysts to collect sufficient data for all combinations in the master orthogonal design.

Results

The confidentiality of the study allows us to present only a portion of the results and those results are disguised. In particular, we do not have the bid variable coefficients. The results we do have can be found in Table 9.5. The different units for each of the variables makes the coefficients difficult (if not impossible) to compare. Furthermore, the aggregate level of the analysis renders any conclusions that we draw tentative. Nevertheless, the statistically significant results in the table can be used as a rough guide for preparing offers to potential clients.

These results include the following:

1. Firms with more managers have a lower image of Holdzer.

2. Clients where the decision makers prefer a cozy environment with effective and neutral service and home-cooked style food are more likely to have a more favorable impression of Holdzer.

3. While á la carte entrees generally increase the chances of Holdzer being chosen, offering hot cereals and dessert dramatically decrease the chances of Holdzer being chosen.

---

13 The responses from each of these segments did not differ significantly. Thus, this categorization does not appear to be useful in segmenting this market.

TABLE 9.5
EFFECTS OF SELECTED VARIABLES ON LIKELIHOOD OF CONSIDERING HOLDZER

Variable	Magnitude of Impact
Number of employees in units of 100 (b_{a1})	1.7
Number of managers and white collar workers in units of 10 (b_{a2})	-1.5^*
Percentage of women in company (b_{a3})	-0.4
Rating on dining environment preference (b_{a4})	-11.2^*
Rating on service style (b_{a5})	-14.4^*
Rating on food preference (b_{a6})	4.7^*
Number of Warm entrees (b_2)	8.8
Á la carte entree available (b_3)	24.9
Salad table available (b_4)	-3.5
Sandwiches available (b_5)	7.1
Hot cereals available (b_6)	-40.0^*
Dessert available (b_7)	-23.8^*
Repetition of weekly menu (b_8)	5.3^*
Lunch price in Marks (b_9)	1.8^*
Company subsidy in Marks (b_{10})	0.6
Catering costs in 1000 Mark units (b_{11})	0.8
Banquet costs in 1000 Mark units (b_{12})	5.6

* Statistically significant at .05 level.

4. Holdzer's chances of being chosen go up for various financial variables.

Implications

These results have several implications for Holdzer in its attempts to reach its market-share goals. These implications come in the areas of market selection and product offering. First, Holdzer should target potential clients that have a higher concentration of blue collar workers relative to white collar workers. Companies that employ blue collar workers are a particularly fertile segment as they have favorable impressions of Holdzer. Second, the company should position themselves as supplying home-style cooked food in an efficient manner. Finally, it should stress the simplicity of their menus (i.e., no desserts, hot cereals, single items). It should offer just full meals and á la carte entrees.

SUMMARY

This chapter has presented a series of examples that should place the reader on firmer footing with respect to applying the techniques described in this book. The applications covered a wide variety of industries (consumer products, consumer services, industrial services), managerial objectives (benefit segmentation, identification of unmet needs, identification of competitors, target market identification, brand name assessment), and tools and techniques (focus groups, perceptual mapping, conjoint analysis). This variety goes a long way towards providing the reader with a foundation to initiate applications that may not perfectly match any of those presented here, but have elements of each.

With the exception of the sports apparel trade study, which was not performed for or by a single, specific company, each of these studies had an impact on the companies involved. Victoria Moore introduced a line of activewear; the photocard has been a major impetus for Citibank's credit card division; and Holdzer catering increased its market share. Analysis is done for a reason: It affects decisions. Even if this book affects only one decision for each reader over the course of a lifetime, it has been worth its weight in gold.

APPENDIX

1. Customer Survey and Detailed Results
for Victoria Moore Study

January 29, 1993

Dear Female Head of Household:

As MBA students at the Leonard N. Stern School of Business at New York University, we are participating in a consulting assignment called the Management Advisory Project. We are currently conducting a market research study for a major fashion designer considering the launch of a new activewear division.

The information we gather from the following survey will allow us to recommend the correct direction and focus on our client's new line. This will also allow our client to better service your needs. This information will be used only for research purposes and will not be forwarded to our client for any reason.

Your time and support in completing this survey will be greatly appreciated. In exchange, we will enter your name in a contest to win one of several prizes including: a designer leather agenda with a retail value of $105 and a designer signature scarf with a retail value of $115. The grand prize will be a designer leather handbag with a retail value of $230. This survey is being distributed throughout the United States with all respondents eligible for the drawing. The drawing will be held on March 1, 1993 so please return your survey and entry form by February 26, 1993.

Thank you again for your help. Good luck!

Sincerely,

Kimberly Banks   Gina Plaia

Tracy Pollastri   Joseph Weglein

Please complete and return with questionnaire:

Name: _____

Address: _____

_____

Final Client Report
– Page B1 –

First, we would like to ask you a few questions about your lifestyle and your activewear purchases. For the purpose of this survey, activewear is defined to incorporate items such as sweatshirts, leggings, and t-shirts. More sports-specific items including tennis skirts, ski pants, and biking shorts would also be represented. This category does NOT include sports equipment or footwear.

1. Do you wear activewear?
    _____ Yes
    _____ No (Please skip to Question 11)

2. When do you wear activewear?
    _____ For sports-related activities only
    _____ For leisure activities only
    _____ For both sports-related and leisure activities

3. How often do you participate in the following activities? (If you do not participate in any of the sports-related activities listed below, please skip to Question 5.)

	Frequently	Occasionally	Rarely	Never
Aerobics/Step Aerobics	_____	_____	_____	_____
Biking	_____	_____	_____	_____
Golf	_____	_____	_____	_____
Rollerblading™	_____	_____	_____	_____
Running	_____	_____	_____	_____
Sailing	_____	_____	_____	_____
Skiing	_____	_____	_____	_____
Swimming	_____	_____	_____	_____
Tennis	_____	_____	_____	_____
Using exercise equipment	_____	_____	_____	_____
Weightlifting	_____	_____	_____	_____
Other_____	_____	_____	_____	_____

4a. Please indicate your FAVORITE activity of those listed above. Please list the types of clothing you wear for this activity and, if possible, their brands.

e.g., Skiing   Overalls (CB), down ski jacket (Bogner), ski sweater (Bogner).
Favorite: Types and brands of clothing

_____   _____

4b. If the activity which you engage in MOST OFTEN is not your favorite, please indicate which it is and the clothing you wear for this activity.

Most Frequent: Types and brands of clothing

_____   _____

Final Client Report

5. Approximately, how much do you spend annually on activewear? Please do not include equipment or footwear in your estimate.

   ____ Under $100

   ____ $100 – $499

   ____ $500 – $999

   ____ $1,000 or more

6. Please rank the following factors from "1" to "6" in order of importance in your decision to purchase activewear for both sports-related and leisure activities. Let "1" represent the most important factor and "6" the least important.

	Sports-related activities	Leisure activities
Brand Name	_____	_____
Comfort	_____	_____
Durability	_____	_____
Fashion/Look	_____	_____
Functionality	_____	_____
Price	_____	_____

7. How do you rate the quality of the following brands of clothing? Please indicate with an "X" the level of quality you associate with the following brands. If you have no experience with a particular brand, please check N/A.

	Lowest Quality 1	2	3	4	5	Highest Quality 6	7	N/A
Adidas	—	—	—	—	—	—	—	—
Bogner	—	—	—	—	—	—	—	—
CB Sports	—	—	—	—	—	—	—	—
Champion	—	—	—	—	—	—	—	—
Ellesse	—	—	—	—	—	—	—	—
Fila	—	—	—	—	—	—	—	—
Head	—	—	—	—	—	—	—	—
Lacoste	—	—	—	—	—	—	—	—
Le Coq Sportif	—	—	—	—	—	—	—	—
Nike	—	—	—	—	—	—	—	—
Reebok	—	—	—	—	—	—	—	—
Sergio Tacchini	—	—	—	—	—	—	—	—
Skyr	—	—	—	—	—	—	—	—
Spider	—	—	—	—	—	—	—	—
Other_____	—	—	—	—	—	—	—	—

8a. What characteristics do you LIKE most about currently available
activewear?

_____

_____

_____

_____

8b. What characteristics do you DISLIKE most about currently available
activewear?

_____

_____

_____

_____

9. Are there any activewear items or attributes you have been looking for
but have been unable to locate?

_____

_____

_____

_____

10. Where are you most likely to shop for activewear? Please check all that
apply.

_____   Department Store (e.g., Saks, Macy's, Bloomingdales)
_____   General Sporting Goods Store (e.g., Herman's)
_____   Pro Shop at my Gym/Health Club
_____   Sport Specific Store (e.g., Golf Store, Tennis Shop, Ski Outlet)
_____   Discount Store (e.g., Marshalls, Filene's Basement)
_____   Dance Supply Store (e.g., Parklane, Capezio)
_____   Specialty Store/Boutique
_____   Catalog (e.g., Road Runner Sports)
_____   Other (please specify) _____

Questions on the following page deal with major fashion designers.

Final Client Report
– Page B4 –

	11. Please indicate all of the designer(s) that you currently wear.	12. If available, which designer activewear line(s) would you consider purchasing? Please check all that apply. *(Note: Not all of the designers listed below currently offer activewear.)*	13. Please indicate the highest price you would be willing to pay for a sweatshirt by the designer(s) you chose in question 12.	14. Please indicate the activities for which you would purchase this activewear. Circle: "S" for sports activities only "L" for leisure only "B" for both activities "NP" for would not purchase
Adrienne Vittadini				S L B NP
Anne Klein				S L B NP
Calvin Klein				S L B NP
Carole Little				S L B NP
Chanel				S L B NP
Christian Dior				S L L NP
Dana Buchman				S L B NP
Donna Karan				S L B NP
Ellen Tracy				S L B NP
Jones New York				S L B NP
Leslie Fay				S L B NP
Liz Claiborne				S L B NP
Ralph Lauren				S L B NP
Saint Gillian				S L B NP
Victoria Moore				S L B NP
Other _____				S L B NP

Now a few questions about yourself.

15. Where did you take your last two vacations?

_____

_____

16. Please indicate your age.
      _____ under 25
      _____ 25–34
      _____ 35–44
      _____ 45–54
      _____ 55 and above

17. Please indicate your household income.
      _____ under $50,000
      _____ $50,000–$59,999
      _____ $60,000–$74,999
      _____ $75,000–$100,000
      _____ over $100,000

18. Please indicate your employment status.
      _____ Full-time
      _____ Part-time
      _____ Not employed (outside the home)

19. Please indicate your marital status.
      _____ Never married
      _____ Married
      _____ Separated/divorced/widowed

Thank you for your time and effort.

	# of Activewear Consumers	% of Activewear Consumers	% of Victoria Moore Active Potential[1]
Region of Country			
Northeast	200	42%	50%
East Central	40	8	8
West Central	69	14	12
South	93	19	15
Pacific	50	10	11
When Wear Activewear			
Sports Only	13	3%	2%
Leisure Only	75	16	11
Sports & Leisure	385	80	87
Activities			
Aerobics	217	45%	55%
Biking	200	42	52
Golf	76	15	15
Running	117	24	34
Sailing	53	11	14
Skiing	104	21	24
Swimming	287	60	64
Tennis	147	28	33
Exercise Eqpmt	289	60	70
Walking	104	22	18
Weights	136	28	40
Annual Expenditures			
< $100	176	37%	30%
$100–$500	257	54	60
$500–$1,000	35	7	5
$1,000+	5	1	3

---

1 People who expressed interest in Victoria Moore Activewear (question 12)

	# of Activewear Consumers	% of Activewear Consumers	% of Victoria Moore Active Potential
Where Shop for Activewear			
Dpt. Store	322	67%	74
Sporting Goods	229	48	61
Pro Shop	54	11	14
Sports Specific	111	23	30
Discount	289	60	57
Dance Supply	65	14	16
Boutique	84	18	21
Catalog	205	43	47
Designers Currently Owned			
A. Vittadini	84	18%	30%
Anne Klein	177	37	62
Calvin Klein	203	42	51
Carole Little	75	16	22
Chanel	30	6	8
Christian Dior	115	24	34
Dana Buchman	26	5	14
Donna Karan	55	11	29
Ellen Tracy	82	17	31
Jones NY	165	34	46
Leslie Fay	129	27	33
Liz Claiborne	303	63	72
Ralph Lauren	135	28	37
Victoria Moore	85	18	40
Intend to Buy Activewear			
A. Vittadini	83	17%	42%
Anne Klein	124	26	58
Calvin Klein	147	31	56
Carole Little	58	12	28
Chanel	48	10	26
Christian Dior	88	18	36
Dana Buchman	34	7	23
Donna Karan	87	18	70
Ellen Tracy	67	14	35
Jones NY	93	19	42
Leslie Fay	82	17	41
Liz Claiborne	203	42	63
Ralph Lauren	118	25	45
Victoria Moore	86	18	69

	# of Activewear Consumers	% of Activewear Consumers	% of Victoria Moore Active Potential
Price Would Pay for Sweatshirt (in \$)[2]			
A. Vittadini		$49	$54
Anne Klein		44	46
Calvin Klein		42	46
Carole Little		48	51
Chanel		47	52
Christian Dior		43	48
Dana Buchman		50	53
Donna Karan		46	48
Ellen Tracy		48	53
Jones NY		45	50
Leslie Fay		41	46
Liz Claiborne		41	45
Ralph Lauren		45	51
Victoria Moore		48	51
When Would Wear Activewear (Sports/Leisure/Both)			
A. Vittadini	3/40/57	1%/8%/12%	2%/16%/26%
Anne Klein	3/59/92	1/12/19	1/22/39
Calvin Klein	7/64/111	1/13/23	4/17/35
Carole Little	5/29/52	1/6/11	1/9/25
Chanel	1/33/46	0/7/10	0/15/22
Christian Dior	3/37/74	1/8/15	1/10/28
Dana Buchman	1/19/32	0/4/7	0/8/21
Donna Karan	4/42/57	1/9/12	2/26/40
Ellen Tracy	1/36/47	0/8/10	1/12/24
Jones NY	2/46/68	0/10/14	0/13/31
Leslie Fay	0/32/87	0/7/18	0/9/34
Liz Claiborne	6/80/154	1/17/32	1/18/44
Ralph Lauren	3/48/102	1/10/21	0/14/34
Victoria Moore	1/26/79	0/5/16	0/14/50
Age of Consumer			
< 25	24	5%	5%
25–34	137	29	44
35–44	161	34	31
45–54	109	23	13
55+	44	9	9

2 The values are ALL average $ amounts, not percents.

	# of Activewear Consumers	% of Activewear Consumers	% of Victoria Moore Active Potential
Household Income			
< $50,000	125	26%	21%
$50,000–$59,999	79	16	14
$60,000–$74,999	76	16	15
$75,000–$99,999	75	16	18
$100,000+	90	19	29
Employment			
Full Time	297	62	66
Part Time	64	13	17
Not Employed	111	23	18
Marital Status			
Single	89	19%	26%
Married	328	68	64
Separated, etc.	55	11	10
Most Frequent Activities			
Aerobics	80	17%	18%
Biking	34	7	6
Golf	14	3	2
Running	29	6	6
Sailing	3	1	2
Skiing	21	4	7
Swimming	58	12	11
Tennis	37	8	6
Exercise Eqpmt	41	9	11
Walking	46	10	11
Weights	10	2	4
Clothes Worn			
Sweatshirt	101	21%	20%
Sweat Pants	93	19	24
T-shirt	147	321	33
Leggings	83	17	17
Shorts	92	19	21
Bodysuit	41	9	11
Tights	30	6	8
Ski Sweater	6	1	2
Brands			
Nike	30	6%	6%
Hanes	22	5	6

	# of Activewear Consumers	% of Activewear Consumers	% of Victoria Moore Active Potential
Important Features/Sports (Median Score)[3]			
Brand		6	6
Comfort		1	1
Durability		4	4
Fashion/Look		4	4
Function		3	3
Price		4	4
Important Features/Leisure (Median Score)[4]			
Brand		6	5
Comfort		1	1
Durability		4	4
Fashion/Look		3	3
Function		4	4
Price		4	4
Available Features Like			
Easy to Wash/Dry	48	10%	14%
Comfortable	210	44	46
Durable	65	14	10
Color Variety	144	30	34
Style Variety	113	24	22
Fabric	79	16	20
Fashionable	73	15	16
Versatile	32	7	8
Available Features Dislike			
Durability	37	8%	9%
Colors	57	12	14
Lack of Sizing	46	10	13

---

3 The values given are the median of a scale of 1 to 6, where 1 represents most important and 6 represents least important.

4 The values given are the median of a scale of 1 to 6, where 1 represents most important and 6 represents least important.

---

2. Discussion Guide Outline for Citibank Photocard Focus Groups

CITIBANK CLASSIC VISA PHOTO CARD
EXPLORATORY RESEARCH

Discussion Guide Outline
October 1990

Prepared for:

CITIBANK

Prepared by:

MCC QUALITATIVE CONSULTING

MEADOWLANDS CONSUMER CENTER INC.
700 Plaza Drive
Secaucus, New Jersey 07094
(201) 865–4900

WARM-UP

- Companies are interested in what people have to say about their products or services.
- Independent market researcher—no vested interest.
- Individual opinions are key—no right or wrong answers.
- Tape/mirror/For marketing research purposes only.
- Any questions.

1. INDIVIDUAL INTRODUCTIONS

- First name, where you live.
- Family composition.
- Occupation.
- What credit cards you currently have, what banks.

2. PHOTO CARD OVERVIEW

- You all mentioned you have a Citibank Photo Card, what I'd like you to do now is WRITE an informal letter to a friend of yours about your Citibank Photo Card. Tell them whatever it is you think they should know. Assume that this friend doesn't live around here and doesn't know anything about this card.

- [EACH RESPONDENT WILL SHARE HIS/HER LETTER] Probe key points as necessary listening for salient benefits/drawbacks.

3. ACQUISITION PROCESS

- Now I'd like to track through the process you went through in acquiring your Photo Card and how you felt about it. First of all . . .

- How did you FIRST HEAR about the Citibank Photo Card?

    ___ What was your initial reaction?
    ___ Why did you feel that way?

- Initially, what BENEFITS did you see in this card?

    ___ How is that important to you?

- What would you say was the key REASON you accepted the offer for the Photo Card?

    ___ How was that important to you?

- Thinking back, what QUESTIONS, if any, did you have?

    ___ What drawbacks, if any, did you think about?
    ___ How did you feel about those?

- Prior to applying, did you talk to anyone about it or not? Who? Why?

- What were the STEPS involved? Walk me through the whole process.

  ___ Probes: Application
               Picture-taking process
               How long to receive, etc.
  ___ How did you feel about each of these steps?

4. <u>USAGE</u>
   - Now let's talk about what it's LIKE HAVING THIS CARD. What thoughts went through your mind when you FIRST RECEIVED the Photo Card?

     ___ What was your initial reaction?
     ___ How did it compare to what you EXPECTED?
     ___ How did you feel about that?

   - How often have you used the card?

   - I'd like you to think back to the first time you used the card. What did you use it for? Where? Why that?

   - How did this initial use compare to what you expected?

   - What were your experiences with merchants when you gave them the card? Did they examine the card? What comments did they make?

   - How did using the card/having the card make you FEEL?

     ___ Why would you say that?
     ___ Listen for end benefits: i.e., Security, safety, prestige, etc.

   - How has having this card CHANGED the way you use other credit cards? (any canceled or usage reduction)

     ___ Why would you say that?
     ___ What is the KEY reason you say that?
         Any other reasons?

   - Did you show the card to your family? How did they react to it? How about your friends.

   - If you were trying to convince someone to apply for this card, what would you say to them?

     ___ What part would the Photo play? How strong do you feel about that? Why?

- You mentioned a number of reasons why you applied for the Citibank Photo Card and why others should [REITERATE REASONS BEYOND JUST THE PHOTO — assuming other mentioned]

    ___ Of all these reasons to get this card, how important is the Photo?
    ___ Why would you say that?

- Are there any DISADVANTAGES you see associated with this card?

    ___ Probe any mentions.

- What does it say about a COMPANY that would OFFER a card such as this?

- If you could, would you CHANGE anything about the process of obtaining the Citibank Photo Card or anything else about it?

    ___ Why that? How would that be a benefit?

- What CONCERNS, if any, do you have that you haven't mentioned?

- As you can imagine, there are ADDITIONAL COSTS to produce a credit card with a picture on it. We've talked a lot about the advantages and benefits of having this card.
  Suppose the annual fee for this card was $____ above what other nonpicture cards are charging.

    ___ How do you feel about that?

  (Alternatively pricing question will be phrased in an open ended manner.)

- Tie up any loose ends.

- Thank you all very much.

Index

A

Abell, dimensions, 101
ABI/INFORM, 160
Abstracting services, 160
Aburdene, Patricia, 140
Achievement motivation, 31
Ackoff, Russell, 16
Action analyses, case examples, 295-334
   introduction, 295-297
   summary, 318-319
Activewear line. *See* Victoria Moore
Activities, interests, and opinions
   (AIO), 26
Actualizer group, 28
ADN. *See* Automatic number
   indentification
Adolph Coors & Co. *See* Coors
Advertising, 244
   data, 159-160
   expenditures, 285
Advertising to sales ratio, 102
ADVISOR, 246, 284
   approach, 285-287
ADVISOR 2, 284
AEA. *See* American
African Americans, 129, 143
Age-specific
   consumption rates, 131, 137
   salesrates, 131, 132
Aggregate
   level, 106
   measures, 74
AHC. *See* Air, hotel, rental cars
AHCR. *See* Air, hotel, rental cars,
   restaurants
AHCRG. *See* Air, hotel, rental cars,
   restaurants, general retailers
AHP. *See* Analytic Hierarchy Process

AIO. *See* Activities, interests, and
   opinions
Air, hotel, rental cars (AHC), 42, 43
Air, hotel, rental cars, restaurants
   (AHCR), 42, 43
Air, hotel, rental cars, restaurants,
   general retailers (AHCRG), 42, 43
Allocation. *See* Resource
   scheme, 276-277
American
   Electronics Association (AEA), 185
   Express, 62, 280, 307
Analogy, 169
   forecasting, 187
   method, 184-187
   technique, 167
Analytic Hierarchy Process (AHP), 246,
   266, 293
   methodology, 248, 250
   methods base, 272-279, 282, 287
   multiple-decision-maker illustration,
   275
   one-decision-maker illustration,
   273-275
Annual fee, 42, 43
Ansoff
   Grid of Competencies, 211
   Product-Market Matrix, 55, 111-112,
   297, 313
Appendix, 320-334
Apple, 82, 121, 212, 228
   MacIntosh, 232
Arco Chemical, 113
Areas. *See* Two
Arm and Hammer, 110
Artificial intellilgence software
   technologies, 143
Asian Americans, 129
AT&T, 50, 88, 90, 142, 143, 310

Attribute(s), 317
  ratings, 66
Auto service systems, 57
Automatic number identification
  (ADN), 56
Availability
  bias, 16
  heuristic, 16
Awareness-image classification
  scheme, 226

B

Background data, 69
Bank. *See* Commercial
  customers, 46. *See* also:
      Convenience-oriented bank
      customers, Service-oriented
      bank customers
  management, 15
  Marketing Association, 79
Bargaining power, 112
Base communication, 65
Base rate bias, 222
Bases. *See* Behavorial, Segmentation
BASICS. *See* Battelle
Bass model of diffusion, 201-203
Battelle
  Consulting Firm, 197
  method, 193, 194
  Scenario Inputs to Corporate
      Strategy (BASICS), 197
    algorithm, 198
    program, 195
    system, 198
Battery discharge, 57
Battles Scenario analysis, illustration,
  197-199
BBDO Advertising Agency, 72, 73
BBDO Worldwide, 227
BCG. *See* Boston Consulting Group
Becks, 33
Behavioral
  bases. *See* Segmentation
  variables, 34, 36
Behaviorally based segmentation, 51
Benefit(s)
  deficiency index, 69, 71
  matrix, 69
  received/wanted, 68
  requirement, 309
  segment(s), 298-303

data collection/procedures,
    298-303
  implications, 303
  segmentation, 37-49
  study, 38
  structure analysis, 61, 62, 67-71
Bibliography, 19-20, 52-54, 94-96,
    117-119, 161, 206-207, 239-241,
    293-294. *See* also: General
Bipolar
  perceived quality, 228
  ratings, 226
  scale, 232, 233
Black & Decker, 88
Boston Consulting Group (BCG), 230,
    251, 252, 261, 262, 276
  business portfolio matrix, 253-255
Bounded rationality, 16, 99
Bowmar Brain, 7
BrainReserve
  group, 140
  Trends, 138-139
Brainstorming, 85, 193
  techniques, 82
Brand(s). *See* Firm marketing brand;
    Multiple brands
  attitudes, 49
  awareness, 225
  data, 159-160
  equity, 221, 225-227, 229, 309-310
    measurement, 224-229
  evaluation, 226
  identification, 10
  image, 225
  knowledge, 225
  marketing expenditures methods,
    283-293
  names, 101, 213, 229
  regression, 106
  switching, 100, 103
Brand-specific constants, 228-229
Brand-switching
  analyses, 102-106, 108, 114
  data, 79
  matrix/matrices, 102-104, 106
  phenonmenon, 102
Brauers-Weber method, illustration,
  196-197
Breakthrough ideas, 92
Bretton-Clark, 46
Bristol-Myers Squibb, 154
Buaron, Roberto, 4

Bureau of Census, 148
Bureau of the Census, 149
Bureau of Labor statistics, 148
Business
    Assessment Array, 255-256, 261, 264
    Screen, 252, 255
    sector prospects, 257-258
    strategy/strategies, 163, 272
Business-to-business marketing, 296, 317
Buyer(s)
    identification, 21-54
        introduction, 21-24
    needs, 6

C

CAD. *See* Computer-aided design
Calgene Inc., 57, 140
Call for Action and the Center for Study of Responsive Law, 80
Capacity expenditures, 267
Capital requirements, 10
Card-sorting task, 303
Carryover, 225
Cash constraints, 271
Cash flow, 269
Cash rebate, 42, 43
CAT. *See* Center for Advanced Technology
Category-primary nature, 304
Caterfone, 143
CATV, 143, 177, 180
    penetration, forecasting, 177-180
Cellular phones/telephones, 56, 143, 172
Census
    Bureau, 22, 129, 134
        . *See* U.S.
    data, 28, 128
    understanding, 127-128
Center for Advanced Technology (CAT), 63
Center for Environmentally Conscious Products, 155
Cerner Corporation, 56
Chevrolet, 81
Choice probabilities, 109
Citibank, 2-4, 8, 9, 11, 12, 15, 17, 296
Citibank Photocard focus group project, 310-313
    discussion guide outline, 331-334

emotional reasons, 312-313
implications, 313
practical reasons, 312
summary, 313
Citicorp, 97
Clairol, 155
Claritas Corporation, 27, 28, 127
Cluster, 197
    analysis, 44, 69, 102, 104, 108
ClusterPlus project, 24
Coca-Cola, 26, 28, 29, 100, 237, 238, 253
Coefficient. *See* Imitation; Learning; Regression
Coefficient of imitation, 184
Coefficient of innovation, 184
Cohort analysis, 133-137
    consumption analysis use, 133-137
    description, 133
Commercial
    banks, 79
    products, 84
    vehicles, 65
Commodity pricing behavior, 257
Communications media, 30
Company information, 157
Compaq, 121, 224, 228
Compatibility, five-point scale, 193
Competition, 4, 98, 107, 252, 309. *See* Five Forces of Competition
    process, 209-241
        introduction, 209-211
        summary, 238-239
Competitive
    advantages, 6, 12, 14, 23, 210, 211, 213, 238
    analysis, 97
    business position, 255, 256
    capabilities, 258-259
    Capabilities/Profit Prospects Matrix, 252
    position, 221-231, 261
        categories, 260
    Position/Industry Maturity Matrix, 252
    pressures, 272
    products, 65
    set, 101
Competitor(s). *See* Potential competitors
    actions, prediction, 115-117
    identification, 97-119. *See also* Industry, Product
    conclusion, 117

introduction, 97-99
responses, 163
variables, 6
Complaint analysis, 61. *See* Customer
CompUSA, 71
Compustat PC Plus, 157
Computer
  industry, 59
  packages, 41
Computer-aided design (CAD), 22, 84
Conditional probability, 102
Conference Board, 153
Confidentiality, 188
Conjoint analysis, 38, 41-44, 169, 198,
    228, 229, 266, 293, 314
  methods base, 277-279, 282-284,
    287-290
  packages, 46
Conjoint part-worth, 47
Consideration set, 108
Consumer(s)
  behavior, 26, 98
  complaint
    analysis, 80-81
    letters, 76
  development labs, 87, 88
  durable goods, 201
  exploratory sessions, 87
  groups, 44-46
  information, 32
  judgment, 98
  markets, 24-30, 159
  needs, 82, 88, 141
  packaged goods, 102, 129
  panels, 76
  perceptions, 303-307
    data collection/procedures,
    303-307
  preference(s), 2, 41, 228
    models, 220-221
  problems, 72, 76, 88
  product marketers, 141
  promotion, 244
  responses, 232
  satisfaction, 79, 81
    study, 79-80
  satisfaction/dissatisfaction (S/D), 76
  surveys, 15, 28, 72, 76. *See* General
  switches, 78
  trends (21st century), 141-142
  variables, 6
Consumer-oriented businesses, 188, 189
Consumer-satisfaction strategies, 91
Consumption, 134

analysis use. *See also* Cohort
behavior, 133, 177
data, 133
habits, 135
rate, 136
Content analysis, 138. *See* Popular
Controlled variables, 92
Convection Corporation, 287
Convenience-oriented bank customers,
  46
Cooking, 142
Coors & Co., Adolph, 97
Cordless telephones, 57, 59
Corning Electronics Delphi Study,
  188-189
Cost function, 267
Cost/experience, 229-231
Creative
  assessment, 138
  resources, customers/experts, 87-88
Creativity, 86
  role, 91-93
Credit
  card industry, 8, 9
  instruments, 114
  services, 114
  unions, 79
Crisis action forecasting, 165
Critical Success Factor (CSF) method,
  215, 217
Cross-classification, 35
Cross-elasticity/cross-elasticities, 280,
  281
Cross-impact
  analysis, 193, 195, 197, 199
  indexes, 198
  matrix, 195
Cross-sectional
  analysis, 135
  forecasts, 136, 137
Cross-tabulation, 69
CSF. *See* Critical Success Factor
CT scanners, 101, 210, 211
  market, 115
Curve-fitting methods, 167
Customer(s). *See* Bank,
  Convenience-oriented bank
  customers, Creative, Potential
  customers, Service-oriented bank
  customers, Target
behavior, 233, 236
complaint analysis, 62
desire, 55-96
  conclusion, 93-94

introduction, 55-60
judgment, 233, 236
    quantitative processing, 233
motivation, 12, 232
requirement variables, 316
satisfaction, 2, 76, 77, 79, 232, 237
    research, 61
satisfaction studies, 76-80
    data sources, 76-77
    measures, 77-79
satisfaction surveys, 62, 232-233
survey. *See* Victoria Moore
        Activewear Line
value, 211, 229
Customer-service representative, 236

D

Data. *See* Advertising; Background;
    Brand; Census; Customer;
    Environmental; External;
    Primary; No; Secondary;
    Techniques
analysis. *See* Regulatory
collection. *See* Benefit, Consumer,
        Holdzer Catering
    instrument, 288
    procedures, 23
    task, 317
collection/procedure, 273
sources, 236 see Demographic,
        Economic, Statistical
terminal market. *See* Nonintelligent
        data terminal market
Datsun, 67
Day, George, 51
DDB Needham Worldwide, 226
DEC, 116
Decision
    maker, 14, 16, 17, 31, 214, 222, 317.
        See Analytic Hierarchy Process
    making, 164. *See* Strategic
    traps, 237
Decision-calculus approach, 279
Decision-making levels, 243, 244
Decline, 6, 8
Decomposition, 285
Dell, 121
Delphi Study. *See* Corning Electronics
        Delphi Study
Delphi technique, 168, 169, 184, 187-189
    advantages, 187-188
    applications, 188-189
    disadvantages, 188

Demographic
    analysis, 127-128, 131
    data, 127, 149
    factors, analysis methods, 127-137
    statistical data sources, 158-159
    trends, 62
    variables, 30
Demographics, 32, 300
Demographics-based segments, 24
Depreciation, 267
Descriptor(s), 50, 195
    dimensions, 31
    variables, 33, 34, 36, 38, 46, 47, 49, 50
Designated market area (DMA), 144,
        145, 159
Development path analysis, 192
Dialog, Business Connection, 160
Differentiation, 210
Diffusion. *See* Product
    path, 186
Digital
    imaging techniques, 92
    techniques, 93
Direct questioning, 38, 40, 44
Directional policy matrix, 252, 256-259,
        261, 264
Directions for Decisions, 298
Discontinuity trend analysis, 140
Discussion groups, 85
Distribution, 223, 287
    channels, 10, 30, 101, 220
    outlets, 273, 275
Diversification, 111, 250
DMA. *See* Designated market area
Dollarmetric approach, 227-228
Donnelly, 24
    Marketing Services, 27
DOS, 56
Dow Chemical, 113
Dow Jones, 127
    News/Retrieval, 157
Dummy variables, 176, 315
Dupont, 88, 116
Durable
    goods, ownership, 203
    product, 204
    sales, forecasting methods, 199-204
Duracell, 223

E

Econometric methods, 279, 291
Economic
    contraction, 199

expansion, 199
factors, analysis methods, 148-153
forecasts, 153
statistical data sources, 158-159
statistics, 148-149
surveys, 149-153
trends, 149
Economies of scale, 10
Economy/performance relationship, 45
Effectiveness skill, 211
EIA. *See* Electronics Industries
    Association
Elasticity/elasticities, 182. *See*
    Long-term; Short-term
    analysis, 218
Electric vehicle energy, 56
Electronics Industries Association
    (EIA), 185
Emergence, 6, 7
E.M.I./EMI, 115, 116, 210, 211
Emigration, 129
Empathetic identification, 86, 87
Encyclopedia of Business Information
    Sources, 160
End-use markets, 113
Energy; see Electric vehicle energy
    Partners, Inc., 56
Entry order, 221, 223-224
Environment. *See* External, Market
    changes, 82
Environmental
    aspects, 258
    changes, 122
    considerations, 295
    factors, 62, 122
        considerations, 124-125
        data, sources, 126-127
        experts, role, 127
        methods, overview, 125-126
        prediction methods, overview,
            124-127
        understanding methods,
            overview, 124-127
    forces, 82, 163
    responses, 163
    scanning, 62, 82
    scenarios, 274
    trends, 122, 143
    understanding, 122-124
    variables, 6
Equifax, 127
Ethnographic techniques, 209
Everex, 228
Existing offerings, problems, 62-81

Experience. *See* Cost/experience
    curve, 230, 231
Experimental methods, 279
EXPERT CHOICE, 275
Expert judgment, 72
Experts. *See* Creative, Environmental
Exponential
    model. *See* Multiple
    trends, 172, 176
Extension-based approach, 228
External data. *See* No, Techniques
External environment
    forecasting, 121-160
    introduction, 121-122
    summary, 156
    understanding, 121-160

F

Factor analysis, 69
Facts, description, 86
Family, definition, 142
FCC, Working Group, 184
Federal Express, 31, 65
Fina Chemicals, 113
Final forecast, 204
Financial
    data, 98
    factors, 222
    institutions, 33, 80
    performance, 2
    success, 93
Firm characteristics, 6
Firm marketing brand, 79
First-person description, 86
Fitting growth curves, 167
Five Forces of Competition, 10
Flexibility, 57
F-measure, 79
Focus groups, 60, 62-65, 83, 84
Food and Drug Administration, 153
Forced
    choice, 108-109
    connections. *See* Morphological
Ford Motors, 51, 106, 310
Forecasts/forecasting. *See* Crisis action
        forecasting; Cross-sectional;
        Economic; External; Final;
        Formal; Genius forecasting;
        Initial; Long-range; Market;
        Population; Purchases; Strategies;
        Technological; Technology;
        Window-blind
    development, 129

illustration. *See* HDTV
methods, 134. *See* Quantitative
   industry use, 170-171
model, 164
process, 165
technology, 164-169
   illustration, 167
   methods, 167-168
Formal forecasting
   alternatives, 165-166
   methods, 169-189
Fort Howard paper company, 112
Fortune
   100 companies, 192
   500 firm, 261
Franchises, 72
Freewheeling, 85
Full-text services, 160
Future Shock, 142-144

G

Gale Research Reports, 127
Gatorade, 26
GCA/David Mann and Company, 84
General
   bibliographies, 160
   Electric, 115, 116, 210, 252, 255
      Corporation, 283
   Foods, 3, 4, 8, 18, 76, 117
   information sources, 160
   Motors, 56, 81, 190, 310
   purpose consumer surveys, 145-148
Genetic engineering, 57
Genius forecasting, 165
Geographic
   areas, 129, 149
   markets, 60
      resource allocation methods, 292
Gillette, 88, 209, 280
Global
   assessments, 81
   Network, 141
Gompertz growth curve, 175-176
Good-life activities, 145
Goodyear Aerospace Corporation, 194,
   196
Governmental structure, 198
Graphical portfolio methods, 251-266
   assumptions, 251-252
   evolution, 265-266
Green marketing trends, 154-155
Group
   approach, 188

discussion
   method, 85
   techniques, 92
   dynamics sessions, 198
   interaction, 63
   moderator, 64
Groups. *See* Consumer, Focus, Strategic
Growth, 6, 7
   curves, 167, 169, 171-176. *See* Fitting
      growth curves; Gompertz; Pearl
   opportunities, 298
   options, 55
   pattern, 182
   potential, 259
Growth-curve equation, 172, 175
Growth-Share Matrix, 261, 264
Growth/share matrix, 276

H

Handbook of Demographics for
   Marketing and Advertising, 159
HDTV. *See* High definition television
Health care industry, 56
Heavy half, 30
Heuristic(s), 16
   . *See* also: Availability
Hewlett-Packard (HP), 100
Hierarchical
   approaches, 104
   clustering, 114
High definition television (HDTV), 2, 7,
   14, 15, 19, 203
   diffusion, forecasting illustration,
      184-187
   market, 11
Hispanics, 129
Historical data, 164, 169, 266
Hofer, Charles, 6
Holdzer Catering, 296, 313-318
   data collection, 317
   implications, 318
   model development, 316
   research approach, 314-315
   results, 317-318
   variables, 314-315
Homogeneity, 63
Honda, 210
HP. *See* Hewlett-Packard
Human
   engineering, 90
   judgment, 99
Humphrey, Hubert, 44
Huntsman, 113

I

IBM, 71, 72, 82, 84, 121, 125, 143, 154, 209, 212, 213, 228
Ice cream industry, 56
Ideal point coordinate, 47
Imaginative speculation, 86
Imitation coefficient, 202
Immigration, 141
Immunization approach, 238
Importance ratings, 298
Improvement potential, 79
Inbound logistics, 215
In-depth interviews, 67
Indexing services, 160
Industrial
    markets, 30-37
    organization economists, 100
    segmentation, 31
Industry
    attractiveness, 255, 256, 262
    category, 283
    category, competitor identification
        inside, 110-115
        outside, 100-109
    feedstock simulation, 257
    information, 157-158
    maturity, 260-261
        categories, 260
        factor, 259
    stages, 6
    structure variables, 6
    study. *See* Sports apparel
    types, 260-261
    utilization, 192
Inflation, 148
Information. *See* Company, Industry
    collection, 236-237
    Resources Inc. (IRI), 50, 51, 103
    sources. *See* General
    system, 77
    technology, 155
        market, 198
Information-processing abilities, 17
Infrastructure, 182
Initial purchases forecasting, 201-203
Innovation, failure/success reasons, 168, 169
Innovation and Development Sessions, 87
Installments loans, 115
Insurance. *See* Rental car insurance, Retail

Intel Corporation, 167
Intentions, methods, 169
Interactive approach, 238
Interations, 187
Interdependence, 244, 279-281
Interdependencies, 190, 193
Internal resources, 236
Interpurchase
    interval, 106
    time analysis, 100
    times, 106-108
Intragroup switching, 104
Intra-industry variability, 100
Investment intensity, 218
IRI. *See* Information
ISDN, 56

J–K–L

Johnson Wax,
Judgment, role, 164
Judgmental
    biases, 237-238
    data, 248, 267, 275

Kansei analysis, 88, 90-91
Kodak, 88

L.A. Gear, 304
Ladder, 47
Laptop computer(s), 71, 143, 167, 211, 224
    business, 125
Leadership, 2
Lead user(s), 82-84
Lead-user
    analysis, 83-85
    research, 82
        methodology, 83
Learning coefficient, 184
Least squares, 175
    method, 171
Leisure time, 142
Libby, 32
Life cycle, 201, 287
    portfolio matrix, 252, 259-261
Lifestyle(s), 300
    analysis, 144-145
    Market Analyst, 144
Light beer industry, 56
Linear
    function, 230
    regression, 107

trends, 172
Linkage analysis, 69
Locating, 65
Log-log graph paper, 230, 231
Longevity, 225
Long-range forecasting, 187
Long-term
    elasticities, 292
    strategic decisions, 110
Lord & Taylor, 232, 233
Lotus 1-2-3, 295
Low-cost strategy, 229

M

M2, 149
Macintosh, 56
MacIntosh. *See* Apple
    platform, 165
MADD. *See* Mothers Against Drunk
    Driving
Mainframe business, 125
Maintenance marketing function, 267
Make-or-buy decision, 113
Mall-intercept method, 76
Managerial judgment, 98, 99, 233-238
Manufacturing process, 11
Mapping. *See* also Perceptual
    study, 65
Marginal benefit, 247
Market(s). *See* Consumer; End-use
    markets; Geographic markets;
    High definition television;
    Industrial; Niche
    areas, 131
    attractiveness, 251
    challenger, 3, 9-10, 12
    development, 111
    dynamics, 122
    entry, 3
    environment
        forecasting, 163-207
        summary, 204
        understanding, 163-207
    evolution, 221
    expansion, 60
    growth, 253, 257, 262, 266
        forecasts, 168
        rate, 218, 255, 259
    leaders, 3, 9, 10, 12
    level, 245
    nicher, 10
    penetration, 55, 111, 310

planned, 69
position; 251, 258
    . *See* Transportation equipment
        division market position
    quality, 257
    research, 93
Research Company of America
    (MRCA), 30
response functions, 248, 249, 267
    methods base, 279-283, 290-292
scope, 6, 8, 12
segment(s), 12, 23, 30, 295, 303
segmentation, 21-54
    introduction, 21-24
share, 9, 37, 67, 100, 102, 216, 221,
        223, 225, 252, 253, 258, 261, 262,
        264, 269, 272, 274, 284, 291
    distribution, 259, 260
    goals, 81
    index, 262
    measurement, 252-253
    position, 238
    stability, 259-260
    situations, 60
    size, 6, 267
    structure, 252
Market-back approach, 220
Marketing. *See* Business-to-business;
        Green; Strategic
    activities, 153
    analysts, 149
    communication methods, 292
    efficiency, 225
    expenditures, 285. *See* Brand(s)
    factors, 222
    investments, 267, 271
    mix, 244, 247, 249, 290
        element, 292
        strategies, 288
        variables, 288
    plan, 117
    research
        firms, 226
        interview question, 108
        survey, 79
    resources, 248
    response function, 246
    stimuli, 50
    strategists, 17, 18
    strategy/strategies, 1, 21, 36, 37, 141,
            144, 149, 295
        analysis, information sources
            guide, 157-160

analyst, 155
trends. *See* Green
variables, 79
MARKPACK, 41
Marriott, 97
Masco Industries, 57
MasterCard, 2, 311
Matrix. *See* Ansoff, Product-Market
structures, 111
Mathematical portfolio method, 267-281
Maturity, 6, 8
Maximum attainable satisfaction, 79
Maxwell House, 4
Mazda, 90, 91
Mazola, 32
McDonalds Corporation, 72, 232, 236,
237
McDonnell Douglas, 97
MCI, 143
Mediamark, 27
Medical supply industry, 101
Megatrends, 138, 140-141
Megatrends, Inc., 82
MEI Marketing Economics guide, 158
Metaphors, 92
Methods. *See* Analogy; Analysis
methods; Brauers-Weber;
Demographic; Durable;
Economic; Environmental;
Forecasts/forecasting; Formal;
Political; Population; Product;
Research; Scenario;
Social/cultural; Solutions; Two
areas; Unmet
Microsoft Excel, 295
Migration, 129
Miniaturization techniques, 211
Minority group, 141
MIPS, 167
Mitsubishi, 97
Mobil Corporation, 154
Mobility barriers, 100
Model. *See* Consumer; Porter; Portfolio;
Preference
development. *See* Holdzer Catering
Modeling variation, 316
Modified A.D. Little Matrix, 261, 264
Monsanto, 84
Moody's, 157
Moore, Victoria. *See* Victoria
Morphological forced connections,
88-90

Motorola, 97, 209
Mothers Against Drunk Driving
(MADD), 148
MRCA. *See* Market
Multicollinearity, 183
Multidimensional scaling, 66
Multi-industry investigation, 219
Multiple
brands, resource allocation, 282-283
exponential model, 180, 182
regression, 43, 46, 169, 171
scenarios, 192
variabes, 133
Multivariate
method, 69
statistical technique, 104
Mystery shopper surveys, 60, 62, 71-72

N

NAFTA, 124
Naisbitt, John, 140
National
Basketball Association, 110
Consumer Study on Service Quality
in Banking, 79
Demographics & Lifestyles, Inc.
(NDL), 144, 145
Family Opinion (NFO), 30
Telecommunications Information
Administration (NTIA), 185
NDL. *See* National
NEC/N.E.C., 224, 228
Needs. *See* Unmet
NFO. *See* National Family Opinion
Niche
marketing, 141
markets, 129
Nielsen, A.C., 50, 51, 103
Nike, 10, 304
Nissan Motor Company, 91
Nixon, Richard, 44
No external data. *See* Techniques
Nonintelligent data terminal market,
35-36
Nonprice problems, 81
incidence, 80
Nonverbal communication, 63
Notebook computer industry, 56
Novell software, 59
NPD, 30
NTIA. *See* National

NYNEX, 88

O

Object-oriented software systems, 143
Occasion-based analyses, 30
Occurrence, frequency, 772
Offerings. *See* Existing
Office of Management and Budget, 31
Ohmae, Kenichi, 21
Open-ended data, 83
Operating costs, 10
Opinion polls, 156
Opportunity
    points, 69
    score, 72, 73
Optical scanners, 50
Optimization, 269, 271
Order of entry. *See* Entry order
OS. *See* Opportunity

P

Packaged goods, 103, 104, 106. *See*
    Consumer
Packard Bell, 228
PAR approach. *See* Profit Impact of
    Market Strategy
Partial factorial orthogonal design, 288
Part worths, 43, 44
Part-worth(s), 316. *See* Conjoint
    functions, 288
    model, 43
Pay phones, 56
PC-MDS, 41
PDA. *See* Personal
Pearl growth curve, 175
Pepsi/Pepsico/PepsiCo, 29, 100, 237,
    244
Perceptual
    map(s), 40, 41, 44, 100, 108, 110
    mapping, 38, 40-41, 65-67
    methods, 60, 62
Performance. *See* Financial
    dimension, 45
    measure, 218
    outcomes, 211, 232-233
Performance/cost ratio, 49
Personal
    computer industry, 56
    digital assistant (PDA), 121
PEST, 121, 122, 124

PETS, 121
P&G. *See* Proctor & Gamble
Pharmaceutical products, 176
Philadelphia Chewing Gum Corp., 34
Philip Morris, 153, 154
Phillip Morris, 116
PIMS. *See* Profit Impact of Market
    Strategy
Planning
    issues, 276
    period, 267, 269
    processes, 16-17, 192
Popcorn, Faith, 138
Popcorn report, 138-140
Political factors, analysis methods,
    153-156
Polysar, 113
Pooled business experience, methods
    base, 283-288
Popular press, content analysis, 138-141
Population
    forecasting methods, 128-129
    structures, 132
    trends, forecasts, 128
Porter, Michael, 10, 229
Porter model, 111-113
Portfolio. *See* Product
    analysis, 262
    developments, 266
    matrix. *See* BCG business portfolio
        matrix, Life cycle portfolio
        matrix
    method; Mathematical
    models, 250. *See* Product
        empirical comparison, 261-265
Positional advantages, judgmental
    evaluation, 221-223
Potential
    competitors, 18
    customers, 1
    identification, 17
    Rating Index for Zip Markets
        (PRIZM), 28
Power-PC, 82
Prediction. *See* Environmental
Predictor variables, 177
Preemptibility, 72
Preference. *See* Consumer
    judgments, 41
Premium buyers, 103
Price
    function, 267

insensitive segment, 51
tiers, 103
variables, 316
Price/cost structure, 6
Price/quality, 44
Price-sensitive retail segment, 51
Primary data, 236
Privacy, 155
PRIZM. *See* Potential
Probabilities, 187
Probability theory axioms, 193
Problem
    detection, 73
        analysis, 72
    evaluation, 72
    generation, 72
    inventory analysis, 72
    perceived importance, 72
    research, 61, 72-76
    score (PS), 72, 73
Problem-detection
    approach, 74
    method, 75
Problem-solving context, 86
Problem-stating context, 86
Proctor & Gamble (P&G), 110, 112, 225,
        245, 280
Product. *See* Competitive; Specialty
    category, 30, 38, 68, 74, 90, 98, 102,
        104, 109, 117, 243, 244, 246, 249,
        283
    category, competitors identification
        inside, 110-115
        outside, 100-109
    characteristics, ratings, 68
    deletion, 108-109
    development, 55, 60, 82, 111, 154, 276
    differentiation, 6
    diffusion, 186
    enhancements, 73
    improvements, 71
    life-cycle, 155
    line, 218
        breadth, 260
    markets, 21, 245
    portfolio, 55
        models, 248, 262
    positioning, 37
    possibilities, 84, 88
    problem detection system, 72
    quality, 2
    research and development, 259
    sales, forecasting methods. *See*
        Durable

usage, 27
Production
    capability, 259
    equipment, 229
Productivity, 272
Product/market, 244, 245
Product-Market Matrix. *See* Ansoff
Product-market selection variables, 101
Products/divisions, 252
Products/markets, 273
Product/service categories, 67
Profit function, determination, 288-290
Profit level, 274
Profit Impact of Market Strategy
        (PIMS), 246, 276, 283-285
    analyses, 218-219, 284
    data, 224
    PAR approach, 250, 284-287
    PAR ROI model, 262, 264
    project, 215
    ROI, 284
Profitability, 51, 218, 264
Project NewProd, 219
PS. *See* Problem
Psuedodiagnostic, 222
Psychographics, 26, 31
PTS PROMPT, 160
Public opinion polls, 155-156
Purchase
    decision, 309
    intentions, 170
    occasions, 78
Purchases forecasting. *See* Inital
PVC products, 84

Q

Quakers Oats, 26
Qualitative interviews, 314
Quantitative
    forecasting methods, 170, 190
    research technique, 62
Questioning. *See* Direct

R

Radio Shack, 91
Railroad industry, 98
Rand Corporation, 197
RAND Corporation, 187
Random
    runs, 89
    switching model, 78
R&D. *See* Research & development

Ready-to-drink tea, 56
Reebok, 2-4, 10-12, 16, 18, 145, 209, 304
Regression, 169, 231
    coefficients, 47, 107, 177, 178
    equation, 183
    function, 163
    model, 46, 176, 180, 284, 285
    procedure, 176-183
    studies, 49
    techniques, 176-183
        precautions, 183
Regulatory
    aspects, 258
    data analysis, 153-154
REM Inc., 197-199
    managers, 198
Renault, 67
Rental car insurance, 42, 43
Replacements, estimation, 203-204
Research. *See* Problem
    approach. *See* Holdzer
    design, 276
    methods, 88-91
    suppliers, 30
    techniques. *See* Quantitative research
        techniques
Research & development (R&D), 154,
    218, 223. *See* Product
    capabilities, 101
    support, 217
Research International, 228
Research labs, 213
Researcher insight, 72
Resource(s). *See* Creative,
    Skills/resources
    allocation, 243-294
        . *See* Geographic markets, Multiple
            brands, Strategic business
            unit
        decisions, 245
        introduction, 243-246
        principles, 247-249
        responsibility, 244
        study, 276
        summary, 292-293
    demand, 274
Retail
    environment, 71
    establishments, 33
    outlets, 145
    purchase insurance, 42, 43
Retirement population, 142
Revenues, 8
Risk-return model, 250

Robbin, Jonathan, 28
ROI. *See* Profit Impact of Market
    Strategy
Rolls-Royce, 117
Roper Organization, 145, 155, 227
Routing, 65
R-square, 177
R-sqaured measure, 183
Ryder Truck Rental, 56

S

Safety/security, 65
Sales
    growth, 272, 274
    performance, 129
    promotions, effects, 79
    response, 288
    volume, 265
SALT. *See* Strategic
Satisfaction
    degree, 81
    impact, 79
    studies. *See* Consumer, Customer
Saturation, 60
Savin, 215
Sawtooth Software, 46
SBU. *See* Strategic business unit
Scan time, 101
Scanner panel data, 98, 100, 106
Scanning. *See* Environmental
Scenario analysis, 196, 199
    . *See* Battles
    alternative methods, 193-194
    methodology, 192-193
    methods, 122, 189-199
    practical issues, 199
    use, case history, 194-196
Scenario-generating procedures, 19
S/D. *See* Consumer
Secondary data, 98, 99, 236
Securities and Exchange Commission,
    157
Segment(s). *See* Demographics-based
    segments, Target
    activity, 101
    description, 46-49
Segmentation, 21, 34. *See* Behaviorally
    based segmentation, Benefit,
    Industrial, Market
    bases, 23-37
    behavioral bases, 49-51
Self-elasticities, 281
Self-moving industry, 56

Self-oriented segment, 300
Self-serving bias, 221
Sensitivity analysis, 215, 217-219
Sensory skills, 91
Sequential predictions, 203
Service
  approaches, 216
  areas, 79
  Gap, 79
  Magnitude, 79
Service-oriented bank customers, 46
Set-up costs, 10
Share of mind, 226
Short-term elasticities, 292
SIC. *See* Standard Industrial
  Classification
Simmons, 27
  Market Research Bureau, 30, 32, 127,
    159
Simon, Herbert, 16
Skills/resources, dimensions, 211-221
Social desirability bias, 40
Social/cultural factors, analysis
  methods, 137-148
Society of Compeititive Intelligence
  Professionals, 237
Soft-drink switching matrix, 104
Solutions, identification methods, 82-88
Sourcebook of County Demographics,
  158
Specialty products, 37
Speculation, 138
Sporting Goods Manufacturers
  Association, 298
Sports apparel, industry study, 297-307
Sports Apparel Products Council, 298
SRDS, 127, 144, 159
Stage-of-industry development, 6
Standard and Poor, 127, 149, 157, 158
Standard Industrial Classification (SIC)
  code, 24, 31, 33, 35, 157
  Manual, 158
Standardization, 143
  technique, 129-137
Stand-alone brands, 225
Stanford Research Institute, 27
Statistical
  Abstract of the United States, 148
  data sources. *See* Demographic,
    Economic
  methodology, 109
  model, 283, 285
  packages, 102
STEP, 121

Stock price, 116
Strategic
  analyst, 126, 164
  Arms Limitation Talks (SALT), 196
  business unit (SBU), 19, 243, 245, 246,
    253, 261, 265, 275, 279, 281-283,
    287
    definition criteria, 250-251
    resource allocation methods,
      249-282
  decision, 163, 244. *See* Long-term
    making, 3, 243
  groups, 100-102
  market planner, 60
  marketer, 82
  marketing, 4
    boundaries, 3-6
    decision, 3
  planning, 196, 275
  Planning Institute, 218, 283
  questions, 12-14
  situations, classification, 6-12
  thinking, analysis/process, 12-17
  variables, 100
Strategy/strategies. *See* Low-cost;
  Marketing
  analysis. *See* Marketing
  implications, 141
  anaylsts, 127
  design, 163-164
  forecasting, 163-164
  formulation, analysis role, 1-20
    introduction, 1-3
  literature, 100
  Sensitive Reports, 284
STRATPORT, 246, 248
  approach, 267-281
Strengths, weaknesses, opportunities,
  and threats (S.W.O.T./SWOT), 18,
  19, 122
Strengths/weaknesses
  analysis, 209-241
  assessment, 221-238
  introduction, 209-211
  summary, 238-239
Substitution. *See* Use
Success factors, 213, 214, 217, 221. *See*
  Critical Success Factor
  judgmental identification, 214-215
  limitation, 219-220
Sun company of Philadelphia, 154
Supplier
  . *See* Research
  integration, 6

variables, 6
Supply control, 113
Surrogates, 101
Survey(s), 61. *See* Mystery
    data, 201
    organizations, 156
    responses, 40
Survey of Buying Power, 159
Survey of Consumer Finances, 152
Survey Research Center (University of
    Michigan), 152-3
Survey-based approach, 67
Switching data, 104
SWOT/S.W.O.T... *See* Strengths,
    weaknesses, opportunities, and
    threats
Syndicated services, 27-30
Synectics, 82, 85-88
Synergies, 282

T

Target
    customers, 1, 308-309
    segments, 23, 37
    selection, 51-52
Technical factors, 222
Technique(s). *See* Delphi, Regression,
    Standardization
    no external data use, 171-176
Technological
    changes, 168
    criteria, 186
    development(s), 168, 190, 245
    domination, 199 forecasts, 166
    innovation, 197
    stability, 260
    trends, 166
Technology. *See* Forecasts/forecasting
    forecasts, accuracy, 168-169
    measurement, 166-169
Telemeter system, 90
Telephone. *See* Cellular
    penetration, forecasting, 180-183
Texas Instruments (TI), 100
Thrifts, 79
TI. *See* Texas Instruments
Time frame, 76
Time trend, 171
Time-series techniques, 167
Toffler, Alvin, 142
Toshiba, 209, 223
Transaction process, 61
Transfer payments, 251

Transportation equipment division
    market position, 275-276
Trend(s). *See* Consumer, Green,
    Marketing, Population
    analysis, 197
    extrapolation, 169, 171
    methods, 167
    information, 135
    variable, 137
TrendBank, 139
T-values, 177
Two areas, comparison method,
    129-133

U

Uncertainty, 164
Uncontrolled variables, 92
Understanding. *See* Census,
    Environmental, External, Market
Unemployment, 148, 197
Univariate method, 69
Unmet customer needs, 121
Unmet needs, 81, 82, 93
    classification, 57-60
    conclusions, 93-94
    identification, 55-96
    introduction, 55-60
    methods, 60-62
    situation characteristics, 60
UPS, 65
Urbanization, 182
U.S. Bureau of Census, 128, 158
U.S. Bureau of Economic Analysis, 159
    Survey of Current Business, 152, 159
U.S. Bureau of Labor, 159
U.S. Census Bureau, 128, 189
U.S. Department of Commerce, 127
U.S. Industrial Outlook, 158
Use analysis, substitution, 114-115

V–W

Valdez Principles, 154
VALS2. *See* Values and Lifestyles
Value chain, 215-216
Value Line Investment Survey, 157
Values and Lifestyles (VALS2), 27,28
Van design, 56
Verbal reports, 90
Vertical integration, 218
Victoria Moore Activewear Line, 296,
    297, 307-310
    customer survey, 320-330

implications, 310
  results, 320-330
Victoria Moore Company, 1, 3, 4, 6, 10,
  11, 13, 14, 18
Video Storyboard Tests Inc., 223
Visa, 2, 311, 313
Volatility, 274, 275
Von Hippel, Eric, 83, 84
Vulnerability, 272

Wal-Mart, 51, 52, 112, 113
Warranty claims, 81
Warranty-claims reports, 81
Weaknesses, analysis. *See*
  Strengths/weaknesses
Wholesalers, 112

Window-blind forecasting, 165
Word for Windows, 60
Working capital, 269
  function, 267

X–Y–Z

Xerox, 2, 4, 19, 215, 216, 237

Yamaha, 50
Yankelovich, Clancey and Schulman,
  27, 145, 156

Zenith, 2, 3, 7, 11, 14, 15, 19, 165
ZMET, 92, 93